Lei Liu

**Organic Service-Level Management
in Service-Oriented Environments**

Organic Service-Level Management in Service-Oriented Environments

by
Lei Liu

Dissertation, Karlsruher Institut für Technologie
Fakultät für Wirtschaftswissenschaften
Tag der mündlichen Prüfung: 15. Juli 2011
Referenten: Prof. Dr. Hartmut Schmeck
            Prof. Dr. Hannes Hartenstein

Impressum

Karlsruher Institut für Technologie (KIT)
KIT Scientific Publishing
Straße am Forum 2
D-76131 Karlsruhe
www.ksp.kit.edu

KIT – Universität des Landes Baden-Württemberg und nationales
Forschungszentrum in der Helmholtz-Gemeinschaft

KIT Scientific Publishing 2011
Print on Demand

ISBN 978-3-86644-730-1

Organic Service-Level Management in Service-Oriented Environments

Zur Erlangung des akademischen Grades eines

Doktors der Wirtschaftswissenschaften

(Dr. rer. pol.)

von der Fakultät für Wirtschaftswissenschaften

des Karlsruher Instituts für Technologie (KIT)

genehmigte

DISSERTATION

von

Dipl.-Inform. Lei Liu

Tag der mündlichen Prüfung:	15.Juli 2011
Referent:	Prof. Dr. Hartmut Schmeck
Korreferent:	Prof. Dr. Hannes Hartenstein

2011 Karlsruhe

Thesis Summary

Dynamic Service-oriented Environments (SOEs) are characterized by a large number of heterogeneous and interconnected service components applying the design paradigm of service-orientation. On the one hand, the runtime behaviour of an SOE is determined bottom-up by individual service components involved in the environment. On the other hand, an SOE is expected to support the business as a whole. Therefore, a top-down business-driven IT service management is desirable to master the continuous changes within and outside of an SOE.

Nowadays, Service Level Agreements (SLAs) are utilised in IT service management as a common means to govern the relationship between a service provider and a service consumer. However, existing approaches consider a given SLA only in the local context of a single service component. They do not cover the fact that a service component may rely on a complex structure consisting of a range of underlying service components. This leads to a situation, where related service components are considered only in a local and isolated context. Correlations between related SLAs are disregarded by existing service management approaches to a large extent.

The present thesis aims at meeting this challenge by providing an automated and multi-level service level management framework based on controlled self-organisation. With a range of given end-to-end operational requirements on the whole IT infrastructure, the introduced framework is expected to autonomously propagate the requirements throughout the complete IT infrastructure. Each related service component is given an appropriate set of operational requirements in accordance with its capabilities, which it has to enforce locally.

Therefore, the framework is designed conceptually on two levels. On the global level, related service components within an SOE collaborate with one another to coordinate their runtime behaviour. In particular, each service component arranges its part to contribute to the end-to-end requirements, so that the overall requirements can be guaranteed by the complete IT infrastructure. On the local level, the arranged requirements are enforced by the respective service component as its operational objectives. It configures its local resources according to the requirements, so that the resulting runtime behaviour of the component complies with the specified requirements.

To facilitate global collaboration, in particular with respect to the distributed, autonomous, and loosely coupled nature of service components, the present thesis models an SOE as a Multi-Agent System (MAS). Each service component is extended with an autonomous management agent that represents the interests of the respective component in the MAS. This management agent carries out collaborative activities on behalf of the respective service component on the global level.

Collaboration between two related service components is done by means of automated bilateral multi-issue negotiation of SLAs. To this end, this thesis introduces a comprehensive negotiation model to guide two management agents to move across their negotiation spaces to reach a mutually acceptable agreement, even if both agents do not share their negotiation preferences.

Resulting SLAs determine the service level targets that a service consumer demands from its service provider. Hence, to enforce the agreed terms in SLAs, the present thesis adopts the generic observer/controller architecture proposed by the Organic Computing research community to establish SLA-driven self-organisation on a service component locally. By doing this, a management agent is aware of the runtime behaviour of the corresponding service component and can proactively perform corrective actions to maintain the runtime behaviour with respect to the SLA.

At last, to evaluate the automated and multi-level service level management framework, the present thesis designed and implemented a simulation-based test bed for SOEs. Based on this simulated evaluation environment, a range of evaluation experiments has been conducted, particularly with respect to the performance of the introduced negotiation model. The experimental results are promising, in particular with respect to negotiation convergence and efficiency of resulting SLAs. In particular, a real-world scenario from the university context was built in the evaluation environment to evaluate the feasibility of the proposed framework.

Acknowledgements

Writing a PhD thesis is a long journey that takes years. And it is not possible to make it alone. While undertaking this PhD thesis project, I have felt extremely fortunate that I have so many people – mentors, colleagues, friends, and my family – to support and encourage me.

Foremost, I would like to profoundly thank my doctoral advisor, Prof. Dr. Hartmut Schmeck, for his invaluable support and guidance throughout the last years. He has been my mentor during the whole PhD thesis and supported me throughout all the stages of the thesis with his long experience in research. In particular, I enjoyed the large freedom he gave me to conduct research in the field that I am interested in. My sincere thanks to him.

Furthermore, I would like to thank Prof. Dr. Hannes Hartenstein, from Karlsruhe Institute of Technology (KIT), who served as second reviewer of my thesis in the examination committee. I am also thankful for his timely review of the thesis despite his busy schedule. Furthermore, I would like to thank Prof. Dr. Andreas Oberweis and Prof. Dr. Svetlozar T. Rachev, both from Karlsruhe Institute of Technology (KIT), for serving as examiner and chairman, respectively, in the examination committee.

I also want to thank my friends and colleagues in the research group Efficient Algorithms for the discussions, advice, help, and inspiration I received during my doctoral days. In particular, I appreciate the valuable and inspiring discussions with Florian Allerding, Prof. Dr. Jürgen Branke, Christian Hirsch, Dr.-Ing. Sanaz Mostaghim, Friederike Pfeiffer, Holger Prothmann, Dr. Urban Richter, Stefan Thanheiser, Dr. Frederic Toussaint, Dr. André Wiesner, and Micaela Wünsche. My sincere thanks to them.

I am also grateful to my long-time friends – Yue Cao, Haipeng Chen, Qing Gong, Lin Jia, Pengyun Ren, and Honggang Zhu. Thank you folks, for enriching my life in Karlsruhe with so many beautiful moments.

Last but not least, I would like to thank my family for their continuous support and encouragement. My wife, Chaojun, stood by me every step of the way and encouraged me continuously during the last years. I feel the same gratefulness to my sisters, Fang and Yan, and my parents-in-law. It is very hard to find words to express my gratitude to my parents, who always put their absolute trust in me and stand by my side with their advice, endless patience, and encouragement. Hence, this thesis is dedicated to all of them for their invaluable support.

Karlsruhe, August 2011   *Lei Liu*

Table of Content

Part I

Motivation and State-of-the-Art

Chapter 1   Introduction

"易，穷则变，变则通，通则久。"
—【周易·系辞下】

"The world is in relentless change; the only way to respond to it is through changes."
(I Ching – Book of Changes, The Great Treatise II, ~1000 B. C.)

1.1 Motivation

Today's businesses are situated within a global and competitive market with continuous changes. As such, they have to arrange backend enterprise IT to streamline and automate business processes to adapt to continuous requirement changes [Dav98]. Alignment between business and IT in support of business agility is one of the central topics for modern businesses to improve their competitive strength in the market [SSW10]. A consistent alignment of business and IT provides businesses with a robust platform for executing business processes in a reliable, scalable, integrated, and unified manner [BBWL05].

In order to reach synergistic business/IT alignment in spite of existing legacy systems, an appropriate approach should provide an adaptive layer between the agile business process and the less flexible IT infrastructure. Service-oriented Architectures (SOA) provide the necessary architectural model to facilitate the business/IT alignment in the desired way. In comparison to existing paradigms for developing enterprise systems, the central focus of SOA is to encapsulate business capabilities as *services* [PH07]. By adopting services in enterprise systems, SOA facilitates manageable growth of large-scale enterprise systems. It provides a simple but scalable paradigm to link business capabilities in IT infrastructure with overall business processes.

Applying SOA helps large organisations to get clear IT Governance with coordinated architecture and infrastructure evolution [But05]. Driven by this, Forrester Research expected already in 2007 that about 75% of Global 2000 organisations were going to implement SOA by the end of 2007 [HF07]. By the end of 2009, 74% of these organisations are using SOA productively; among all the organisations being sur-veyed, this number is about 56% [HLA10]. This shows the potential of SOA to streamline strong business/IT alignment, especially for organisations with large-scale distributed IT infrastructure.

While SOA makes IT infrastructures more flexible, it increases simultaneously the complexity of the resulting system – sometimes to such an extent that undertaking SOA projects causes more cost and efforts than conventional approaches would. It is not without cause that voice came up like "SOA is dead" [Man09], which has caused a large debate in the field [KL09]. Most of all, businesses implementing SOA are frus-trated by additional complexity in service-oriented systems.

Fiadeiro denotes this type of complexity in collaborative service-oriented systems as "social complexity", which "arises not from the size of applications but from the number and intricacy of interactions" [Fia07]. The increasing number of autonomous, distributed, and mostly heterogeneous components in service-oriented systems raises the need to manage large scale IT systems as a whole. Fiadeiro quoted Erickson on the challenge to manage systems with high social complexity *[Fia07]*:

"When you build an application you look at it in isolation. When you build a service, you have to look at who will use it and how they will use it. It re-quires new skills and a new mindset."

Erickson's statement characterises the situation of a highly connected and hetero-geneous environment with complex consumer/provider relationships between compo-nents. To cope with the increasing social complexity, "being able to monitor and con-trol systems or environments is an important part of designing software intensive sys-tem" [Fia07]. In other words, software/hardware components involved in software intensive systems must be measurable and manageable, which is addressed by *SOA Governance* as well as *SOA Management*.

SOA Governance provides organisational measures to reduce inherent complexity of IT infrastructure at design time. It is the logical evolution as well as specialisation of IT Governance [WR04] in the context of service-oriented environments [SS07]. SOA Governance intends to ensure alignment between business and enterprise IT by defining "an enforceable set of policies for building, deploying, and managing ser-vices" [Win06]. Those policies define guidelines for carrying out top-down to-be analysis with respect to business requirements, such as determining organisation structure, clarifying responsibilities, or defining service level objectives.

SOA management is responsible for managing and controlling technical components at runtime. By applying various management standards (such as the *Web Service Distributed Management* (WSDM) standards published by the OASIS [BV06, WS06] and the *Web Services for Management* (WS-Management) standard by the DMTF [DMTF10a]), technical components can be managed by several management systems with a single set of instrumentation. Together with traditional management systems, such emerging management standards help to increase manageability of a service-oriented system.

In short, SOA Governance defines from top-down operational objectives for the underlying IT infrastructure. SOA Management determines from bottom-up runtime behaviour of technical components within the IT infrastructure. Hence, in order to align runtime behaviour of the IT infrastructure with the business requirements, an additional component is needed. In the context of business/IT alignment, *Service Level Management* (SLM) is responsible for this task, as illustrated by the non-functional view in Figure 1-1.

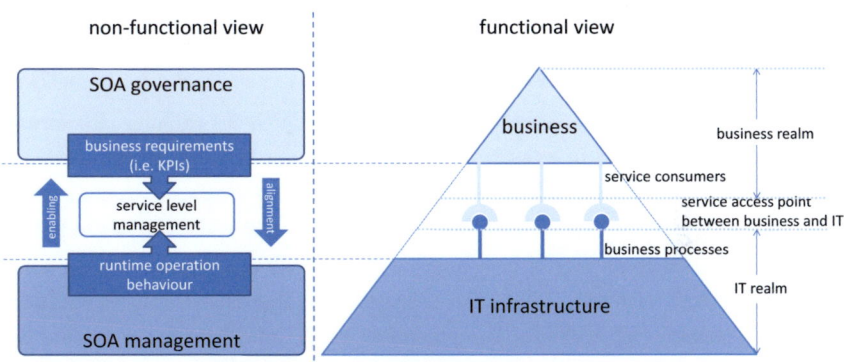

Figure 1-1: End-to-end Service Level Management

Office of Government Commerce (OGC) defines SLM as:

"...the process responsible for negotiating Service Level Agreements, and ensuring that these are met. SLM is responsible for ensuring that all IT Service Management Processes, Operational Level Agreements (OLAs), and underpinning Contracts, are appropriate for the agreed Service Level Targets. SLM monitors and reports on Service Levels, and hold regular Customer reviews." [RL07]

According to this definition, SLM ensures that all IT service management process-es defined in SOA Governance are appropriate to agreed service levels between the business and the IT infrastructure. Among other things, SLM includes negotiating Service Level Agreements (SLAs) between consumers and providers, as well as en-forcing SLAs with suitable management approaches at runtime.

Therefore, the alignment problem between a business's operational objectives and an IT infrastructure's runtime behaviour can be transferred to an *end-to-end Service Level Management* problem. That is, how top-down operational objectives of a busi-ness and operational execution of its supporting IT infrastructure can be aligned in an efficient and effective way.

The term *end-to-end* refers to the fact that service levels defined by SLM cover the operational behaviour of the entire underlying infrastructure. Such end-to-end service levels are associated with service access points between the business as *service con-sumer* and the business processes – the topmost components of the underlying IT in-frastructure - as *service providers*, as shown in the functional view in Figure 1-1. To address the end-to-end characteristic between business and IT, Koch cited the state-ment of Weill: "The business doesn't care about 99.9 per cent uptime unless you're talking about the uptime of a business process or an end-to-end capability" [Koc07].

The essential challenge for establishing end-to-end SLM is the complex structure of IT infrastructure involved in a business process. Although IT infrastructure operates as a black box for business, it involves a set of technical components to complete a single business process. For example, a business process may invoke several Web services. A Web service may in turn involve several technical components to com-plete its execution, such as a Web server for hosting it, or a database server for man-aging data. Hence, each technical component of an IT infrastructure may have the roles *service consumer* and *service provider* simultaneously. Such recursive functional dependences between technical components exist across the complete service-oriented system and set up a kind of functional dependence chains across the IT infrastructure.

The existence of such functional dependence chains determines that the runtime behaviour of a business process at the top of an IT infrastructure depends on all relat-ed technical components in support of it. Hence, although the performance of a top-most business process is determinant for end-to-end SLM, it still has to incorporate all underlying components into the corresponding SLM process. However, current man-agement approaches support end-to-end SLM only to a limited extent:

- Traditional approaches for SOA Management provide – if at all – only very limited capabilities to support business/IT alignment. They focus mainly on specific systems and applications with respect to particular management aspects, such as fault management, configuration management, and performance management [HAN99]. These approaches are crucial to enforce agreed service levels at runtime, however only in a local context. Due to high heterogeneity of these management approaches, they cannot provide comprehensive support to manage all related technical components at runtime. This is, however, one of the prerequisites to enable end-to-end SLM in service-oriented environments.

- Further, existing management approaches do not prevent human participants from being strongly involved in managing such environments. They have to design, implement, configure, and maintain complex distributed IT landscape with dozens of distributed and heterogeneous technical components. In addition to the fact that human participants are the leading cause of failures, cost for maintaining large-scale IT infrastructure is reported to be five to ten times the purchase price of software and hardware [PBB+02].

- A comprehensive SLM framework demands support for negotiating service levels between related technical components. Recursive functional dependences between technical components determine that the corresponding negotiation process should be carried out in a multi-layered manner. Starting from business processes at the top of the IT infrastructure, a negotiation process should be propagated top-down systematically across the complete IT infrastructure. Currently, this propagation process is in the majority of cases initiated and accomplished manually. That is, human participants have to negotiate SLAs in a point-to-point manner for each consumer/provider pair.

- Furthermore, the common practice in SLM is to establish generic point-to-point SLAs for each provider/consumer pair. Such a generic SLA prevents a provider from differentiating its service offers by providing value-added services to specific consumers.

- In practice, negotiating SLAs can be a very complex process involving a group of stakeholders from both providers and consumers to determine their expectations and responsibilities [Lab02]. This process often lasts over a long period, depending on complexity of services, number of parties involved, relationships between these parties, expectations of all parties, and prior experience of the parties with SLA negotiation.

Hence, existing SOA management approaches are not yet mature enough to support comprehensive end-to-end SLM largely. Limited support for automated end-to-end SLM in service-oriented environments reduces agility of these environments at runtime. One of the characteristic advantages of SOAs in comparison to conventional distributed computing approaches is their flexible and agile response to changes in their environments. Therefore, demands on flexible and fully automated end-to-end SLM arise continuously, as more and more businesses begin to apply SOA to increase efficiency of their IT landscapes. This remains one of the key challenges to enable adaptive SOAs with respect to continuous changes in their environments [PTDL07].

1.2 Approach

As motivated in Section 1.1, SLM is the core concept to control quality of service delivery within service-oriented environments. In dynamic and fully automated service-oriented environments, it is desirable to utilise SLM across all related technical components to align business needs and IT capabilities. However, high social complexity within such service-oriented environments prevents an active and consistent realisation of end-to-end SLM.

A plausible way out of this dilemma is to provide technical components with the ability to organise themselves – so-called *self-organisation*. That is, software components are expected to organise autonomously their activities considering given operational objectives and thus leave human participants in most cases uninvolved. To cope with increasing cost and administrative overhead for managing such systems, there are growing expectations that technical components within a service-oriented system can adapt flexibly to changes in their environments on their own, in particular with respect to non-functional requirements in terms of *service levels* [BKM+04, BMK+05].

Hence, in order to realise automated end-to-end SLM in a service-oriented environment, the major approach of the present thesis is:

With appropriate adoption of self-organisation, technical components in support of a service-oriented environment can collaborate with one another in order to produce a desired runtime behaviour complying with requirements given by the business, even in the presence of high social com-

plexity within the environment. Using such an approach, a service-oriented architecture is expected to respond adaptively to changes in its environment – with respect to both functional and non-functional aspects of those changes.

To establish this concept within service-oriented environments, a technical component must have two fundamental capabilities:

- *Being able to organise itself with respect to given operational objectives*: A service provider has the responsibility to deliver its services complying with service level targets specified in SLAs. Hence, a technical component should be capable to organise itself to guarantee agreed service level targets.

- *Being able to collaborate with other components*: The IT infrastructure supporting SOA contains more than one component. To ensure that the emerging runtime behaviour of the IT infrastructure is aligned with requirements of the business, it is desirable that all components have to coordinate their runtime behaviour in a seamless way.

The remainder of this section reviews the problems for enabling end-to-end SLM with self-organisation, and outlines the challenges. Moreover, it introduces the measures to meet the challenges with respect to the two fundamental capabilities of a self-organising technical component as described above.

1.2.1 Scenario and Objectives

The clear claim of this thesis is to automate end-to-end SLM within a service-oriented environment. Ideally, given business requirements should be propagated autonomously and independently across all service providers within the environment, so that they can collaboratively fulfil the business requirements that a business has on its IT infrastructure in an efficient way. The term "efficient" means that each service provider can guarantee its service delivery without over- and underutilisation of its resources.

Hence, in order to achieve the desired balance, service providers and service consumers are required to collaborate with one another. On the one hand, a service consumer has to specify its expectations on the quality of service delivery; on the other hand, a service provider has to be aware of its capabilities to deliver services. As such, SLM is concerned with bringing the consumer's expectations and the provider's service capabilities together. Figure 1-2 illustrates briefly the typical process of SLM

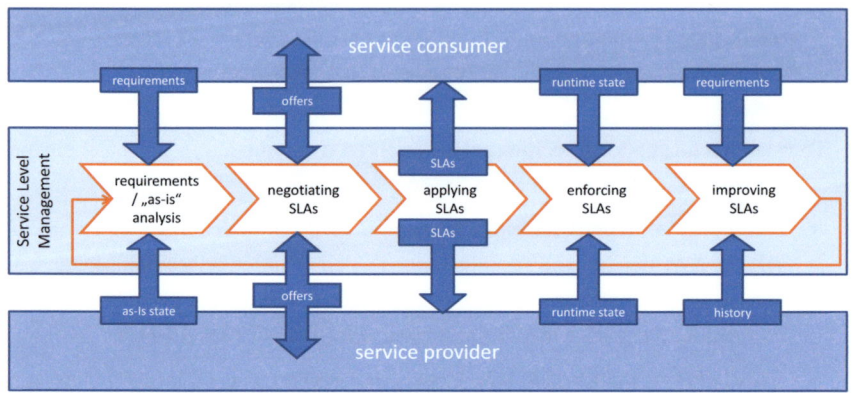

Figure 1-2: Service Level Management with consumer-facing IT providers

along with interactions between service providers and service consumers. A more detailed description of SLM is given in Section 3.2. In general, the life cycle of SLM consists of the following five phases:

- *Requirements/"As-Is" Analysis*: In this phase, SLM maintains a status quo by doing quantitative assessments on what a service consumer expects and what a service provider can deliver. The result of this phase is clear definitions in terms of quantitative measures.

- *Negotiating SLAs*: With the result from the analysis phase, a service consumer and a service provider begin to negotiate with each other. The goal in this phase is to find a compromise on the determined service objectives from the analysis phase. In this way, a service consumer and a service provider can find appropriate trade-offs between their interest conflicts.

- *Applying SLAs*: In this phase, a service provider applies the negotiated SLA to configure its local resources. The main aspect of the provider is to ensure the required quality of service delivery with an appropriate amount of resources. For a service consumer, it documents the agreed SLA locally, in order to check compliance of the quality of service delivery with the agreed service objectives at runtime. At the end of this phase, a service consumer begins to invoke the service of its provider.

- *Enforcing SLAs*: At runtime, SLM is responsible for enforcing the agreed SLAs between a consumer and a provider. In this phase, a service provider has to achieve consistently the service levels specified in the SLAs. Therefore, the key responsibility of SLM in this phase is to evaluate runtime events from both service consumer and service provider and quantify quality of service delivery in terms of predefined metrics. If necessary, SLA can take appropriate actions to ensure that SLAs are continuously met by the provider.

- *Improving SLAs*: SLM is a continuous process. On-going interactions between the SLM process, the consumer, and the provider increase visibility of SLA compliance of service delivery. Historical information collected in the previous phase provides the foundation for continuous improvement of service levels. Using such information, SLM can identify problems as well as determine related aspects for improvements. If necessary, it performs correcting actions to solve problems while taking changing requirements from the environment into consideration.

Hence, SLM is an on-going process with permanent interactions between service providers and service consumers. In doing so, IT infrastructure can guarantee that services are being delivered consistently in compliance with business requirements, so that business can achieve its desired objectives and outcomes. To automate such an SLM process with continuous and iterating life cycles, a sophisticated approach must address the following challenges:

- *Awareness of runtime state*: SLM has to ensure that consumer's expectations are met consistently by the provider. Hence, it must be aware of operational events from both consumer and provider and evaluate those events to estimate effectiveness of the SLM process. This provides the prerequisite for proactive reactions to problems.

- *Self-adaptive SLM*: As aforementioned, SLM is an on-going process with continuous improvements, in particular with respect to changing requirements from the business. In addition, with continuous monitoring of runtime states, SLM is aware of the compliance of service delivery with regard to SLAs. Hence, an automated SLM approach has to respond to changes or problems reactively or even proactively at runtime.

- *Automated negotiation support*: negotiating SLAs between providers and consumers is the core of SLM. With negotiated SLAs, a service consumer and its provider can balance their interest conflicts. On the one hand, this ensures that business requirements of a consumer can be met. On the other hand, a service provider delivers its service efficiently, in particular with respect to the amount of resources needed for service delivery. Therefore, an automated SLM approach must provide support for automated negotiation of service levels.

- *Involving related underpinning components*: business processes are consumer-facing. That is, it has direct interactions with the business as a service consumer. Hence, runtime behaviour of business processes is the determinant factor for controlling the end-to-end SLM process between business and IT. However, each business process is supported by a range of technical components from the IT infrastructure. The runtime behaviour of a business process depends on the behaviour of all underpinning components. Therefore, the end-to-end SLM should involve all related technical components in the process. This is the only way to ensure that IT as a whole can deliver the required services in alignment with desired objectives of the business.

- *Mapping business requirements to IT-centric metrics*: Section 1.1 describes the recursive functional dependences between technical components based on provider/consumer relationships. Hence, it requires that an end-to-end SLM approach should provide a top-down mechanism to link business requirements to underlying IT-centric metrics. By creating such links recursively across the entire service-oriented environment, business requirements can be gradually broken down into IT-centric service levels for each supporting component.

- *Autonomy of technical components*: each technical component within a service-oriented environment is autonomous. That is, a service-oriented component has the full freedom to make its own decisions without external interventions. Therefore, it has full control over its own runtime behaviour. From the viewpoint of an automated SLM approach, it is required that each technical component can keep its autonomy independent from other related components in the environment.

- *Heterogeneity of technical components*: as discussed in Section 1.1, a service-oriented environment is heterogeneous. Each technical component in the environment may differ from other components in many ways, such as technical standards they utilise, organisational models they rely on, and management standards they use. Hence, a comprehensive approach for end-to-end SLM should provide the possibility to include all related components into the process with reasonable efforts – in spite of their heterogeneous natures.

- *Adaptive management of technical components in compliance with service levels*: since technical components are autonomous, they are required to manage themselves in compliance with service levels defined in the SLM process. With self-organising capabilities, each technical component ensures that its runtime behaviour for service delivery complies with the agreed service levels.

In a word, to enable automated end-to-end SLM in a service-oriented environment, each technical component is expected to collaborate with related technical components to arrange service levels between them and organise itself in compliance with the arranged service levels. In this process, the approach has to take characteristics of a service-oriented environment into consideration, in particular, autonomy and high heterogeneity of technical components in the environment.

1.2.2 Approach

The focus of this thesis is to find appropriate approaches to facilitate end-to-end SLM within service-oriented environments. That is, how service levels can be established and enforced between each pair of service consumer and service provider at runtime, so that the overall runtime behaviour of the IT infrastructure can satisfy the end-to-end requirements of the business. In particular, this thesis investigates how a technical component can be included in the global SLM process in an automated manner.

Therefore, this thesis does not address how a technical component can be instrumented to deliver management capabilities at runtime, in particular from the viewpoint of distributed system management. Instead, it is assumed that each technical component is locally instrumented for management purposes by utilising a number of management technologies. Furthermore, it is assumed that each technical component exposes a manageability interface to external applications. Through those manageability interfaces, a management application can communicate with the corresponding technical component. Activities, such as reading management metadata, monitoring runtime events, configuring management objects, are done through the manageability interface. These assumptions assure that an external management component can monitor and control each technical component at runtime.

Another assumption on the IT infrastructure is the extended and consistent implementation of service-orientation on all technical components. That is, the service concept is not restricted to business processes or Web services. Underlying technical components in support of Web services, in particular hardware components, such as physical servers or network connectivity components should be service-oriented, too. Technically, this assumption is reasonable and realistic, in particular with respect to the emergence of *Cloud Computing*. As later discussed in Section 2.1.3, Cloud Computing promotes the provision of infrastructure components as network services. Thorough enforcement of the design principles of service-orientation across the entire IT infrastructure ensures that the approach described in this thesis can be applied to each technical component in the IT infrastructure, from business-facing processes down to IT-centric infrastructure components.

To realise automated end-to-end SLM in a service-oriented environment, as discussed in the motivation, this thesis proposes an approach on two different levels:

- On the *local* level, a technical component organises itself according to service levels it agrees upon with its consumer(s). To establish controlled self-organisation on a technical component, this thesis utilises the generic Observer/Controller (O/C) architecture from the Organic Computing research community [BMM+06]. Section 3.4 provides a detailed insight into the generic O/C architecture. With the generic O/C architecture, each technical component is expected to control adaptively its runtime behaviour in compliance with SLAs it closes with its service consumers.

- On the *global* level, a technical component collaborates with related components in its environment – either service consumer or service provider respectively – to coordinate their runtime behaviour. With recursive collaborations between related components top-down from business-centric processes to IT-centric components, requirements on business processes can be gradually broken down into requirements on each technical component. These IT-centric requirements derived from business requirements are in turn applied to each component individually by its local O/C architecture.

Concisely, the key characteristic of the approach is to enable end-to-end SLM by facilitating collaboration between all related technical components in a service-oriented system. Collaborative activities between technical components are carried out by means of automated negotiation of SLAs between service providers and service consumers. In this way, end-to-end service level requirements can be automatically propagated across the complete landscape without any manual efforts of human participants. In addition, SLAs as abstracted and homogeneous messages ensure that the proposed approach can be applied to technical components, in spite of their heterogeneous implementations.

1.3 Contributions

In brief, this thesis contributes to the current research in the field of automated Service Level Management for service-oriented systems. Among other things, this thesis makes the following major contributions:

- This thesis analyses the characteristics of service-oriented systems and outlines the objectives for enabling automated SLM in service-oriented systems. As the main environment for applying the approach, this thesis reviews the concept of service-orientation and its applications in the enterprise IT. In particular, it places an emphasis on the recent development in Service-oriented Computing (SOC), especially on Cloud Computing. Moreover, this thesis also reviews the research areas of self-organisation and Multi-Agent Systems (MAS) that are closely related to the approach of the present thesis. Among other things, it reviews the existing concepts in MAS to enable collaboration between agents.

- This thesis proposes an architecture that enables end-to-end SLM in service-oriented systems. Based on the generic observer/controller architecture introduced in the Organic Computing community, this thesis extends the architecture with the necessary capabilities to accelerate collaboration between technical components. In particular, it addresses how the extended observer/controller architecture can be applied to technical components to achieve automated end-to-end SLM in a service-oriented system.

- This thesis investigates the characteristics of SLAs in service-oriented systems and introduces an automated negotiation model to facilitate collaboration between technical components. There is a range of existing mechanisms that can be applied to realise negotiation between technical components. Hence, the design of a particular negotiation mechanism is subject to the characteristics of end-to-end SLM within a service-oriented system. The present thesis reviews the specific requirements of end-to-end SLM on automated negotiation and designs an automated negotiation model with respect to this requirement analysis.

- This thesis designs and implements a high-level simulation environment for evaluating solutions for service-oriented systems. In order to evaluate the proposed approach, an appropriate evaluation environment has to be able to deliver an operating service-oriented system that can be flexibly adjusted in accordance with objectives of particular evaluation experiments. Since physical environments satisfy this requirement only to a limited extent, a high-level simulated environment is designed and implemented in the present thesis. The resulting simulation environment is able to produce realistic runtime behaviour of a service-oriented system with respect to both functional and non-functional aspects of such a system.

- This thesis evaluates the proposed approach and outlines the application of automated SLM to manage a service-oriented system. In the simulated evaluation environment, the present thesis evaluates the proposed automated negotiation model towards its performance and efficiency. Moreover, the present thesis also evaluates the applicability of the proposed multi-level SLM approach with a real world scenario from the university.

1.4 Thesis Outline

The present thesis is organised with respect to a conventional software engineering approach. Beginning with motivation and state-of-the-art for end-to-end SLM, the design of the proposed architecture is introduced and evaluated within a simulation environment. The last part of this thesis summarises the work and provides an outlook on possible further development of the concept.

Figure 1-3 illustrates the roadmap of the present thesis. The first part, Motivation and State-of-the-Art (Part I), motivates the main problem addressed by the present thesis and reviews the current development in the related research fields.

Chapter 1 introduces the recent development within SOC and enlightens the need to establish a self-organising SLM for service-oriented system. Chapter 2 reviews the main research fields that are closely related to the approach of this thesis. It reviews the most recent development in the field of SOC, which is the target application field of the thesis. In addition, it reviews various approaches that aim at establishing self-organisation in technical components. At last, it discusses existing approaches in MAS to facilitate collaboration between agents, which plays a key role in the approach of this thesis.

The second part, Design (Part II), introduces the design of the architecture to enable self-organising SLM in a service-oriented system. Chapter 3 introduces the fundamental means to realise the multi-level framework to enable automated SLM. Among other things, it establishes a common understanding of service-oriented environments as well as the process involved in SLM for the present thesis. In addition, it introduces the basic model to enable automated negotiation between a service consumer and a provider and outlines the generic observer/controller architecture in detail.

Chapter 4 reviews a real service-oriented scenario from the university context and analyses the requirements and challenges that the self-organising SLM approach of this thesis has to address.

Chapter 5 introduces a reference architecture to enable automated end-to-end SLM in a service-oriented environment. In particular, this chapter outlines how the concepts described in Chapter 3 can be combined to establish a framework for realising automated end-to-end SLM.

Chapter 6 focuses on collaboration between a service consumer and its providers, which is crucial for establishing service relationships dynamically. Particularly, this chapter is concerned with the underlying automated negotiation model and introduces the negotiation protocol to facilitate bilateral negotiation between management agents. Moreover, this chapter describes a range of negotiation strategies that can be applied to find optimised SLAs in the course of negotiation.

The third part, Evaluation (Part III), is concerned with evaluating the proposed framework to enable automated end-to-end SLM.

Chapter 7 focuses on the evaluation environment to assess the feasibility of the negotiation-based SLM approach. Among other things, this chapter outlines the overall architecture of the evaluation environment and describes how the simulation environment can produce the runtime behaviour of a service-oriented system both on the macroscopic and microscopic level.

Chapter 8 is concerned with the evaluation results of the present thesis. It outlines the design considerations of the evaluation environment and provides the evaluation results to show the feasibility of the proposed approach in this thesis.

The last part, Conclusion and Outlook (Part IV), summarises the thesis and describes how the proposed approach has addressed the design objectives determined in

Chapter 4. In addition, this part outlines the possible research directions and extensions of the proposed framework for future work.

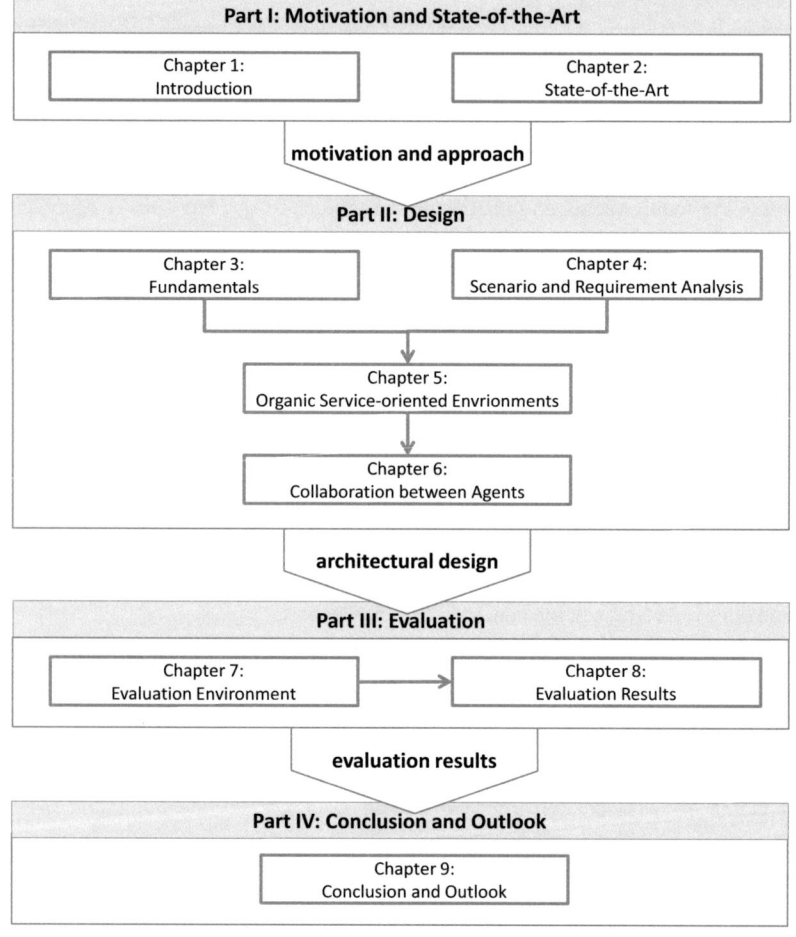

Figure 1-3: Structure of the present thesis

Chapter 2   State-of-the-Art

"知人者智，自知者明。"
— 【道德经，三十三章】

"The one who knows others is learned; the one who knows oneself is enlightened."
(Tao Te Ching, Laozi, ~ 470 B.C.)

The present thesis envisions automating SLM processes between all related service providers and service consumers in a service-oriented environment. The approach to realise this vision is to combine local self-organisation of a technical component with global collaboration between components, as described in Section 1.2. Hence, this chapter provides an overview on current research in the related research fields, in particular with respect to service-oriented systems and self-organisation.

Section 2.1 introduces the concept of service-orientation and its application in enterprise IT. In particular, this section places an emphasis on the recent development in Cloud Computing that provides the ideal environment for applying the approach of this thesis due to its service-oriented design. Section 2.2 focuses on approaches realising self-organisation. Among other things, the observer/controller architecture from the Organic Computing research community is highlighted in this section. The last section, Section 2.3, addresses the foundation of Multi-Agent Systems (MASs). In particular, this section is concerned with automated negotiation between agents in MAS and provides an overview on how negotiation can be applied in service-oriented environments.

2.1 Service-oriented Computing

Service-oriented Computing (SOC) is an emerging distributed computing model to build business applications that usually span several organisational units. It provides the fundamental means to design, implement, deliver, and consume business capabilities as *Services*. As the name *SOC* already says, services play a key role within SOC.

In the context of SOC, services are self-contained units that provide business capabilities via well-defined interfaces.

However, such units of business capabilities exist already in other similar computing paradigms, such as objects in object-oriented programming or components in component-oriented programming. To distinguish the concept of services from other encapsulation mechanisms, design and implementation of a service must follow the design paradigm of *service-orientation*. That is, how such self-contained units can be built on top of given business capabilities. To this end, service-orientation defines a range of design principles, such as using abstracted and well-defined interfaces to realise loose coupling between related components, or using coordinated interactions to implement value-added service compositions on top of basic services.

In this way, business capabilities become reusable services that can be invoked dynamically by other components. Figure 2-1 illustrates the relationships between all the artefacts of Service-oriented Computing.

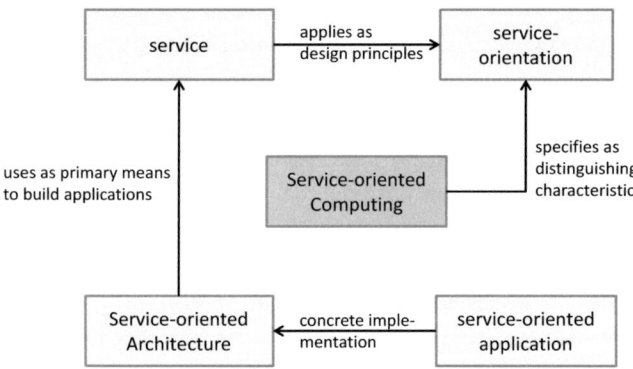

Figure 2-1: Artefacts of service-orientation

Service-oriented Architecture (SOA) specifies the way in which such flexible and reusable services are organised to implement end-to-end business solutions. In general, an SOA defines the architectural model that organises the various artefacts to realise required business functionalities at a conceptual level, such as business processes, (Web) services, applications, and components. Based on this conceptual model, *service-oriented applications* can be implemented. Each service-oriented application consists of a combination of technologies, products, platforms, and various other parts. Due to different operational contexts of such applications, each deployed SOA is always unique. Nevertheless, there is usually a common set of technologies, in particular standardised communication protocols, to ensure the interoperability between different SOA implementations.

The remainder of this section focuses on the design principles of service-orientation, and outlines their impact on developing business applications. In addition, the reference architecture of SOA is introduced to show the essential architectural parts that are highly relevant to the approach introduced in this thesis. At last, this section gives an insight into service-oriented infrastructure, in particular Cloud Computing, which utilises the concept of service-orientation to provide a novel way to deliver and consume hardware-based services.

2.1.1 Service-orientation

As the requirements for tighter alignment between business and IT infrastructure increase permanently, the design paradigm of service-orientation emerges as the ultimate solution. In a business, IT infrastructure is responsible to deliver business solutions to automate business processes. The widely established approach to build business solutions adopts the concept of "separation-of-concerns." It consists of several tasks, including identifying business tasks to be automated, defining business requirements for these tasks, and building appropriate business capabilities to satisfy the defined requirements. However, business solutions built in this way are less flexible and reusable, because business capabilities are closely tied to specific business scenarios and requirements associated with them. In case of changed business requirements, significant changes to these business solutions are often not avoidable.

To reduce the time needed to adapt business applications to changing requirements, the design paradigm of *service-orientation* has emerged. It is concerned with reusable and flexible encapsulation of business capabilities as *services*. By applying service-orientation to enterprise IT, business requirements are no longer met by building or extending existing business applications. Instead, new requirements are addressed by changing the composition of existing services in accordance with these requirements. This kind of agility enables IT infrastructure to adapt to changing conditions in business and its environment on demand [CGH+05].

The idea of encapsulating business capabilities as logic units is not new. Similar approaches, such as Object-oriented Programming or Component-oriented Program-

21

ming, uses this concept, too. To distinguish services from objects or components, service-orientation defines a set of design principles. Service-orientation addresses mainly the way in which such business capabilities can be encapsulated as reusable services for remote access. Box defined four fundamental tenets for creating services, in particular in comparison with object-orientation [Box04]:

- *Boundaries are explicit*: each service has an explicit boundary to the outside world. Services interact with each other explicitly by exchanging messages through the boundaries. Such an explicit boundary allows each service to do implementation-independent interactions with predefined messages.

- *Services are autonomous*: autonomy of a service appears in several facets throughout a service development process, in particular during deployment and versioning. During this process, each service is expected to behave reasonably as an independent entity. In other words, each service is free to choose the platform, middleware, or coding languages to implement its logic.

- *Services share schema and contract, not class*: each service interacts with its consumers through messages specified by schema and behaviour defined by contract. A service contract defines the structure and ordering constraints of messages exchanged between a service and its consumer. Hence, contracts are used to verify message integrity at runtime. In addition, in order to ensure long-term relationships between a service and its consumers, contracts and schema have to remain stable over time. In contrast, the respective service provider can change its service implementations autonomously.

- *Service compatibility is determined based on policy*: both service consumer and service provider have policies on operational requirements to control interactions between them. Therefore, they express their capabilities and requirements in terms of policy expressions. Before a provider and a consumer enter a long-term relationship, they must be able to satisfy each other's policy requirements.

Box's definitions emphasise the explicit boundaries between services and the autonomous behaviour of services behind the boundaries. Erl extended this view on service-orientation towards design principles concerned with adopting services in enterprise IT, in particular with respect to federated interoperability and vendor independence of services. Based on analysis of best practices and similar design approaches, Erl summarises the following eight design principles for service-orientation – with a partial overlap with the definitions of Box [Erl08]:

- *Standardised service contracts*: similar to the previous definition of Box, each service shares a formal contract with its consumers. A formal contract can be composed of legal and technical information, such as interaction interface, constraints, usage policies, and so on.

- *Service loose coupling*: a service and its consumers retain a minimal level of coupling. The term coupling refers to the level of dependence between a service and its consumer. Ideally, a service and its consumers depend on each other only on the base of an agreed service contract. This ensures maximal flexibility of the resulting architecture in case of changes.

- *Service abstractions*: from the viewpoint of a service consumer, a service operates as a black box. The only information of a service available to its consumers is the published service contract. This design principle helps to reduce dependence between a service and its consumer and thus makes the loose coupling between them possible.

- *Service reusability*: this principle requires that the design of a service cannot be bound to a particular process task. Instead, a service has to attain an effective level of reusability to become generic enough for being involved in other processes. This ensures that the resulting service-oriented environment can be extended and adapted beyond particular business solutions.

- *Service autonomy*: similar to the previous definition given by Box, service autonomy emphasises the governance by the underlying implementation by a service provider.

- *Service statelessness*: the essential difference between service-orientation and object-orientation is that a service has no state. Runtime state information is only specifically bound to the current process instance. This principle allows a service to be integrated into different business processes without any changes to the underlying implementation.

- *Service discoverability*: this aspect is new in comparison to the previous definitions given by Don Box. Discoverability is the prerequisite to facilitate consumption of a service by potential service consumers. It can be done by automated interpretation and evaluation of abstract service contracts that provide metadata on the target services to potential service consumers.

- *Service composibility*: a service composition represents coordinated consumption of a set of services. This allows service providers to produce value-added services on top of a set of underlying services. In fact, this principle is the direct result of service reusability and statelessness.

While the definitions of Box are restricted to a single service, the definitions given by Erl have extended their view to the architectural design principles.

Figure 2-2 summarises the relationships between all design principles discussed in this section. *Standardised service contracts* abstract implementation details of a service and provide metadata about the service for *discovery* purpose. *Service abstraction* allows a service to operate as a black box and thus retain its *autonomy* in the course of interactions with its consumers. To achieve a *loose coupling* between a service and its consumers, the service is expected to reduce its dependence with its consumers. This is ensured by the principles of *service abstraction, autonomy*, and *statelessness. Service abstraction specifies* that the service only shares interface information with its consumers and no implementation details. *Service autonomy* specifies that each service is responsible for its own runtime behaviour. That is, from the viewpoint of service implementation, a service and its consumers are fully independent from each other. This also requires that a service is *stateless*. Only *stateless* services can be easily disconnected from existing service consumers and be connected to other potential consumers. In this way, a service increases its *reusability* for other potential consumers. Together with service *discoverability, statelessness*, and *reusability*, services can be composed to value-added services. This possibility addresses the design principle of service *composibility*.

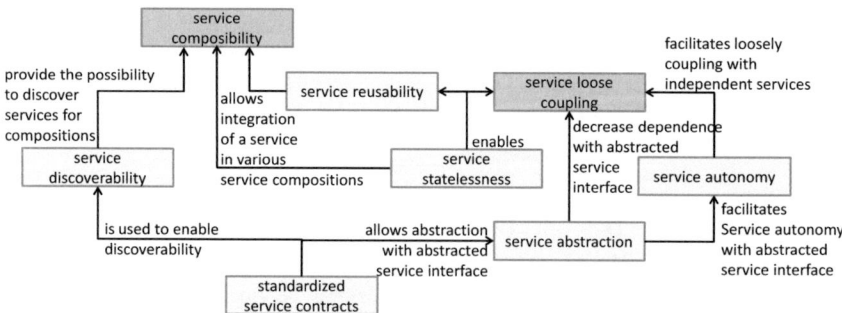

Figure 2-2: Relationships between the design principles of service-orientation

By reviewing the service principles, it is obvious that service autonomy is of particular interest for SLM. With service autonomy, a service has awareness and full control over all its local resources. Such control exists in all facets of service development, in particular during deployment and versioning. It allows a service to specify independently the underlying implementation logics required to realise the business capabilities exposed by the service contract. By doing so, a service can autonomously govern its local resources to tune runtime behaviour of its business capabilities – e.g., reliability, availability, and performance in compliance with SLAs closed with its service consumers. In this context, services are similar to the behaviour of agents in multi-agent systems that are further discussed in Section 2.3.3.

2.1.2 Service-oriented Architecture

Service-oriented Architecture defines an architectural style that has services as core architectural elements. It provides a set of standardised messaging protocols, interface definitions, workflow modelling languages, as well as management policies. These artefacts of SOA address the necessary connecting pieces to compose services to business processes that satisfy given business requirements. As aforementioned, SOA has different objectives than service-orientation. Service-orientation focuses on the abstracted design principles for defining how services can be constructed out of given business capabilities. It does not address the way, in which such services can be composed to realise a particular business process. In contrast to this, SOA provides the architectural framework around services. By using the artefacts specified by SOAs, business can compose the required business logic out of existing services without having to care about the barriers caused by heterogeneous technical platforms.

Although it has been applied by numerous organisations, there is no widely accepted definition for SOA. Instead, there is a number of competing definitions proposed by various industrial consortia and software vendors. Each definition has its emphasis on different aspects. The W3C defines a Service-oriented Architecture as "a set of components which can be invoked, and whose interface descriptions can be published and discovered" [HB04]. This definition addresses the basic parts of an SOA as a set of discoverable and callable components. However, it restricts an SOA as a set of components that exist already in other similar design paradigms. Furthermore, the W3C's definition of SOA covers mainly development and deployment aspects and addresses less architectural aspects of service-oriented systems [SW04].

The OASIS defines SOA as "a paradigm for organizing and utilizing distributed capabilities that may be under the control of different ownership domains"

[MKL+06]. In addition, the OASIS views SOA as an ecosystem that provides "a medium for exchange of value between independently acting participants. Participants (and stakeholders in general) have legitimate claims to ownership of resources that are made available via the SOA; and the behaviour and performance of the participants are subject to rules of engagement which are captured in a series of policies and contracts." [ELMT09]. It is noteworthy that this definition uses the term *participant* to denote the artefacts within an SOA. In comparison to the narrow definition given by the W3C, the OASIS' definition includes not only services, but also machines and people in the context of SOA. Each of those participants has some control and influence on the overall service-oriented system. Furthermore, this definition clarifies the architectural aspect of SOA that provides the space between participants to facilitate interactions between them. It also implies that in order to enable consistent communication between participants, SOA needs a number of standards and policies to guide interactions between services and their consumers. Such policies determine the behaviour and performance of participants during their interactions with other stakeholders.

Erl defines SOA as "a form of technology architecture that adheres to the principles of service-orientation. When realised through the Web services technology platform, SOA establishes the potential to support and promote these principles throughout the business process and automation domain of an enterprise" [Erl05]. This definition emphasises the capabilities of services in compliance with the design principles of service-orientation introduced in 2.1.1. In addition, it clarifies the relationship between Web services and SOA. That is, as a subset of services, Web services provide the necessary means to help to realise SOA. Further similar definitions on SOA are given by Colan [Col04], the Open Group [OG09], Papazoglou and van den Heuvel [PH07], as well as Sprott and Wilkes [SW04].

The variety of definitions shows that it is not trivial to give a precise and commonly accepted definition of SOA. It depends on different views on target systems employing service-orientation. For the present thesis, it is sufficient that an SOA definition can address the following characteristics:

- SOA provides an architectural paradigm for organising a network of independently participating artefacts including services, machines, and people that operate, use and govern these services and machines. Each artefact may affect or be affected by the system.

- In a system applying SOA, none of the participating artefacts owns the system. Instead, each of them controls and influences part of the system.

- Services follow the design principles of service-orientation.

- SOA provides the necessary standards and policies to facilitate interactions between services and their consumers. These policies place unique requirements on the infrastructure to ensure interoperability in a heterogeneous environment.

With the SOA definition as guidance, the more interesting aspect is what an SOA-based system can look like. To address this aspect, several organisations have worked on various reference models as well as reference architectures to provide architectural patterns for building SOA-based systems [KE09]. The W3C defines Web Services Architecture as an architectural model that identifies the functional components within such an architecture and specifies relationships between those components [BHM+04]. However, the architectural model of the W3C focuses mainly on the implementation details of Web services in support of SOA. In particular, it outlines the Web Services Architecture stack as a set of layered and interrelated technologies. To this end, it identifies the necessary communication protocols (such as HTTP and SMTP) together with a number of emerging standards (e.g., XML for encoding information, SOAP for transporting messages, WSDL for describing interfaces, etc.). A standard-based Web Service Architecture stack increases interoperability between heterogeneous components in a service-oriented environment. However, it provides less information on how such a service-oriented environment should be built. Similarly, the reference architecture foundation hosted by the OASIS uses a similar view to provide the fundamental model of SOA [MKL+06, ELMT09]. However, in comparison to the W3C approach, the OASIS reference architecture provides only abstract and fundamental models on the meta-level. Other than the W3C approach, one cannot use directly the OASIS reference architecture to implement SOA-based systems.

A more concrete reference architecture intended to support understanding, design, and implementation of SOA-based systems is provided by Arsanjani et al. of the Open Group [AZE+07, AK09]. This reference architecture provides the blueprint of an SOA-based system, including integral architectural parts of an SOA. For organisations implementing SOA, they can directly use this reference architecture to make architectural and design decisions.

The reference architecture of the Open Group divides a service-oriented architecture into nine independent layers, five horizontal layers and four vertical crossover layers, as illustrated in Figure 2-3. The five basic layers are from top-down the *consumer interfaces* and *business processes* layers with consumer concerns, the *services* layer, the *service components* layer, and the *operational systems* layer with provider concerns. The *operational systems* layer is composed of technical infrastructure needed to operate an SOA-based environment, e.g., operational hosting environments of system components. The *service components* layer consists of software components that provide implementation of services. The *services* layer includes all services defined within the given service-oriented environment. The *business process* layer contains service orchestrations and compositions in compliance with business requirements. At last, the *consumer interface* layer provides interfaces to connect the IT capabilities with end users, such as Web portals, or rich clients.

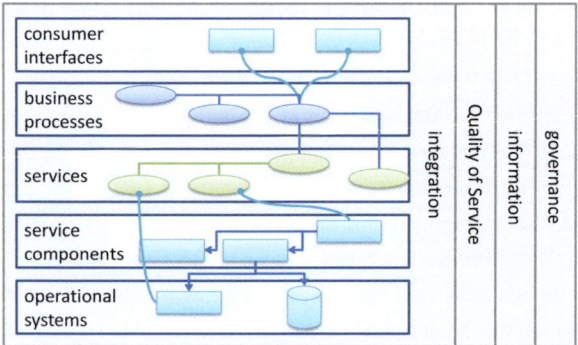

Figure 2-3: SOA Reference Architecture of the Open Group (see [AK09])

The four vertical layers cut across the five basic layers and support the aspects of *integration*, *quality of service*, *information*, and *governance* in the environment. The *integration* layer provides the fundamental communication platform to connect service providers with service consumers. The *quality of service* layer provides the necessary capabilities to support the life cycle processes of non-functional policies, e.g., reliability, availability, and security. The *information* layer focuses on the information aspects of the entire service-oriented environment and provides the basis for creating business intelligence, e.g., by using data warehouse. The *governance* layer ensures that the entire service-oriented environment is aligned with defined corporate and IT policies, guidelines, and standards.

Other layered approaches similar to the Open Group's reference architecture are the *Integrated Service-oriented Architecture* (iSOA) introduced in the Karlsruhe Integrated InformationManagement (KIM) project [FLM+06, KIM10] and the *extended Service-oriented Architecture* (xSOA) proposed by Papazoglou [Pap05]. The reference architecture iSOA distinguishes between four different architectural parts: *technical infrastructure* for providing infrastructural support, *basic services* for offering simple business functionalities, *application services* for provisioning value-added service compositions, and a *service portal* for enabling interactions with end users.

However, both iSOA and xSOA do not include the underlying physical and hardware-centric components in the architecture. For real world implementation of SOA in support of dynamic business, agility of IT infrastructure is important to guarantee a consistent and comprehensive support of service-oriented solutions. The emerging trend to combine the design paradigm of service-orientation with IT infrastructure, as later introduced in Section 2.1.4, provides the prerequisite to increase agility of the complete service-oriented solution, including hardware-centric components.

2.1.3 Cloud Computing

Cloud Computing is the emerging paradigm for provisioning infrastructure services over the Internet. The basic idea behind Cloud Computing is to provide scalable and flexible computing resources on demand to satisfy real-time usage requirements on computing resources of business [Hay08]. In comparison to traditional computing resources, such as local installed software and hardware components, Cloud Computing provides a shift in the geography of computation. Instead of getting computing tasks done locally, Cloud Computing processes computing tasks on unseen computing resources in the cloud, possibly scattered around the globe.

As pointed out by Erdogmus [Erd09] and Vaquero et al. [VRM+08], there are a number of definitions of Cloud Computing with different focuses on this technology, such as in [BYV08, Dej08, McF08, AFG+09, BYV+09, Gee09]. Most of the definitions outline the major characteristics of Cloud Computing: *virtualisation*, *Internet centric*, *scalability*, *pay-per-use*, and *service/infrastructure SLAs*. This thesis aligns itself to the definition given by Buyya, Yeo, and Venugopal [BYV08] that covers most of these characteristics and suffices for the purpose of the present thesis:

> *A Cloud is a type of parallel and distributed system consisting of a collection of inter-connected and virtualized computers that are dynamically provisioned and presented as one or more unified computing resource(s)*

based on service-level agreements established through negotiation between
the service provider and consumers.

According to this definition, Cloud Computing can be considered with respect to the following aspects:

- *On demand service provisioning*: Cloud Computing provides a vast resource pool with on-demand resource allocation. This is the most significant difference of Cloud Computing in comparison to traditional enterprise IT. From this point of view, Cloud Computing follows the idea of Utility Computing [BCL+04], where infrastructure providers make computational resources available and customers can rent computational resources as needed.

- *Abstraction via virtualisation*: Virtualisation provides the technological foundation for Cloud Computing. Computational resources on demand imply that infrastructure providers can dynamically change resource allocation of a particular consumer or transparently moving an existing consumer from one physical server to another. This requires service consumers to be decoupled from the underlying hardware, which is not possible without virtualisation. By organising physical resources, (e.g., storage, computing power, network connectivity) in a resource pool, virtualisation allows service providers to get an abstract and logical view on those resources. Individual requirements from consumers on computational resources can be satisfied by providing resources directly from the virtualised and logical resource pool. As summarised by Baun et al. [BKNT10], from the viewpoint of infrastructure providers, virtualisation allows them to realise greater ROI by improving the average resource utilisation rate of hardware components. From the viewpoint of consumers, they can achieve more dynamic on providing their applications on top of scalable and high available computational resources.

- *SLA-driven*: Provisioning infrastructure services in Cloud Computing is controlled by SLAs negotiated between infrastructure providers and consumers. In this case, underlying computational resources are dynamically managed by terms defined in SLAs. For example, an SLA may define how quickly incoming requests should be processed, or how much a respective consumer should be priced for using particular services. For infrastructure providers, SLA-driven management of resources allow them to relocate efficiently computational resources to individual consumers to fulfil their requirements. On the other hand, dynamically negotiated SLAs ensure that consumers are fairly priced for cloud services they consume on the base of pay-per-use.

- *Network-centric*: Infrastructure services provided in Cloud Computing are accessible over network or Internet, depending on the type of the clouds [AFG+09]. In general, depending on the accessibility of services provided in the cloud, a cloud infrastructure can be either private, hybrid, or public [AFG+10].

- *Self-healing*: physical resources in clouds are managed transparently to consumers. Various software and hardware components are autonomously reconfigured, orchestrated, and consolidated as virtualised resources to consumers. Based on the concept of virtualisation, a virtualised instance can be replaced in case of failures by a new as well as backup instance. All failover measures of virtualised resources are performed autonomously and transparently in the background.

- *Service-oriented provisioning*: computational resources in clouds are provided as services. Clouds, especially public clouds, provide necessary interfaces based on standardised communication protocols, such as Web services or RESTful services, to their consumers. This allows asynchronous and message-based communication between service providers and service consumers [BKNT10c].

To sum up, Cloud Computing provides architectural and technical foundations to provision IT infrastructures, software platforms, and applications as network-centric services. Meanwhile, there have been a number of cloud providers on the market, such as Amazon Elastic Compute Cloud (Amazon EC2) providing virtual servers, Amazon Simple Storage Service (Amazon S3) providing online storage, or Microsoft SQL Azure providing fully relational database in the cloud [BKNT10a].

To get a better overview on various technologies and services in the cloud, Baun et al. worked out a architecture stack for Cloud Computing, as illustrated in Figure 2-4 [LKN+09, BKNT10b]. They distinguish between four different layers in the architecture stack. The lowest layer in the stack manages a set of hardware-centric resources, such as storage, network connectivity, or computing power (e.g., automated setup and tear-down, demand-based scaling, fail-over, etc.). These resource sets are provided as virtualised infrastructure services (i.e., IaaS) to upper software-related layers.

The PaaS layer provides programming and execution environments (e.g., Java or .NET environments) for running applications. The SaaS layer contains all applications provided to end-users. The applications services offer basic business capabilities that can be further orchestrated by applications to provide value-added functionalities.

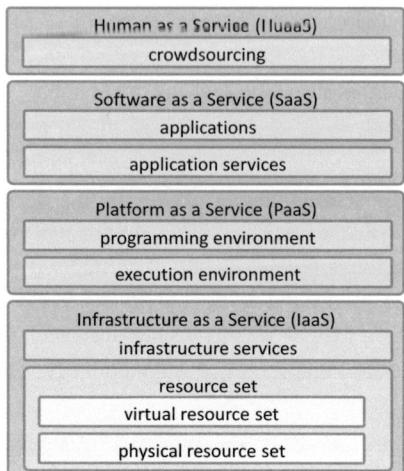

Figure 2-4: Cloud Architecture Stack (see [BKNT10b])

The topmost layer in the stack, HuaaS, helps to involve human intelligence into service offers. It is well known that in spite of advancement in Artificial Intelligence, there are tasks (e.g., pattern recognition) that cannot be efficiently processed by computers. HuaaS allows in such case to incorporate human intelligence into software-based services to solve given problems, as promoted e.g. in the Amazon Mechanical Turk service [BC06].

2.1.4 Service-oriented Infrastructure

The evolution of enterprise architectures from traditional two/three-tier architectures to Service-oriented Architectures is driven by increasing demands on tight alignment between business and enterprise IT in face of ever-changing market environments. Recent research so far focuses mainly on software-centric aspects to increase agility of related IT infrastructure. That is how service-oriented applications can respond quickly and efficiently to changes in business. The service-oriented approach to orchestrate atomic capabilities to business processes, as promoted in SOA, can solve this problem effectively – from the viewpoint of functional aspects.

However, from the viewpoint of non-functional aspects, such as performance or availability, software-based adaptation is not sufficient to improve the agility of the whole IT infrastructure. For example, to satisfy an unexpected peak of service requests for a given business process, adapting service compositions has only limited efficiency. In this case, the underlying technical components in support of the respective business process must be reconfigured to get rid of increasing requests, such as by assigning more computational capacities to the process. Hence, it is obvious that in order to provide highly agile IT infrastructure, hardware-centric components should be included in the comprehensive SOA, too. That is, applying the design principles of service-orientation to link service levels of higher-level business processes with those of the underlying hardware-centric services, such as network connectivity, storage, and servers. The resulting IT infrastructure is denoted as Service-oriented Infrastructure (SOI).

SOI is characterised by defining and provisioning IT infrastructure in terms of services. That is, hardware-related SOI undergoes the same life cycle as software-related SOA to design, implement, provision, operate, and manage services. The resulting infrastructure services run on top of a pool of physical resources governed by a centralised management system that keeps the balance between service delivery and service demand.

Cloud Computing provides the suitable example to demonstrate how such an SOI can work. As outlined in 2.1.3, Cloud Computing provides virtualised hardware components, technology platforms, and network-centric applications as services. These services can be orchestrated as needed to provide appropriate runtime environments for an SOA-based system. Varia has demonstrated the simplicity and strength of SOI to run applications on top of orchestrated Cloud services [Var08]. Based on a set of Amazon Cloud services, he built an application to do pattern-matching across millions of Web documents. In each run, his application draws the necessary computational resources on demand (up to hundreds of virtual servers), runs a parallel computation on them, and then shuts down all involved virtual servers after task completion to free resources in the Cloud. All of these tasks are done transparently through abstracted Web service interfaces. This scenario demonstrates clearly the strength of service-oriented infrastructure to construct highly agile and resilient network-enabled applications.

Although the idea of applying design principles of service-orientation to the hardware-centric infrastructure emerged only a few years ago, there are already several efforts in industry and academia towards realisation of SOI. The most representative works are the SOI Reference Framework proposed by the Open Group [OG08], the

SLA@SOI project supported by the EU [The08], and Intel's research on SOI with a
prototypical implementation [CLC+06].

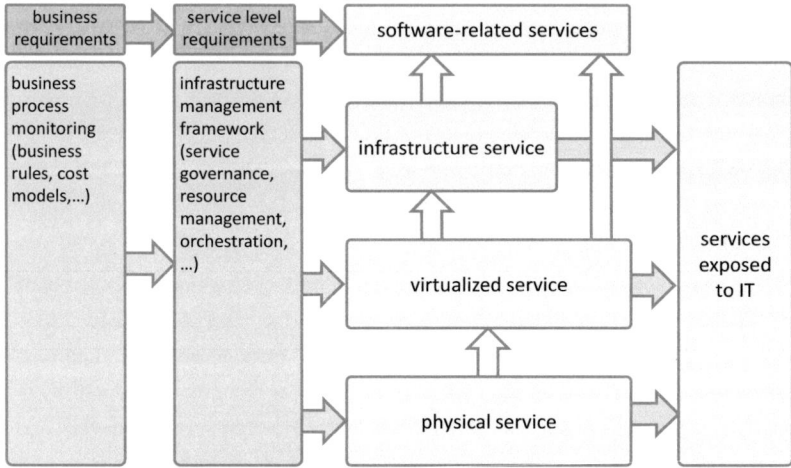

Figure 2-5: SOI reference model by the Open Group (see [OG08])

Figure 2-5 illustrates the SOI reference model proposed by the Open Group with all
its conceptual building parts [OG08]. *Business Requirements* capture all business requirements from both the business and the IT in terms of SLAs, such as business process performance, security requirements, cost models, and so on. Based on those giv-
en business requirements, *Business Process Monitoring* derives a set of rules, cost
models, and other artefacts to control the *Infrastructure Management Framework*.
Service Level Requirements are derived from given business requirements. They define service levels for each service delivered by the infrastructure. The *Infrastructure
Management Framework* consists of a set of software, processes and procedures to
plan, build, and run IT resources in accordance with Service Level requirements and
other business rules. By doing this, this framework governs the underlying physical
resources and encapsulates them as services. The *Physical Services* represent hardware-related resources on the atomic level, such as storage, computing power, and
operating systems. On top of those atomic physical resources, *Virtualised Services*
abstract physical resources by providing interfaces to enable consistent access to
them. *Infrastructure Services* compose virtualised services to provide unique capabilities with value-added functionalities. The IT manages all services and the underlying

IT infrastructure via the particular management services exposed by the Infrastructure Management Framework.

In short, the Open Group's reference model provides a functional view on service-oriented infrastructure and specifies the necessary integral parts with less reference to SOA. Driven by high-level business requirements, SOI has to define appropriate service levels to satisfy overall business demands. Provisioning physical resources as services is controlled by centralised management systems with the fundamental approach of virtualisation. With increasing degree on abstraction, SOI provides access to physical services, virtualised services, and composed infrastructure services.

Another comprehensive framework considering interactions between SOI and SOA is proposed by the EU's SLA@SOI project. Initialised with the vision to provide "*a business-ready service-oriented infrastructure empowering the service economy in a flexible and dependable way,*" the research project aims to provide fundamental support to enable service-oriented economy. IT-based service can be flexibly traded and consumed as economic good between loosely coupled service consumers, service providers, and infrastructure providers. To gain the desired flexibility, SLA@SOI utilises a holistic SLA management framework in combination with adaptive SLA-aware infrastructure. The multi-layer SLA management framework provides support to specify, negotiate, and monitor SLAs between related stakeholders in an *end-to-end* manner. The behaviour of corresponding infrastructural resources is then controlled and enforced by negotiated SLAs. More details on SLA@SOI are available on the project website [SLA10]. The difference between the approaches utilised in SLA@SOI and the SOI reference model of the Open Group are their different scopes of their frameworks. While SLA@SOI intends to provide a comprehensive SLA-driven framework covering both hardware-centric and software-centric services, the Open Group's SOI reference model focuses mainly on essential parts to enable hardware-centric services, i.e., an implementation guide for enterprise IT.

2.1.5 Concluding Remarks

The emergence of service-orientation facilitates the shift of enterprise IT from product-oriented economy to service-oriented economy. Applying service-orientation to enterprise IT, businesses can gain increasing agility in their enterprise IT. Section 2.1 outlines the basic concept of service-orientation and reviews the development of Service-oriented Computing in the last years. The largest benefit of adopting SOA is that enterprise applications can flexibly reorganise themselves in response to changes in their environments. However, SOA addresses the desired agility only for changing functional demands from business. In order to get service-oriented applications responsive to changing demands in the environment, the design principles of service-orientation are applied to hardware-related IT infrastructure, too. The resulting Service-oriented Infrastructure provides business on demand access to computational resources within a single data centre or across several data centres in an adaptive manner.

In brief, service-oriented enterprise IT has the following characteristics that are of interest for the purpose of this thesis:

- *Consistent service-orientation across IT infrastructure*: service-orientation is not limited to software-related enterprise applications any more. The occurrence of SOI allows business to apply the same design principles of service-orientation consistently across the complete IT infrastructure, down to physical resources.

- *Distributed components*: with consistent application of service-orientation, a business process can run on top of an IT infrastructure distributed across organisational boundaries. In particular, the emergence of Cloud Computing facilitates the shift from locally installed data centres into Clouds possibly scattered across the globe.

- *Autonomy of technical components*: artefacts within a service-oriented IT infrastructure are autonomous. Each technical component operates in the IT infrastructure as a black box with standardised and abstracted interfaces. IT capabilities, independent of their types (such as computing power or business capability), can be consumed via such interfaces in a standardised way. Behind the abstracted interfaces, each technical component is autonomously responsible to design, implement, deploy, and manage its service.

- *Heterogeneity of IT infrastructure*: artefacts within a service-oriented IT infrastructure are heterogeneous, from the viewpoint of technology platforms, organisational affiliations, and management standards. However, heterogeneous service consumers and service providers can interact with one another, as long as they leverage interoperable communication standards for their interactions.

- *SLA-driven IT infrastructure*: a service-oriented IT infrastructure is driven by SLAs. Each pair of service consumer and service provider arranges their expectations and obligations with an SLA. Such an SLA defines exact conditions, under which the corresponding service is delivered. A service provider enforces the arranged SLAs at runtime by allocating its local technical resources in accordance with the terms agreed in the SLAs.

Hence, in the remainder of this thesis, the term *service-oriented environment* (SOE) is used to denote a complete IT infrastructure, from software-centric business processes down to hardware-centric infrastructural components. All technical components within an SOE are expected to conform to the design principles of service-orientation. This ensures that all technical components can interact with one another unambiguously via standardised communication protocols. Therefore, these technical components are referred to as *service components* in the remainder of this thesis.

2.2 Self-organisation

Today's technical systems become more and more complex. Especially, the increasing combination of traditional mechanical engineering and electronic engineering in technical systems let human efforts to maintain such technical systems get out of hand. For example, the latest breakdown statistics of the German automobile club ADAC shows, meanwhile around 40 per cent of all registered car breakdowns are reducible to electronic problems [ADA10]. To cope with increasing complexity of technical systems, there is a considerable amount of research efforts in industry and academia focusing on the capability of technical systems to self-organise themselves.

This section focuses on the concept of self-organisation. After a short introduction on self-organisation in Section 2.2.1, Section 2.2.2 provides an insight into approaches adopting self-organisation in technical systems, in particular from the viewpoint of SOA. Section 2.2.3 focuses on some generic approaches to establish self-organisation in technical systems, including the aforementioned research efforts from the Organic Computing community, while Section 2.4 summarises the section.

2.2.1 Overview

Self-organisation is a phenomenon often seen in nature. In the thesis of Gershenson [Ger07], he summarises works on self-organisation from different disciplines, such as in cybernetics [VF60, Ash62], mathematics [Len64], computer science [HG03, MMTZ06, Pol08], etc. Analogically, it is not trivial to give a common definition precisely on self-organisation. For distributed systems with interconnected and autonomous components, Richter adopts the following definition made by Gershenson to describe self-organisation [Ric10]:

A system described as self-organising is one, in which elements interact in order to dynamically achieve a global function or behaviour.

Another similar definition is made by Camazine et al. to format self-organisation as emergent effects on the global level resulting from local interactions between autonomous components [CDF+01]:

Self-organisation is a process in which pattern at the global level of a system emerges solely from numerous interactions among the lower-level components of the system. Moreover, the rules specifying interactions among the system's components are executed using only local information, without reference to the global pattern.

Both definitions capture an important aspect of a self-organising system: the behaviour of a system emerges from *interactions* of underlying low-level components of the system. In particular, this global behaviour is *not* the result of an external influence. Instead, it is caused by interactions between a set of interconnected low-level components within the system. With the motto *"the whole is greater than the sum of its parts,"* interactions between interconnected components contribute collaboratively to the global behaviour of the system.

The other important aspect of a self-organising system is the local view of each component. Each component in the system has no global view on the overall behaviour of the system. Instead, they make decisions to interact with other components or to control their own behaviour only based on information available locally. This is in fact one characteristic advantage of self-organisation in contrast to centralised control systems. In case of changes, centralised control system often needs a large amount of computational time to find an optimal solution from the global view, in particular for systems with large state space. For components with local self-organisation, global management problems can be delegated to a set of distributed components. Hence, such delegation restricts the size of the state space that a single component has to deal with. From this viewpoint, self-organisation allows reducing necessary response time of a single component to solve problems.

The increasing need for self-organisation within technical systems can be explained threefold:

- Firstly, from the viewpoint of *economic* aspects, self-organisation helps to reduce operational cost for maintaining technical systems and increase so the ROI of IT infrastructure. As pointed out by Patterson et al., meanwhile the cost for maintaining IT infrastructure is five to ten times the purchase price of software and hardware [PBB+02]. A similar statistic is also given by Ganek et al. [GHS+04]. They figured out that four out of five IT dollars are spent on operations, maintenance, and minor enhancements.

- Secondly, from the viewpoint of *human* aspects, self-organisation is expected to eliminate the need for human interventions at runtime. Apart from the fact that over 40 per cent of all errors within technical systems are caused by human participants, each system administrator spends in average 25 per cent to 40 per cent of the time to determine problems and solve them [GHS+04].

- Lastly, from the viewpoint of *complexity* aspects, self-organisation provides means to cope with increasing complexity of technical systems. As already mentioned in Section 1.1, increasing connectivity between components challenges traditional engineering approaches to build distributed systems. As pointed out by Zambonelli and Rana [ZR05], the large amount of networked components makes it impossible to rely on a priori information about their execution context. In addition, the high dynamic and decentralisation of such components make it difficult for engineers to perform a strict micro level control over them.

Therefore, in order to cope with increasing complexity in technical systems, such system should be able to self-organise their internal activities and thus reduce the number of necessary human interventions at runtime. According to Zambonelli and Rana, such self-organising technical systems are expected to [ZR05]:

- adaptively self-configure their execution parameters depending on the current characteristics of the operational environment,

- In addition, survive the unpredictable dynamics of the operational environment by preserving specific structural properties and quality levels.

Hence, it is necessary to get an appropriate balance between design and runtime self-organisation of engineering technical systems. Prokopenko addressed the possible design space for self-organising applications [Pro08]. He figured out the contradictory character between design and self-organisation. The former approach often follows a top-down process to break down given requirements step-by-step to concrete statements with predictable outcomes, where the latter involves nondeterministic spontaneous dynamics with emergent features.

A promising balance between design and self-organisation is provided by generic architectures to enable self-organisation within technical systems. By applying such generic architectures, the role of software engineers changes to ensure that the resulting system can correctly evolve in compliance with predefined operational goals. In this way, a technical system can deal with unpredictable dynamics from the system's environment. For example, this is achievable by utilising appropriate reinforcement learning techniques to associate unpredictable dynamic situations with adequate actions. Section 2.2.3 introduces some representative approaches to enable self-organisation in technical systems.

2.2.2 Self-organising SOA

As pointed out by Liu, Thanheiser, and Schmeck, an SOE has inherent social complexity due to the large number of interacting components and the highly dynamic behaviour of components within the environment [LTS09a, LTS09b]. This makes it impossible to manage such an SOE at runtime by relying on a priori information about the environment at design time. Furthermore, the large number of distributed and heterogeneous service components prevents establishing a consistent management approach across the complete environment. Hence, it is reasonable to incorporate self-organisation into service components of an SOE. With self-organisation, components are expected to organise their activities autonomously and thus leave human participants in most cases uninvolved.

In the last few years, a considerable amount of research has been conducted to enable self-organisation within SOA. In general, there are two major research directions in the community. One research direction focuses on the self-adaptation of global structures of an SOE to address changes from business, such as discovering, composing, and invoking appropriate Web services in a fully/partly automated manner. The other research direction focuses on the adaptive and SLA-driven management of a particular service component. Most of these research efforts investigate how resource management can be performed efficiently in compliance with given SLAs.

Garlan et al. designed a generic approach to enable architecture-based self-adaptation with a reusable adaptation infrastructure [GCH+04]. Their framework utilises a common set of architectural styles that can be applied to a distributed system at runtime to change its behaviour. By monitoring the target system at runtime, their framework is aware of the system's behaviour. If the framework detects any violation, such as broken server links, the adaptation infrastructure autonomously triggers appropriate adaptation strategies to solve problems. Such a strategy applies a new appropriate architectural style to the target system to change its behaviour with respect to detected failures in the system. For example, in case of a broken server link, the affected client can be relocated to another server group. In other words, in the approach of Garlan et al., self-organisation is realised by changing the architecture of the target system in dependence upon the current operational context. Similar approaches can be found in [OGT+99, FHS+06, WH07, HWH08].

Kim and Lin proposed an approach to combine intelligent agents with technical components [KJ06] to enable automated composition of semantic services. By consulting additional metadata provided by semantic descriptions of a service, an agent can autonomously orchestrate several existing semantic Web services and invoke the resulting service composition. To this end, each agent uses a centralised service broker agent to compose semantic services to satisfy given functional requirements. Similar centralised approaches are [ADK+05], [NPTT06], and [GKS+08].

The works cited above focus mainly on realising self-organisation by changing architectures of target systems in an automated and *centralised* manner, as surveyed by Rao and Su [RS05]. A more general way in compliance with the distributed nature of services is to enable automated service composition in a decentralised way, such as the approach proposed by Falou et al. [FBMV09]. Their model utilises a set of service agents, where each of them has a number of services organised in a graph. In order to provide a service composition satisfying given functional requirements, each of these service agents proposes a partial plan out of the graph it has. Then these agents coordinate with each other to generate the best global plan based on the partial plans submitted by each agent. Similar decentralised approaches with multi-agent systems are [CDS06], [MKB06].

These works are majorly concerned with adaptive behaviour of an SOE on the global level rather than on the local level. Since an SOE is composed of a set of underlying service components, it is desirable to have such components self-organise their runtime parameters in dependence of the current operational context. That is, each technical component can monitor its own behaviour and perform adaptive reconfiguration to react to changes in their environments [MFZH99]. Activities, such as configuring local resources or adjusting resource capacity are carried out autonomously and independently by technical components.

Many works are done in this research field, such as [Kon00], [LYFA02], [Hua04] , [PSGS04], and [BDHT06] - just to name a few of them. A representative work is done by Buchard et al. [BHK+04] in the context of Grid Computing. They proposed an SLA-aware architecture for a plan-based virtual resource manager. To support SLAs between a resource and its consumers, a resource manager can establish runtime responsibility with advanced reservations throughout the lifetime of a computational job. By doing this, the corresponding grid infrastructure can easily allocate failures or outages of resources and process corrective measures if needed to solve them.

It is noteworthy that automated resource management has been applied to technical systems of modern daily life. For example, the online e-mail service Hotmail that serves over 350 million people worldwide with over 1.3 billion inboxes utilises automated deployment and configuration management in its IT infrastructure [Haa09]. Running on over 10,000 servers spread around the globe, Hotmail applies closed control loops with permanent monitoring of underlying software/hardware infrastructure. This allows Hotmail to correlate changes of a particular server's configuration automatically with corresponding effects on the overall behaviour of the system. Such correlation enables Hotmail to automate the process to detect, isolate, and trouble-shoot failures by itself [Hof06]. Similar automated management approaches can be found in other server applications, see [XHL+03, Hua04, BBK+05, WSW+05]. More overview on existing approaches to enable self-organisation in service-oriented systems is given by Salehie and Tahvildari [ST09] in a survey.

2.2.3 Approaches with Self-organisation

This section focuses on the engineering aspect of self-organising systems and provides an insight into some representative approaches that intend to establish self-organisation within technical systems.

Organic Computing

As outlined in Section 1.1 and Section 2.2.1, increasing (social) complexity of technical systems demands new engineering approaches. The traditional top-down design principles to develop technical systems based on given functional behaviour do not suffice the continuously changing context, within which these technical systems have to operate. In these deterministic technical systems, unknown situations at runtime can lead to behavioural problems due to missing procedures to deal with them. On the other hand, a set of connected technical systems may result in new and emergent properties on the global level that are difficult to anticipate at design time. Hence, it is necessary to find an appropriate balance between the top-down deterministic behaviour and the bottom-up emergent behaviour of technical systems.

The desired balance between top-down control over technical systems and bottom-up self-organisation of technical systems is addressed as one of the central research interests of the research initiative Organic Computing. The term *Organic Computing* (OC) is firstly introduced in 2002 by a workshop focusing on future technologies to engineer technical systems. In 2003, the vision of OC is manifested in a joint position paper published by the section of *computer engineering* (*Technische Informatik*) of the *Gesellschaft für Informatik* (*German Association for Informatics*, GI) and the *Informationstechnische Gesellschaft* (*German Association for Information Technology*) [ACE+03]. In 2005, the German priority research programme Organic Computing granted by the *German Research Foundation* (*Deutsche Forschungsgemeinschaft*, DFG) is launched. Within the project period of six years until 2011, a range of granted projects work on various topics on controlled self-organisation. In particular, these projects investigate theoretical foundations addressing emergence and self-organisation within technical systems (such as in [MSS08], [BS08]) and establish technological foundations to design technical systems with controlled self-organisation (such as using the generic observer/controller architecture introduced in [MS04, BMM+06, RMB+06]). Another emphasis of the priority programme is to apply design principles of OC in technical systems. Herein, a set of projects in the priority programme are engaged in realising technical systems with controlled self-organisation across a range of technical domains, such as organic traffic control [PRT+08, TPR+08] and system-on-chip design [BZS+06]. Information on the priority programme and the projects funded in the programme is available on the Website of the priority programme [OC10].

OC claims to incorporate *controlled self-organisation* into technical systems. The term *controlled* indicates the difference of self-organisation claimed in OC from other similar approaches. Rather than realising fully self-organising technical components, organic technical systems provide a designated interface to the outside world, in particular to the higher control instance in the outside world, e.g., human participants. Through this interface, a control instance of the higher level (e.g., a human being) has the possibility to influence operational behaviour of an OC system by setting an externally provided goal. With respect to such a goal, an OC system controls its behaviour to adapt to environmental changes, even in the presence of unanticipated and possibly undesired emergent behaviour.

To enable adaptive behaviour of an OC system, it is crucial that the underlying technical system is monitored and controlled continuously. To this end, a generic observer/controller architecture is introduced in OC to provide a reference architecture determining the necessary components for establishing controlled self-organisation. Figure 2-6 illustrates the simplified view of the generic observer/controller architecture according to Richter [Ric10]. This generic architecture is introduced in detail in Section 3.4.

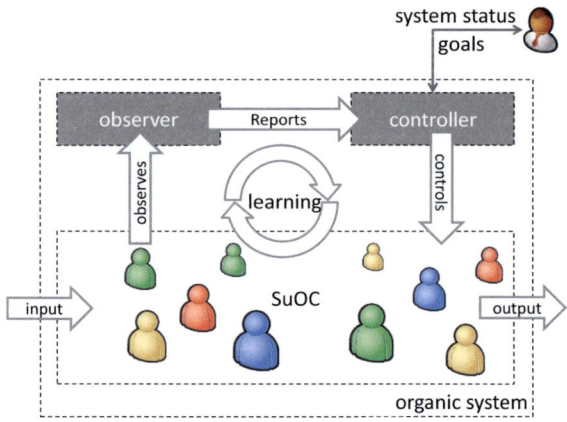

Figure 2-6: Simplified view of the generic observer/controller architecture (see [Ric10])

As illustrated in Figure 2-6, the generic observer/controller architecture utilises a closed control loop to monitor and control the underlying technical system(s). In general, the architecture contains the following components:

- *System under Observation and Control (SuOC)*: SuOC defines the scope of technical systems that are actively managed by the corresponding observer and controller. Hence, an SuOC has clear boundaries to its environments. The runtime behaviour of the system within the boundaries are monitored and controlled by the observer and the controller.

- *Observer*: the observer monitors runtime events of the SuOC, collects relevant attributes about runtime behaviour of the system, and aggregates them to situation parameters. Situation parameters concisely describe the observed runtime behaviour from the viewpoint of the observer.

- *Controller*: the controller receives situation parameters that represent the current operational context of the SuOC, analyses them, and decides whether the current runtime behaviour complies with the given external goal. If not, it performs corresponding corrective actions upon the underlying system to influence its behaviour with respect to the desired operational goal. The results of such interventions are in turn observed by the observer, which leads to another control loop between observer, controller, and SuOC.

- *External goal*: the behaviour of the observer and the controller is determined by the external goal. An external goal defines the desired state space, within which the SuOC has to operate. Any deviation from optimal states leads to corresponding corrective actions of the controller through the closed control loop.

An important aspect of the generic observer/controller architecture is learning. Learning is a characteristic property of technical systems that are capable to deal with situations that are unknown a priori at design time. In OC, continuous execution of control loops over the underlying technical system(s) allows the observer and controller to build up their knowledge base about the target system. In particular, through permanent monitoring of the target system, the controller can get feedback on the performance of actions it executed. This kind of *trial-and-error* feedback enables the controller to get accurate correlation between situations and actions and to build up its own knowledge about the underlying systems through learning.

To summarise, Organic Computing focuses on increasing complexity in a range of interconnected technical systems, from traffic light control, to robot control, to enterprise servers. With the generic observer/controller architecture, Organic Computing allows incorporating controlled self-organisation into technical systems. In contrast to fully self-organising technical systems, the generic observer/controller architecture provides human participants with an abstracted, dedicated, and consolidated interface, through which they can influence the runtime behaviour of organic systems.

Autonomic Computing

With a similar focus on self-organising systems, *Autonomic Computing* (AC) was firstly introduced by IBM's Autonomic Computing initiative as its response to increasing complexity in computer systems, in particular in complex enterprise server systems [GHS+04]. In the manifesto given by P. Horn [Hor01], complex computer systems are compared to a complex human body that has an autonomic nervous system to regulate the body without self-conscious actions of the human. Hence, IBM suggests that complex computer systems should also have autonomic properties that can maintain regular administration tasks by themselves. By doing this, complex computer systems are expected to reach the same level of self-regulation as the human's nervous system does while hiding the increasing system complexity from end users and system administrators.

In the meantime, the concept of Autonomic Computing has evolved to a widely accepted concept for dealing with increasing system complexity. Various research in industry and academia has focused on solutions and technologies that exhibit the self-x properties [HMC08]. However, there is still a lack of a commonly accepted definition of "Autonomic Computing." Lin, Macarthur, and Leaney have tried to establish a common definition for AC [LML05]. They carried out a survey on publications in the field and studied various definitions for Autonomic Computing. The most commonly referenced definitions in the literature contain the following *self-x* properties that an Autonomic Computing system must have (see also [KC03] and [BBC+03]):

- *Self-configuring*: self-configuring is a system's capability to configure itself dynamically, such as adding components from the system or applying software updates, to achieve the desired operational goals.

- *Self-healing*: from the perspective of reactive systems, self-healing is the system capability to discover, diagnose, repair, and recover from system faults when they occur. From the viewpoint of predictive systems, self-healing contains mechanisms to predict and thereby prevent system faults by monitoring vital parameters of the target system.

- *Self-optimizing* refers to the capability to measure system performance against predefined objectives and to attempt to improve performance by controlling efficiently allocation and utilisation of resources available in the system.

- *Self-protecting* describes the capability of a system to anticipate and detect external malicious attacks and to protect itself in case of attacks. It means that the system must be aware of potential threats and be able to take actions to avoid completely or at least mitigate partly the effects caused by external attacks.

To support these self-x properties, an autonomic system should be aware of itself (*self-awareness*) and of the environment around it (*context-awareness*). The system monitors its internal state by collecting management information from its functional components and evaluates the collected data to identify its vital status. Furthermore, a network-enabled system is not isolated from its environment. For example, a Web service is related to its hosting environment, or to other Web services involved in the same business process. More or less, functional states of the related systems have impact on the system itself. Therefore, an autonomic system knows the way to interact with its neighbouring systems for sharing functional state information. To achieve cooperation between different systems in a possibly heterogeneous environment, the autonomic system must implement open standards to enable an unobstructed communication with other systems.

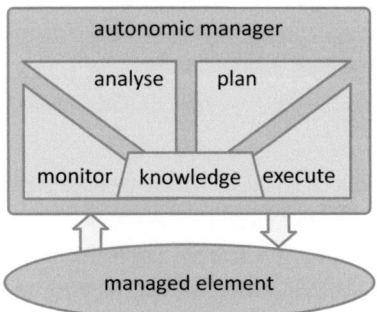

Figure 2-7: Structure of an autonomic element in Autonomic Computing (see [KC03])

In order to build autonomic systems with the aforementioned self-x properties, IBM proposed a reference model with a closed control loop consisting of four processing steps: monitor, analyse, plan, and execute (MAPE) ([KC03, IBM05]), as illustrated in Figure 2-7. The reference model for autonomic systems consists of the following building blocks:

- The managed element represents the underlying system that should be managed by an autonomic manager. A managed element (e.g., a Web server, a database, a device, etc.) provides a standardised manageability interface for the autonomic manager, so that the manager can sense and effect behaviour of the managed element.

- By using various sensors that connect with the managed element, the monitor function collects data (for example, instrumentation metrics or runtime events), filters it, aggregates it and reports the results that represent the current runtime state of the managed element to the analyse function.

- The analyse function correlates the data being reported by the monitor. Based on this, it tries to model complex situations of the managed element.

- The analysis result is consumed by the plan function, which selects or constructs appropriate actions matching the current runtime state of the managed element based on the analysis and on predefined operation policies.

- The execute function controls the execution of an action plan using effectors, which are connected to the managed element via its manageability interface.

- The knowledge component holds the accurate rules base of the managed element. That is, which action should be executed under which circumstances to get the operational state of the system to comply with given requirements. Such rules may come from external sources, such as human experts from their day-to-day operation of the system. Otherwise, they can also be collected by the autonomic manager independently through continuous observation of management actions at runtime, e.g., by adopting reinforcement learning in the control loop [DCCC06].

One of the ultimate goals of AC is to automate management processes of complex distributed systems applying the traditional multi-tier architectural pattern. To this end, IBM has developed several reference implementations of the MAPE control loop, such as the Autonomic Computing Toolkit [IBM06] and the Agent Building and Learning Environment (ABLE) [BSP+02]. Both toolkits provide the foundation to build an autonomic manager in the reference model for specific artefacts within a multi-tier architecture. For example, Melcher and Mitchell extend the Autonomic Computing Toolkit to create network services with autonomic service configuration [MM04]. Bigus et al. uses the ABLE environment to tune Apache Web servers automatically [BSP+02]. Rutherford et al. build the MAPE control loop into the application tier to enable reconfiguration of application servers at runtime [RAC+02].

The research cited above focuses on incorporating autonomic behaviour into particular server components. Alternatively, some approaches in the research community seek to build autonomic behaviour into the entire multi-tier system instead of particular server components within the system. For example, Ungaonkar et al. utilises a global autonomic manager to determine the appropriate resource allocation among all tiers to improve the overall performance of the system [USC+08]. Wang et al. follow a similar way to provide autonomic multi-tier service delivery in an virtualised environment [WDCL08].

To conclude, the main application domain of AC is enterprise server systems. There is a considerable amount of similar research investigating autonomic behaviour of server components within complex distributed systems. In particular, many of the works focus on efficient allocation of computational resources, such as computing power, storage, or network, to multiple applications.

Viable System Model

Organic Computing and Autonomic Computing introduced in the previous sections have strong technical focuses. However, as mentioned at the beginning of Section 2.2.1, self-organisation is also studied in many other natural sciences, e.g., in cybernetics. A representative work in this research field is the *Viable System Model* (VSM) developed by S. Beer in the 1970s [Bee79, Bee81, Bee85]. He developed the VSM model to describe the essential parts of a viable system, with strong reference to an organisation, such as a business with a set of interconnected organisational units. In the VSM, a *viable* system is one that is robust against internal malfunction or external disturbance, i.e., it has the ability to respond and adapt to unexpected stimuli, allowing the system to survive in a changing and unpredictable environment [BSTL06]. To maintain the viability of the overall system, the VSM identifies five interconnected and hierarchically arranged subsystems, as illustrated in Figure 2-8:

- *System 1* (operation): All the operating components in the system are referred to as System 1. In other words, System 1 in a viable system may have several instances. Each instance in System 1 is autonomous and can operate according to its local environmental situation with limited view to the environment.

- *System 2* (coordination): System 2 establishes the necessary communication channel to facilitate coordinating activities between various System 1 instances. Through appropriate stabilising and coordinating facilities such as schedule or standardised information in System 2, System 1 instances can reduce possible conflicts between one another.

- *System 3* (control): System 3 is responsible for immediate supervision and control of all activities in System 1 instances from a local perspective. In addition,

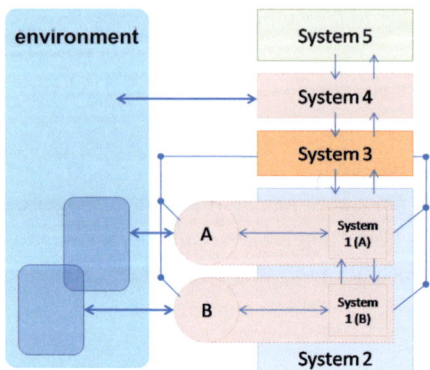

Figure 2-8: The Viable System Model, (see [Bee79, Bee81, Bee85])

it also supervises the coordination activities of the System 2. So far, with System 1, 2, 3, the system is capable of dealing with immediate internal concerns taking place in the local environment.

- *System 4* (intelligence): To adapt to changes in the global environment, the VSM employs a further System 4 to control and predict the overall system behaviour based on information collected from both global and local environments. To this end, System 4 creates a model of system capabilities of the entire local organisation based on information collected by System 3. In addition, System 4 generates a model of its global environment via interactions with its environment. Based on internal system capabilities and external environmental changes, System 4 develops actions plans for the whole organisation.

- *System 5* (policy): System 5 guarantees the balance between the internal operational state and the given external operational goal. With given operational policies, System 5 supplies and enforces logical policies to the entire system. From this point-of-view, it creates an interface for superior systems to control the system behaviour externally. With System 4 and System 5, the entire system is capable of controlling itself based on externally given policies as well as on situations in the global environment.

Furthermore, the VSM can be applied in a recursive manner - in other words, each System 1 may contain a viable subsystem consisting of all five subsystems mentioned before.

Beers developed the VSM model as an application of system theory in the field of organisation management. Although the VSM is founded in cybernetics, Beers claims that VSM is more generally concerned with "the existence of laws or principles of control that apply to all kinds of complex systems, whether animate or inanimate, technical or societary" [Bee85]. Indeed, the VSM has been applied in technical systems as intelligent control paradigm to enable adaptive runtime behaviour. It is obvious that VSM can be used to design business processes due to the tight connection between business processes and enterprise organisations. For example, Vidgen uses the VSM as the theoretical and practical base for designing enterprise process architecture [Vid98]. According to him, the VSM has a significant contribution "to make in helping enterprises to align purpose, policies, and organisation structure such that identity and viability are maintained."

A more general application of the VSM is given by Herring and Kaplan, who construct on the base of VSM a viable system architecture as a reference architecture to engineer complex applications with adaptive control [HK00, HK01]. Similarly, Bustard et al. incorporate the VSM to develop design models of an autonomic system and its environment [BSTL06]. In those approaches, the VSM is used to refine the design of an autonomic system to ensure that it contains adequate management controls.

2.2.4 Concluding Remarks

This section focuses on the concept of self-organisation. First, an insight is provided into the current development of approaches to enable self-organisation within technical systems. Because of the increasing complexity of technical systems, there is currently a considerable amount of efforts in both industry and academia on research of self-organisation. All those efforts have the ultimate goal to get technical systems to cope with increasing complexity with minimal intervention of human participants using self-organisation. Next to the approaches OC, AC, and VSM introduced in this section, a range of other approaches such as the HP Converged Infrastructure [HP10], the Microsoft Dynamic System Initiative [Mic04], or the Forrester Organic IT [GRS+02] shows the large interests of vendors in the research field of self-organisation.

The three approaches introduced in this section are representative for the current research on self-organisation. While the generic observer/controller architecture of OC and the MAPE control loop of AC are more technology-oriented, the VSM has its origin in organisation system theory and provides more high-level guidelines on how viable systems can be designed.

Furthermore, the underlying concepts of OC and AC are similar to each other, in particular with respect to the similar constructs of the generic observer/controller architecture and the MAPE control loop. However, the application domains of both concepts differ strongly, as pointed out by Richter [Ric10]. As aforementioned in Section 2.2.3, AC focuses on management scenarios in IT systems with interconnected and diverse components. A large amount of research done in AC discusses concepts on monitoring and controlling runtime behaviour of enterprise server systems. In particular, most of this work deals with efficient resource management, where an autonomic manager dynamically allocates technical resources among several servers in accordance with strategies established by human participants.

In contrast to AC, OC focuses on technical systems with large collections of intelligent devices that provide services to humans and adapt themselves to the current requirements of their execution environment [Sch05]. That is, OC focuses more on technical systems and their interactions among one another. For example, traffic light control is one of the domains, to which the concept of OC is applicable. With decentralised coordination of traffic lights across several urban road nodes, OC shows promising results to reduce average waiting time of vehicles [TPR+08]. Furthermore, in comparison to AC, OC emphasises interactions between technical systems and human participants. Through explicit interfaces, human participants can influence runtime behaviour of the observer/controller architecture by performing corrective actions if necessary. In this context, a self-organising system remains under control of human participants. Therefore, OC promotes the establishment of *controlled* self-organisation within technical systems. This differs from the vision of AC with focus on capabilities of self-management.

An important aspect that is not explicitly addressed by both OC and AC is collaboration between self-organising technical systems. Although both approaches envision the possibility to arrange several managing elements (either observer/controller instances or autonomic managers) in a hierarchical manner [BMM+06, IBM05], where a higher managing element can delegate management tasks to lower managing elements, they do not address how collaboration can take place among managing elements to impact their local behaviour. This missing aspect is however addressed by the VSM. In spite of its focus on organisational theories, the VSM addresses interactions of essentials parts of a viable system with its environment. In particular, the VSM identifies subsystems that are influenced by such interactions with the environment. Hence, it is reasonable to use the VSM as a complement to OC/AC to guide the design of collaboration mechanisms between self-organising systems.

2.3 Multi-Agent Systems

With its origins in distributed artificial intelligence, the concept of Multi-Agent Systems (MAS) is concerned with a collection of autonomous agents that have the ability to cooperate, coordinate, and negotiate with each other [Woo02]. Given the distributed and dynamic nature of service-oriented systems and the autonomy of components in such systems, MAS provides a promising way to model the social relationships between components within SOA. Hence, this section provides a brief overview on agents in MAS and discusses the possibility to combine MAS with SOA. Furthermore, this section outlines the ways, in which agents can collaborate with each other, in particular how agents with conflicting interests can negotiate with one another to solve conflicts.

2.3.1 Overview

The concept of MAS has been intensively studied since about 1980. It gained widespread recognition since about the mid-1990s, driven by the increasing connectivity in technical systems, such as large-scale distributed systems (e.g., the Internet). In particular, MAS is considered as the appropriate software paradigm to understand and build a wide range of so-called *artificial social systems*. An artificial social system contains a number of autonomous systems that are capable of interacting with one another. Such interactions are done not only by simply exchanging data, but also by carrying out social activities analogously to humans' daily life, such as *communication*, *coordination*, *negotiation*, and so on [Woo02].

Hence, it is obvious that research of MAS has both microscopic and macroscopic focuses. The microscopic focus studies the autonomous behaviour of an agent. That is, how each agent can satisfy given design objectives by deciding by itself what actions are to be executed for which situations. Macroscopic research is interested in social behaviour of autonomous agents within a society of agents, so that they can work together to solve problems in spite of possible conflicts. The remainder of this section provides a brief insight into both aspects. Among other things, this section explains common characteristics of agents and outlines possible ways they can interact with one another.

In spite of the significant research efforts on agents and MAS, there is no common definition for agents. H. Nwana pointed out that the term *agent* has been an umbrella term for a heterogeneous body of research and development in the field [Nwa96]. This leads to a role-specific classification of agents [Kin95] that confuses the common understanding of agents. For the purpose of the present thesis, the definition of Wooldrige and Jenning seems to be appropriate. After having taken a range of similar definitions into consideration, they defined an *agent* as a hardware or (more usually) software-based computer system that has the following properties [WJ95]:

- *Autonomy*: agents operate on their own behalf without any direct intervention of other agents. Therefore, agents control their actions and internal states by themselves.

- *Social ability*: agents can interact with other agents via some kind of communication language.

- *Reactivity*: agents perceive their environment and respond to changes in the environment in a timely manner.

- *Proactivity*: agents do not simply react to changes in their environment. Instead, they can behave goal-directed by taking the initiative.

In short, an agent is an autonomous system that behaves proactively on behalf of its owner. An agent is aware of changes in its environment, e.g., by perceiving information from the environment, and it performs reactive actions to respond to such changes. In addition, an agent lives in a society of agents. It has the necessary social abilities to interact with other agents in its environment, for example in order to solve problems collaboratively.

The key characteristic distinguishing MAS from traditional artificial intelligence is its emphasis on social behaviour of autonomous agents. That is, how agents communicate with each other, how they coordinate their activities to solve problems, and how they negotiate among one another to eliminate conflicts. Therefore, research on social behaviour of agents covers mainly macroscopic aspects. That is, rather than investigating the behaviour of a particular agent, the related research focuses on issues concerning the entire agent society. The shift of research from individual agents to an agent society is driven by increasing connectivity and scale of technical systems.

Green et al. summarises the main motivations for the increasing interest in the social behaviour of agents in a society [GHN+97]:

- To solve problems that are too large for a centralised single agent to deal with, e.g., due to limited resources or risk of single point of failure

- To provide a way to facilitate interoperations among multiple existing systems and to link knowledge of them, e.g., between various expert systems or decision support systems

- To provide a way to cope with inherent distribution of technical systems, e.g., traffic light control in urban road networks

- To provide conceptual clarity and simplicity of design based on the modularity of MAS

The prerequisite for successful interactions between agents is communication. It is only possible through explicit usage of an *agent communication language* (ACL), such as the *Knowledge Query and Manipulation Language* (KQML) or the ACL developed by the *Foundation for Intelligent Physical Agents* (FIPA) [CDD02]. Analogous to speech act, ACL, such as KQML, is comprised of two parts: an outer language to define various acceptable performatives, such as *perform*, *tell*, *reply*, etc.; and an inner language for expressing message content. In this way, agents can exchange information among one another to coordinate their activities at runtime.

In addition, M. Wooldridge pointed out that there are two general ways to support interactions between agents, a centralised way and a distributed way [Woo02]. First, agents can utilise a centralised blackboard as shared storage, where they can submit or retrieve any information. The other way is to use peer-to-peer message passing. For example, agents can share information through the *publish/subscribe* pattern, where an agent can decide selectively the set of information that it is interested in.

Agent communication languages provide the prerequisite to enable interactions between agents, in particular to coordinate their activities at runtime. The following sections provide an overview on the major approaches to facilitate coordination and negotiation between agents.

2.3.2 Coordinating Agents

Coordination is the key to facilitate teamwork between agents in MAS. Green et al. pointed out that coordination helps to prevent chaos within MAS [GHN+97]. Limited views, goals, and knowledge of an agent may interfere with other agents' activities instead of supporting them. Hence, coordinating activities between agents from a global point of view is vital to prevent chaos caused by conflicts between agents and to meet global constraints at the same time. In general, depending on the degree of cooperation, researchers distinguish between two types of agents in MAS [Woo02]:

- *Cooperative* agents: cooperative agents follow the same interest. In this case, all agents are constructed by a single designer to help each other whenever possible. Thus, the common interest of the MAS is to increase the social welfare of the entire MAS other than welfare of individual agents. For example, by considering an SOE as a MAS and the service components in the SOE as agents, then it is obvious that technical components within the same organisation are interested in providing optimal performance to support business goals. In this case, all technical components are cooperative in their interactions with one another.

- *Self-interested* agents: the more general case is that agents in a MAS represent different individuals or organisations. In that case, it is not reasonable to assume that all agents are benevolent. Instead, agents are assumed to act in order to defend their own interest, even - where applicable - at the cost of other agents. Using the example of SOA, if a service-oriented application consumes a PaaS service in the public cloud, then it is reasonable, if both components share different interests. As the application is interested in improving its performance with low cost, the interest of the PaaS is to increase its profit as much as possible.

Both cooperative and self-interested agents need to be coordinated at runtime. In order to exploit possibilities provided by MAS to solve collaboratively given problems by a collection of agents, there are still coordination problems to solve. That is, how activities of agents with different capabilities can be coordinated, so that each of them can contribute to sort out a given problem.

As summarised by Green et al. [GHN+97], a range of approaches have been proposed in the last years to address coordination problems in MAS. *Organisational* coordination leverages an agent that has a wider perspective of the system, including the organisational structure of the system. Hence, this agent can act in a classic master/slave manner to perform centralised coordination among slave agents. That is, the master agent collects information from other agents, creates action plans based on the given problem and the capabilities of slave agents, and assigns tasks to individual agents to guarantee global coherence. In this centralised approach, a master agent with a global view on the organisational structure of the MAS is required. This is however not always possible in realistic applications with distributed agents. In particular, this approach assumes cooperative agents that are willing to share their intentions and beliefs, which is only valid in limited scenarios.

Alternatively, agents can also utilise a decentralised approach to coordinate their activities, such as by following the *Contract Net Protocol* proposed by Smith [Smi80]. In this approach, a decentralised market structure is assumed, with agents either as manager or as contractor. The basic idea of a Contract Net is that if an agent cannot solve a problem locally with its resources, it can decompose the problem into sub-problems (as *manager*) and try to find other appropriate agents (as *contractors*) that have the necessary resources and are willing to solve such sub-problems. To this end, the manager utilises a contracting mechanism to assign sub-problems to contractor agents. The contracting mechanism includes, among other things, announcing tasks by the manager agent to potential contractor agents, submitting bids by interested contractor agents in response to the announcement, evaluating the submitted bids by the manager agent, and awarding contracts to contractor agents with most promising bids.

Due to its simplicity and flexibility, Contract Net is often utilised in MAS to realise dynamic task allocation. As Contract Net does not require that each agent has to respond to task announcement messages, agents are free to decide whether they should bid, e.g., in dependence of their current load. Hence, it is obvious that Contract Net can realise a kind of load balancing between agents, which allows efficient resource utilisation in the MAS.

The limitation of Contract Net is its restricted support for negotiation. In fact, the Contract Net Protocol is rather a coordination protocol than a negotiation protocol, as determined by Smith [Smi80]. There is no negotiation process between a manager agent and its contractor agents. On the one hand, a manager agent has no minimal condition on the potential bidders; on the other hand, the bidders do not get a second chance to submit their bids again. Hence, there is no mutual decision between a manager agent and its contractor agents, which is however characteristic for negotiation purpose. Other approaches to coordinate activities of agents in MAS are to use multi-agent planning [WC09] or similar decentralised approaches [ME05], but they are out of the scope of this thesis.

2.3.3 Negotiation between Agents

In the field of computer science, in particular in MAS, negotiation is utilised to find mutually beneficial agreements on given negotiation objectives between negotiation parties. This section provides an overview on existing research in the field, with a focus on negotiation in SOEs.

Overview

In general, negotiation is defined as "a process by which a joint decision is reached by two or more agents, each trying to reach an individual goal or objective" [HS00]. Raiffa specifies that such a process is concerned with "situations in which two or more parties recognise that differences of interest and values exist among them and in which they want (or in which one or more are compelled) to seek a compromise agreement through negotiation" [Rai82].

From the both specifications, a negotiation process contains the following structural aspects (cf. [Rai82, BS97, Reb01, LWJ03, Bue06]):

- *Negotiator*: each negotiation involves two or more parties, i.e., negotiators, which have conflicting interests on a given set of negotiation objectives. Conflicts between negotiators are prerequisite for a negotiation situation; otherwise, involved parties can easily find an agreement by simply selecting a mutually agreed optimum of negotiation objectives. Depending on the number of participating negotiators in the negotiation process, Büttner differentiates between bilateral, one-sided multilateral and double-sided multilateral negotiations [Bue06]. In bilateral negotiation, two negotiation agents interact with each other (e.g., a service consumer and a service provider). One-sided multilateral negotiation involves a single master agent and a set of slave agents (e.g., a single service consumer and several service providers or vice versa). This type of negotiation corresponds to the auction mechanism applied in eBay, where a set of buyers bid for an article of a single seller. Analogously, double-sided multilateral negotiation involves on both sides a set of agents that interact among as well as between one another.

- *Negotiation issues*: all negotiation issues span the negotiation space, within which negotiators try to reach a consensus about the issues. In a negotiation process, negotiators can either negotiate over a single issue from the negotiation space each time (single-issue negotiation), or handle all negotiation issues in a single negotiation round simultaneously (multi-issue negotiation, e.g., all issues defined in an SLA).

Because negotiation is a complex task, in particular with respect to the high degree of dynamic of negotiation processes, various computational models are developed to facilitate negotiation process. The level of automation of these models varies from fully automated to partly automated [Reb01]. In a fully automated negotiation, autonomous agents can interact without external interventions to reach an agreement. In partly automated models, human participants are required to make final decisions with decision supports given by such models.

In fact, automated negotiation has been subject of intensive research over the last few decades, especially in the field of MAS with respect to their decentralised nature. Various approaches and models from different domains, such as game theory, economic models (e.g., auctions), and learning mechanisms from artificial intelligence are applied to facilitate automated negotiation. In general, automated negotiation research consists of the following aspects:

- *Negotiation protocols* to guide interactions between negotiation parties. Rosenstein and Zlokin [RZ94] define a protocol as "the public rules by which agents will come to agreements". More specifically, a negotiation protocol specifies "the rules of the negotiation, the rules by which the agents will come to a consensus, agreeing to carry out one of the deals in the negotiation set" [RZ94]. Negotiation protocols are designed to support negotiation processes in particular target scenarios. For example, the simplest form of such a protocol can be auctions for allocating goods, tasks, or resources. The different types of auctions, such as English auctions, Dutch auctions, or First-price sealed-bid auctions [Woo02], vary in their protocol design, in particular, the number of negotiation rounds, the way bidders interact with an auctioneer, and mechanisms to determine the auction winner at the end.

- Given a negotiation protocol, the second aspect, *negotiation strategy*, is concerned with how an agent should behave in a negotiation process. First, negotiation strategies specify decision-making models that provide support to negotiators for determining their actions for given situations in the course of negotiation (i.e., accept/reject an offer, or propose a counter offer). The goal of negotiation strategy design is to reach an agreement after a negotiation process, while ensuring that a negotiator's individual welfare is assured in the negotiation. Therefore, selecting an appropriate negotiation strategy is critical for a negotiator with respect to its negotiation behaviour and, hence, to the outcome of the negotiation. Among other things, a negotiation strategy influences the willingness of a negotiator to cooperate with other negotiators.

Designing mechanisms to support automated negotiation depends strongly on the characteristics of particular negotiation scenarios. For example, a suitable protocol for English auctions is not necessarily applicable to multilateral negotiation scenarios with multiple issues. Hence, negotiation mechanisms have to be designed in compliance with requirements of the target problem domains. In addition to such specifically characterised requirements, negotiation mechanisms should have the following desirable properties (cf. [Woo02], [LWJ03], and [San00]):

- *Pareto Efficiency*: a negotiation outcome is then Pareto efficient (or Pareto optimal), if there is no other outcome that improves one negotiator's utility without deteriorating that of another one. Obviously, if an outcome maximises the overall social welfare of all negotiators, i.e., the sum of all negotiators' utilities, it is Pareto efficient. In this case, if the sum of all negotiators' utilities is maximised, a negotiator can only increase its utility by decreasing another negotiator's utility.

- *Computational Efficiency*: an ideal negotiation mechanism should be computationally efficient. In other words, a negotiation mechanism should be designed in a way negotiators need as little computation as possible to take an active part in a negotiation process.

- *Communicational Efficiency*: communicational efficiency addresses communication cost between negotiators in the course of negotiation. It is desired that a negotiation process generates only reasonable communication traffic as necessary. For example, broadcasting to all involved negotiators for exchanging negotiation messages is not reasonably efficient, if the same task can be completed using dedicated end-to-end communication.

- *Distribution*: distribution is another desired property of negotiation mechanisms, in particular with respect to increased robustness and availability of such distributed mechanisms. In comparison to centralised mechanisms, a distributed negotiation mechanism reduces the risk of a single-point-of-failure and avoids a performance bottleneck.

- *Individual Rationality*: a negotiation mechanism is individually rational to an agent, if the resulting utility of an agent from negotiation is not less than the utility that the agent would get without negotiation. In other words, because agents that do not participate in a negotiation get no additional utility, a negotiation process with individual rationality provides agents with an incentive to participate in a negotiation process.

All these properties are desirable for an efficient negotiation protocol/strategy. However, these properties should be considered relatively and always in the respective context of target negotiation scenarios. For example, communicational efficiency and distribution are two conflicting properties: a distributed negotiation protocol requires generally more communication efforts than a negotiation protocol with a centralised mediator. On the other hand, a distributed negotiation protocol increases the robustness of a negotiation process and, hence, is preferable in contrast to a centralised approach. From this point-of-view, the properties discussed afore provide common design guidance for negotiation mechanisms and have to be individually prioritised according to the requirements of particular negotiation scenarios.

Automated Negotiation

As afore mentioned, automated negotiation builds often the foundation for automating processes to solve conflicts between various parties within an MAS. Hence, there is a considerable amount of research on approaches to facilitate automated negotiation in MAS.

Büttner reviewed most of the current approaches and classified them using the following criteria [Bue06]:

- Information situation: each negotiation agent has its preferences on the negotiation issues. However, it is not automatically assumed that each agent is also aware of preferences of its negotiation partners. Information situation refers to the amount of information that an agent has about itself, its negotiation partners, and its environment. Hence, knowledge about the information situation is crucial for designing negotiation mechanisms. It is obvious that an agent that knows the preferences of its negotiation partners behaves differently than an agent that is not aware of the preferences of its partners. Lomuscio, Wooldridge, and Jennings distinguish between complete and incomplete information situation [LWJ03]. In a complete information situation, all agents are aware of the negotiation preferences of their negotiation partners. Analogously, in an incomplete information situation, each agent has only partial or even no information about its negotiation partner, or its environment. In this case, each agent can only presume the negotiation behaviour of its partners based on information it observes in the course of negotiation, for example incoming offers proposed by its partners.

- Negotiation time: negotiation behaviour of agents in the course of negotiation is influenced by time. Suitably selected time limits for negotiation places appropriate pressure on agents, e.g., to force agents to make larger concessions as the predefined negotiation deadline is approaching. Stuhlmacher and Champagne investigated impacts of time pressure on negotiation behaviour of agents [SC00]. To this end, they examined impact factors by leveraging a variety of methods, including objective measures (e.g., number of offers), and constructed measures (e.g., utility). They found out that time pressure has little impact on the utility of the negotiators' first offers. They justified this with the argument that subjective time pressure has little influence at the beginning of negotiation. Such influence increases only as the given deadline approaches. Furthermore, although agents under time pressure tend to make more concessions in utility, it results, however, in less exploration in the negotiation space than with less time pressure. This leads to implications for the quality of the resulting agreements.

- Mediation: a mediated negotiation process between negotiation parties is carried out via a trusted third party, the so-called mediator. To enable an accurately mediated negotiation, each party submits its preferences to a mediator. The mediator makes decisions based on information submitted by the negotiators. Obviously, in a mediated negotiation process, trust between the mediator and other agents plays an important and fundamental role for a successful negotiation. In contrast, a non-mediated negotiation is conducted via direct peer-to-peer interactions between negotiators. In this case, a trusted third party is not involved in the negotiation process.

- Negotiation Access: a public negotiation process is open to all parties that are interested to take part in the negotiation process. In a closed negotiation process, only selected/invited parties are allowed participating in the negotiation. No additional participants can join the negotiation process as soon as it has been triggered.

- Theoretical foundations: agents need negotiation strategies to guide their behaviours in the course of negotiation. To design such negotiation strategies, various theory foundations from AI and mathematics have been utilised, such as fuzzy logic, optimisation, game theory, etc. Jennings et al. categorised three general theoretical foundations to design negotiation strategies [JFL+01]:

o *Game theory*: approaches based on game theory (e.g., work done by Zlotkin and Rosenschein [ZJ89]) aim at finding optimal strategies among a set
   of rational and autonomous agents by analysing the equilibrium conditions
   of all possible deals. To do this, each agent is equipped with a utility function to estimate the value of achieving a goal and the price for this. Using
   such utility functions, a pay-off matrix with utility values for each outcome
   for each agent can be calculated. This pay-off matrix is known to both negotiation partners a priori before the negotiation process. In the course of
   negotiation with alternating offers and counter offers, each agent tries to
   choose the deal based on the pay-off matrix to maximise its outcome. From
   this viewpoint, game theory provides a good foundation to investigate strategic interactions between self-interested agents. Nevertheless, it does not
   suffice for realistic scenarios, as pointed out by Nwana [Nwa96]. The assumption that in a negotiation all participating agents are rational is not realistic in the real world. Furthermore, this approach requires that the pay-
   off matrix is available a priori. This requirement is obviously rarely true in
   most negotiation scenarios, where agents have only an incomplete information situation about their negotiation partners.

o *Heuristic*: heuristic-based approaches aim to reduce computational cost and
   accelerate the negotiation process by searching the negotiation space in a
   non-exhaustive manner (e.g., the model proposed by Sierra, Faratin, and
   Jennings [SFJ97]). The key idea of such an approach is to model the decision-making process of an agent heuristically. The negotiation space is
   spanned by all possible agreements for agents. The value of each possible
   agreement to an agent is estimated by a utility function. Hence, generating
   an offer for the opposing agent turns out to be a task of searching for an
   appropriate agreement in the negotiation space. Each agent uses appropriate decision-making mechanisms to search for possible offers. Faratin et al.
   classified two general decision-making mechanisms: *responsive* and *deliberative* [FSJB99]. The former mechanism generates offers by manipulating
   utility of agreements. That is, an agent uses the responsive mechanism to
   concede by moving from its optimum agreement and thus reducing its ex-

pectation of utility. The latter mechanism is to find trade-offs that are more attractive to the opposing agent, e.g., by providing offers that are closer to the opponent's last offer. In comparison to approaches based on game theory, heuristic-based approaches are based on realistic assumptions about target negotiation scenarios, in particular incomplete information situation between agents. This makes this approach applicable to a wider range of possible application domains. However, outcomes of heuristic-based approaches are in the majority of cases only suboptimal. This is majorly caused by the fact that an agent's search for offers does not explore the full negotiation space due to their limited information situation.

o *Argumentation-based*: both game-theoretic and heuristic approaches assume that agents' preferences are fixed in the course of negotiation. However, in some real world scenarios, agents can benefit from revising their preferences during negotiation. Nevertheless, the negotiation process of humans is accompanied by on-going acquisition of new information, and a revision of preferences based on newly acquired information. Hence, an argumentation-based approach aims to address this by augmenting a common negotiation protocol with an additional argumentation protocol that allows exchanging supplementary information in addition to offers between agents [RRJ+03]. Such additional information may have a number of possible forms to explain the opinion of an agent. For example, if an agent rejects an offer, it can inform its negotiation partner, why the offer is not acceptable. Upon receiving such argumentation, the negotiation partner can, e.g., identify the region in the negotiation space that is less promising for the opponent. Alternatively, such argumentation may persuade the negotiation partner to alter its preferences and thus change its negotiation space. Due to its additional ability to enable flexible dialogues, an argumentation-based approach gains increasing popularity in the research. Rahwan reviews in his thesis [Rah04] a range of existing argumentation-based approaches and figures out that such approaches are more complex than game-theoretic and heuristic-based approaches, and add a considerable overhead to the negotiation process.

From the discussion in this section, it is clear that there is no universal approach to facilitate automated negotiation in every application domain. Rather, there is a set of possible approaches that are modelled based on different assumptions about the environment and the agents in the negotiation. Hence, for each application domain, the corresponding approach to support automated negotiation should be individually chosen based on characteristics of the target problem domain.

Negotiation in Service-oriented Environments

In MAS, negotiation is essential to solve conflicts between agents, e.g., between sellers and buyers. With negotiation, self-interested agents can find mutually acceptable agreements that are beneficial to both sides. The same scenario applies also to SOEs, where service providers and service consumers have to reach agreements regarding service delivery. In particular, a dynamic and liberated SOE needs a service market, where service providers can advertise services they provide, and consumers can request services they need. It is obvious that in a highly dynamic SOE where customers' demands continuously change, fixed quality of service delivery reduces largely the competitiveness of corresponding service providers. Hence, to better fulfil demands that service consumers have, service providers deliver their services with different quality levels for different prices. As pointed out by Elfatatry and Layell [EL04], negotiation in SOEs is used as a means to tailor software needs dynamically for service consumers.

Elfatatry and Layell have done conceptual work on how negotiation can be carried out in an SOE. Figure 2-9 depicts the three phases of negotiation that they identified in their work. They divided the negotiation process into three main phases: *prenegotiation*, *negotiation*, and *delivery*. The *prenegotiation* phase is concerned with preparation tasks for the main negotiation phase, in particular identifying a set of potential service providers that satisfies the functional and non-functional requirements of a consumer. *Service selection* determines the target service type with functional requirements. Since potential service providers deliver their services with different quality levels, they need to be further filtered during *provider selection* by using non-functional attributes. At the end of this phase, initialisation information, including a list of service providers and the consumer's expectations on service delivery (e.g., QoS, cost, etc.), is forwarded to the next phase. In the *negotiation* phase, service consumer interacts with potential service providers to agree upon quality of service delivery. An issue that must be addressed in this phase is the way to compose functionalities of several service providers. That is, given a set of functional requirements and a number of service providers, negotiation should provide a way to coordinate these providers to get the best composition that meets the desired requirements. If the *negotiation* phase results in a set of service contracts with respective service providers, the *service delivery* phase is concerned with applying the agreed contracts at runtime. In this phase, service delivery of providers is observed and evaluated. Such information can be used in the next *prenegotiation* phase to select potential service providers.

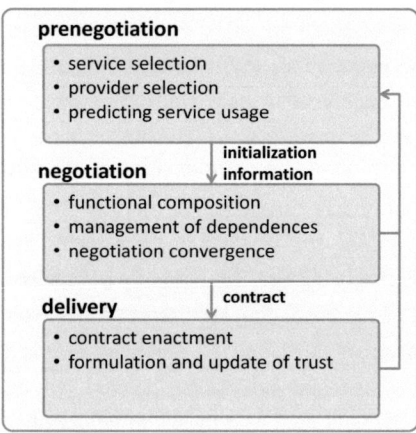

Figure 2-9: Conceptual negotiation model in SOA (see [EL04])

A similar conceptual model is provided by Lin [Lin08], too. In contrast to the abstract negotiation model proposed by Elfatatry and Layell, Lin focused in his model on the process aspect of automated negotiation between service providers and service consumers, and modelled the negotiation process using a range of UML diagrams. In particular, he modelled the collaboration between various stakeholders within a negotiation process in a much more fine-granular level of details than the rather abstracted model of Elfatatry and Layell.

Both works focus mainly on the negotiation process between service consumers and service providers in an SOA in a software-centric manner. As discussed in Section 2.1, increasing support for service-oriented infrastructure facilitates establishment of service-orientation across the complete IT infrastructure. Hence, it is desired to use negotiation as the fundamental measure to enable loosely coupled provider/consumer relationships across the complete IT infrastructure down to the hardware-centric layer. This aspect is covered by the EU's SLA@SOI project [The08, SLA10].

The SLA@SOI project proposes a multi-level SLA management approach for service-oriented infrastructures [TYB08]. In their approach, SLA is used as a means to specify conditions under which a service provider provisions its services. Objectives of such an SLA cover a variety of IT management areas, such as service and application management. Based on automated negotiation between corresponding service providers and service consumers, the SLA@SOI project aims at realising stepwise mapping of high-level SLA requirements onto low-level SLAs for hardware-centric components.

Figure 2-10 illustrates the top-down SLA management process in an SOE. The overall management process involves several stakeholders in such an environment, including consumers, software providers, service providers, and infrastructure providers. Given the recursive nature of an SOE, high-level SLA requirements from customers are mapped to low-level SLAs for hardware-centric components step-by-step in the negotiation phase. After that, negotiated contracts are monitored and enforced bottom-up to ensure delivery of business processes to customers as agreed in contracts.

In a word, the SLA@SOI project is concerned with integrated provisioning of services in an SOE that involves a set of stakeholders (service provider/consumer, infrastructure provider, etc.), various service level aspects (security, performance, etc.), and considerations of the complete service life cycle (engineering, provisioning, negotiation, monitoring, etc.). Negotiation is explicitly used as a measure to control runtime behaviour of particular hardware-centric components with low-level runtime requirements derived from high-level business requirements.

The work discussed so far is mainly conceptual work. Negotiation is considered mainly as a means to facilitate dynamic relationships between service providers and consumers. Hence, no insight is provided into the negotiation process, in particular how negotiation between related service provider and service consumer can be carried out to realise automated SLA management in an SOE. To date, there is a range of ongoing research on SLA management, but most of the relevant issues regarding automated negotiation are still open, as pointed out by Theilmann, Yahyapour, and Butler [TYB08]. The remainder of this section provides a brief overview on this work.

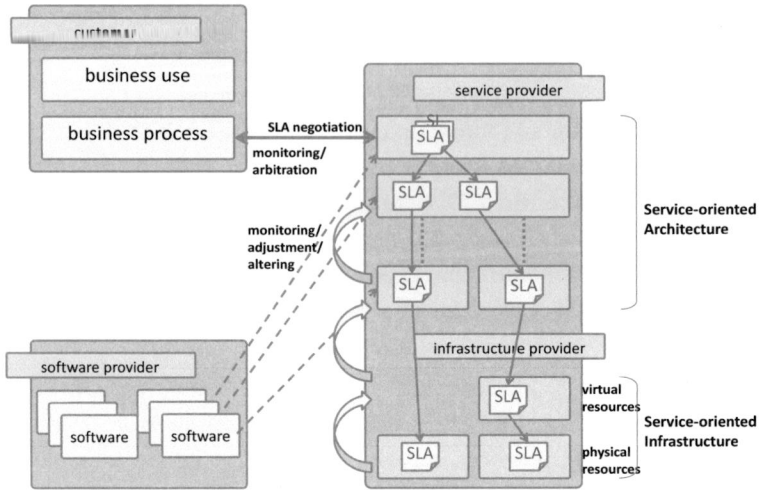

Figure 2-10: Overview of the SLA management process in SLA@SOI (see [TYB08])

The foundation for SLA management is to model SLAs computationally. To this end, several approaches have been proposed. WS-Agreement [ACD+07] provides an extensible framework for specifying agreements between negotiation parties within SOA. Next to the capabilities to model SLAs, WS-Agreement also includes a simple negotiation protocol that covers only a simple one-shot negotiation scenario. That is, a negotiator makes an offer to its opponent, and the opponent can either accept or reject the offer. No further multi-rounded negotiation in the form of counter offers is supported in WS-Agreement. Similar approaches for specifying and monitoring SLAs for Web services can be found in Web Service Level Agreement (WSLA) by Keller and Ludwig [KL03] as well as Web Service Management Network Agent (WSMN) by Sahai et al. [SMS+02]. These frameworks focus on providing approaches to create and monitor SLAs rather than to automate negotiation of SLAs at runtime.

Yan et al. proposed an agent-based approach to facilitate negotiation of SLAs for service compositions [YKL+07]. The focus of their work is to establish agreements on QoS constraints for individual services in the composition. Hence, they introduced a compatible iterated negotiation protocol to enable coordinated negotiation between agents with respect to given end-to-end QoS requirements. Based on this protocol, agents are able to find a set of appropriate SLAs for individual services, which can conjointly guarantee the QoS constraints for the overall service composition. In addition, they design the necessary Web service interfaces with respect to their negotiation protocol.

Another similar approach for negotiating SLAs for Web services is proposed by [ZMCW08]. They applied the negotiation model proposed by Sierra, Faratin, and Jennings [SFJ97]. As the negotiation protocol, they used a subset of the existing FIPA Contract Net Interaction Protocol [FIP02a] and constructed a specification schema for specifying negotiation policies on the basis of WS-Policy[VOH+07]. Their work focused on architectural design of the overall negotiation process and, hence, lacked in-depth investigation of negotiation strategies.

Ludwig et al. introduced a framework for automated SLA negotiation in service grids using dedicated third-party negotiators [LBKF06]. In their work, they applied the WS-Agreement specification and modelled the stakeholders involved in a negotiation process, i.e., service providers for arranging agreements, service providers for negotiation protocol, and service providers for decision-making support, as stand-alone third-party negotiation service providers. Based on these dedicated service providers for negotiation purposes, related service providers and service consumers in the grid apply the FIPA *Iterated* Contract Net Interaction Protocol to reach consensus on quality of service delivery [FIP02b].

All works cited above consider the SLA negotiation problem between consumers and providers as a bilateral, multi-issue, private, and non-mediated negotiation process. In these approaches, negotiation information, e.g., negotiation preference, is private to the respective negotiators and, hence, not shared with others.

Another way to carry out automated negotiation between related service components is to use the aforementioned mediated negotiation, where both negotiation parties delegate their negotiation-related activities to a trusted third party, the *mediator*. Comuzzi and Pernici introduced such an approach [CP05]. In their work, both service consumer and service provider submit their preferences on QoS parameters together with their negotiation strategies to a dedicated mediator. The negotiation mediator performs negotiation based on this information and delivers the resulting SLAs back to the respective service components. In case one negotiating party does not trust the negotiation mediator, a specific semi-automated negotiation model is designated, so that the other party can utilise the mediator for partial negotiation support.

In contrast to non-mediated negotiation, mediated negotiation requires specific infrastructure support. Furthermore, both service components must a priori establish trust relationships with the third-party mediator, before the actual negotiation process can take place. However, such a network of trust relationships is not always available, in particular in an SOE that spans several organisational boundaries.

Next to the works cited above, there is a set of other similar research on automated negotiation conducted in the field of SOA or Grid Computing. Most of this work concentrates only on SLA negotiation within the context of composite services and, hence, addresses issues of bilateral SLA negotiation between service provider and service consumer only to some limited extent. Further issues concerning the design paradigm of *service-orientation* are not taken into account at all, such as autonomy, dependences between services, and dynamism. In addition, existing works in the field lack an in-depth investigation of efficiency and effectiveness of such negotiation models.

Beyond that, the present thesis desires to propose a *controllable* and *business-driven* negotiation model with respect to global business objectives. The resulting SLAs should help to enforce these business objectives on the global level. For example, if the global business objective is defined as maximising customer satisfaction, the negotiation process should place focus on finding agreements with high availability and short response time. In this case, cost does not play a critical role in the negotiation. From this point-of-view, a comprehensive SLA negotiation framework across all related service components in support of a service-oriented system is desired [LS10], which takes global business objectives as high-level goal into consideration.

2.3.4 Concluding Remarks

This section reviews the basic concept of multi-agent systems, and provides a common accepted definition on agents with some characteristic properties. Furthermore, an insight is provided into existing mechanisms to enable interactions between agents in MAS. In particular, existing approaches to coordinate activities of a set of agents in MAS are reviewed. To solve possible conflicts between agents in their interactions, the research community of MAS developed a considerable amount of negotiation mechanisms. This section places an emphasis on the theoretical foundations adapted to enable automated negotiation, namely game theoretic, heuristic, and argumentation-based approaches. As aforementioned, each approach has its merits and drawbacks. Hence, a given problem domain has to be analysed to select the suitable negotiation technique.

Furthermore, this section correlates the characteristics of autonomous agents to those of services in an SOE. The distributed and autonomous nature of services corresponds strongly to the characteristics of agents in MAS. Nevertheless, the W3C states, "a Web service is an abstract notion that must be implemented by a concrete agent. The agent is the concrete piece of software or hardware that sends and receives messages, while the service is the resource characterised by the abstract set of functionality that is provided" [W3C04]. In this definition, the W3C correlates the concept of services with agents. This correlation is of particular interest for the present thesis, especially from the viewpoint of the agent-oriented design of the architecture later discussed in detail in Section 5.1.

2.4 Summary

This chapter reviews the state-of-the-art of three main research fields that relate strongly to the present thesis. Section 2.1 reviews at first the concept of service-orientation and explains the design paradigm of Service-oriented Computing. Furthermore, this section outlines the current development in the fields of Cloud Computing and Service-oriented Infrastructure. These technological evolutions introduce the concept of service-orientation also to hardware-centric components in IT infrastructure, which is crucial for the present thesis. Thorough realisation of service-orientation across the complete IT infrastructure provides the prerequisite to apply the concept proposed in this thesis to an SOE.

Section 2.2 reviews the concept of self-organisation and outlines the typical problems to engineer self-organising applications. In addition, this section provides a brief insight into existing approaches to establish self-organisations in technical systems, including OC, AC, and the VSM. These approaches are compared with one another regarding their capabilities and possible application domains. Furthermore, this section gives an overview on existing approaches to realise self-organisation in SOEs.

The last focus of this chapter is, in Section 2.3, to review the concept of Multi-Agent Systems. MAS has been intensively studied in the last few decades, in particular with respect to the interaction-related aspects between agents. That is, how agents can be coordinated, so that they can solve a global problem collaboratively. To this end, a considerable amount of research has been done to facilitate social interactions between agents. This section places an emphasis on existing approaches to enable coordination and negotiation between agents. Such techniques are of particular interest to the present thesis, among other things, from the viewpoint of collaboration between various service components in SOA. Furthermore, this section illustrates the characteristics of agents, which correspond strongly to those of services in an SOE. This correlation between MAS and SOC stimulates strongly an agent-oriented design of the concept proposed in this thesis, which is discussed later in detail.

Part II

Architecture Design

Chapter 3   Fundamentals

"千里之行，始于足下。"
—【道德经 · 六十四章】

*"A journey of thousand miles begins with the first step; the highest eminence is to be
gained step by step."*
(Tao Te Ching, Laozi, ~ 470 B.C.)

The focus of the present thesis is to provide a multi-level framework to enable automated end-to-end Service Level Management between business and enterprise IT.
SLM defines the fundamental concept to bring requirements of business and capabilities of IT infrastructure together. Appropriate realisation of multi-level SLM facilitates efficient allocation of technical resources in compliance with business requirements. This contributes to a strengthening of competitive advantages on the market.

The concept of SLM revolves mainly around SLAs. It covers the complete life cycle of SLAs, from negotiating SLAs at design time to enforcing them at runtime. In
the context of SLM, SLAs are mutually accepted contracts between a service provider
and its consumer(s). They specify rights and obligations of providers and consumers
to enable successful cooperation between them. With automated negotiation of SLAs
as well as self-organisation of individual service components in order to fulfil agreed
SLAs, they provide the fundamental means to facilitate collaboration between service
components in a coordinated manner.

Hence, this chapter is concerned with the fundamental means to realise the two-
level approach introduced in Section 1.2. As stated there, the approach combines the
local SLA-driven self-organisation with the *global* automated SLA negotiation to enable automated multi-level SLM in SOEs. Section 3.1 provides a common understanding of an SOE and outlines its main architectural layers. Section 3.2 gives an
overview on the basic concept of SLAs in the context of service-oriented systems, in
particular the formal model and the life cycle of SLAs. Section 3.3 introduces the
basic model to enable bilateral multi-issue negotiation between agents, particularly
with respect to automated negotiation of SLAs between service provider and consum-

er. Section 3.4 focuses on the local SLA-driven self-organisation of a technical component. It introduces the detailed observer/controller architecture to establish controlled self-organisation of a service component in compliance with negotiated SLAs. The last section concludes the chapter and address how the fundamental means introduced in the chapter relate to one another.

3.1 Service-oriented Environments

Service-orientation allows IT components to expose their business and technical capabilities to their environment as reusable services, while keeping their autonomy concerning the internal realisation and maintenance of these capabilities. Section 2.1 reviews the current development of service-orientation in the context of enterprise IT, in particular service-oriented applications on top of SOAs and SOIs. In particular, the trend towards virtualisation technologies facilitates the implementation of service-orientation in enterprise IT, which results in new service-oriented technologies, such as Cloud Computing.

Traditionally, SOA is regarded as software-centric approach to connect business with enterprise IT. That is, SOA specifies how business processes can be composed out of a set of services that encapsulate capabilities provided by external business applications. On the other hand, SOI is regarded as hardware-centric approach to provide operational environments for software applications. It addresses how underlying hardware components, such as network connectivity, computing power, or storage can be virtualised and managed as reusable services for business applications. Obviously, both concepts themselves address only part of a service-oriented enterprise IT. However, both concepts together cover all artefacts that typically make up enterprise architectures. Hence, as stated in Section 2.1.5, the present thesis uses the term *service-oriented environment* (SOE) to denote the entire operational environment of business processes in the IT infrastructure that adopt the design principles of service-orientation in its technical realisation.

An SOE involves a set of artefacts across the business/IT stacks of enterprise IT. For example, the business-related artefacts of such an SOE are business process, business governance, or capacity management, which aim at facilitating business-driven support on top of enterprise IT. IT-related artefacts like applications, servers, platforms, and hardware build technically the operational foundations in support of business. Because of the high variety of artefacts involved in an SOE, this section provides a general multi-layered architecture to describe SOEs. In particular, it outlines the provider/consumer relationships between service components that characterises the service-oriented nature of such an environment.

It is worth noting that the multi-layered architecture introduced in this section focuses mainly on the technical aspects of an SOE. Because of the high synergy between business and enterprise IT, this section focuses partly on the impact of business objectives on the IT stack, in particular from the viewpoint of business-driven IT management. Other business-related aspects, such as Corporate Governance [SV97] are out-of-scope of the present thesis.

3.1.1 Multi-layered Architecture

An SOE consists of a set of possible technical artefacts in support of business, and applies service-orientation. Each service component in an SOE has in general two views. From the viewpoint of a provider, a service component has one or more business/technical capabilities that can be delivered as services to customers. From the viewpoint of a consumer, a service component has to make use of services from other components to enable its functional requirements. Based on such provider/consumer relationships, business can builds up service-oriented applications synergising business and enterprise IT.

Combining the reference architectures introduced in Section 2.1 for SOA and SOI, the present thesis introduces a multi-layered architecture of an SOE with essential concerns. This multi-layered architecture intends to establish a common understanding of an SOE for the present thesis. Figure 3-1 illustrates the multi-layered architecture with five horizontal layers and three vertical layers. The layers in the architecture separate effectively various concerns of an SOE.

It is noteworthy that the architecture depicted in Figure 3-1 covers only technical aspects and part of business aspects within an SOE. Organisational aspects, such as organisational memberships of the artefacts involved, are not considered in the multi-layered architecture. The common case is that all artefacts belong to the same organisation. However, along with the shift of enterprise IT towards service-oriented systems, an SOE may involve components from other organisations. Hence, one organisation might completely be a service consumer, and another a service provider.

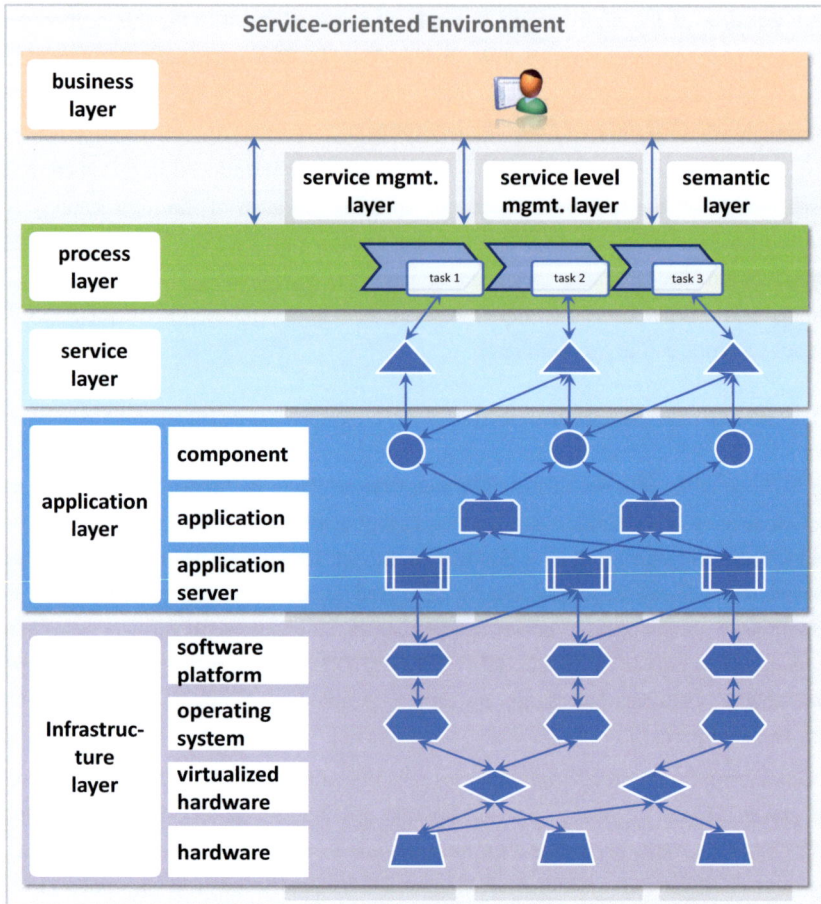

Figure 3-1: Multi-layered architecture of a service-oriented environment

The five horizontal layers of the multi-layered architecture contain all functional components that are required to provide business capabilities to end users. From the top down, the layers have decreasing business values and increasing IT focuses:

- The business layer represents end users that consume business capabilities provided by enterprise IT to carry out their day-to-day activities in their organisations. Hence, the business layer has end-to-end functional as well as non-functional requirements on the underlying process layer. These requirements are derived from the business and its environment, for example, business processes, legal restrictions, market conditions, and so on. The underlying enterprise IT has to arrange its components to meet these requirements. This shows the supporting role of enterprise IT in business.

- The process layer builds up the connecting piece between the business and the enterprise IT. On the one hand, the process layer takes over functional as well as non-functional requirements that the business layer has on the entire enterprise IT. On the other hand, it orchestrates services from the underlying service layer to meet requirements from the business layer. Hence, the process layer provides the fundamental means to guide end users through various activities involved in business processes. In particular, business process engines adopting standards for modelling business processes (e.g., Business Process Modelling Notation (BPMN) or Business Process Execution Language (BPEL)) allows agile changes in business processes by modifying the corresponding models at runtime. From this viewpoint, the process layer establishes an adaptation layer between the dynamic business layer and the comparatively less flexible service layer. This capability is crucial to enable business-driven IT infrastructure, in particular to get business demands of the business layer and technical capabilities of the underlying enterprise IT seamlessly aligned. Furthermore, because of the specific role of the process layer between the business and the enterprise IT, it plays an important role with respect to IT Service Management. It is obvious that the runtime behaviour of the process layer directly influences user experience of the business layer that interacts with the enterprise IT. Hence, non-functional requirements on quality of service delivery of the process layer should be considered as the end-to-end non-functional requirements on the complete enterprise IT, including the process layer and all underlying layers.

- The service layer establishes an abstract layer on top of the physical implementations of business capabilities provided by the application layer. Hence, the service layer is composed of services delivered by various organisations. Each service component in this layer complies with the design principles of service-orientation, in particular service abstractions and service autonomy. These design principles allows services being discoverable, remotely executable, and able to be choreographed into business processes at runtime. It is noteworthy that services in the service layer are not restricted to Web services, which are the most popular representation of services in SOA. Instead, services may differ from one another in their types, realisation, interaction style, and so on. The present thesis distinguishes between two different types of services that a business process can invoke: services with user interfaces for human participants and services with programming interfaces (so called APIs). The former service type provides a necessary frontend interface (e.g., rich clients or Web portals) to allow end users in the business layer to interact with the corresponding processes. Such user interfaces are essential to support interactive human activities in a business process [TGWD09]. The latter service type is associated with reusable business capabilities that are encapsulated as services. These business capabilities are realised by the underlying backend applications, such as business unit specific components, project specific components, or other enterprise scale components.

- The application layer is the layer within the architecture that is responsible for realising business capabilities and maintaining runtime behaviour of exposed services with respect to quality of service delivery. Hence, each application in the application layer reflects both the QoS and functionality of the services it exposes. On the one hand, each application represents a stakeholder in the layered architecture and ensures that its implementation along with services from the underlying IT infrastructure align with its service descriptions. Given the recursive nature of the SOA, an application can build its implementation on top of other applications from the same layer. By applying this recursive scheme, the application layer can be divided into several sub-layers, such as a sub-layer with software components, a sub-layer concerning applications, and a sub-layer with container-based servers (e.g., application server or Web server). On the other hand, each application represents an enforcement point for ensuring conformance of runtime behaviour of a particular service with agreed SLAs. In particular, container-based server applications play a key role in influencing non-functional behaviour of software components at runtime. To this end, each server application has a range of configuration possibilities to determine directly QoS of corresponding software components they host (e.g., response time, availability, throughput, etc.).

- The infrastructure layer provides the necessary technical environment to host applications in the application layer, including software platforms (.NET, Java, etc.), operating systems, and underlying hardware-centric components (network connectivity, computing power, storage, and so on). Hence, similar to the application layer, the infrastructure layer can be divided into several sub-layers, too. On the bottom is the sub-layer with hardware components in support of service-oriented applications. These hardware components are normally virtualised, so that they can be organised in resource pools with on demand resource allocation. The sub-layer with virtualised hardware components provides an abstraction layer to enable unified and consistent access to underlying hetero-geneous hardware components. Hence, the sub-layer with operating systems can access virtualised computational resources in a consistent and transparent manner. On top of operating systems, software platforms are responsible to set up basic execution environments for the application layer.

The design principles of service-orientation are inherent in the multi-layered archi-tecture. Components in the various layers provide a range of possible service types (e.g., implementation services, hosting services, Web services, and so on) to other components in the same or upper layers. For example, Web services or frontend ap-plication services are service providers for business processes in the upper *process* layer. Similarly, software components providing technical implementations to services in the *service* layer consume in turn hosting services from the sub-layer of container-based servers. From this viewpoint, service-orientation is one of the common proper-ties that each component in an SOE has.

Accordingly, service-related aspects are integral parts of such a multi-layered archi-tecture to describe an SOE. There are no separate stakeholders for these aspects in the horizontal layers, as introduced previously. Instead, layers addressing service-related aspects cut across all horizontal layers in the architecture (as illustrated in Figure 3-1): the *service management* layer covers capabilities, functionalities, and processes for managing services over their entire life cycle. The *service level management* layer regulates all provider/consumer relationships between related technical components using mutually agreed contracts. The *semantic* layer ensures that all components in-volved in the SOE have a common understanding on service-related issues, such as QoS terms, their metrics, and measurement of these metrics at runtime.

Service management is essential for businesses that adopt service-orientation to de-sign and implement components in their enterprise IT, e.g., business processes, IT applications, or hardware components. Hence, the *service management* layer provides a set of organisational and technical capabilities for managing services in the way that they can provide expected values to their consumers. These capabilities cover the en-tire life cycle of a service, including strategy, design, implementation, operation, and continuous improvement. To this end, a range of possible measures, such as appropri-ate organisational structures, processes, or management systems, are utilised to coor-dinate and control the life cycle of a service. Such management tools can span the complete organisation (e.g., processes to guarantee organisation-wide service strate-gy) or be restricted to particular service components in the architecture (e.g., management systems to control one or more service components). Hence, it is important that the *service management* layer continuously links service management processes of related components closely together, from the *process* layer down to the *infrastructure* layer. This is vital to enable consistent management and maintenance of services in accordance with requirements from the *business* layer.

A tighter relationship between service providers and service consumers is formed by SLAs. As a fundamental means to regulate expectations of service consumers and capabilities of service providers on quality of service delivery, SLAs ensure that runtime behaviour of service provides complies with QoS terms agreed in contracts with their consumers. Hence, while service management is concerned with particular service component(s) in the architecture, service level management deals with provider/consumer relationships between related components across the architecture, in particular with respect to their non-functional runtime behaviour. The *service level management* layer is cutting across all horizontal layers. It provides a consistent foundation to facilitate comprehensive SLM between related providers and consumers at runtime. To this end, this layer provides a service the necessary means to negotiate, establish, and document operational targets of service delivery with their consumers, and enforce them by monitoring and producing reports on services' ability to deliver the agreed service levels. Given the recursive nature of the SOA and the continuous adoption of service level management from the *process* layer down to the *infrastructure* layer, the *service level management* layer allows services providers to tailor their capabilities with respect to requirements that the *business* layer has on the entire enterprise IT.

Semantics is of great importance for all stakeholders in an SOE. One of the prerequisites for successful collaboration between related service providers and service consumers is their unambiguous understanding of terms involved in their collaboration. In particular, from the viewpoint of service level management, both service provider and service consumer must have the same definitions for QoS issues that are specified in an SLA. Hence, the *semantic* layer provides the necessary ontologies about the SOE, in particular for terms involved in service level management (such as QoS issues, time units, related metrics, and so on). By establishing such global ontologies in an SOE, components can unambiguously collaborate with one another to facilitate service level management across the entire IT landscape.

As aforementioned, the target of the multi-layered architecture in this section is to establish a common understanding of major architectural layers and building blocks of an SOE. In comparison to other similar reference architectures of SOA, as introduced in Section 2.1, the architecture introduced in this section focuses mainly on two aspects. The first one is the connection between the underlying enterprise IT in support of service-oriented applications and the *business* layer with end users of the enterprise IT. This connection allows modelling and establishing business-driven management of the entire IT landscape. The second aspect is the focus on service-related artefacts in a service-oriented enterprise IT. That is, services are treated as first-class citizen in the landscape to increase the agility of the entire enterprise IT. Furthermore, it is noteworthy that the multi-layered architecture introduced in this section is not claimed to be complete concerning all possible artefacts within an SOE. There are certainly aspects, such as service integration or service governance, which are not included in this multi-layered architecture. For the purpose of the present thesis emphasising on service level management, this architecture indeed includes all service-related building blocks in an SOE. Hence, this abstracted multi-layered architecture suffices for further analysis in the present thesis.

3.1.2 Provider/Consumer Relationship

An SOE is characterised by provider/consumer relationships between related components. By consistently adopting service-orientation across the complete IT landscape, services build the conjunction part between related technical artefacts in the multi-layered architecture. Given the recursive nature of an SOE, runtime behaviour of the *process* layer depends on behaviour of all underlying layers in support of the *process* layer. Throughout all underlying layers, a single business process involves a set of service components that span a *hierarchical dependence chain* based on recursive provider/consumer relationships, where the business process is the root of the chain.

Therefore, the provider/consumer relationship plays a fundamental role for proper functionality of service-oriented systems. Figure 3-2 shows the relationships between major stakeholders in an SOE that are involved in a provider/consumer relationship.

The core of a provider/consumer relationship is of course the *service provider* and the *service consumer*. However, before they can interact with each other, a *service consumer* has to retrieve a *service provider* that can fulfil its functional and non-functional requirements. To this end, service providers publish meta-level information about their services (i.e., *service contracts*) to a *service broker*. Using this meta-level information, a *service broker* can respond to inquiry requests, i.e., both functional and non-functional requirements on the target service type, from service consumers.

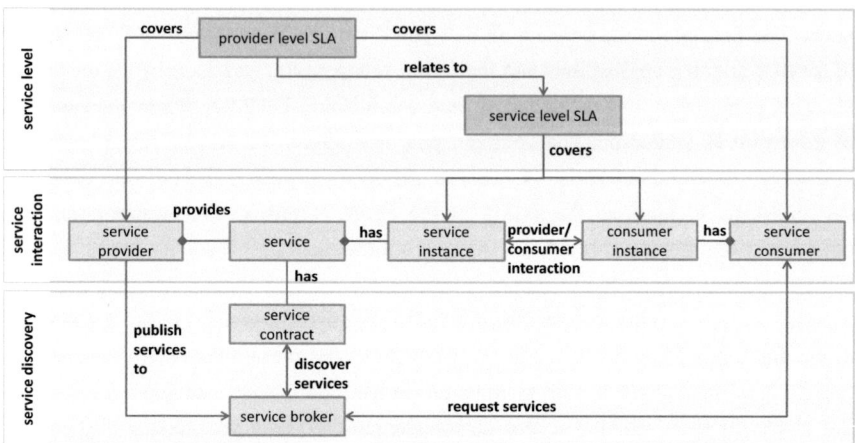

Figure 3-2: Provider/consumer relationship in a service-oriented environment

After a *service consumer* has identified the *service provider* it wants to interact with, they have to reach an arrangement on service levels. To this end, SLAs are used to document service level targets and responsibilities of a *service provider* and its *service consumer* during their interactions. By doing this, a *service provider* can ensure that delivery of its services is aligned with business requirements and meets the expectations of the consumer in terms of service quality.

The present thesis utilises a multi-level SLA approach. That is, next to the explicit *service level* SLA assigned to each provider/consumer relationship, there is a framework agreement on the *provider level*. Alternatively, such a framework agreement can also be closed on the business unit or even corporate level. The function of such a framework agreement is to cover all generic and static service level issues appropriately for each service of the service provider (or respectively of the business unit or of the corporate unit). For example, a framework agreement can regulate the legal aspects of all related electronic SLAs on the service level that are stable over the time. Section 3.2.1 is going to discuss the needs of such a multi-level approach in detail.

Such a multi-level structure allows a separation of concerns within all SLAs. On the one hand, each SLA is clearly defined and has a manageable size without having to duplicate unnecessary contents in each agreement. On the other hand, moving generic parts that are less variable from service level SLAs to higher-level SLAs reduces the need for frequent updates of SLAs, which is usually associated with additional administrative overhead.

With established *provider level* and *service level* SLAs, interactions between a *service provider* and a *service consumer* can take place. It is assumed that a service provider offers a range of various services to potential consumers. However, for each provider/consumer relationship, there is only a single service involved. By all means, it is possible that a *service provider* and a *service consumer* have more than one provider/consumer relationship between each other. Hence, for each provider/consumer relationship, there is a dedicated *service instance* of the corresponding service at the side of the *service provider*. Respectively, the *service consumer* has a *consumer instance* of the corresponding provider/consumer relationship. By using such a service-provisioning concept on the instance level, a *service provider* can provide a single service with differentiating capabilities, i.e., different performance or security levels. Analogously, a *consumer instance* allows a *service consumer* to consume simultaneously several services from different service providers. Hence, the actual interaction between a *service provider* and its *consumer* takes place between the *service instance* and the corresponding *consumer instance*. Hence, the service level SLA is associated with the respective *service instance* and the *consumer instance*. Their behaviour at runtime is decisive for management processes involved in the SLM.

In the remainder of this thesis, except for explicit annotations, the terms *service provider* and *service instance*, *service consumer* and *consumer instance* are used as synonymously. In particular, in the discussion of automated negotiation of SLAs, service levels of a provider/consumer relationship refer to IT-related non-functional aspects between a service instance and its corresponding consumer instance.

3.2 Service Level Agreements

This section outlines the basic idea of SLAs and their impacts on service-oriented systems. Furthermore, this section provides an insight into formal approaches for modelling SLAs electronically, which is crucial to enable automated negotiation between related components. Then, a set of common QoS parameters associated with service-oriented systems are introduced in this section. The last part of this section covers the life cycle of an SLA in the context of SLM.

3.2.1 Overview

Service-orientation is increasingly adopted to build mission-critical distributed applications spanning several autonomous organisations, for example, applications for supply chain management in industry or applications for scientific computing in academia. As already mentioned in the motivation (see Section 1.1), such a service-oriented system depends not only on the functionality, but also the quality of services involved in the system (e.g., performance and availability). Hence, in order to operate a service-oriented system in a predicable way, contracts are used to govern relationships between related service consumers and service providers. In particular, such contracts define mutual responsibilities of consumers and providers with respect to quality of service delivery. Hence, these service contracts are considered as a predictable level of assurance with respect to quality of service delivery of the provider.

In the context of SLM, such clauses are referred to as Service Level Agreements (SLAs). An SLA is a written contract between IT service provider and its consumer(s) that defines the key service targets and responsibilities for both sides. ITIL defines an SLA as [RL07]:

...an agreement between an IT service provider and a customer. The SLA describes the IT service, documents service level targets, and specifies the responsibilities of the IT service provider and the customer. A single SLA may cover multiple IT services or multiple customers.

Given the definition above, SLA are used to regulate obligations and rights of service providers and service consumers in their interactions. In fact, SLAs play an important role in IT service management. McConnell and Siegel summarise the strategic values of SLAs for providers and consumers [MS04a]:

- The related parties have an explicit agreement that specifies the scope of the cooperation, the related services, the desired performance of the provider, the measurements to assess provider performance, and the penalties for agreement violation. The clarity of SLAs removes much of the ambiguity in the provider/consumer relationship.

- SLAs help customers to control their cost reasonably by allocating their IT spending efficiently based on differentiated service provisioning.

- SLAs help providers to allocate their resources efficiently based on consumer demands. SLA-driven resource management helps to avoid over- or underutilisation of their resources.

In traditional IT service management, an SLA is a written document between a service provider and its consumer(s). The content of an SLA varies from case to case, depending mainly on requirements and capacities of particular agreement parties, in particular, service provider, service consumers, and end users.

Nevertheless, in analogy to commerce contracts, an SLA in general covers both technical and business aspects of service delivery. Next to the meta information about an SLA, e.g., scope of agreements, period of validity of an agreement, and service descriptions, an SLA defines a range of technical service level targets, where each service level target addresses one QoS parameter about the service delivery, e.g., response time, availability, or security level. Furthermore, an SLA specifies metrics to assess the degree that service delivery complies with the agreed service level targets.

The other focus of an SLA is to specify business aspects of the contract. Among other things, an SLA provides details on charging formulas used, charging period, reference to external charging policies, as well as invoicing procedures. Furthermore, an SLA specifies procedures to do service reporting and reviewing: how often service reports should take place, content of service report, and frequency of service reviewing meetings to manage changes of SLAs. An important aspect during service level management is to determine responsibilities of the various parties involved in the agreement. In addition, an appropriately negotiated agreement should give a provider appropriate incentive to guarantee its service delivery quality. On the other hand, it should provide a consumer with the necessary incentive to consume the specified service(s) as contracted. Hence, an agreement specifies penalties for both service consumer and service provider. If a service consumer violates limits agreed in an SLA, e.g., maximal number of requests submitted per time unit or maximal amount of data processed per time unit, then a consumer is required to pay a higher price. Vice versa, if a service provider cannot deliver its service(s) as arranged in the agreement, e.g., minimal throughput per time unit, or maximal response time, then the corresponding consumer receives compensation for contract violation by the provider.

SLAs determine obligations, permissions, and responsibilities between a service provider and its consumer(s). It is obvious that in order to enable SLA-driven business scenarios between technical systems, electronic contracts mirroring paper documents exchanged between businesses are required. Indeed, there is a range of possible approaches that provide the basic concepts for modelling electronic SLAs between technical systems, e.g., WS-Agreement introduced in detail in Section 3.2.2. Electronic SLAs provide technical systems with the possibilities to create, negotiate, apply, and enforce restrictions on behaviour of providers and consumers in an automated and flexible manner.

However, a potential obstacle to prevent the application of such electronic contracts is the legal implications of electronic SLAs. For the purpose of this thesis, it is therefore important to investigate how such obstacles can be overcome in service-oriented systems, where electronic SLAs lay the cornerstone for the approach of this thesis.

First, it is obvious that legal aspects of SLAs cannot be completely ignored for service-oriented systems. In particular, in the context of Cloud Computing, SLAs closed between a cloud service provider and its consumers must cover legal aspects. It is crucial that cloud service providers are trustworthy enough for their consumers, that businesses would outsource their critical business data to external cloud services. Hence, cloud service providers must be able to demonstrate that those business data are processed and stored in the way that their consumers specify. Such guarantees are given on the one hand by means of technical measures, which are specified in SLAs, such as using certain security standards. On the other hand, SLAs must be legally binding for both service providers and their consumers, before service consumers enter into partnerships with cloud service providers. This additionally enforces the guarantee levels that technical measures can provide.

The concept of incorporating legal aspects into electronic SLAs will fail, as long as the question if intelligent agents can be held accountable for contracts they close is not clarified. Furthermore, an important advantage that electronic SLAs offer is that they can be dynamically negotiated and adjusted at runtime in dependence of the current operational context. However, legal aspects of electronic SLAs are rather fixed and restrictive, as opposed to what electronic SLAs allow.

Therefore, a more promising way to combine legal binding with flexible electronic SLAs is to use multi-level SLAs, as introduced in Section 3.1.2. That is, service provider and service consumer can adopt one or more additional high-level SLAs signed by human representatives on top of electronic SLAs negotiated by software agents. This enables businesses to address legal constraints in their interactions, while they can still benefit from the flexibility and simplicity provided by intelligent agents.

High-level SLAs, which are framework agreements for the underlying electronic SLAs, are in general non-electronic. Such contracts are usually arranged and signed by human representatives from the agreement parties. The main purpose of high-level framework agreements is to govern legal aspects of all interactions, in particular software-based automated negotiation, between intelligent agents from related businesses. Among other things, a framework agreement specifies the scope of automated negotiation, including acceptable penalties, required capabilities, and administrative boundaries of intelligent agents. Furthermore, a framework agreement also defines accountabilities and responsibilities of all parties involved in the agreement, which are legally binding with respect to traditional contracts exchanged between businesses.

In the remainder of the present thesis, it is assumed that legal aspects are covered by framework agreements that are closed a priori, before automated negotiation between related service components takes place. Hence, the scope of the present thesis is restricted to electronic SLAs with technical aspects (e.g., QoS parameters) of interactions between service providers and service consumers. Correspondingly, the following subsections discuss the conceptual model of SLAs, common QoS parameters used in SLAs, and the typical life cycle of SLAs within SOEs.

3.2.2 Formal SLA Model

The prerequisite of automated negotiation and enforcement of SLAs is to model and describe them formally in a common language that is unambiguously understandable for intelligent agents. As mentioned in Section 2.3.3, there have been several efforts in the research field that intend to provide the foundation to facilitate agreement set-up between service providers and service consumers, such as WSMN [SMS+02], WSLA [KL03], or SLAng [SLE04]. The most recent effort is the WS-Agreement specification [ACD+07] published by the Open Grid Forum as a proposed recommendation, which incorporates a range of existing concepts proposed in the WSLA framework. WS-Agreement specification focuses on creating and monitoring SLAs between a service provider and its service consumer. This section introduces the basic formal SLA model defined in the WS-Agreement.

Figure 3-3 illustrates the distinct parts of an agreement defined in the WS-Agreement specification. The optional *name* section provides the possibility to specify a name for the agreement, so that it can be uniquely identified if needed. The *context* section contains meta-data about the entire agreement. Among other things, it provides information about both negotiation parties, namely the agreement *initiator* that initialises the negotiation request and the agreement *responder* that responds to the negotiation request. In addition, the *context* section specifies the service provider, which is normally either an agreement initiator or an agreement responder. Another focus of the *context* section is to specify the lifetime of an agreement, in particular, the expiration time of the agreement, when it is no longer valid.

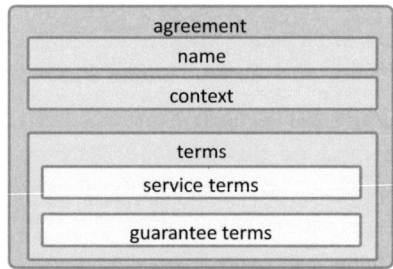

Figure 3-3: Structure of a service level agreement (see [ACD+07])

In order to better control the content of an agreement at runtime, WS-Agreement uses agreement templates with predefined context information. Hence, the *context* section can optionally provide information about the template, based on which this agreement is created. It is noteworthy that the *context* section is extendable by default. It is therefore possible to add further domain specific information about the agreement to the *context* section. For example, it can contain a reference to the framework agreement that settles the general legal restrictions. By extending the context section with custom information, it can provide further expressive information on the respective agreement.

The main body of an agreement is composed of *terms*. A *term* refers to some consensus or obligations of a party. The WS-Agreement defines two types of terms: *service terms* and *guarantee terms*. A *service term* contains information about services, to which the agreement pertains and to which the guarantee terms apply. To this end, a service term consists of references to the respective service and its service descriptions that provide further functional information about the service. Furthermore, it is possible to extend a service term with domain-specific service properties, which can be used to describe its non-functional aspects.

Guarantee terms are the part in an agreement that specifies assurances about quality of service delivery given by a service provider to its consumer(s). Each *guarantee term* is associated with one or more service terms to determine their scope. For example, the service scope can contain a single operation of a service or multiple services to which the guarantee term applies. Each guarantee term contains a *service level objective* determining a particular service attribute, such as average response time, service availability, or service throughput. To each service level objective, the guarantee term specifies also its *service level target* that provides quantitative assertion on the respective *service level objective*.

A further aspect addressed by a guarantee term is business values of the respective service. The WS-Agreement specification determines four general business value types: *importance, penalty, reward,* and *preference.* The element *importance* is used to express the relative importance of meeting an objective. The elements *penalty* and *reward* are used to state the penalty of not meeting an objective and the reward of meeting an objective. The element *preference* allows both parties to specify a list of possible alternatives concerning the service level objective. In addition to these four *business value* types, a range of custom business values can be defined in a guarantee term, which allows service providers and their consumers to arrange their domain-specific business values.

Table 3-1 illustrates a simple XML document sample in accordance with the WS-Agreement specification.

The sample document is an agreement offer sent from the service consumer *CompetenceFieldsWorkflow* (cf. line 5) to the service provider *PersonService* (cf. line 6). The given agreement expires at the end of 2011. The agreement covers the operation *Read* of the Web service *PersonService* (cf. lines 14 and 15).

The guarantee term (cf. lines 18 and 19) in the agreement offer provides an assurance over response time for the operation *Read*. It defines that each request must be pressed within 10 seconds (i.e., response time of the provider must be less than 10 seconds, cf. lines 22~25).

Table 3-1: Sample SLA based on the WS-Agreement specification

```
 1   <?xml version="1.0" encoding="UTF-8"?>
 2   <wsag:AgreementOffer sag:AgreementId="negotiation_sample_PersonService_offer"
        xmlns:tns="http://www.w3.org/2005/08/addressing"
        xmlns:wsag="http://schemas.ggf.org/graap/2007/03/ws-agreement"
        xmlns:wsrf-bf="http://docs.oasis-open.org/wsrf/bf-2"
        xmlns:xml="http://www.w3.org/XML/1998/namespace"
        xmlns:xs="http://www.w3.org/2001/XMLSchema"
        xmlns:xsi="http://www.w3.org/2001/XMLSchema-instance"
        xsi:schemaLocation="http://schemas.ggf.org/graap/2007/03/ws-
agreement.xsd"
        xsi:type="wsag:AgreementType">
 3   <wsag:Name>PersonService_Negotiation_Sample</wsag:Name>
 4   <wsag:Context>
 5     <wsag:AgreementInitiator>CompetenceFieldsWorkflow<wsag:AgreementInitiator/>
 6     <wsag:AgreementResponder>PersonService</wsag:AgreementResponder>
 7     <wsag:ServiceProvider>PersonService</wsag:ServiceProvider>
 8     <wsag:ExpirationTime>2011-12-31T12:00:00</wsag:ExpirationTime>
 9   </wsag:Context>
10   <wsag:Terms>
11     <wsag:All>
12       <wsag:ExactlyOne>
13         <wsag:All>
14           <wsag:ServiceDescriptionTerm wsag:Name="Read"
15                 wsag:ServiceName="PersonService"/>
16         </wsag:All>
17       </wsag:ExactlyOne>
18       <wsag:GuaranteeTerm wsag:Name="ServiceResponseTime"
19             wsag:Obligated="ServiceProvider">
20         <wsag:ServiceScope Name="PersonService">Read</wsag:ServiceScope>
21         <wsag:ServiceLevelObjective>
22           <wsag:KPITarget>
23             <wsag:KPIName>ResponseTime</wsag:KPIName>
24             <wsag:Target><10s</wsag:Target>
25           </wsag:KPITarget>
26         </wsag:ServiceLevelObjective>
27         <wsag:BusinessValueList>
28           <wsag:Penalty>
29             <wsag:AssesmentInterval>
30               <wsag:TimeInterval>Weekly</wsag:TimeInterval>
31             </wsag:AssesmentInterval>
32             <wsag:ValueUnit>EUR</wsag:ValueUnit>
33             <wsag:ValueExpr>1</wsag:ValueExpr>
34           </wsag:Penalty>
35           <wsag:Reward>
36             <wsag:AssesmentInterval>
37               <wsag:TimeInterval>Daily</wsag:TimeInterval>
38             </wsag:AssesmentInterval>
39             <wsag:ValueUnit>EUR</wsag:ValueUnit>
40             <wsag:ValueExpr>0.5</wsag:ValueExpr>
41           </wsag:Reward>
42         </wsag:BusinessValueList>
43       </wsag:GuaranteeTerm>
44     </wsag:All>
45   </wsag:Terms>
46   </wsag:AgreementOffer>
```

In order to provide incentives for the provider to fulfil this guarantee term, the agreement specifies business values for the provider and the consumer. In the example, the offer states that for any violation of the guarantee term in the period of a week, the service provider is obligated to pay a penalty of one EUR (cf. lines 28~34). Otherwise, if the service provider can deliver the service in compliance with the guarantee term, it is going to receive an additional reward of 0.5 EUR, in addition to the actual service cost (cf. lines 35~41).

3.2.3 Quality of Service

SLAs uses service level objectives to determine the scope of non-functional attributes that are of interest for both contract parties. Hence, it is necessary for both parties to specify which non-functional attributes should be included in an SLA, so that the quality of service delivery can be assessed at runtime. In fact, Quality of service (QoS) of technical systems has been subject of active research for several decades. The international quality standard ISO 9000:2005 describes quality as *"degree to which a set of inherent characteristics fulfils requirements"* [ISO05]. Starting from related research concerning real time issues in telecommunication networks, QoS provides the basic means to address non-functional aspects of technical systems. In the context of this thesis, the definition given by ISO refers to the *quality of service delivery* of a service provider that provides distinguishing features to fulfil functional requirements of its service consumers. Hence, in order to estimate the degree of requirement fulfilment by a service provider, QoS consists of a set of non-functional attributes to estimate quality of service delivery of the provider.

In the field of SOC, QoS plays the fundamental role to allow service providers and service consumers to express their non-functional requirements and capabilities. In particular, SLAs utilise QoS to specify service level objectives and their targets. Hence, one prerequisite for using QoS in SOEs is to determine the set of non-functional attributes that are of interest either to service providers or to service consumers. Van Moorsel analysed the quantitative metrics to evaluate Internet-based services [Moo01]. He recognised that there are different types of QoS parameters with respect to their objectives. By considering the multi-tier architecture of Internet applications, van Moorsel proposed the terms *Quality of Business*, *Quality of Experience*, and *Quality of Service*. Respectively, each type of quality has a different focus for evaluating quality of service delivery. While *Quality of Service* is concerned with technical metrics, the other two quality types address more end-to-end aspects of In-ternet-based services on service level. That is, they concentrate on experience that business and end user perceive during their interactions with an IT-based system. By using this categorization, van Moorsel distinguished explicitly between QoS parame-ters from the perspective of service providers and QoS parameters from the perspec-tive of service consumers.

Cubera, Khalaf, and Mukhi investigated QoS in SOEs and identified the necessary protocol stack to support QoS in SOA-based systems, including WS-Agreement, WS-Security, and WS-Coordination [CKM08]. Based on their analysis, they summarised that the use of middleware protocols in support of QoS and the aggregation of QoS parameters in service compositions are two areas that require active research and de-velopment. However, they do not investigate the set of QoS parameters that are of interest for SOEs. Cardoso et al. reviewed the common QoS parameters involved in service compositions (i.e., workflows and Web service-based business processes) [CSM+04]. For each identified quantitative QoS parameter, such as task response time, cost, and reliability, they specified the measures to estimate those QoS metrics. Furthermore, they also provide formulas to estimate composite values of several QoS parameters of services that are orchestrated by using workflow patterns, such as se-quential or parallel execution of tasks.

The work of Cubera et al. and Cardoso et al. focuses mainly on QoS parameters in workflows. In contrast, Menascé reviews research issues associated with QoS evalua-tion of Web services in SOEs [Men02]. To this end, he analyses the issues both from the perspective of a service provider and that of a service consumer, and figures out the differences between these two perspectives on QoS parameters. From his view-point, in order to differentiate services from various service providers, users and pro-viders need to engage in QoS negotiation. With negotiated QoS, consumers and pro-viders can enter into long-term relationships with consequent enforcement of agreed-upon SLAs. However, he did not analyse the set of QoS parameters associated with Web services.

The variety of research on QoS issues shows that determining the set of non-functional attributes to assess quality of service delivery depends on respective per-spective and problem domain. Perspective specifies from which viewpoint QoS is ob-served. In addition, problem domain specifies the specific environment, within which QoS is evaluated. Hence, it is not possible to define a common set of non-functional attributes exhaustively that are of interest for all stakeholders and problem domains. The remainder of this section introduces a set of common QoS parameters that are frequently referred to in the context of service delivery. As aforementioned, the list of QoS parameters introduced in the following is by no means complete.

Runtime-related QoS parameters: this category contains all non-functional attributes that can be used to estimate runtime behaviour of a technical system. On the other hand, those parameters also reflect the experience of service consumers with related service provisioning. Depending on the different alignments of QoS parameters, there are two general sub-categories, namely performance-related and dependability-related parameters.

Performance-related QoS parameters are measured over a range of service invocations during some predefined sampling period. They indicate the abilities of a service provider to provision the desired services. Thus, performance-related QoS parameters are measured on the level of service operations. In the context of service-oriented applications, the following QoS parameters are often used:

- *Response time* indicates the average time units between the point in time t_{input}, at which a service request is received, and the point in time t_{output}, at which the respective response is sent by a service provider within a given measurement period. Sometimes, this QoS parameter is also referred to as *completion time* of a request. To estimate the average response time of a service, one has to observe the start and end points in time of n requests, and calculate the durations and their average, namely $\sum_{i=1}^{n}(t_{output}^{i} - t_{input}^{i})/n$.

- *Throughput* indicates the average number of requests completed by a service within a given time period. To this end, it is necessary to estimate the number of requests n processed within a given measurement period t, then the average throughput of a service is determined by n/t per time unit.

Dependability-related QoS parameters state the probability that a service provider runs into exceptions at runtime. Hence, in contrast to performance-related parameters, these QoS parameters are measured on the service level. In general, the following QoS parameters are of particular interest for service-oriented applications:

- *Availability* indicates the probability that a service is up and running within a given measurement period. To calculate the availability of a service, it is necessary to observe the total time t_{up} during which the service is up and the total time t_{down} during which the service is down during the measurement period.

Then the availability of a service during a given measurement period is determined by $\frac{t_{up}}{t_{up}+t_{down}}$ per cent.

- *Reliability* indicates the ability of a service to perform its predefined operations for a given measurement period. In general, reliability can be measured by using *Mean Time Between Failure* (MTBF) as well as *Mean Time To Repair* (MTTR). MTBF indicates the average number of time units it takes until the next failure occurs. Hence, if $n_{failures}$ failures occur during a measurement period $t = t_{up} + t_{down}$, then MTBF can be calculated with $MTBF = t_{up}/n_{failure}$ time units. Correspondingly, MTTR indicates the average number of time units it takes to repair a failure in the service, and can be estimated by using $MTTR = t_{down}/n_{failure}$ time units.

Configuration-related QoS parameters: this category contains non-functional attributes that relate to the configuration management of a service. Other than the QoS parameters discussed previously, configuration-related QoS parameters are mostly qualitative and therefore cannot be expressed by metrics. In the context of SOEs, configuration-related QoS parameters often cover standards that a service complies with (e.g., communication standards, such as HTTP, FTP, or SMTP; or various versions of a particular standard, such as SOAP 1.1 or SOAP 1.2). Such QoS parameters are crucial to establish interoperable communication between service providers and service consumers.

Business-related QoS parameters: this category contains QoS parameters that cover especially economic aspects of a service. Hence, such QoS parameters are in general quantitative, unambiguous, and precise.

- *Cost* indicates the price for a service being invoked by a service consumer. Since a service provider intends to differentiate its service delivery by providing its service with different service quality levels for different prices, cost is usually determined by other QoS parameters. To this end, a service consumer and a service provider have to unambiguously agree upon the related service, the range of acceptable values of related QoS parameters (such as availability, performance, and so on), and the base for calculating cost (e.g., either per request or per time unit).

- *Penalty* indicates the cost for a service provider, if it cannot deliver its services in compliance with the agreed quality guarantees. Similar to cost, penalty needs to be explicitly specified between a service consumer and a service provider. In particular, they have to determine under which circumstances a service provider has to face the penalty.

Security-related QoS parameters: this category contains QoS parameters necessary to guarantee trustworthiness between service providers and service consumers. In particular, for service-oriented applications, where critical business data is passed across technical systems spanning organisational boundaries, security-related QoS parameters are crucial for service consumers to ensure secure access to business information.

- *Authentication* specifies the way in which a service provider and a service consumer can verify their identities mutually. For example, WS-Security defines mechanisms to use either user name tokens, X.509 certificate tokens, or SAML tokens to verify identities of communication partners.

- *Authorisation* determines which principals can access critical information and data of a service. As a QoS parameter, authorisation defines access control policies of a service. When a service consumer tries to access information provided by a service, the access control process checks that the respective consumer is authorised to access the resource based on the principle of least privilege.

- *Auditability* indicates the possibility to trace interaction history between a service provider and a service consumer. By tracing the complete information about every step in the course of interactions, technical systems can verify access to their resources and detect eventual security threats using such information.

- *Data encryption* specifies how technical systems can encrypt messages in their communication channels as well as in their local data storage. By using this QoS parameter, a service provider can express all possible mechanisms it supports (such as using symmetric keys or public keys), and a service consumer can express a list of desired encryption mechanisms to secure its data.

A critical issue of using QoS parameters to specify service level objectives in an SLA is consistent interpretation of these QoS parameters across the entire SOE. For example, the QoS parameters *response time* and *completion time* refer to the same non-functional attribute of a service. Without further semantic information, it is impossible for a service provider or consumer to distinguish between these two terms. Furthermore, service level targets specified in an SLA depend strongly on the interpretation of corresponding service level objectives. For example, a service level target for availability with the same value but different time units is ambiguous for both contract parties. Hence, it is important that a service consumer and a service provider must have the same understanding on QoS parameters specified in an SLA. In addition, in order to enable automated negotiation of SLAs between service providers and service consumers, it is also important that both parties can achieve the necessary level of understanding with respect to the corresponding QoS parameters.

This requirement is covered by a common ontology for QoS with rich semantic information, such as QoSOnt proposed by Dobson, Lock, and Sommervile [DLS05]. They developed an extensible ontology around the core of a base QoS ontology to enable semantic description of QoS. The basic element in the based QoS ontology is a QoS attribute that can be either measurable (e.g., performance) or immeasurable (e.g., security standards). Respectively, there is a set of quantitative metrics to estimate values of measureable attributes. Furthermore, QoSOnt also addresses the units associated with a QoS attribute and provides the necessary conversion rules to convert values of the same QoS attribute with different units. Starting from the base QoS ontology, Dobson et al. demonstrated in their work how a domain-specific QoS ontology could be built.

In comparison to the abstract QoS model presented by Dobson et al., Mabrouk, Georgantas, and Issarny worked out a more concrete QoS model for SOEs [MGI09]. Similar to the work of Dobson et al., they defined the necessary constructs to specify quality attributes, their taxonomy, and the way they can be estimated. Based on these basic constructs, they build further ontologies to specify quality attributes related to infrastructural components, applications services, and users.

In the remainder of this thesis, it is assumed that service consumers and service providers have the same understanding of QoS parameters denoted in an SLA. That is, service level objectives specified in an SLA are interpreted consistently across all negotiation parties. For example, this can be ensured by using a single QoS ontology service that is deployed globally within the respective SOE.

3.2.4 Life Cycle of SLAs

The previous sections introduced the concept of SLAs and outlined the main constructs of SLAs to regulate expectations and obligations of service providers and service consumers within their interactions. Another important aspect about SLAs is their dynamics at runtime. That is, how an SLA is constructed, negotiated, enforced, and terminated at runtime. Obviously, dynamics of SLAs are tightly associated with the process of Service Level Management, as introduced in Section 1.2.1.

Figure 3-4 depicts the states of an SLA in relationship to the phases of SLM.

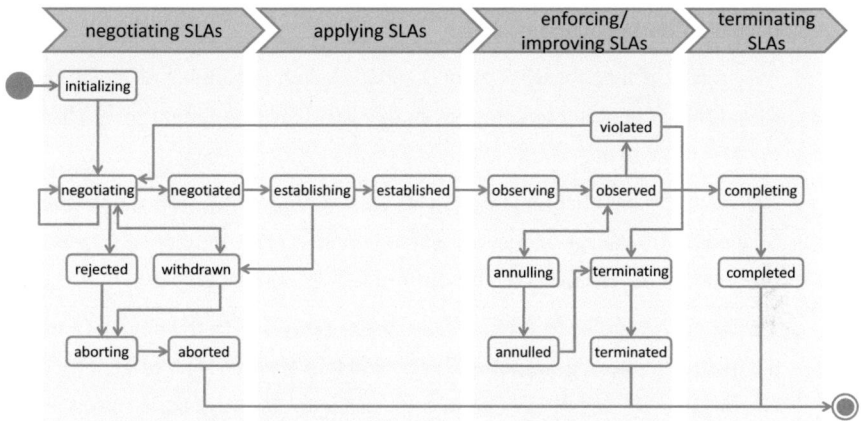

Figure 3-4: Life cycle of SLAs in service-oriented environments

As shown in the picture, an SLA runs through a range of possible states in the course of SLM:

- *Negotiating SLAs*: in this phase, a service consumer and a service provider seek to find a mutually acceptable agreement on a set of predefined QoS parameters. The process can be triggered by either the service consumer or the service provider, depending on the protocol applied in the negotiation. For example, the set of QoS parameters can be retrieved from a given SLA template made available by a human administrator.
  - o *Initialising*: in this state, the initiator of a negotiation process (either a service provider or a service consumer) determines the set of QoS parameters for negotiation, retrieves initial values of related QoS parameters from the previously determined negotiation space, prepares the SLA offer with the initial values, and sends the initial offer to its negotiation partner.
  - o *Negotiating*: this state indicates that the current SLA is being negotiated between a service consumer and its provider. Depending on the negotiation protocol applied, there can be either a *single-round* or a *multi-round* negotiation.

In a single-round negotiation, the recipient of an SLA offer can only decide to accept or reject the incoming offer. The recipient cannot respond with a counter offer. A multi-round negotiation allows negotiation parties to send counter offers to each other. In this case, the state of an SLA remains *negotiating* until the end of the negotiation process.

o *Negotiated*: if a negotiation party is satisfied with conditions of an incoming SLA offer, it is going to accept it. In this case, the negotiation party changes the SLA state to *negotiated* to signal its willingness to accept the offer.

o *Rejected*: if a negotiation party rejects an incoming offer, then it changes the SLA state from *negotiating* to *rejected*. In this case, the active negotiation process will be terminated by the corresponding negotiation party.

o *Withdrawn*: in order to provide negotiation parties with the ability to exit a negotiation process, a negotiation party can withdraw its SLA offer. That is, it can suggest its negotiation partner to terminate the negotiation process by withdrawing its proposed agreement. The respective negotiation partner can decide independently, whether to follow the suggestion or to deny it. Hence, the negotiation partner can either abort and terminate the negotiation process or return to the process.

o *Aborting*: if an SLA offer is rejected or withdrawn by a negotiation party, the state of the corresponding SLA is changed to *aborting*. By doing this, both negotiation parties have the possibility to free resources utilised in the negotiation process and prepare themselves for the termination of the negotiation process.

o *Aborted*: the SLA state *aborted* signals that both negotiation parties are ready to terminate the negotiation process. Form this point in time, both negotiation parties can exit the respective negotiation process. Thus, the negotiation process is terminated.

• *Applying SLAs*: if both negotiation parties have expressed their willingness to accept a mutually negotiated SLA offer, they are going to apply it to their local technical infrastructures.

- o *Establishing*: an SLA with the state *establishing* designates that the corresponding service component (either provider or consumer) is applying the SLA to its underlying technical system. That is, for a service provider, it has to configure its local resources in accordance with QoS terms specified in the SLA so that it can ensure the negotiated service levels at runtime. During this phase, it is possible for either of the negotiation parties to withdraw a negotiated agreement. For example, if a service provider experiences any problems while configuring its local resources that prevent it from guaranteeing the negotiated service level, it can withdraw the agreement to avoid runtime disturbance proactively. It is noteworthy that this action should be associated with certain penalty for the party that withdraws a negotiated agreement.

- o *Established*: after both negotiation parties have configured their local technical components in compliance with the negotiated agreement, they change the state of the SLA to *established*, which signals their readiness to start active invocations of services offered by the service provider.

- • *Enforcing/Improving SLAs*: in this phase, the applied SLAs are actively monitored and enforced at runtime. To this end, the quality of service delivery of the provider is continuously monitored and controlled by both the provider and the consumer.

- o *Observing*: this SLA state indicates that both service provider and service consumer are configuring their monitoring infrastructures according to conditions derived from the SLA, so that they can, at runtime, monitor the compliance of the service delivery of the provider.

- o *Observed*: the state *observed* shows that the negotiated SLA is monitored and controlled actively by both service provider and service consumer. During this phase, the corresponding monitoring infrastructure can use various patterns, such as the publish/subscribe pattern, to actively capture runtime events of the underlying technical system and process them to consolidated QoS values indicating the current service delivery status of the service provider.

- o *Violated*: if either service provider or service consumer detects any SLA violation at runtime, they change the state of the corresponding agreement to *vio-*

lated. This leads to an adaptation of the negotiated SLA by starting a renegotiation process, in which the service provider and the service consumer affected by the violated SLA begin to find a more appropriate replacement that better fits the up-to-date operational context. Alternatively, a contract partner can decide to terminate the violated SLA without a renegotiation process.

o *Annulling*: it is of course possible for a negotiation party to exit an active partnership regulated by an SLA. For example, if a service provider has technical difficulties to guarantee the agreed service levels or a service consumer decides to abort its operation earlier than planned, they can annul an observed SLA by sending an annulment request to their contract partner. In this case, the state of the corresponding SLA is changed to *annulling*. The contract partner is free to decide whether to accept the annulment or deny it and go back to the *observed* state.

o *Annulled*: this state indicates that both contract partners have agreed to annul the applied SLA. In this case, both service provider and service consumer can start their internal process to terminate the annulled SLA.

o *Terminating*: before service provider and service consumer terminate an actively observed SLA, they switch the state of the SLA to *terminating*. This state indicates that the technical systems affected are preparing to terminate the corresponding SLA. To this end, the service provider is going to free all technical resources allocated to guarantee the given SLA. In addition, both service provider and service consumer reconfigure their monitoring infrastructures to free any additional resources.

o *Terminated*: if the service provider and the consumer have finished reconfiguring their local components and are ready to terminate the corresponding SLA, they change the state of the SLA to *terminated*. In this case, the contract partners exit the loose provider/consumer relationship and the corresponding SLM process is terminated.

• *Terminating SLAs*: each agreed SLA has a negotiated period of validity. If the agreed contract comes to a natural end and no further contract is negotiated, then the related SLA will be terminated, too.

- o *Completing*: similar to the *terminating* state in the last phase, the *completing* state shows that the related SLA has been successfully guaranteed in the period of validity specified in the SLA. Hence, after an SLA comes to its predefined end, the affected service provider and consumer have to free their local resources allocated to support the completed SLA.

- o *Completed*: after the related service provider and consumer have freed all allocated resources, they change the state of the SLA to *completed*. Hence, the corresponding service provider and consumer can exit their partnership and terminate the corresponding SLM process.

By considering the life cycle of SLAs introduced in this section, it is obvious that a well-functioning and fully automated SLM requires active support from the following viewpoints:

- Both the service provider and the service consumer must have the ability to perform automated negotiation over a set of non-functional QoS parameters. By supporting this, a service provider and a service consumer have the possibility to enter an active partnership regulated by automatically negotiated SLAs.

- The underlying technical systems must support SLA-driven resource management. This is crucial for a service provider to offer differentiated quality of service delivery in an efficient manner. That is, a service provider can proactively avoid over- or under-utilisation of its resources at runtime.

- The underlying technical systems must provide the necessary manageability interfaces to allow exporting runtime events to external monitoring infrastructure, so that an active and proactive monitoring of agreement compliance at runtime can be carried out.

- There must be a continuous process to monitor vital signs of the underlying technical systems and perform necessary corrective control actions to get the system behaviour compliant with the agreed SLAs.

Hence, in order to enable a fully automated and end-to-end SLM across the entire SOE, the points discussed above are functional requirements that must be addressed by the approach proposed in the present thesis. Chapter 4 will discuss the functional requirements on an automated SLM approach in detail.

3.3 Bilateral Multi-issue Negotiation

The main negotiation scenario considered in the present thesis is automated SLA negotiation between a service provider and a service consumer. Figure 3-5 depicts a sample negotiation scenario in an SOE. In this scenario, a provider and a consumer negotiate over two QoS parameters, cost and response time. The negotiation spaces of the negotiation parties overlap partly, as illustrated in Figure 3-5. The service provider and the service consumer seek to find a mutually acceptable agreement in the common area of their negotiation spaces. Since both negotiation parties are not aware of negotiation preferences of their opponent, the key challenge in this negotiation scenario is how the negotiation parties can find the overlapping area in their negotiation spaces and further find an agreement in this area.

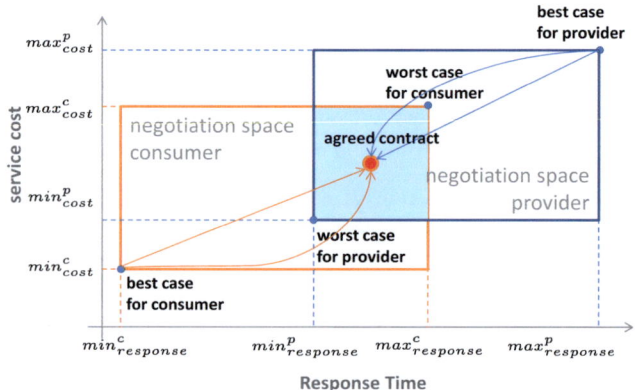

Figure 3-5: Sample negotiation scenario between a service provider and a consumer

By considering the negotiation scenario illustrated in Figure 3-5, it has the following characteristics:

- The service consumer and the service provider have conflicting interests on the QoS parameters involved in the negotiation.

- Each negotiation process involves only one service provider and one service consumer. That is, the negotiation scenario is bilateral.

- The negotiation parties argue over the whole set of QoS parameters at the same time. That is, they consider in each negotiation round all QoS parameters, instead of arguing over them one after another. This allows the negotiation parties to make trade-offs between two or more QoS parameters. Hence, the negotiation scenario contains a multi-issue negotiation.

To sum up, the present thesis is concerned with scenarios leveraging bilateral multi-issue negotiation between a service consumer and one of its service providers. Section 6.3 justifies the choice of this negotiation type in detail. As mentioned in Section 2.3.3, there is a large number of existing approaches for enabling automated negotiation. In the remainder of this section, one representative approach to support bilateral multi-issue negotiation, the service-oriented negotiation model proposed by Sierra et al. [SFJ97], is introduced in detail. This negotiation model builds the theoretical foundation for further investigation of negotiation behaviours of autonomous service components in this thesis.

3.3.1 Basic Negotiation Model

On the basic negotiation model of Raiffa [Rai82], Sierra et al. introduced a service-oriented negotiation model to formally describe a negotiation process between two or more parties [SFJ97]. In their model, a negotiation involves two (i.e., bilateral) or more (i.e., multilateral) parties. All parties collaborate with one another to reach mutually acceptable agreements on predefined negotiation issues (e.g., cost, penalty, performance, and so on). Communication between negotiation parties is governed by a commonly acknowledged negotiation protocol, until either they reach a consensus regarding negotiation issues or the negotiation process is aborted due to certain constraints (e.g., a predefined negotiation deadline t_{max} is exceeded).

Sierra et al. models a bilateral negotiation between two agents a and b on multiple negotiation issues $\{1, 2, ..., n\}$. For each negotiation issue $j \in \{1, 2, ..., n\}$, there is a continuous value range with $x_j \in [min_j, max_j]$. The value range defines the set of valid values of x_j that a negotiation party can assign to the corresponding issue. The value ranges of all negotiation issues span the negotiation space of a negotiation party in the course of a negotiation.

Obviously, an agent's value range of the issue j overlaps with the one of its opponent for the same issue, i.e., $[min_j^c, max_j^c] \cap [min_j^p, max_j^p] \neq \emptyset$ for an issue j, otherwise both agents are not able to reach an agreement on j. Furthermore, an offer that is sent from agent a to agent b at time t is denoted as $x_{a \to b}^t = (x_{a \to b}^t[1], x_{a \to b}^t[2], ..., x_{a \to b}^t[n])$ with $a, b \in \{c, p\}$, $t \in [1, t_{max}]$, and $a \neq b$. Correspondingly, $x_{a \to b}^t[j]$ represents the value of the issue j in the offer $x_{a \to b}^t$. Based on these definitions, a negotiation thread between agents a and b is defined as a finite sequence of $\{x^1_{s_1 \to d_1}, x^2_{s_2 \to d_2}, ..., x^{t_i}_{s_i \to d_i}, ..., x^{t_k}_{s_k \to d_k}\}$, where $s_i, d_i \in \{c, p\}$, $s_i \neq d_i$, $s_{i+1} = d_i$, $t_1, t_2, ..., t_k \in [1, t_{max}]$, and $t_i \leq t_j$ if $i \leq j$.

Each agent i has a utility function $V^i_j : [min_j, max_j] \to [0, 1]$ that assesses the preference agent i has for a value of the negotiation issue j in its value range. To reflect the relative importance of a particular issue j to an agent i, each negotiation issue j is assigned with a weight ω^i_j with $\sum_{j=1}^{n} \omega^i_j = 1$. Based on these definitions, an agent's utility function V^i to estimate the quality of a given agreement $x^t_{a \to b}$ is defined as:

$$V^i(x^t_{a \to b}) = \sum_{j=1}^{n} \omega^i_j \cdot V^i_j(x^t_{a \to b}[j])$$

.

It is obvious that negotiation parties have conflicting interests in negotiation issues. For example, a service consumer prefers higher availability with low cost, while its provider tends to offer services with lower availability for high price. Hence, in the course of negotiation, two negotiation agents have to move stepwise towards each other by leaving their respective optimum in the negotiation space. As a consequence, for a negotiation issue $j \in \{1, 2, ..., n\}$, conflicting interest of agents on the same issue can be expressed by (3.3.1), where $t, t' \in [1, t_{max}]$, $a, b \in \{c, p\}$, and $a \neq b$:

$$V^a_j(x^t_{a \to b}[j]) \leq V^a_j(x^{t'}_{a \to b}[j]), \text{ iff } V^b_j(x^t_{a \to b}[j]) \geq V^b_j(x^{t'}_{a \to b}[j]) \tag{3.3.1}$$

A bilateral negotiation process alternates between two negotiation parties by exchanging offers and counter offers. In each negotiation round, each agent has to decide which action it should take for the incoming offer. That is, it can either accept the incoming offer or propose a counter offer to its opponent. For an offer sent from agent b to agent a at time t, Sierra et al. introduced an interpretation function to support decision-making of an agent a for the incoming offer $x^t_{b \to a}$:

$$I^a(t + 1, x^t_{b \to a}) = \begin{cases} accept & \text{if } V^a(x^t_{b \to a}) \geq V^a(x^{t+1}_{a \to b}) \\ x^{t+1}_{a \to b} & \text{otherwise} \end{cases} \tag{3.3.2}$$

In other words, for each incoming offer $x^t_{b \to a}$ to agent a, it generates a counter offer $x^{t+1}_{a \to b}$. If the counter offer has equal or less utility than the incoming offer, then agent a accepts the offer; otherwise, agent a sends its counter offer $x^{t+1}_{a \to b}$ to its negotiation partner. This alternate process runs, until either a mutually acceptable SLA is found or one of the negotiators terminates the process due to predefined termination rules, such as the predefined deadline t_{max} is exceeded.

3.3.2 Conceding Strategies

In order to reach a compromise on the negotiation issues, both negotiation agents have to move from their optimum in favour of their opponents. To this end, Sierra et al. defined a tactic-based conceding strategy in their model [SFJ97]. A tactic is defined as *"a set of functions that determine how to compute the value of an issue (...), by considering a single criterion (time, resource, ...)"* [SFJ97]. In the case an agent has to consider more than one criterion to compute the value of an issue, they proposed a weighted combination of tactics covering all given criteria to generate values. By taking common issues of negotiation processes into consideration, they developed three families of tactics:

- *Time-dependent tactics* model the fact that an agent is likely to concede more strongly as a given deadline approaches. As time constantly proceeds towards the given deadline, an agent may get more conceding pressure than at the beginning of the negotiation progress.

- *Resource-dependent tactics* model the pressure to reach an agreement in relationship to some limited resources, e.g., money, or other potential negotiation partners in the environment. In fact, time-dependent tactics are a subset of resource-dependent tactics. Resource-dependent tactics allows involving more resources with different usage patterns other than the one of time, whereas time proceeds straightforwardly towards its deadline.

- *Behaviour-dependent tactics* enable an agent to align its negotiation behaviour to its negotiation partner. In a competing environment, an agent using imitative tactics can avoid being exploited by its negotiation partner and thus getting disadvantaged in a negotiation process; however, in a cooperative environment, agents can utilise imitative tactics to move more rapidly towards each other and thus reach a more satisfying agreement by negotiation.

Considering characteristics of SLA negotiation scenarios (see Section 6.2), it is obvious that time-dependent and behaviour-dependent tactics are the most applicable to these scenarios. In a bilateral multi-issue negotiation between a service consumer and its provider, the only resource constraint is time – a given deadline defines the maximal amount of time units that an agent can spend to reach an agreement with its counterpart. Therefore, in the following, the function models for time-dependent as well as behaviour-dependent tactics are introduced. For a detailed introduction of all other function families please refer to [SFJ97].

Given a negotiation deadline t_{max}, time t with $0 \leq t \leq t_{max}$, and an issue j for an agent a with $x_j \in [min_j^a, max_j^a]$, the value proposed by agent a to agent b at time t is determined by:

$$x_{a \to b}^t[j] = \begin{cases} min_j^a + \alpha_j^a(t) \cdot (max_j^a - min_j^a) & \text{if } V_j^a \text{ is decreasing} \\ min_j^a + (1 - \alpha_j^a(t)) \cdot (max_j^a - min_j^a) & \text{if } V_j^a \text{ is increasing} \end{cases} \quad (3.3.3)$$

The utility function V_j^a is decreasing, if utility of the issue j decreases, as its value increases. Vice versa, V_j^a is increasing, if utility of the issue j increases, as its value increases. In addition, $\alpha_j^a(t)$ with $0 \leq \alpha_j^a(t) \leq 1$ defines a range of time-dependent functions with $\alpha_j^a(t) \leq \alpha_j^a(t')$ for $t, t' \in [0, t_{max}]$ and $t \leq t'$, $\alpha_j^a(0) = 0$, and $\alpha_j^a(t_{max}) = 1$. This ensures that calculated values using (3.3.3) are always located within the value range of x_j, i.e., $x_{a \to b}^t[j] \in [min_j^a, max_j^a]$. Furthermore, $\alpha_j^a(t)$ determines the extent of concession of the agent a in dependence of the negotiation time t. That is, the larger the value of $\alpha_j^a(t)$, the more concession the agent a will grant in favour of its negotiation partner.

Sierra et al. identified two families of functions to estimate the value of $\alpha_j^a(t)$ in dependence of t:

$$\alpha_j^a(t) = \begin{cases} \kappa_j^a + (1 - \kappa_j^a) \cdot (\frac{t}{t_{max}})^{1/\beta} & \text{polynomial functions} \\ e^{(1 - \frac{t}{t_{max}})^\beta \cdot \ln \kappa_j^a} & \text{exponential functions} \end{cases} \quad (3.3.4)$$

In (3.3.4), β is a parameter to control the time-dependent degree of convexity of the function. κ_j^a defines a constant determining the initial value of issue j in the initial offer at time $t = 0$. That is, if V_j^a is decreasing, then the initial value $x_{a \to b}^0[j]$ of issue j is $min_j^a + \kappa_j^a \cdot (max_j^a - min_j^a)$. If V_j^a is increasing, then the initial value is $min_j^a + (1 - \kappa_j^a) \cdot (max_j^a - min_j^a)$.

Figure 3-6 illustrates the curves of both families of functions with $\kappa_j^a = 0.2$ and varying β. The curves show that the function families given in (3.3.4) have different conceding behaviour for the same β. For $\beta > 1$, a polynomial function concedes more quickly than an exponential one (i.e., the corresponding curve rises more quickly than the one of an exponential function with the same β); In contrast, for $\beta < 1$, a polynomial function waits longer than an exponential function with the same β, before it begins to concede.

Time-dependent tactics use negotiation time as the single criterion to compute values of issues in the next offer. Because negotiation time as a parameter does not differ from negotiation to negotiation, a negotiation agent behaves homogeneously in all negotiation threads, as long as it uses the same function to calculate counter offers. Hence, negotiation behaviour of such an agent does not take the negotiation behaviour of its counterpart into consideration.

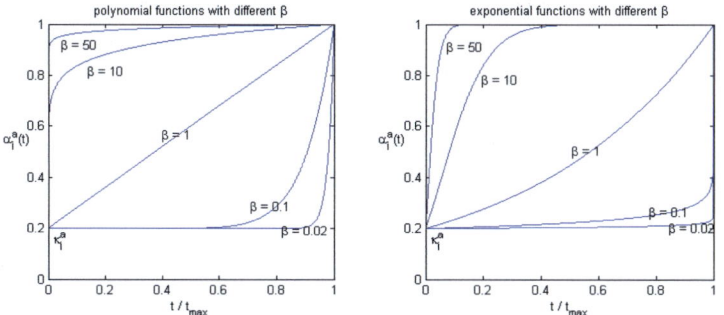

Figure 3-6: Polynomial and exponential functions to compute the value of $\alpha_j^a(t)$ (see [SFJ97])

Such undesired behaviour of an agent can be avoided by adopting behaviour-dependent tactics in the decision-making processes. A behaviour-dependent tactic allows an agent to generate offers with respect to its opponent's behaviour. Sierra et al. identified three different types of behaviour-based tactics to compute an issue's value:

- *Relative Tit-for-Tat*: an agent a reproduces in percentage terms the behaviour of its opponent performed $\delta \geq 1$ steps ago, namely the relationship between the offers of its counterpart, agent b, at time $t_{n-2\delta}$ and time $t_{n-2\delta+2}$:

$$x_{a \to b}^{t_{n+1}}[j] = min(max(\frac{x_{b \to a}^{t_{n-2\delta}}[j]}{x_{b \to a}^{t_{n-2\delta+2}}[j]} \cdot x_{a \to b}^{t_{n-1}}[j], min_j^a), max_j^a), n > 2\delta$$

- *Random absolute Tit-for-Tat*: similar to the tactic with relative Tit-for-Tat, but in absolute terms. That is, this tactic considers the absolute difference between the offers of the agent b at time $t_{n-2\delta}$ and time $t_{n-2\delta+2}$ to calculate the corresponding value in the counter offer:

$$x_{a \to b}^{t_{n+1}}[j] = min(max((x_{b \to a}^{t_{n-2\delta}}[j] - x_{b \to a}^{t_{n-2\delta+2}}[j]) + x_{a \to b}^{t_{n-1}}[j], min_j^a), max_j^a), n > 2\delta$$

- *Average Tit-for-Tat*: an agent uses the change in percentage between the current offer of the agent b, i.e., $x_{b \to a}^{t_n}[j]$, and the offer proposed $\lambda \geq 1$ time units ago, i.e., $x_{b \to a}^{t_{n-2\lambda}}[j]$, to compute its next offer:

$$x_{a \to b}^{t_{n+1}}[j] = min(max(\frac{x_{b \to a}^{t_{n-2\lambda}}[j]}{x_{b \to a}^{t_n}[j]} \cdot x_{a \to b}^{t_{n-1}}[j], min_j^a), max_j^a), n > 2\lambda$$

Depending on the type of imitation, behaviour-based tactics enable an agent to align its negotiation behaviour to that of its opponent.

At runtime, different negotiation tactic delivers different values for the same issue j in the counter offer. Hence, in order to involve more than one tactic to generate a counter offer, the final value for the issue j is estimated as the weighted combination of all values of related negotiation tactics. That is, for a finite set of tactics $\{1, 2, ..., m\}$, each tactic k is executed separately to calculate a value τ_k. Then the final value for the issue j in the counter offer is determined by:

$$x_{a \to b}^{t_{n+1}}[j] = \sum_{k=1}^{m} \gamma_k \cdot \tau_k, \text{ where } \sum_{k=1}^{m} \gamma_k = 1 \qquad (3.3.5)$$

Thus, given a negotiation thread $\{x_{a \to b}^1, x_{b \to a}^2, x_{a \to b}^3, ..., x_{b \to a}^n\}$ between management agent a and management agent b, where $x_{b \to a}^n$ is the last offer that agent a receives from its counterpart b, the agent can utilise (3.3.5) to compute the value of an issue j in the offer. Furthermore, given a finite set of tactics $\{1, 2, ..., m\}$, each issue can have different negotiation behaviour by weighting the corresponding tactics differently in the calculation. From this viewpoint, at time t, an agent has a local strategy matrix Γ to determine assignment of tactics $\{1, 2, ..., m\}$ to a particular issue $j \in \{1, 2, ..., p\}$:

$$\Gamma_{a \to b}^t = \begin{bmatrix} \gamma_{11} & \gamma_{12} & \cdots & \gamma_{1m} \\ \vdots & \vdots & \vdots & \vdots \\ \gamma_{j1} & \gamma_{j2} & \cdots & \gamma_{jm} \\ \vdots & \vdots & \vdots & \vdots \\ \gamma_{p1} & \gamma_{p2} & \cdots & \gamma_{pm} \end{bmatrix} \qquad (3.3.6)$$

By dynamically changing the value of γ_{ij} for one or more issues in the strategy matrix (3.3.6) in the course of negotiation, an agent can flexibly align its negotiation behaviour with its environment. For this purpose, Sierra et al. defined a negotiation strategy as a function of an agent's mental state MS_a^t and its strategy matrix $\Gamma_{a \to b}^t$ at time t:

$$\Gamma_{a \to b}^{t+1} = f(\Gamma_{a \to b}^t, MS_a^t)$$

That is, an agent can review in each negotiation round its mental state – state information that an agent perceives from its own operation as well as from its environment – to adjust its negotiation strategy dynamically by changing the weights of particular tactics in the strategy matrix. The simplest form of a negotiation strategy is to define an initial strategy matrix at the beginning and keep $\Gamma^t_{a\to b} = \Gamma^{t+1}_{a\to b}$ in the course of negotiation.

Concisely, the tactic-based negotiation model introduced by Sierra et al. represents a comprehensive method to determine the degree of concession of an agent dynamically at runtime. The basis for decision-making to compute QoS values of a counter offer can either be negotiation time remaining until a given negotiation deadline or imitation of the opponent's negotiation behaviour. Combining several tactics linearly enables an agent to use several criteria simultaneously to support its decision-making process. In addition, by changing weights of particular tactics in the course of negotiation, an agent can adapt its negotiation behaviour to the most recent context of the environment.

3.4 Generic Observer/Controller Architecture

Dynamic SOEs contain a set of technical components that are interconnected with one another based on loosely coupled provider/consumer relationships. Such a dynamic environment is characterised by a large number of heterogeneous service components and their interactions with one another. Performance of the entire service-oriented system is determined *bottom-up* by runtime behaviour of individual components in the system. From the viewpoint of business, IT systems involved in an SOE are expected to support given business requirements as a whole. That is, business demands a holistic understanding and management of IT systems to fulfil business objectives. Such *top-down* business-driven IT management is desirable in order to cope with a continuously changing environment, within which business has to operate.

As motivated in Section 2.2, self-organisation of technical systems provides an efficient means to deal with increasing complexity within service-oriented systems. Business-driven IT management requires that such bottom-up self-organisation must be accompanied with top-down control derived from business objectives. To achieve such controlled self-organisation, each technical component is endowed with an additional observation and control layer called *observer/controller architecture*, as introduced briefly in Section 2.2.3 [Sch05].

It is noteworthy that the present thesis adopts the generic observer/controller architecture introduced by the Organic Computing initiative. Of course, the desired property of controlled self-organisation can be realised by using other similar approaches, such as the MAPE control loop of Autonomic Computing or the VSM. However, in comparison to other approaches, the observer/controller architecture envisions native support for *controlled* self-organisation. To this end, it provides a generic architectural pattern to enable agent-based design of technical systems. Furthermore, the generic observer/controller architecture provides a particular interface to facilitate interactions between human participants as a high-level control instance and the underlying technical systems. This functional design addresses one of the central aspects of an SOE that involves a large amount of interactions between human participants (e.g., administrators or end users) and technical systems. Based on these considerations, the present thesis leverages the generic observer/controller architecture to support multi-layered and self-organising SLM in service-oriented systems. The remainder of this section introduces the observer/controller architecture in detail. This section is mainly based on [BMM+06, RMB+06, Ric10].

3.4.1 Observer

In the generic observer/controller architecture, the observer is responsible to monitor runtime events of the SuOC, consolidate them, draw particular behaviour patterns of the underlying systems in the SuOC based on these consolidated events, and predict their behaviour in the future.

To this end, the observer collects raw data from the SuOC and pre-processes the collected data by removing irrelevant and noisy data. Based on the pre-processed data, the observer can perform different analysis methods on the data to get an overview of the current operational state of the SuOC. In addition, it can use the collected data to predict future development of the operational state of the SuOC. Both prediction and analysis results are aggregated to build a system-wide fingerprint of the SuOC, which serves as the base for decision making of the controller, concerning how to influence runtime behaviour of the SuOC.

Figure 3-7 depicts the generic constructs of the observer to realise the desired capabilities, in particular the capabilities to characterise runtime behaviour and to predict future behaviour of the SuOC.

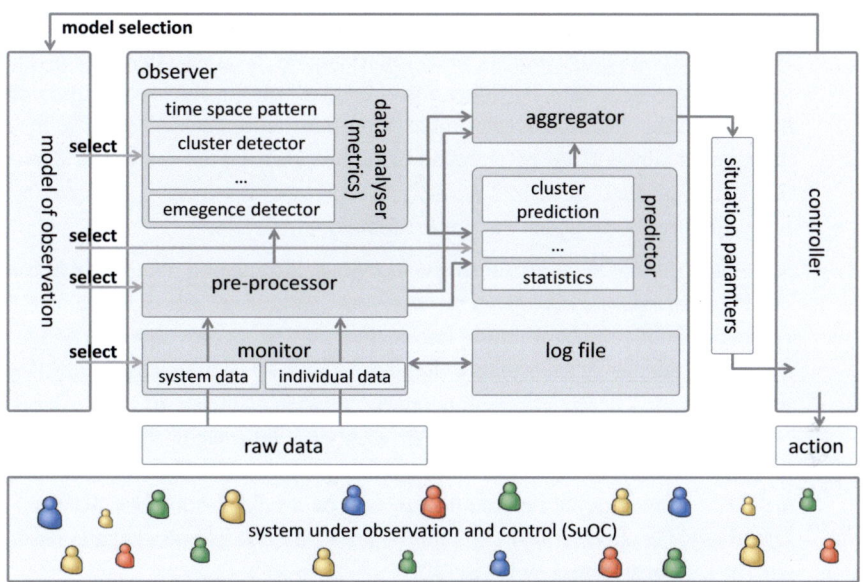

Figure 3-7: Generic observer architecture (see [Ric10])

Among other things, the observer involves the following generic components:

- Model of observation: the components defined in the observer are generic. That is, they are expected to be able to process a range of possible events and data that the underlying SuOC delivers. This generic approach however has two possible drawbacks that may affect the performance of the observer negatively. On the one hand, the SuOC may deliver a large amount of runtime information to the observer that cannot be processed within reasonable time with reasonable resources by the components. On the other hand, the aggregated situation parameters can contain in addition to necessary information a set of unused situation information that increases the state space unnecessary, within which the controller has to operate. Hence, it is desired that the observation behaviour of the observer can be adjusted depending on the current operational focus of the controller. To this end, the observer employs an additional component, the model of observation, which determines the operation mode of particular components in the observer with respect to the preferences of the controller. The controller provides feedbacks on the situation parameters it gets from the observer, in particular information that it needs to make decisions. Based on such evaluation information from the controller, the component model of observation specifies the range of raw data the observer should collect from the under-lying SuOC (e.g., scope of data, sampling frequency, etc.) and appropriate tools to process collected data. By doing this, it ensures that the observer can provide the information that is most relevant to the controller for decision-making. Fur-thermore, it allows efficient operation of the observer and the controller, in par-ticular in case both of them have only limited local resources (i.e., computa-tional resource, storage, etc.) to use at runtime.

- Raw data: the SuOC is instrumented to deliver information about its runtime behaviour to external authorised management applications. For example, in the context of SOEs, instrumentation information may be metrics about service in-vocations (number of invocations, duration of each invocation, communication partner (s), etc.) or specific runtime events (warnings, errors, or other signifi-cant occurrences). To collect such instrumentation information from the target SuOC, the observer can uses the manageability interface it offers. For example, a SuOC can provide its runtime information on a publish/subscribe basis. Al-ternatively, the observer can also poll the SuOC for changes on a regular basis, such as heartbeat testing on the SuOC.

- Monitor: this component is one of the two components that connect the generic observer/controller architecture to the SuOC. The monitor is responsible for perceiving the SuOC by collecting runtime information specified by the obser-vation model. It is noteworthy that runtime information exposed by the SuOC depends strongly on the type of instrumentation of the SuOC. This determines the type and the amount of available information that the monitor can request. The generic observer/controller architecture distinguishes between two general raw data types: system data and individual data. System data describes the global behaviour of the underlying SuOC, while individual data refers to a par-ticular component within the SuOC.

- Log file: The SuOC's runtime information collected by the monitor is archived in the log file in a chronological order. Historical information stored in the log file is particularly of interest for the data analyser as well as the predictor, which can do time series analysis based on archived data to address the long-term aspects of runtime behaviour of the SuOC.

- Pre-processor: The pre-processor is responsible to remove unnecessary and noisy data from the collected runtime information and perform data consolida-tion on the cleaned data. The observation model controls how the pre-processor processes the raw data. For example, the pre-processor can derive response

time of a particular service request by using the point in time at which the request is sent and the point in time at which the corresponding response is received. Hence, the pre-processor prepares raw data for further processing by
the data analyser and the predictor. This helps to reduce the amount of data that
the components in the processing pipeline have to deal with in the next step.

- Data analyser: the data analyser intends to understand the pre-processed system
  information and draw conclusions about how the SuOC behaves currently as
  well as during a limited time window in the past. To this end, the data analyser
  utilises a set of mathematical as well as statistical models to analyse the system
  behaviour of the SuOC. For example, the data analyser can perform time series
  analysis on the historical data to understand the development of a particular
  system attribute in the past. In addition, the data analyser can utilise the emergence detector to discover emergent effects on the global level of the SuOC.
  These analysis tools result in a series of quantitative metrics that characterises
  the system behaviour of the SuOC during the last sampling period.

- Predictor: in order to give the controller the possibility to make anticipatory
  decisions for a limited time window into the future, the observer/controller architecture utilises an additional component to predict future behaviour of the
  SuOC. To this end, the predictor consumes the consolidated information from
  the pre-processor as well as the data analyser. Based on this information, it performs quantitative prediction using different mathematical and statistical models for a given time horizon (short-term, middle-term, or long-term prediction).
  The resulting data reflects the observer's expectation of the development of
  particular system attributes for a given time horizon – based on the observer's
  most recent understanding of the system behaviour of the SuOC.

- Aggregator: the last processing step in the observer is performed by the aggregator. It is responsible for consolidating quantitative metrics delivered by the
  pre-processor, the data analyser, and the predictor into a set of data vectors.
  Furthermore, the aggregator has the last possibility to filter results and remove
  noise. The output of the aggregator is composed of situation parameters that
  represent the understanding of the observer of the current system behaviour of
  the SuOC based on runtime information it collects.

In a short, the observer is the part in the generic architecture that perceives the system behaviour of the SuOC at runtime. To this end, it utilises a set of components,
including the *pre-processor*, the *data analyser*, the *predictor*, and the *aggregator* to
process stepwise metrics and events the *monitor* collects from the SuOC. The process

to handle collected information is a process of data consolidation. This results in a set of situation parameters that reflect clearly the current state and dynamics of the SuOC. This consolidation process reduces the state space that the controller has to deal with to a reasonable extent. It enables the controller to make efficient decisions based on cleaned and appropriately consolidated situation parameters.

3.4.2 Controller

With the situation parameters prepared by the observer, the controller is the part in the observer/controller architecture that establishes controlled self-organisation in the SuOC. To this end, the controller has three interfaces outwards. One interface to the observer allows the controller to be aware of the current operational state of the Su-OC. The second interface to human participant(s) makes the controller controllable for high-level goals. The third interface to the SuOC gives the controller the possibility to influence the behaviour of the underlying SuOC if necessary. The intelligence to enable self-organisation is provided by autonomous learning mechanisms that map incoming situation parameters to selected actions on the SuOC.

Figure 3-8 illustrates the main constructs of the controller with two-level learning. That is, the controller organises its learning process on two levels with a different degree of abstraction: a first level that learns *offline*, based on an abstracted simulation model and a second level that learns *online*, evaluating the results of actions with the real-world system.

Level 1 is responsible to make ad hoc decisions on actions to execute upon the Su-OC –depending on given situation parameters delivered by the observer. To this end, *level 1* utilises online learning to build up and maintain its knowledge base on the Su-OC. Hence, *level 1* holds a repository of rules that map situation parameters of the SuOC into possible actions that can be executed for the given situations. In this case, the repository of rules represents the up-to-date understanding of the controller of the SuOC. Such knowledge reflects the experience of the controller with the SuOC so far.

To choose an action for given situation parameters, *level 1* utilises an *action selector* that implements a mapping function F_i to select the best suitable action A_i for the current situation C_i. The mapping function intends to provide quick response to incoming situation parameters in real time. Therefore, it does not involve any learning mechanisms in its mapping process. Instead, evaluating actions selected and executed by the controller is done in the *evaluation* component with a time-shift of Δt. The *evaluation* component uses history information, in particular the archived action A_i executed at time t and the situation parameters at time $t + \Delta t$, to check the performance of the corresponding rules. Rules that induce positive effects in the SuOC, i.e., desired changes of the operational state, receive rewards from the *evaluation* component. This results in an update of fitness values of corresponding rules in the mapping.

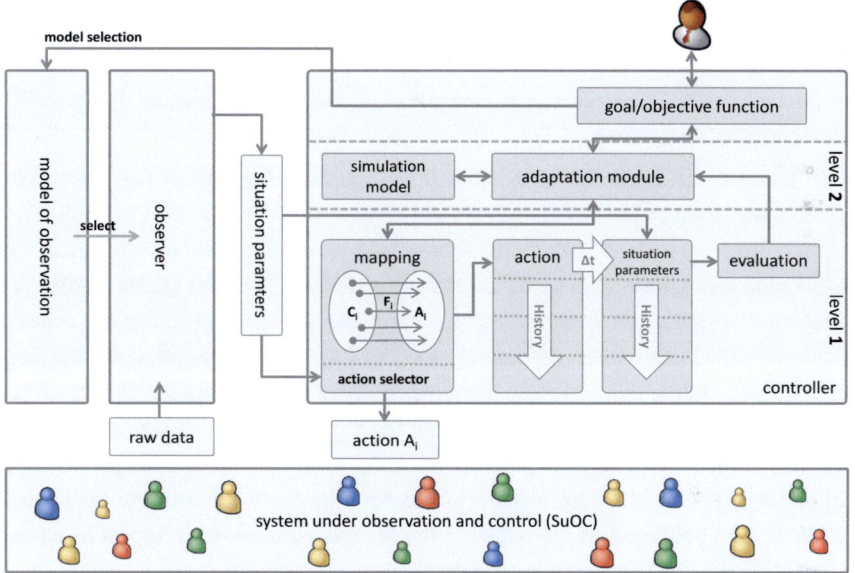

Figure 3-8: Generic controller architecture with two-level learning (see [Ric10])

Level *2* is the part in the controller that generates rules for previously unknown situations in the SuOC using offline learning. The state space of the SuOC may contain situations that the controller is not aware of, in particular in the early stages of the self-organising process. In this case, the controller has to generate new rules that combine unknown situations with appropriate actions by applying various machine-learning mechanisms, such as learning classifier systems (LCSs), reinforcement learning (RL), and so on. To this end, level 2 contains an *adaptation module* and a *simulation model*. The adaptation module applies online learning based on existing rules in level 1.

However, the accuracy of new rules generated by the *adaptation module* cannot be guaranteed. This uncertainty is especially not desired in critical application domains, where wrong rules may result in serious damages, as in the case of traffic control. Hence, in addition to online learning, the *adaptation module* in combination with the *simulation model* performs a second offline learning loop, where possible impacts of newly generated rules are predicted within the simulation model of the SuOC. This type of offline learning using simulation models decouples the time-intensive learning process from the real-time control process with prompt response. In addition, impacts of newly generated rules are verified in the simulation model, before they are applied to the real SuOC. This additional step prevents damage to the underlying SuOC caused by inaccurate rules.

In a word, the controller is the part in the generic architecture that influences runtime behaviour of the SuOC with respect to operational goals given by high-level control instances, such as human participants. To accurately correlate situations of the SuOC with appropriate actions, the controller combines online and offline learning to build up its knowledge about the SuOC, while keeping the probability for making wrong decisions caused by inaccurate rules as low as possible. Various learning mechanisms, such as reinforcement learning, or neural networks, enable the controller to evolve its knowledge about the underlying SuOC continuously, in particular in case of changes in the SuOC itself or in its environment. Based on this knowledge base, the controller can select the most suitable action for a given situation of the SuOC that guides system behaviour of the SuOC in the desired direction with respect to operational goals provided by human participants.

3.4.3 Application of the Generic Architecture

The generic observer/controller architecture provides the fundamental architectural pattern to design technical systems that expose the behaviour of controlled self-organisation. How the observer/controller architecture should be applied to technical systems depends strongly on the characters of the respective application domains. Hence, the scheme to apply the generic architecture may vary from fully centralised self-organisation to fully distributed self-organisation. In addition, individual components in the generic architecture must be adjusted to match the particular application domain, within which the SuOC has to operate.

Hence, for software engineers, their task changes from implementing an application explicitly with all predictable eventualities to implementing the specified components of the generic observer/controller architecture in the application that enable controlled self-organisation, in particular to balance the degree of top-down control with the degree of bottom-up self-organisation. Following the instructions first outlined by Schmeck [Sch05], Richter summarises the main challenges to engineer organic systems [Ric10]:

- It should be ensured that self-organising systems based on OC principles do not show unwanted (emergent) behaviour. This is particularly important for safety critical systems. Therefore, engineers have to derive an appropriate set of rules and behaviour patterns for an organic system. Such rules should enable the organic system to control its behaviour on the local level in such a way that the system shows the desired behaviour on the local level while eliminating undesired behaviour at the global level.

- It should be ensured that the overall system behaviour of an organic system is monitored and influenced by human participants. Therefore, an organic system should have a user interface for its human users, so that corrective actions can be performed to control the system, as needed.

- An organic system should provide context sensitive information via its user interface. That is, it has to filter information and services appropriately, according to the current situation or the user's needs, before such information and services are presented to human participants.

Furthermore, an organic system should have the appropriate degree of freedom to realise its adaptive behaviour. However, organic systems with too much degree of freedom may operate out of control and result in uncontrollable situations on the global level. Hence, it is crucial to determine the necessary degree of freedom for organic systems. That is, system engineers have to determine an appropriate balance between external control and internal self-organisation.

A further question that has to be addressed is the appropriate definition of the SuOC. The generic observer/controller architecture does not provide a statement on the granularity of the underlying SuOC, i.e., technical systems in the SuOC. For example, in a traditional multi-tier server application, each single component within the architecture can be an SuOC. Alternatively, components of the same tier (e.g., the presentation tier, the business logic tier, or the database tier) can be organised as a single Su-

OC. Additionally, it is also possible that a single observer/controller instance manages the components of all tiers. That is, the complete multi-tier server application is controlled as an SuOC.

Obviously, different granularity levels have both pros and cons. An SuOC involving less technical systems has a controllable state space that allows efficient monitoring and control at runtime. However, due to limited correlation to other server components that are out of scope of an observer/controller instance, it can only make decisions based on information it collects from the local SuOC. Therefore, due to the limited view of the global operational context, it is possible that such decisions are only suboptimal on the global level. This deficit can be eliminated by a global observer/controller instance over the complete server landscape. This guarantees the observer/controller instance can make optimal decisions on the global level. However, due to a too large state space an observer/controller instance has to deal with, it may need more time and computational resources to find optimal solutions, which is less desirable in time-critical systems.

To this end, Branke et al. suggest three general approaches to apply the generic observer/controller architecture in technical systems - depending on corresponding scenarios [BMM+06]:

- *Central* approach: a single observer/controller instance for the entire technical system. For example, Wuensche et al. apply the observer/controller architecture to machine management systems in off-highway machines [WMS+10]. By using a centralised observer/controller instance, all interconnected components within a single off-highway machine (e.g., traction drive, power take-off, or hydraulic system) are monitored and controlled as a whole SuOC in real time. Input from the SuOC is composed of a set of information about the machine and its environment (e.g., fuel, driver interactions, or changing subsoil). Based on this monitored information, the observer/controller instance can adjust particular components in the machine to keep efficiency of the whole machine at a desired level (e.g., to reduce overall fuel consumption of the machine).

- *Decentral* approach: an observer/controller instance for each component in a technical system. For example, Prothmann et al. applied the generic architecture to road traffic signals in an urban area in a fully distributed manner [PBS+09]. In their approach, traffic light controllers are extended by observer/controller instances that reconfigure the controllers depending on the current traffic volume. In addition, an organic traffic light controller has the possibility to collaborate with neighbouring controllers in a decentralised manner. This decentralised collaboration between related traffic light controllers allows more traffic-responsive signal systems that take traffic volumes of several interconnected intersections into consideration.

- *Multi-level* approach: an observer/controller instance on each component as well as one for the entire technical system. In this way, a hierarchy with multi-level observer/controller instances is built. Tomforde et al. proposed a hierarchical application of the generic observer/controller architecture to improve performance of interconnected self-configuring traffic light controllers [TPB+10], as a further improvement of the decentralised approach proposed by Prothmann et al. [PBS+09]. On top of a set of collaborative organic traffic light controllers, a global observer/controller instance is adopted to coordinate behaviour of individual controllers that have only a locally limited view. Such a hierarchical approach enables coordination of related observer/controller instances on the global level and therefore helps to improve the quality of decisions made by each individual observer/controller instance. Similarly, Becker et al. utilise a multi-level approach with several observer/controller instances to facilitate decentralised energy management in smart home [BAR+10]. In their approach, each intelligent household appliance is controlled by a local observer/controller instance, and a centralised observer/controller instance coordinates the interconnected local observer/controller instances from a global viewpoint. The local observer/controller instance consists of simple software/hardware modules to control the corresponding devices. The centralised observer/controller instance captures runtime information of local devices, such as power charges of each appliance, a device's degree of freedom, or other related device profiles. Based on this information, the centralised observer/controller instance can create a global schedule that specifies and predicts the behaviour of power consumption of related appliances. For example, such power forecast is of particular interest to avoid an unexpected peak in the electricity network caused by simultaneous charging of all appliances.

3.5 Summary

The focus of the present thesis is to provide a framework enabling self-organising multi-level Service Level Management in an SOE. To this end, the framework is expected to combine local objective-driven self-organisation within a single service component with global collaboration between related service components, as described in Section 1.2. Hence, this section is concerned with the fundamental means that relate strongly to the proposed approach in the present thesis.

Figure 3-9 illustrates the relationship between the fundamental concepts introduced in this chapter. The target application domain of the present thesis is an SOE. In comparison to existing models for software-centric SOAs, SOEs in the present thesis consists of both software-centric and hardware-centric service-oriented components within enterprise IT, where each technical component provides particular service(s) to other components in the environment.

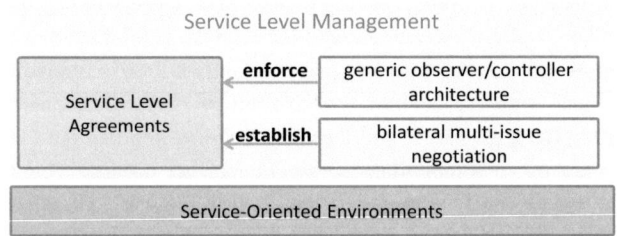

Figure 3-9: Fundamental concepts for multi-level self-organising SLM

Hence, Section 3.1 aims at establishing a common understanding of SOEs with respect to recent development in the field of service-oriented infrastructure, in particular Cloud Computing. To this end, the section reviews an SOE from both a macroscopic viewpoint and a microscopic viewpoint. The macroscopic view identifies the major building blocks of an SOE, which results in a multi-layered architecture with five horizontal and three vertical architectural layers. The microscopic view focuses on the characteristic provider/consumer relationship between service components and identifies the main artefacts involved in consuming services by a service consumer.

Based on the model of SOEs, the other three concepts are concerned with Service Level Management in SOEs. Hence, Section 3.2 addresses the essentials of Service Level Agreements. In particular, the section describes a formal SLA model that is required to model electronic service level contracts. The other focus of the section is put on the life cycle of SLAs and the roles of service consumers and service providers in the life cycle. In addition, this section also provides an overview on common QoS parameters in an SOE.

By considering the life cycle of SLAs between service consumers and service providers, there are two essential activities involved in the life cycle: *negotiating SLAs and enforcing SLAs at runtime*. Therefore, Section 3.3 addresses the former issue and introduces a formal model to facilitate automated bilateral negotiation with multiple issues. Section 3.4 introduces the generic observer/controller architecture from the Organic Computing research community, meant to enable controlled self-organisation of service components in an SOE. That is, the generic observer/controller architecture is expected to enable SLA-driven management of the underlying service component (i.e., from the viewpoint of system management).

To conclude, this chapter outlines the essential fundamentals to enable self-organising SLM in SOEs. On top of the multi-layered architecture for an SOE, this chapter covers the basic concepts of SLAs and introduces the two fundamental approaches to support SLA negotiation and SLA enforcement at runtime. The following chapters in the remainder of Part II focus on the design of the proposed approach and describe its architecture and implementation in detail.

Chapter 4   Scenario and Requirement Analysis

"学而不思则罔，思而不学则殆。"
— 【论语·为政，孔子】
"Learning without reasoning leads to confusion, thinking without learning
is wasted effort."
(Analects of Confucius, Confucius, 551 B.C.-479 B.C.)

So far, the vision of self-organising SLM in SOEs has been introduced on an abstract level. For example, the layered architecture introduced in Chapter 3 identifies the major building blocks and architectural layers of SOEs. Now, the present chapter introduces a real service-oriented scenario from the university context and analyses the challenges and requirements that the self-organising SLM approach of this thesis has to face.

Correspondingly, this chapter is organised as follows: Section 4.1 introduce a real scenario from the university context to demonstrate the direct relevance of self-organising SLM to SOEs. Based on this scenario, Section 4.2 identifies the main problems and challenges that a self-organising SLM approach has to address in its design. Section 4.3 outlines the main functional and non-functional requirements of the approach, while Section 4.4 summarises the chapter.

4.1 Target Scenario

In 2005, the Karlsruhe Institute of Technology (KIT, former University of Karlsruhe) launches a university-wide integration project called Karlsruhe Integrated InformationManagement (KIM) [KIM10]. The vision of the KIM project is to provide a portal-based information centre for employees and students by integrating a range of information distributed throughout the campus, such as study-related information from the central administration or literature information from the library. From within the central information portal, students can perform a range of activities related to

their studies, such as browsing lecture timetables, subscribing to workspaces of particular lectures, and enrolling for exams.

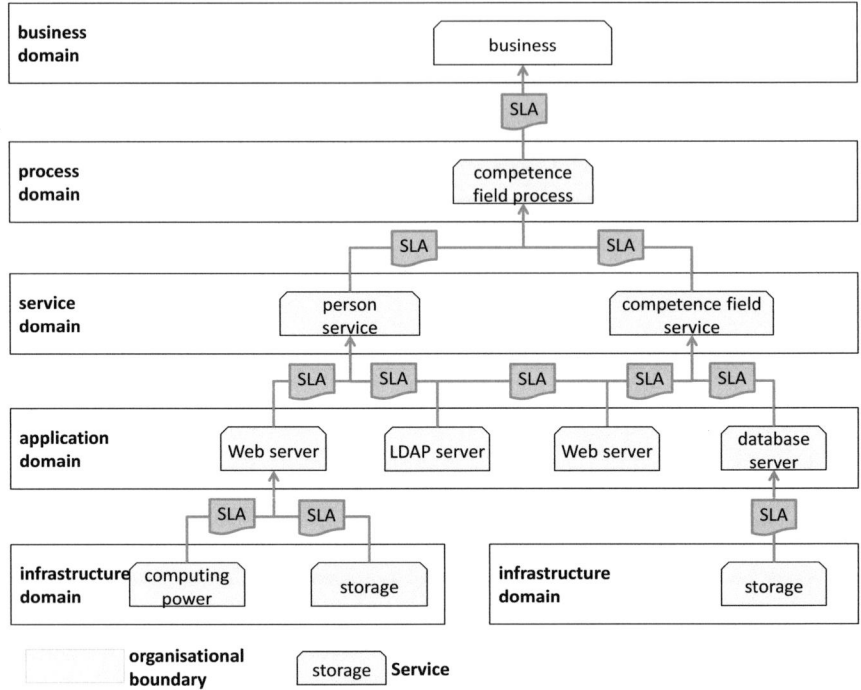

Figure 4-1: Sample scenario of a service-oriented environment (SOE)

One of the services that are implemented by the KIM project is the *competence
field* process, as symbolically illustrated in Figure 4-1. The process is described in
detail in Section 8.3.1. Figure 4-1 is by no ways complete. For simplicity and clarity,
it contains only essential provider/consumer relationships from the implemented scenario. Briefly, the competence field process allows employees at KIT to assign themselves to particular competence fields. The technical realisation of the competence
field process is simple. It is provisioned as a business process within a Web portal.
Internally, the competence field service involves two underlying Web services to get
the necessary information. The *person* service provides the capability to deliver personal information (e.g. name, surname, affiliation, etc.) to the process. The *competence field* Web service enables the process to store and retrieve competence infor-

mation of a particular employee. The Web services in turn consume services from the application layer. That is, both Web services are hosted by a Web server with two separate server instances. In addition, the *person* service leverages a *LDAP* server to authenticate service requests. Similarly, the *competence field* service utilises a database server to manage its application-specific data. In turn, all servers in the application domain consume services from the underlying infrastructure layer. At runtime, the Web server consumes *computing power* and *storage* services from the infrastructure layer for hosting Web services. Similarly, the *database* server consumes *storage* service in the infrastructure layer to store data.

The scenario shows clearly the layered architectural style of service-oriented systems, as introduced in Section 3.1.1. The business layer consists of end users (e.g., university employees or students) of the competence field process. The business process in turn build its implementation on top of two separate Web services that consume hosting services and data management services from the application layer. The Web server and the database server leverage technical capabilities from the infrastructure layer, i.e., computing power and storage, to accomplish their functions.

In addition, the scenario clarifies the provider/consumer relationship between service providers and service consumers in SOEs. Such provider/consumer relationships are not restricted to business processes and their supporting Web services. Indeed, by extending the narrow definition of Web services to services that provide "a means of delivering value to consumers by facilitating outcomes customers want to achieve [RL07]", relationships such as those between Web services and their hosting Web Server are provider/consumer relationships, too. In these provider/consumer relationships, proper functionality of service consumers relies strongly on that of providers.

The recursive nature of service-orientation, where a service provider (e.g., the person service) can be consumer of other service providers (e.g., the Web server), correlates all related provider/consumer relationships to a hierarchical structure. On top of the hierarchy is the relationship between a business process and its end users, which in turn involves the relationships between the business process and its underlying Web services. Such recurrence continues top-down to the hardware-centric infrastructure layer, where infrastructural components do not depend functionally on other components. That is, they do not need to consume other services to carry out their desired capabilities.

This hierarchical dependence chain determines that the operational behaviour of a business process, for example the competence field process, relies not only on the related Web services, but also on all technical components from all underlying layers that are involved in the hierarchical dependence chain. It also determines the correlation between the non-functional behaviour of different technical components in the hierarchy. For example, the performance of a business process is partly dependent on the performance of Web services it invokes.

To keep runtime behaviour, in particular non-functional behaviour, of business processes manageable and in compliance with business objectives, service levels are utilised to regulate the requirements of the consumer and the capabilities of the provider in a relationship. In the example of the competence field process, the business layer, i.e., end user, closes an SLA with the competence field process. Because of the hierarchical dependence chain between the process and its underlying IT components, this SLA places non-functional end-to-end requirements on the business process and the underlying technical components. That is, all technical components in the hierarchical functional chain are involved to support collaboratively the end-to-end SLA between the process and its end users, as illustrated in Figure 4-1. The end-to-end SLA closed between the competence field process and end users is supported by SLAs between the process and the involved Web services. The SLA between the process and the Web service is supported by the SLA between the Web service and the Web server. This scheme is applied recursively down to the infrastructure layer.

Hence, the vision of this thesis is to enable automated SLM between related components in a hierarchical functional chain, so that they can jointly contribute to the desired behaviour of a business process at the top of the chain. That is, in case of the present scenario, given a set of end-to-end non-functional requirements on the competence field process, the proposed approach can autonomously propagate corresponding requirements of the process to all related components by means of automatically negotiated SLAs.

Appropriately negotiated SLAs help technical components determine their operational targets at runtime. By enabling SLA-driven management of the corresponding components, technical components get the possibility to align their local resource configurations to requirements of their consumers, which leads to efficient allocation of resources avoiding over- or underutilisation. For example, if the database server needs more computational resources, it only needs to increase its local resources for the particular service instance, or if necessary, arrange with its computing power provider to get more computational resources.

4.2 Problem Analysis

Service-orientation provides the fundamental means to orchestrate business data and applications to business processes in a loosely coupled manner. Technically, applying service-orientation to traditional n-tiered applications is not problematic with the newest shift in IT, as promoted in Cloud Computing. This can be done by tearing apart traditional n-tier architectures and spinning each tier into the corresponding layer in the SOE. With further specialisation of third party IT providers in the cloud, it is even imaginable to deploy the layers of an SOE across several cloud infrastructures, as long as the business objectives of the business layer can be met by the underlying layers. As mentioned in the motivation section 1.1, an architecture with loosely coupled layers greatly increases flexibility and resilience of the resulting service-oriented applications. If one involved service in the architecture is heavily used, it is merely necessary to replicate and load-balance the affected service in the system. Other parts in the corresponding service-oriented applications remain unaffected from this procedure.

Hence, the problem within SOE consists not in technologies and their capabilities to realise service-oriented applications, but rather in approaches to manage such a distributed service-oriented infrastructure that is dispersed across several organisational and technological boundaries. The design paradigm of service-orientation does not provide adequate ways to enable tightly coupled control over the services and resources involved in the environment. Changes applied to a single service in the environment can raise unexpected outcomes in other related components in the dependence chain.

Hence, despite the benefits of service-orientation to align business and enterprise IT, in particular in terms of flexibility and ability to scale on demand, service-orientation exhibits a set of characteristics that complicate management tasks of service-oriented systems. Parts of these characteristics are inherited from traditional distributed paradigms; others are more specific to service-oriented systems. In the following, the problems and challenges to enable self-organising SLM are addressed in accordance with characteristics of a service-orientated environment.

Service autonomy: As one of the fundamental design principles for service-orientation, *autonomy* refers to the desired behaviour of services to be responsible for their own operational state. Therefore, services may autonomously vary their implementation, deployment, operation, and management independently of their consumers. Generally, service autonomy raises the question of how to establish a proper operational state on the system level, especially in presence of possible failures in the underlying service components along the dependence chain. Service autonomy prevents technical components from actively influencing behaviour of other components in the dependence chain. This makes a tightly coupled control over several services and resources in certain circumstances (e.g., different organisational units) partly or even completely impossible.

Dependence is a phenomenon frequently observed in service-oriented applications. As already discussed in the target scenario in Section 4.1, dependence exists bi-directionally between service providers and service consumers. In the abstract layered architecture for SOEs, services build the conjunction part between a consumer and its underlying providers in the architecture. In this context, services top-down along with business processes, applications, and infrastructural components build a vertical functional dependence chain between functionally interrelated components in the environment. All components involved in the dependence chain are functionally dependent on each other.

Apart from direct functional dependences, there are weak dependences between components that are indirectly related to each other. A weak dependence occurs, if two independent components functionally depend on the same component in the system (e.g., two Web services running on the same application server) or if they support the same component (e.g., a Web server and a database server supporting the same Web service). Weak dependence does not play a critical role for proper operation of service-oriented applications. However, since runtime behaviour of a consumer depends on all its providers, providers with weak dependences to one another can use such information to exploit possibilities to decompose and allocate the overall non-functional requirements of the consumer in terms of QoS metrics among them.

Decentralisation and distribution: service-orientation can be regarded as an evolution of traditional concepts of distributed applications. It imposes decentralisation by utilising business capabilities provisioned by various distributed organisational units. Related components are distributed across organisational boundaries with different technology standards. From a system management point-of-view, decentralisation requires appropriate management approaches to cope with the distributed nature of service-oriented applications and to avoid drawbacks like resource bottlenecks or single-point-of-failure. Furthermore, management approaches have to move away from centralised monitoring and control. This requires implicitly that distributed management systems have to coordinate and cooperate with each other to reach global objectives.

Dynamism can be partly derived from service autonomy: the open architecture of SOE allows for introducing/removing services as autonomous functional units to/from the system at any time, while each service is free to adapt its behaviour autonomously to environmental changes. A similar level of dynamism can be observed in the environment on the system level, in particular with respect to global emergent behaviour resulting from behaviour of local components. Dynamism complicates the efforts of management applications to monitor and control technical components. Continuous changes require agile reactions of management applications.

Heterogeneity and interoperability. IT landscape of service-oriented applications is heterogeneous with respect to the variety of types of components in the environment, i.e., business process, service, applications, and infrastructure components. Each of them differs from one another with respect to their platforms, technologies, and capabilities. Although industry standards help to reduce the impact of heterogeneous technologies on system management approaches, this characteristic remains a challenge for designing generic self-organising management approaches. Furthermore, the decentralised and distributed nature of service-oriented systems determines that these management approaches have to deal with heterogeneous interfaces when interacting with target technical components, while keeping their own capabilities to collaborate with one another.

Robustness. As aforementioned, a self-organising approach for SLM has to face a dynamic and decentralised environment. Both characteristics make it difficult to ensure the overall optimal behaviour of the approach, which can only exist in a static and centralised environment. Hence, the self-organising approach has to balance between optimal but strongly restricted central management and suboptimal but robust decentralised management of technical components.

Scalability. A service-oriented application may scale from simple applications leveraging a few services to large-scale enterprise-level applications involving a set of back-end systems (e.g., CRM, ERP, and so on) and a range of organisational units. It is obvious that approaches that works well in a small environment are not necessarily applicable to a large-scale environment, in particular from the viewpoint of agile responses to changes in the environment. Hence, a solution for enabling self-organising SLM has to be able to deal flexibly with various scalability levels of the targeted service-oriented applications.

Transparency. This characteristic refers to the willingness of an autonomous technical component to reveal information about itself and to accept external operational objectives. The background for this request is the necessary collaboration between interrelated components at runtime. In such a scenario, a component can decide autonomously if it is willing to reveal its internal information and choose the way to reveal it. Depending on the different degrees of willingness, technical components can be generally distinguished between

- *fully transparent* - if a component reveals its (consolidated) internal information to other components and is ready to cooperate with them,

- *partly transparent* - if a component only reveals part of its internal information to components with functional dependences,

- and *non-transparent* - if a component acts as a black box that does not expose any internal information except the predefined service messages.

From the viewpoint of service autonomy, each component can autonomously determine their degree of transparency. This presents a problem for the self-organising SLM approach of this thesis that is forced to enable collaboration between related distributed components. If a technical component is not willing to expose information and react on instructions, it is not possible for an external component to influence its behaviour.

To sum up, service-oriented applications can benefit from the design paradigm of service-orientation, in particular with respect to agility of service-oriented systems to respond to changes; however, it does not address necessary means to manage such SOE. It is obvious that centralised management approaches are not suitable for large-scale service-oriented applications. The distributed nature of large-scale service-oriented systems and dependences between technical components in such systems demand decentralised and collaborative management of those components. On the other hand, autonomy and heterogeneity of those components prevent an active collaboration between them. In particular, non-transparent components are impossible to integrate into such a collaborative management federation. Hence, the self-organising approach for SLM proposed in this thesis must appropriately address these issues in its design, which are summarised by means of functional requirements of the approach in the following section.

4.3 Requirements Analysis

The previous two sections outlined the target scenario and the main problems that must be addressed by the approach for self-organising SLM in this thesis. Before the architecture for self-organising SLM is introduced in the next chapter, this section outlines the general requirements on its design. In particular, the requirements are derived from the problems identified in Section 4.2. This section is partly based on the joint work of Liu and Schmeck [LH06].

While reviewing the target scenario, it is obvious that requirements for establishing automated end-to-end SLM can be considered on both local and global levels. Requirements on the local level are concerned with capabilities of particular components in an SOE, while requirements on the global level focus on collaboration between components in such an environment. Hence, in the following, the requirements are specified on these two levels.

At the local level, it is firstly required that *a service component needs to know itself*. The knowledge of a service component about itself can be acquired at two levels – the *meta*-level and the *instance* level. At the meta-level, a component should know its functionalities, its interfaces to the external world, and a way to describe them. For example, Web Service Description Language [CCMW01] (WSDL) provides a meta-model to describe syntactically interfaces of a service. A further example of such a meta-model is OWL-S [MBH+04] that specifies is a Web service ontology based on Ontology Web Language (OWL) [MGVH04] and describes semantically what a service does, how it works, and how to access it. At the instance level, a service component should have detailed knowledge about its internal components and their runtime state. This is the basic requirement for a managed service component to be self-aware. To this end, the component must be technically instrumented to expose runtime management information and provide a set of interfaces to access them. For example, Common Information Model (CIM) [DMTF99] provides a syntactical as well as semantic base for modelling management objects using object-oriented constructs.

Based on CIM, external management applications can access management information of an instrumented component via common communication protocols, such as HTTP or FTP. It is noteworthy that various management approaches based on CIM, such as Web-Based Enterprise Management (WBEM), have been applied to a range of technical systems, including various operating systems (e.g., Windows), business applications (e.g., SAP business applications), and hardware-centric components. Via suitable manageability interfaces, external management applications (such as the observer/controller instance) can monitor and control the runtime behaviour of the corresponding components.

Secondly, It is required that *a service component should be able to control its own behaviour to meet its own operational goal.* A service component has an operational goal that can be specified either internally during initialisation or by a related component in the environment as part of an agreement. Furthermore, if a service component is involved in a business process, there will be some global goals for the whole business process. In this case, a component has to adjust itself to contribute to the given global goal. Generally, there are two possible ways to adjust a service's behaviour: Either a service component can configure its own parameters locally or it can rely on its dependences (i.e., service providers) in its environment. For example, in order to increase the performance of a service instance, a service component can increase the amount of resources assigned to this specific instance; or it can adjust its performance by influencing the behaviour of its providers, such as encouraging them to increase the processing priorities of its requests. It is noteworthy that this requirement relies on the previous requirement of manageability interfaces. Modifying runtime configuration of a particular service component is generally carried out via such manageability interfaces.

Thirdly, it is required that *a service component should be able to take over external directives and align its behaviour to these directives, if applicable.* For a service component in SOEs, external directives are only requests and the requestor cannot assume that the target service component is going to follow them. According to the service design principle of autonomy, a service component can autonomously determine how to deal with such directives, depending on its internal policies with respect to the types of these directives. For example, service components that belong to a single organisation are, in all probability, going to cooperate rather than compete with each other. That is, in this case, the service components are willing to follow global business objectives to ensure that these objectives can be met. However, if two service components belong to two different organisations, such as a business consumer and an external IT provider, then they are expected to behave in a more self-interested manner. In this case, their relationships can only be governed by a service level agreement. It is noteworthy that both of them are required to align their behaviour to this agreement, which acts as external directive for both contract parties.

Briefly, the first three requirements are concerned with capabilities of service components to organise themselves from a local perspective. In order to be self-aware, a service component needs to be correspondingly instrumented to expose management information and to receive control instruments. Furthermore, a service component is aware of its own capabilities that can be expressed with help of various modelling languages, such as WSDL or OWL-S. In addition, each service component is expected to organise itself with respect to internal objectives and, if applicable, external directives. This allows realising controlled self-organisation on local components.

The requirements on the global level focus on the abilities of service components to communicate and collaborate with one another in the environment. Functional and non-functional dependences between related distributed service components demand intensive collaboration between them to ensure desired behaviour of the complete enterprise IT at the global level, where service components are expected to exchange messages among one another to facilitate collaboration.

Hence, it is required that *a service component should be able to expose meta-level information, and if applicable, part of its instance-level information to other related components*. The meta-level information is crucial for other elements to determine the capabilities of a particular service component in the environment, in case that a relationship should be established between them. This is especially important for service discovery at design time, where a service consumer looks for its potential service providers with respect to a set of search criteria (e.g., functional, non-functional, or QoS requirements). At runtime, a service component can get an overview about its environment based on information exchanged with its dependences and take actions, if necessary, to ensure its operational goal. Furthermore, establishing automated SLM has to take into consideration the willingness of a service component to expose its runtime information. This should allow service components that do not expose instance-level information to other related components to participate in the global collaboration. This is crucial for enabling automated SLM in SOEs, where each related component must be included in the solution, despite its willingness.

Secondly, it is required that *a service component should be context-aware*. A service component should at least know its neighbourhood (i.e., its service providers and service consumers with provider/consumer relationships) in an SOE. The previous requirement on exposing meta-level and instance-level information provides the foundation for a service component to discover its neighbourhood. Such information allows service components to get an overview over existing components in its environment (e.g., to discover potential service providers/consumers). Through regular exchange of information with its neighbourhood, a service component is aware of its environment and take necessary actions, if the environment changes. Furthermore, a service component must have knowledge about specific infrastructure services (i.e., a global ontology service or a central service registry) available in the environment, of which it may make use, if necessary. This requirement is the prerequisite to enable collaboration between related service components. By doing this, a service component can identify the appropriate collaboration partner at runtime, and respond to changes in its environment with respect to its operational objectives.

Thirdly, it is required that *a service component should be able to establish and maintain relationships with other service components in the SOA*. The previous two requirements provide the basis for building new relationships between related components in the environment. The most essential relationship in an SOE is a provider/consumer relationship, which is regulated by one or more service level agreements between a service consumer and its service provider. In this case, both parties must understand the terms specified in the agreements and, if necessary, negotiate them with each other. Once two parties can close an agreement, they must abide by the defined terms to maintain their relationship. It is necessary to remark that a component that is not willing to expose its runtime information to other related components must be covered by this requirement, too. That is, relationships should not only be built between cooperative, but also between self-interested and therefore less cooperative service components.

Lastly, it is required that *a service component should use interoperable communication standards while building up relationships with related service components*. The largest obstacle to facilitate intensive collaboration between related service components is the high degree of heterogeneity of those components. Base on the design principle of service autonomy, service components may differ from one another in their design, implementations, technical realisation, and other related artefacts. An effective way to overcome this obstacle is to utilise interoperable communication standards, such as WS-* specifications, SOAP, XML, etc. These communication standards allows service components to communicate using predefined and standardised vocabularies, which are in turn individually interpreted and implemented by particular service components.

To conclude, these four requirements are concerned with collaboration between related components on the global level to guarantee the desired global behaviour of the entire IT infrastructure. By consuming information exposed by other service components, a service component is aware of its environment, in particular its (potential) service providers and service consumers. Based on this information, related service components can use interoperable communication protocols to build up provider/consumer relationships.

4.4 Summary

The focus of this chapter is to review the target scenario of this thesis, analyse the existing problems to establish self-organising SLM in SOEs, and specify the requirements on the architecture to enable self-organising SLM. To this end, this chapter reviews a real service-oriented scenario from the university context to demonstrate how end-to-end SLM works in an SOE. Hierarchical dependence chains between related service components demand a comprehensive approach that includes all related components systematically in a global SLM process. However, inherent characteristics of SOEs, in particular those derived from the design paradigm of *service-orientation* prevent an effective implementation of such a comprehensive SLM approach. In particular, service autonomy and service heterogeneity require additional considerations in the architecture design for enabling self-organising SLM. Such considerations are analysed and specified in terms of functional requirements at both the local and global levels. Requirements at the local level are mainly concerned with monitoring and control of the behaviour of particular service components, while requirements at the global level focus on collaborations between related components. Based on these requirements, the following chapter describes the architecture to enable self-organising SLM in SOEs, the core of this thesis.

Chapter 5   Organic Service-oriented Environments

"日新之谓盛德。"
— 【周易 • 系辞上】

"Bringing forth novel ideas continuously lays a corner stone for moving forwards the human beings."

(I Ching – Book of Changes, The Great Treatise I)

Today's ever paced and changing business world calls for consistent support of business by enterprise IT. Emerging technologies, in particular SOC, drive a further convergence of existing isolated IT systems towards integrated enterprise-level business applications. In this context, the design paradigm of *service-orientation* provides the fundamental means to construct business logics on top of distributed capabilities provisioned by various IT systems. This leads to a tighter alignment between business and IT. However, this design paradigm does not address necessary means to handle system complexity resulting from increasing integration of technical systems, such as a large amount of interactions between related systems or continuous changes in a system and its environment. In particular, existing engineering approaches lack sufficient support to predict and handle all eventualities of an SOE at runtime. Hence, human participants are still strongly involved in managing large-scale distributed systems, in order to cope with increasing system complexity.

As motivated in Section 1.2, a plausible way out of this dilemma is to utilise software components exhibiting the capabilities of *controlled self-organisation*. Such software components are able to operate autonomously in their environment, while still being under control of human participants in the system. Automating tasks to monitor and control software components establishes a range of self-x properties in the system. These self-x properties allow corresponding software components to adapt their behaviour transparently to their up-to-date operational context in the environment. At the same time, the behaviour of these self-organising technical systems can still be influenced by human participants through external policies or high-level system objectives.

This chapter introduces a *reference architecture* to enable automated end-to-end SLM in SOEs. In software engineering, a reference architecture serves as "an architectural blueprint for constructing software systems targeting particular problem domain(s) with specific functional, behavioural, and quality attribute requirements" [KCB03]. It outlines a set of necessary software components, their externally viewable interfaces, as well as interrelationships between them (e.g., data flows). The major effort of this chapter is to apply the design paradigm of Organic Computing, i.e., the generic observer/controller architecture, to an SOE. In this way, the resulting architecture is expected to establish a framework for self-organising end-to-end SLM, while keeping the system complexity hidden from human participants.

Hence, the remainder of this chapter is organised as follows. Section 5.1 outlines the agent-oriented design of the framework on the macroscopic level. The distributed and autonomous nature of service components stimulates usage of design principles from multi-agent systems to facilitate collaboration between them. Hence, this section justifies the agent-oriented design of the architecture and provides an insight into collaboration between service components in the context of end-to-end SLM. Section 5.2 focuses on the architecture of a management agent on the micro level. It addresses the integral parts of the architecture in detail and provides a rationale with respect to the design requirements discussed in Section 4.3. Section 5.3 concludes the chapter.

5.1 Agent-oriented Design

As discussed in Section 2.3, a multi-agent system is characterised by its autonomously operating agents and social-like interactions between these agents. Interactions are not carried out simply by exchanging data, but by performing social activities similar to humans' daily life, such as coordination or negotiation. Furthermore, software architectures based on multi-agent systems are open and dynamic in the sense that agents operate in a changing environment, which they can join or leave at any time. The high degree of architectural similarity between MAS and SOEs makes it promising to investigate how far the concepts of MAS and SOEs can be combined to facilitate collaborations between service components. It is noteworthy that the term collaboration is not limited to simple provider/consumer relationships between service components, as described in Section 3.1.2. Moreover, the term covers necessary interactions between service components to achieve some given tasks jointly, in particular from the viewpoint of end-to-end SLM.

Hence, this section is concerned with the agent-oriented design of the architecture. Section 5.1.1 introduces the agent-oriented design of a management overlay that aims at facilitating collaborations between related service components. Section 5.1.2 focuses particularly on collaborative activities between service components to enable SLM. Section 5.1.3 provides a rationale for the agent-oriented design with respect to problems and design requirements discussed respectively in Section 4.2 and Section 4.3.

5.1.1 Management Overlay with Autonomous Agents

Services in SOEs are limited with respect to their ability to collaborate actively with other services. That is, services applying the design paradigm of service-orientation are passive in their nature, until they are invoked by other service components in the environment. Before a service is actively consumed, it is not aware of its consumers and possible interactions with them. In other words, services are not designed to operate in an extensively autonomous manner, which is however one of the prerequisites to enable self-organisation in an SOE.

Furthermore, the design paradigm of service-orientation does not address how a service can design and carry out its social activities with other related components. Hence, they are not expected to collaborate proactively with other related service components to reach some global objectives, such as providing jointly composed services to meet given functional requirements. However, in order to reduce administrative efforts of human participants in an SOE, service components are indeed expected to self-organise their own activities, including carrying out social interactions with related components. In the light of the emphasis of MAS on facilitating social interactions between agents, it is of particular interest to investigate how far the concept of MAS can be applied to design a self-organising SOE.

The idea of combining the concepts of MAS and SOC has been intensively studied in the research community for years. Petsch, Nissen, and Traub investigates the potential of applying intelligent agents in SOA [PNT06]. They found out that there are two general ways to consider relationships between agents and services, namely agents as service providers and agents as service brokers. In the former category, agents operate as Web services. Indeed, the W3C defines a Web service as *"an abstract notion that must be implemented by a concrete agent. The agent is the concrete piece of software or hardware that sends and receives messages, while the service is the resource characterised by the abstract set of functionality that is provided.*" That is, an agent is considered as a service provider for a particular service. Based on abstracted service interfaces, agents can autonomously implement their services that can be consumed by other components in the environment.

In the second category, intelligent agents are utilised to monitor, control, and orchestrate services, from the viewpoint of a service broker. Advanced research in MAS aims to facilitate autonomy, social ability, reactivity, and proactivity of software agents. These capabilities help services to be aware of themselves and their environments and to operate actively in such environments. In contrast to the passive operation mode determined by the design paradigm service-orientation, agent-oriented design provides services with the necessary intelligence to operate more actively in their environments. In particular, the fact that services can only realise their values in an SOE affirms the importance of social abilities of services. This allows services to respond collaboratively to external demands and changes at runtime. Indeed, most of the research in this category focuses on automated orchestration of services matching given functional and non-functional requirements, as introduced in Section 2.2.2. By applying the agent-oriented design, service components are expected to become more dynamic, flexible, and robust [LKH06].

The focus of the present thesis is to enable end-to-end SLM in SOEs. Hence, the interrelated nature of services determines that they must, on the one hand, collaborate globally with other related services. On the other hand, services must be capable of performing autonomous actions locally to meet their operational objectives, i.e. their service levels. By comparing these requirements with the characteristics of the multi-level SLM approach of the present thesis, it becomes reasonable to apply agent-oriented design to the architecture to enable multi-level SLM.

The result of applying the agent-oriented design in an SOE is a management overlay, as illustrated in Figure 5-1. As the name says, the management overlay operates on top of an SOE. The management overlay separates the management concern from the operational context of an SOE. That is, activities associated with service level management are carried out mainly in the management overlay, in particular by intelligent agents deployed in the management layer. In the remainder of this thesis, these

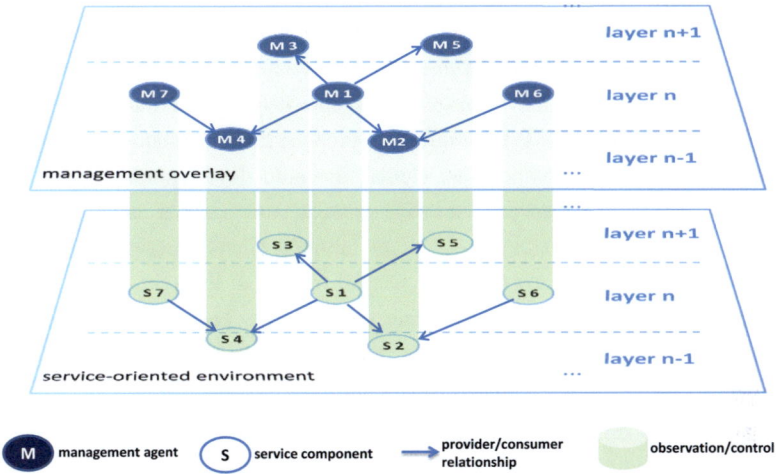

Figure 5-1: Management overlay with autonomous management agents

agents are referred to as management agents to distinguish them from agents offering services to other components.

Figure 5-1 illustrates the management overlay with abstracted service components and their management agents. In the abstract model, each technical component in a real SOE, e.g. a Web service or a database server is abstracted to a service component in the figure with incoming/outgoing relationships to other components. An incoming relationship indicates that the corresponding component consumes services from other components. Analogously, an outgoing relationship indicates that the component de- livers services to other components in the system. For simplicity, without loss of gen- erality, it is assumed that each service component from layer n consumes only ser- vices provided by service components located in layer $n-1$ and delivers services to service components in layer $n+1$.

The challenge is to determine how management agents can be attached to service components in the underlying environment. The vertical dependence chain, as dis- cussed in Section 4.1, requires a compatible management approach in the overlay. Considering the three architectural patterns specified by the generic observ- er/controller architecture (cf. Section 3.4.3), the centralised approach would imply that the complete underlying environment is organised by a single management agent. This approach does not satisfy the fine-granular and dynamic nature of service-oriented systems. Therefore, it involves the risk of losing control over the complete system due to a 'single-point-of-failure'. The decentralised approach satisfies the fine-granular and scalable nature of service-oriented systems. However, since the decentralised approach implies that management agents may operate independently from each other, it does not provide the ability to reproduce the aforementioned dependence chains between service components. Hence, the multi-level approach provides the necessary support with respect to the fine-granular and scalable nature of SOA. In addition, constructing hierarchical structures between related management agents allows the management overlay to reflect vertical functional links between corresponding service components in the underlying environment. Therefore, all management agents, i.e., observer/controller instances of these agents, are organised in a multi-level manner corresponding to that of their underlying components.

Consequently, each service component in the operational layer is monitored and controlled by a dedicated management agent in the management overlay. The connection between a service component and its dedicated management agent is implemented individually by the management agent. That is, management agents utilise individual manageability interfaces offered by corresponding service components to communicate with them. It is noteworthy that such manageability interfaces can be heterogeneous. Service components are free to design and implement their instrumentation mechanisms internally by applying various management standards, such as CIM or WBEM. These manageability interfaces provide external management agents an insight into the runtime behaviour of their corresponding service components. In addition, such interfaces enable management agents to perform, if necessary, corrective actions on these components to influence their behaviour. The way, in which a management agent communicates with its service component, depends on the particular implementation of manageability interfaces of the component, e.g., by using WSDM or WS-Management. Section 5.2.1 discusses the internal architecture of a management agent in detail.

As a result, the structure of the underlying service-oriented layer, in particular the hierarchical structure spanned by vertical dependence chains between service components is fully mapped to the management overlay. That is, two management agents are related to each other, if their corresponding service components in the service-oriented layer have a direct provider/consumer relationship with each other. Thus, management agents are aware of other related management agents in their environment. This allows them to carry out context-aware collaboration with respect to corresponding rela-tionships in the underlying operational layer. In particular, management agents can determine their collaboration partners precisely, with which they can jointly fulfil some given functional and non-functional requirements. It is noteworthy that two col-laborating management agents are not equivalent with respect to their roles in collabo-ration. In other words, a management agent has either the role of a *provider agent* or a *consumer agent*, depending on the role of the service component it manages. Such distinction of roles is important for management agents to determine their activities in the course of collaboration, as later discussed in Section 5.1.2.

The management overlay along with the underlying SOE separates three essential concerns of multi-level SLM, namely *operational context, management context,* and *environment context*. With respect to the operational context, each service component delivers service(s) to other service components in its environment, e.g., encapsulated business capabilities, hosting services, or platform/infrastructure support. Managing those service components is achieved by management agents in the overlay, with re-spect to the management context of the environment. In addition, each management agent maintains information about its immediate neighbourhood in the overlay, which has direct influence on its behaviour. In particular, a management agent's limited view of the environment restricts the number of communication partners, with which it has to interact. This restriction of environment context helps to reduce communication efforts of a management agent and induces a less complex state space that it has to deal with at runtime.

The organisation of the management overlay is designed in accordance with the de-sign paradigm of *service-orientation*. The autonomous nature of each management agent corresponds to that of a service, as defined in the design paradigm. Despite the high similarity between management agents and services (e.g., service abstraction, loosely coupling, service reusability, etc.), the largest motivation of applying service-orientation in the management overlay is the resulting homogeneous collaboration environment for management agents. Communication between management agents is carried out via standardised Web service protocols, such as the specifications of the Web services technology stack discussed in [BHM+04]. In particular, specifications for enabling distributed management (e.g., WSDM) and electronic contracts (WS-Agreement) are of particular interest to management agents. By using these specifica-tions, management agents can unambiguously exchange messages among one another.

The management overlay establishes a homogeneous and scalable collaboration layer on top of heterogeneous SOEs. On the one hand, as discussed in Section 3.1, recursive functional dependences determine that all related service components have to collaborate with one another to ensure desired functionalities on the global level. That is, they have to coordinate their activities in a way, in which service providers support their consumers to accomplish their operational objectives. On the other hand, management agents are autonomous with respect to their behaviour in the management overlay. Each management agent is only responsible to its corresponding service component in the underlying service layer. In other words, a management agent represents interests of its respective service component in the management overlay. Therefore, related agents in the management overlay have to facilitate collaborations with one another, so that their respective service components can achieve a given operational objective in a well-coordinated manner.

The following section is concerned with collaboration between management agents. Among other things, Section 5.1.2 investigates the character of the management overlay and determines appropriate collaboration mechanisms in the overlay.

5.1.2 Collaboration between Management Agents

So far, the previous section has outlined the necessity to establish collaboration between related management agents in the management overlay. Different organisations may design service components in an SOE for varying purposes. This leads to the fact that service components do necessarily share common operational objectives. However, in order to deliver value-added services (e.g., business processes) to end users with given operational objectives, service components have to be orchestrated. That is, various service components have to collaborate with one another, so that they can act strategically to achieve desired outcomes on the global level.

Furthermore, a dynamic runtime environment demands that service components have to adapt their runtime behaviours dynamically in accordance with their environment. Hence, their management agents are expected to act autonomously to decide what to do at runtime, rather than having all situations as well as corresponding reactions hard-coded in their implementations. In particular, related management agents have to coordinate their activities to control runtime behaviour of their respective services components.

Hence, this section is concerned with issues related to collaboration between management agents. In detail, this section addresses:

- organisational patterns to organise management agents in the overlay,
- possible forms of collaboration between management agents,
- and how management agents can collaborate with one another to facilitate end-to-end SLM in an SOE.

Organisational patterns applied to a multi-agent system have significant impact on the collaborative behaviour of the agents at runtime. As pointed out by Carley and Gasser [CG99], they determine roles of various agents, relationships between them, and a structure to organise them. In addition, an organisational pattern specifies how agents can interact with one another to realise a particular goal on the global level. Hence, appropriate organisational patterns are crucial to organise a group of independent agents systematically to exhibit more complex behaviour patterns on the global level.

The basis for choosing the appropriate organisational pattern for a management overlay is the recursive provider/consumer relationship in the underlying SOE. As discussed in Section 4.1, recursive provider/consumer relationships span a hierarchical dependence chain between related service components across an SOE. The example of the *competence field* process illustrated in Figure 5-2 shows this dependence. In the sample scenario shown in Figure 5-2, the provider/consumer relationship between the business process and its end users is governed by an end-to-end SLA. This SLA specifies guarantees with respect to quality of service delivery of the business process. As aforementioned, the business process operates on top of a range of service components in the IT infrastructure. Therefore, the negotiated agreement between the process and its end users determines the desired runtime behaviour of both service providers in the service domain to some extent. Both service providers run in turn on top of their supporting servers from the application layer.

Such a recursive consumption scheme is applied top-down until the lowest layer of an SOE, whose components do not have any further providers for their part. In this way, the top-down hierarchical dependence chain spans a finite tree structure involving all supporting service components for a particular business process. The business process itself builds the root of the tree. Each connection between two nodes in the tree structure indicates that a service component of an upper layer consumes some service from a service component of a lower layer. By doing this, a service component

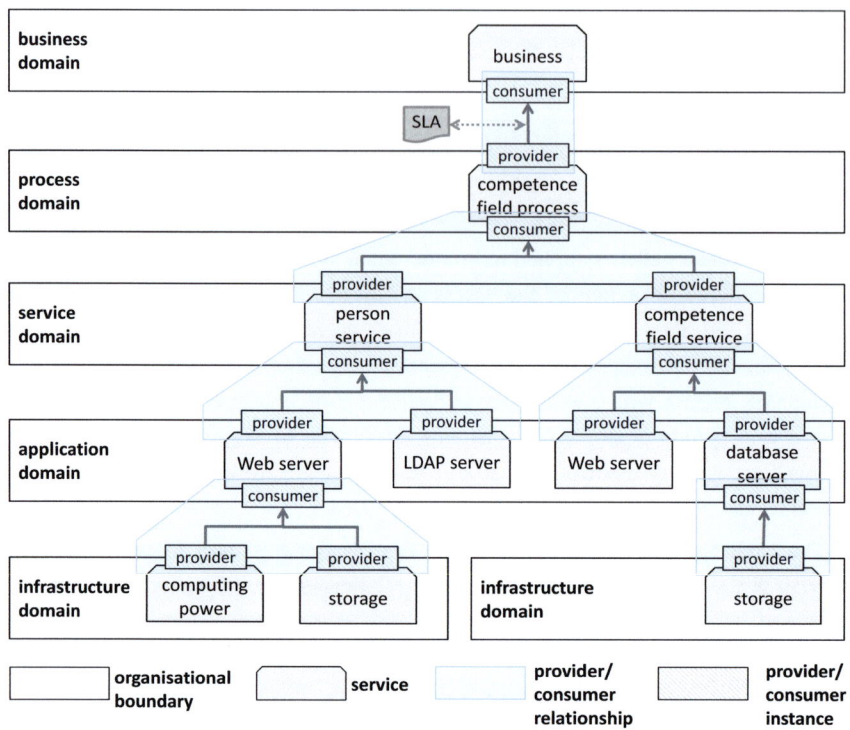

Figure 5-2: Hierarchical provider/consumer relationships by means of a sample SOE

can delegate part of the implementation of its functionalities to a service component in the lower layer.

From this consideration, it is imperative for a service component to make sure that its service providers deliver their services in an acceptable range, in particular with respect to objectives specified by its consumers. Therefore, to enable a consistent and holistic service level management across all related service components, all related components in the hierarchical dependence chain must be included in the corresponding SLM processes. As pointed out by Liu, Thanheiser, and Schmeck [LTS07, TLS07], the hierarchical dependence structure of an SOE requires a hierarchical organisational pattern to facilitate collaborations between management agents. The management agent of a business process forms the root of the hierarchy. Management agents of service components that do not consume any other services form the leaves of the hierarchical tree. All other management agents form intermediate nodes between the root and the leaves.

At runtime, the agent of a business process triggers collaborations between management agents within a hierarchical dependence chain. This is determined by the fact that as the root of a hierarchical chain, a business process closes a service level agreement with its end users. Since a business process delegates part of its functionalities to its providers, it has to ensure that not only itself but also its service providers must operate in conformance with quality terms defined in the agreement. Therefore, their respective management agents have to collaborate with one another to coordinate their activities. In this way, a service consumer can ensure that its underlying service components can jointly enforce quality terms specified by the agreement.

Recursive provider/consumer relationships in a hierarchical dependence chain require that the initial collaboration triggered by a business process has to be propagated top-down to all related service components in the lower layers. For example, as shown in , a Web service provider of the competence field process, e.g., the person service, depends functionally on servers located in the application layer. Hence, its management agent has to collaborate with agents of those servers, so that they can cooperate to ensure overall runtime behaviour of the person service. In this way, all service components are gradually involved in the global collaboration, top-down, and layer-by-layer.

In addition, it is worth noting that not all participating management agents involved in the collaboration are equivalent in their roles. The management agent for a service consumer plays the *master* role in the collaboration. That is, it has to fulfil binding QoS terms in the agreements it closes with its consumers. To this end, it has to involve its providers by delegating part of the specified QoS obligations to them. That is, the management agent has to encourage its supporting providers to commit to certain non-functional obligations, so that it in turn can meet its assurance to its consumers. Therefore, management agents of service providers play a *slave* role in the course of collaboration. They are expected to respond to requests of their consumers regarding quality of service delivery. By doing this, a service component (i.e., with the master role) with the help of its supporting service components (i.e., with the slave role) can ensure to deliver its service in compliance with quality terms it has agreed on with its consumer.

Hence, the objective of each service component in the collaboration is to coordinate its activities and those of its service providers appropriately with respect to its operational objectives. It is therefore of particular interest to determine how management agents can cooperate with one another. Among other things, an appropriate collaboration allows a master management agent influencing the runtime behaviour of its slave management agents, while these slave management agents can maintain their autonomy and individuality in the collaboration. In other words, slave management agents are not expected to give up control over their local resources partly or even completely to their master agent in the collaboration.

Furthermore, it is worth noting that existing collaboration mechanisms in MAS, such as task sharing, cannot be applied directly to management agents. First, task sharing implies that slave agents are going to execute any task that the master agent distributes to them. In this way, they lose a large part of their control over their local resources. Secondly, task sharing requires that slave management agents are homogeneous to a wide extent. Only so, they can accomplish assigned subtasks unambiguously. This is however not achievable in a heterogeneous SOE. In addition, task sharing does not provide any assurance on non-functional aspects of how the tasks are accomplished. In contrast, in an SOE, it is desirable that collaboration between management agents should help to maintain long-term relations between related service components, in particular in terms of service contracts. In this way, a service consumer can reach certain stability in the construct of its underlying service providers.

Therefore, the present thesis uses the concept of SLAs in a uniform way, in particular in the context of multi-level SLM within an SOE. SLAs only contain abstract terms regarding quality of service delivery, as discussed in Section 3.2. Hence, under the assumption that related service components use the same QoS ontology model, SLAs are generic enough to unambiguously transfer information regarding service levels between service components. Therefore, they are suited to be used as homogeneous messages between a set of collaborating heterogeneous management agents.

If a service provider has negotiated an SLA with its consumer, it can interpret the agreement individually in its local context. In this sense, negotiation is of particular importance for service providers. Via negotiation, they do not simply follow requests from their consumer. Instead, they can give their views on negotiation issues. From this point of view, a slave management agent does not lose its autonomy in the collaboration. Furthermore, a negotiated SLA between a service consumer and its provider regulates the obligations and prohibitions of them in the course of their interactions. Therefore, a negotiated SLA as a contract leads to a long-term relationship between the related components.

Collaboration between related management agents is concerned with establishing SLAs between related service components. Figure 5-3 illustrates collaboration between the management agent for a consumer, i.e., the master agent, and the agents for its providers, i.e., the slave agents.

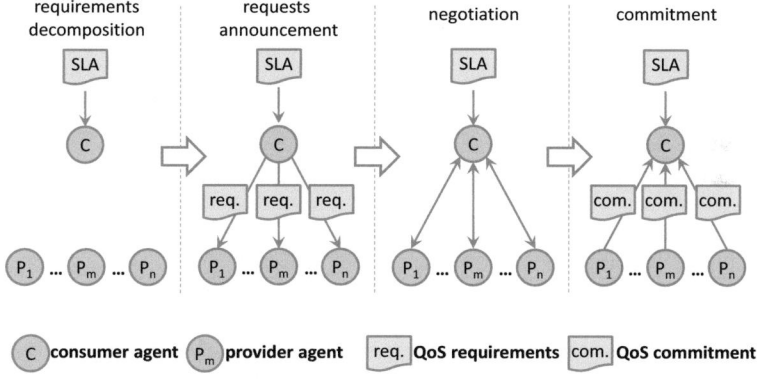

Figure 5-3: Collaboration between master/slave management agents

At the beginning of the collaboration, a service consumer receives an SLA with a set of non-functional requirements. These requirements represent the overall requirements on the runtime behaviour of the consumer and its providers. That is, both the consumer and the providers are requested to coordinate their activities so that they can jointly meet these requirements. The master agent decomposes the incoming requirements into a range of sub-requirements, depending on individual capabilities of its providers. These sub-requirements are then submitted to the corresponding management agents as base for further negotiation. In the negotiation phase, the master agent and the slave agents exchange offers and counter offers between one another, until they find mutually acceptable agreements. In the last stage of collaboration, the providers commit to the negotiated agreements with their consumer. From this point in time, they build a long-term relationship with each other regulated by the closed agreements, whereupon the consumer begins to invoke functionalities offered by its providers. The suitable negotiation protocol with detailed description of collaborative activities between a service consumer and its providers is defined in Section 6.5.

In a word, collaboration between management agents is carried out in the form of negotiation. Within negotiation, both master agent and slave agents maintain their autonomy. Differences of opinions between collaborating management agents are settled by using negotiation. Offers exchanged in the course of negotiation only contain platform-independent SLAs, which can be interpreted individually by management agents in their local context. Once a consumer finishes negotiating an SLA with its provider, they establish a long-term provider/consumer relationship. Both contract parties are expected to contribute jointly to enforce the negotiated SLA.

5.1.3 Design Rationale

Extracting management-related concerns from the operational service-oriented layer into a separate management overlay enables a clear separation between management-centric and service-centric communication. In the management overlay, communication between various management agents allows them to cooperate with one another to coordinate activities of their respective service components in the underlying service-oriented layer.

In the management overlay, each management agent simultaneously has a local and a global context. Locally, each management agent interacts with its corresponding service component in the underlying layer to provide self-organising capabilities. Globally, each management agent is situated in an environment consisting of other related management agents with functional dependences. These management agents in the neighbourhood are potential cooperation partners at runtime. To facilitate cooperation at runtime, each management agent exposes a range of services to other management agents in the overlay while keeping its internal autonomous behaviour unaffected. To this end, service-orientation is applied to the management overlay to improve the interoperability of the management agents and its responsiveness at runtime.

Furthermore, employing design principles of service-orientation in the management overlay keeps it flexible with respect to changes in the underlying service-oriented layer. Any changes in the service-oriented layer result in respective change(s) in the management overlay. For example, if a new service component is introduced to the service-oriented layer, its corresponding management agent is added to the management overlay, too. Furthermore, the open architecture of the service-oriented management overlay allows integrating further management agents with specific capabilities into the management overlay. For example, a management agent can provide decision support service in case of uncertainties/conflicts to other management agents.

In addition, as pointed out by Liu, Thanheiser and Schmeck [LTS07], in order to cope with complexity associated with distributed SLM, there are three general strategies: *abstraction*, *delegation*, and *variability reduction*. By considering these strategies, the agent-oriented design of the management overlay reduces the complexity of the multi-level SLM approach in the following way:

- *Abstraction*: Using abstract SLAs hides implementation details from other management agents. SLAs contain only abstracted information on particular QoS parameters regarding service delivery of a service provider. Hence, terms specified in an SLA have no direct reference to the underlying technical details of a respective service component, e.g., configurations of local resources. Therefore, both management agents in the collaboration can keep their negotiation on an abstract level, without having to consider underlying technical details, which obviously imposes additional complexity in SLM processes.

- *Delegation*: Negotiation allows a service consumer delegating part of its responsibility to its service providers. Through collaboration, a master management agent can coordinate its activities with those of its slave management agents. By doing this, all management agents can ensure that the overall runtime behaviour of the consumer complies with its external objectives. From the viewpoint of SLM, delegation helps a provider to reduce its efforts to enforce external objectives.

- *Variability reduction*: This strategy focuses on reducing system complexity by downsizing the system variability. An abstract SLA covers a limited part of service level objectives that a respective service component exposes. From the viewpoint of other management agents, this reduces the variability that those agents have to deal with to a minimal extent.

In addition, applying service-orientation and agent-oriented design to the management overlay addresses a large part of the architectural design challenges discussed in Section 4.2. Among other things, this approach covers the following challenges:

- *Decentralisation and distribution*: In an organic SOE, distributed management agents organised in compliance with the design principles of service-orientation enables decentralised control of a service-oriented application. This streamlines decentralised control essentially to cope with the inherent distributed characteristic of an SOE.

- *Dynamism*: A management overlay employing the design principles of service-orientation reveals the dynamic characteristics of SOA-based systems. Various approaches from service-orientation help the management overlay to cope with high dynamism of the underlying service-oriented layer, such as the WS-Discovery specification for discovering services. Any ad-hoc change in the underlying SOE can be reflected to the management overlay on the fly. In this way, the management overlay is kept up-to-date with the underlying landscape.

- *Heterogeneity and interoperability*: The underlying service-oriented layer is heterogeneous with respect to technical platforms and supporting technologies. The design paradigm of service-orientation resolves the problems caused by heterogeneity by employing a set of standards, such as XML, SOAP, and WSDL. Applying service-orientation and abstract SLAs to the management overlay ensures that communication and collaboration between management agents in the overlay can take place independently of their heterogeneous technical implementations.

- *Scalability*: any change in the underlying service-oriented system results in an analogous change in the overlay. This allows the management overlay to scale in accordance with the underlying SOA-based system.

- *Service autonomy*: Using agent-oriented design in the management overlay allows service components to retain their autonomy in the SLM processes. Related management agents representing interests of corresponding service components collaborate among one another to guarantee some given external objectives jointly. Hence, negotiation allows a management agent to solve conflicts with other related management agents, in particular in case of different operational objectives. From this viewpoint, service components can maintain their autonomy to control their local technical resources.

- *Dependence*: Management agents are aware of their direct neighbourhood with related agents in the environment. They use this dependence information to determine their collaboration partners and their roles in the collaboration, i.e., either the master agent that distributes requests or the slave agent that responds to incoming requests. In this way, the functional dependence chain in an SOE is fully considered in the SLM processes.

However, in comparison to traditional centralised management solutions, the decentralised and distributed architecture of the management overlay implies some limitations. Obviously, decentralised control applied in the management overlay requires more communication and coordination efforts, which may negatively affect the performance of the whole system. In contrast to this, a centralised management system can make decisions based on globally available information and resources.

Moreover, each management agent has only a limited view of the entire system, which may lead to suboptimal decisions without reference to global objectives. Decisions made by a management agent optimally address the local situation of the underlying service component. However, these decisions may not be optimal with respect to other related service components on the global level. However, these limitations are compensated by the robustness that the management overlay has, in contrast to single-point-of-failure of centralise management solutions.

5.2 Management Agent

Management agents are the part in an organic SOE that connects the management overlay with the underlying SOE. On the global level, a management agent collaborates with other related agents in the management overlay to coordinate their activities. On the local level, a management agent controls its underlying service component autonomously in compliance with SLAs negotiated with its providers/consumers.

Hence, this section is concerned with the internal architecture of a management agent. It outlines how the functional parts of the architecture work together to establish collaboration on the global level as well as locally controlled self-organisation on a particular service component. Therefore, Section 5.2.1 provides an insight into the overall architecture of a management agent. The sections 5.2.2 to 5.2.5 introduce the functional parts of the architecture in detail. Section 5.2.6 undertakes a review on the architecture with respect to the design requirements, summarised in Section 4.3.

5.2.1 Architecture

As discussed in Section 5.1, a management agent is responsible to collaborate with other related management agents to coordinate their activities as well as those of their respective service components via negotiation. In addition, a management agent has to establish controlled self-organisation in the underlying service component driven by the negotiated SLA. Hence, a management agent is composed of two major parts: one for conducting global collaboration and the other for locally realising SLA-driven self-organisation. This section focuses on these two parts and, on a higher level, addresses the major functional parts of the architecture for a management agent. This section is based partly on the work by Liu, Thanheiser, and Schmeck [LTS07] as well as [LTS08].

Figure 5-4 depicts the high-level architecture of a management agent. In the architecture, the SuOC of a management agent represents the local operational context of a management agent. It contains all operative service components that carry out predefined business capabilities, such as a business process that provides process-level support to end users, or a Web server that provides hosting services for Web services. Business capabilities define functionalities that a service component offers to other service components in the service-oriented layer. A consumer can access business capabilities through their service interfaces.

A *service interface* separates the invocation aspect of a service component from its operational aspect. As defined in accordance with the design principles of service-orientation, a service interface abstracts technical implementations of a service component for potential service consumers. A service consumer can only access a provisioned service via its predefined service interface. This explicit separation between a specified *service access point* and its underlying technical implementation allows a service provider and its consumer to define artefacts explicitly related to service invocation, such as SLAs. These artefacts only refer to runtime behaviour of a service experienced by a service consumer at the service access point, which are determinative for estimating metrics for SLM processes.

One prerequisite for involving a service component into the global management context is that this service component has to provide manageability capabilities to its management agent. Only via these manageability capabilities, a management agent can monitor the operational state of its respective service component and influences its runtime behaviour by reconfiguring it in an automated manner. These manageability capabilities can be exposed via an abstracted and standardised *management interface*, where external management applications like a management agent can access them (e.g., in alignment with WS-Management or WSDM). Similar to the role of a service interface, a management interface represents the single access point for external management applications to get access to management functionalities.

In addition, it is worth noting that both a service interface and a management interface do not have any reference to the global context or other operative components in the environment. In particular, management capabilities provided by a management interface operate only on the technical resources of the SuOC in a local context, such as increasing the amount of resources assigned to a particular service instance, or decreasing the priority of incoming requests from a particular consumer instance. Similarly, a management interface provides only access to the runtime information of the local SuOC, i.e., the underlying service component. Hence, the local focus of a manageability interface limits the state space that a management agent needs to deal with at runtime. This limitation leads to an efficient decision-making process of the agent. Furthermore, strict definition of the management domain in the SuOC allows a clear design of the management agent. This helps to avoid undesired dependencies between management agents due to overlap of their management domains.

A management agent operates on top of the SuOC. Communication between a management agent and its SuOC is achieved by using the aforementioned manageability interface of the SuOC. Via this interface, a management agent collects runtime information from its underlying service component. Monitored information gives a management agent an insight into the operational states of the underlying SuOC. However, such management information is generally composed of a large amount of

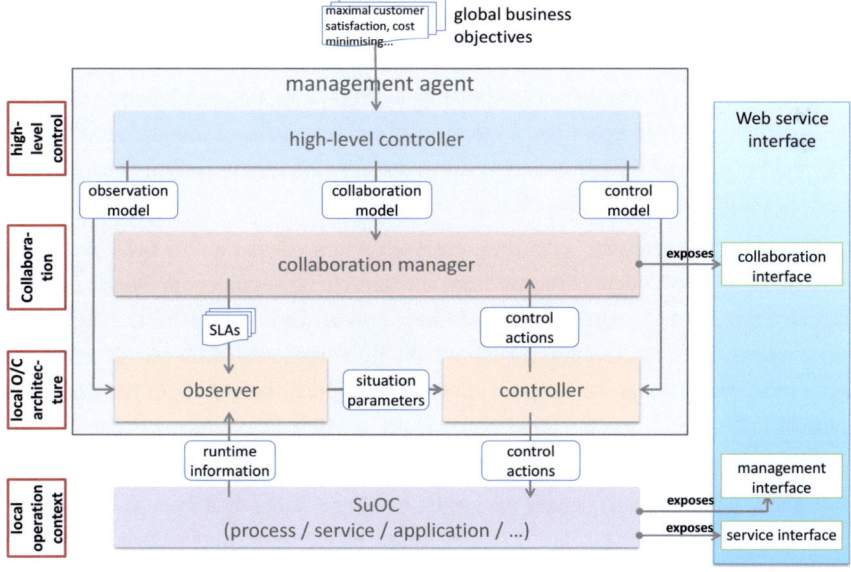

Figure 5-4: Architecture of the management agent

raw data describing operational states of the SuOC, e.g., information about processing incoming requests (request arrival time, queuing time, processing time, and completion time). This raw data with less quality provide a management agent with a very restricted view of the current state of the SuOC. Hence, a management agent utilises a set of further components internally to process incoming management information, to consolidate it, to analyse it, and to make decisions to perform necessary corrective actions on the SuOC, with respect to given objectives. On the other hand, a management agent needs further components to interact with other related agents in the management overlay. Hence, the remainder of this section describes the main components of a management agent bottom-up and outlines interactions between them.

The local O/C architecture on top of the SuOC is the component that performs local management activities immediately on the SuOC, if necessary. To this end, the local O/C architecture is composed of two components - the *observer* and the *controller*, as specified in the observer/controller architecture introduced in Section 3.4. Both components operate in the local context of the SuOC with no reference to other components in the environment. They make decisions only based on locally available information the *observer* collects from the underlying SuOC. In turn, actions that the controller chooses for execution only affect the SuOC itself. It is not desired that the *controller* considers runtime states of components from other SuOCs during its decision-making process. It is a necessary design decision to maintain the autonomy of technical components in the service-oriented layer. Following this restriction consequently, each management agent has a clearly defined management domain consisting of the underlying SuOC. Each agent has the necessary authority to control the underlying service component without breaking its autonomy.

The *observer* measures, quantifies, analyses, and predicts runtime behaviour based on raw management data collected from the underlying service component. As such, the observer uses manageability capabilities provided by the SuOC to collect low-level management information at runtime. As aforementioned, such raw data provides poor information about the current system-wide status of the SuOC, in particular with respect to QoS parameters. Obviously, it is not possible to use raw management data directly to draw conclusions about operational states of the service component.

Hence, this raw management data must be consolidated to a system-wide fingerprint that depicts system states of the respective service component on the global level. For example, a fingerprint may make an assertion about whether the current SLA is violated by a provider. To this end, the observer utilises a range of analysis tools to consolidate the raw management data. This process may include steps:

- to consolidate collected raw data with respect to given management objectives,
- to search pre-processed data for recognisable patterns with help of various mathematical and statistical methods,
- or to forecast the next system-wide behaviour of the observed component.

In addition, in order to assess conformance of current operational states of a service component with the service contract it closes, the observer is aware of the corresponding SLA. QoS parameters defined in an SLA represent target values of the operational states, where consolidated management data represents actual values of the state. Using these values, the observer can determine conformance of the current operational states with those target values defined in the SLA. The observer forwards the resulting fingerprint consisting of the current operational states and SLA conformance information as so-called *situation parameters* to the controller.

Upon receiving situation parameters from the *observer*, the controller has to choose the best appropriate actions accordingly. The ultimate goal of the controller is to guide the SuOC to show the desired behaviour in compliance with its operational objectives. To this end, the controller is composed of two integral subcomponents. The heart of the controller is an adaptation module that utilises various learning algorithms to correlate situations with appropriate actions. For example, a learning classifier system can be used to classify incoming situation parameters and to map particular situation(s) to appropriate actions in a learning-by-doing manner. However, in critical business applications, wrong control actions can lead to serious damages in the business. Hence, the second subcomponent in the controller is responsible to generate accurate classifier rules by learning algorithms based on offline simulation models. As such, the controller can test the accuracy of particular rules offline before they are applied for live control on the real SuOC.

The controller and the observer together enable an underlying service component to adapt to its operational environment in accordance with given operational objectives specified in an SLA. As aforementioned, this type of adaptive control is carried out in the local context of the underlying service component. Hence, a management agent has to collaborate with other related management agents to coordinate their activities. To this end, the *collaboration manager* operates on the global level to facilitate collaborating activities with other related management agents. It helps a management agent to understand its role and responsibilities in the global management over-lay. Such global context is incorporated by the local O/C architecture to support its local decision-making.

The collaboration manager has an understanding about its environment. That is, it is aware of other related management agents that have provider/consumer relation-ships to the current management agent. These related management agents are potential collaboration partners of the current agent. The focus of collaboration between two related management agents is to negotiate and establish an SLA between them, which gives a consumer some assurances regarding quality of service delivery. For a service provider, an appropriately negotiated agreement makes it possible to perform proac-tively SLA-driven management of its local technical resources. Such configuration takes place not only during initialisation of the whole environment, but also during operation at runtime.

Service-oriented design of a management agent is addressed by the *collaboration interface* based on Web services. Thus, management agents can take advantages of the Web service technology stack to enable reliable, interoperable, and robust communi-cation among one another. Furthermore, the service-oriented collaboration interface decouples related management agents from one another, which results in increasing flexibility and scalability of the entire management overlay. In combination with other approaches such as dynamic discovery, the collaboration interface helps to keep the management overlay up-to-date without any manual procedures.

Until now, the local O/C architecture and the collaboration manager provide a management agent with the necessary abilities to self-organise. However, a manage-ment agent still lacks an appropriate interface for human participants to influence its behaviour as well as that of its service component. For example, it is assumed that a business intends to provide their IT services with maximal customer satisfaction. Hence, the related service components should correspondingly configure their local resources to enhance service level objectives that are directly related to user experi-ences, such as reduced response time or increased availability.

Hence, a management agent uses an additional component, the *high-level control-ler*, to realise the interface to human participants. As input, the high-level controller receives business objectives from human participants. It is noteworthy that business objectives express only abstract business goals that are less correlated with the under-lying technical implementations of a service component. A possible business objective may be to maximise customer satisfaction, or to maximise financial profits of the IT infrastructure. These business objectives are translated by the high-level controller, depending on its knowledge about correlations between high-level business objectives and low-level technical details.

Therefore, the high-level controller influences the behaviour of the local O/C architecture and the collaboration manager, while they in turn control the behaviour of the underlying service component in the SuOC. Hence, from given business objective(s), the high-level controller derives an *observation* model for the observer, a *collaboration* model for the collaboration manager, and a *control* model for the controller, respectively. These models specify how the corresponding components have to behave at runtime. For example, an observation model states the set of management information that the observer has to collect from the underlying SuOC. A collaboration model guides the collaboration manager in its negotiation by specifying priorities of particular QoS parameters. The control model supports the controller to make decisions in accordance with global business objectives.

With the high-level controller, a management agent is able to establish *controlled self-organisation* in technical service components, with respect to given service levels. The following sections provide a detailed insight into the internal structures of the components discussed in this section.

5.2.2 High-Level Controller

The high-level controller is the brain of a management agent. Its primary responsibility is to guide runtime behaviour of a management agent in accordance with external business objectives. Hence, it derives necessary control models from given business objectives and forwards them to the collaboration manager and the local O/C architecture for further enforcement at runtime. Such control models provide statements about operational objectives regarding desired quality of service levels. For example, given a business objective to maximise satisfaction of end users with IT services, control models derived may place emphasis on QoS issues associated directly with user experiences, such as availability of IT services for business days/holidays, or average response time during peak time.

The design of the high-level controller depends strongly on the type of business objectives received from the high-level control instance (i.e., human participants). Herein, it is noteworthy that business objectives can be either business-centric (such as *increasing revenue generated by the enterprise IT*) or IT-centric (such as *minimising cost of business processes*). As figured out by Thanheiser, Liu, and Schmeck [TLS08], different layers in the enterprise IT, from the *corporate governance* layer down to the *infrastructure* layer, have varying objectives depending on their views on the enterprise IT.

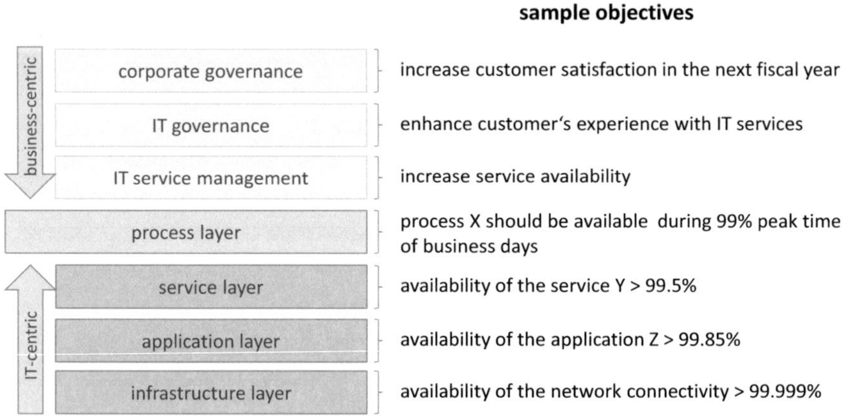

sample objectives

business-centric corporate governance	increase customer satisfaction in the next fiscal year
IT governance	enhance customer's experience with IT services
IT service management	increase service availability
process layer	process X should be available during 99% peak time of business days
IT-centric service layer	availability of the service Y > 99.5%
application layer	availability of the application Z > 99.85%
infrastructure layer	availability of the network connectivity > 99.999%

Figure 5-5: Hierarchy of business objectives (see [TLS08])

Similar objectives are defined in the ITIL framework [RL07], where the management policies are organised vertically from the viewpoint of varying management focuses, such as availability management, capacity management, change management, and so on. Figure 5-5 depicts the recursive delegation relationships between such objectives for the layers.

As depicted in , objectives of various layers are not isolated from one another. Indeed, objectives of two neighbouring layers have a kind of delegating/supporting relationship. Objectives of a lower layer are set to support those objectives of a higher layer, which delegates part of its responsibility downwards to service providers in the underpinning layer. From this viewpoint, all objectives across all layers are linked to one another tightly through the recursive delegation relationships between them.

The *corporate governance* layer consists of a set of processes to control the way in which the whole organisation is administered. Hence, corporate governance works with objectives that are highly aggregated and less related to particular technical aspects of the enterprise IT, such as "increasing customer satisfaction in the next fiscal year." Thereby, the connecting piece between corporate governance and enterprise IT is *IT governance*. It derives IT-related objectives from given objective for *corporate governance* and defines which strategies the underlying IT infrastructure should pursue to archive business objectives of corporate governance. For example, for the previously used sample objective to increase customer satisfaction, the derived objective for the IT governance could be "enhancing customer's experiences with IT services."

The *IT service management* layer is the one in enterprise IT that manages life cycles of IT services to meet the needs of a business. Hence, it works with IT-related metrics that quantify operational states of the underlying IT infrastructure, such as availability, response time, throughput, and so on. To this end, the *IT service management* layer must address the issue of linking business-oriented layers with IT-oriented layers. Questions like how a given business objective is supported by the underlying IT infrastructure or how the underlying IT infrastructure influences the business-oriented layers, are considered in this layer. For example, the sample objective of IT governance in Figure 5-5 can be interpreted as "to increase availability of IT services" or "to reduce average response time of IT services." To this end, the IT service management layer utilises a range of models and tools to estimate dependences between business-related metrics and IT-related metrics quantitatively. It uses such quantified correlations to improve alignment between business and enterprise IT.

Mapping between business objectives and IT-related metrics is however out of scope of the present thesis. The key issue related to the present thesis is to determine the type of objectives with appropriate granularity that affects control behaviour of management agents. Because of the IT-centric nature of management agents and their close relationships to services, it is reasonable that management agents work with IT-centric objectives rather than more abstracted business-centric objectives. That is, a management agent gets its high-level objectives from the *IT service management* layer. Such IT-centric objectives guide a management agent to control its underlying service component in compliance with global business objectives on corporate governance level.

A management agent can derive the following control models from high-level objectives given by the *IT service management* layer:

- *Observation* model: An observation model defines measures to collect and aggregate raw data from the underlying SuOC. It determines a set of relevant raw data that the observer must collect from the SuOC at runtime. In addition, it

specifies procedures to aggregate the collected data, and a set of situation parameters that should be passed to the controller. Thus, an observation model restricts the amount of information passed through to the controller to a minimal
set. This procedure reduces the state space that a management agent has to deal
with for making decisions. As such, it increases efficiency of a management
agent to process comprehensive runtime states of the SuOC.

• *Control* model: A control model guides the behaviour of the controller to maintain desired operational states in the underlying service component, i.e., the
SuOC. In particular, a control model defines operational goals of the service
component with respect to objectives it receives from the IT service management layer. Among other things, these operational goals specify a set of non-
functional (i.e., QoS) parameters that are of particular importance for the controller. By respecting these specified parameters, the controller can ensure to
align its maintenance activities to global business objectives.

• *Collaboration* model: A collaboration model provides the collaboration manager with necessary guidance on how to negotiate with other management
agents in the environment. Among other things, the collaboration manager can
use the model to determine priorities of non-functional parameters involved in
a negotiation process. For a negotiation process with identical conditions, pri-
oritising non-functional parameters differently may lead to completely different
outcomes of negotiation. Hence, while a given SLA is acceptable for a management agent, the same agreement may be unacceptable for another agent
with different control models.

In brief, the high-level controller provides an interface between an autonomous
management agent and other high-level control instances (e.g., human participants) in
the environment. Via this interface, high-level control instances supply a management
agent with external directives (i.e., those derived from global business objectives). As
such, high-level control instances can influence the decision-making processes of a
management agent that otherwise operates autonomously. This enables underlying
service components to act locally in a self-organising manner, while keeping their behaviour in alignment with global business objectives.

5.2.3 Collaboration Manager

The *collaboration manager* is the part of a management agent that connects it to its
neighbourhood in an SOE. The loosely coupled nature of service components in such

an environment and the resulting functional dependences between them determine that service components have to work together to achieve global business objectives.

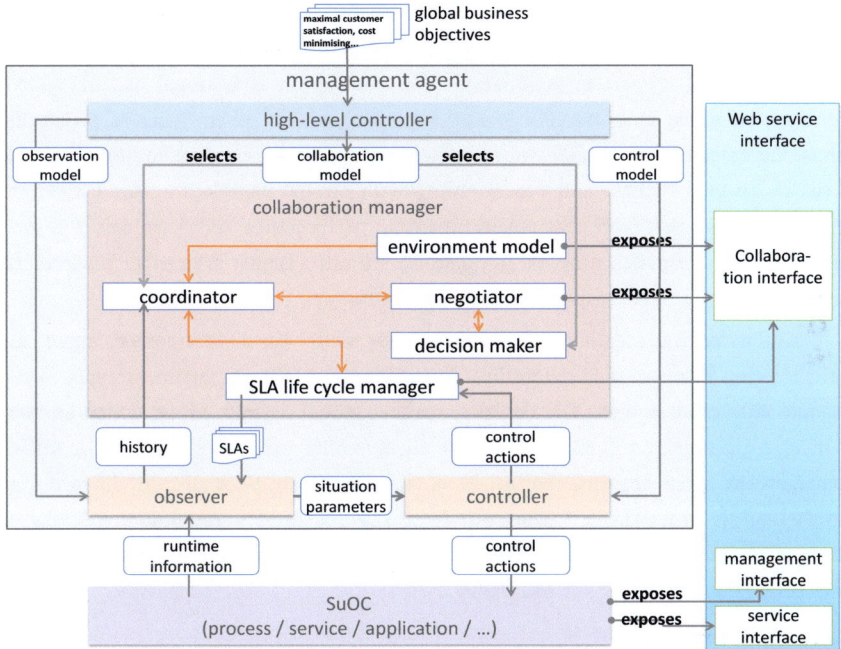

Figure 5-6: Structure of the collaboration manager

The collaboration manager is mainly responsible to get aware of an agent's environment, determines a set of potential management agents to collaborate with, carries out negotiation activities with them, and maintains service level agreements with related service components. To this end, the collaboration manager utilises a range of interacting functional subcomponents, as illustrated in Figure 5-6. The remainder of this section introduces the functional subcomponents briefly. The more detailed description of the functionalities of each subcomponent is provided in Chapter 6. In particular, Chapter 6 focuses on negotiation capabilities within the collaboration manager and outlines how they are implemented to facilitate negotiation activities between related management agents.

Collaboration Model

The *collaboration model* specifies primarily an agent's behaviour in the course of collaboration with other agents. In particular, it characterises negotiation strategies of a management agent, i.e., utility functions for estimating an SLA's quality as well as decision-making support in negotiation. For example, it is assumed that the global business objective is to maximise user experiences with given business processes. Thus, the collaboration model can select an appropriate negotiation strategy that emphasises on performance and dependability with limited negotiation time constraint. This determines that QoS parameters regarding performance and dependability, such as availability, response time, or throughput, are rated higher than other parameters, e.g., service cost, in the respective negotiation strategy.

Furthermore, by selecting a decision making model for a management agent, the collaboration manager also determines the willingness of a management agent to co-operate with other agents. The decision making model defines, under which circumstances a management agent can accept an incoming offer. For example, a selfish management agent requires that an acceptable incoming SLA A^t must have higher utility than its own offer A^{t+1} (i.e., $utiltiy(A^t) > utility(A^{t+1})$); while a cooperative management agent is going to accept an incoming offer, if it has the same utility as its own offer (i.e., $utiltiy(A^t) \geq utility(A^{t+1})$).

Environment Model

Briefly, the environment model specifies a set of related management agents in the neighbourhood, their relationships to the current management agent, and their relationships among one another. That is, for any given agent in its neighbourhood, a management agent is aware of whether it is a service provider, a service consumer, or some other artefacts. In particular, if a service component consumes services simultaneously from several providers, its corresponding management agent is aware of all service providers and their relationships to the component.

The environment model can be built by adopting various discovery mechanisms, such as WS-Discovery or UDDI. These discovery mechanisms allow a management agent to explore its environment for potential communication partners and keep such information up-to-date at runtime.

Furthermore, in a self-organising SOE, a service consumer is expected to autonomously determine its service providers and compose their services to realise a value-added service. Hence, each service consumer is previously equipped with a meta-model. Such a model describes the set of service capabilities it needs, pre-conditions and after-conditions of these capabilities, and compositions of these service capabilities at design time, e.g., by using WSDL and OWL-S. Such logical composition models precisely describe relationships between all related service providers. Based on this, a corresponding agent can build up an accurate model of its environment.

Coordinator

The *coordinator* is the engine of the collaboration manager. Since each service component may have several service providers or service consumers simultaneously, there are in general several parallel negotiation threads between a management agent and its service providers/consumers. In particular, a service consumer has a given set of QoS requirements that should be delegated to its service providers via automated negotiation. Hence, these parallel negotiation threads must be appropriately triggered and coordinated by a central instance, so that the resulting SLAs are aligned with the given QoS requirements.

To this end, the coordinator requires several inputs to initiate parallel negotiation threads. The first input is the environment model that delivers an overview of available collaboration partners. By means of this model, the coordinator determines the set of management agents, with which it intends to negotiate.

Secondly, in order to negotiate with other agents, the coordinator must be aware of functional capabilities of the underlying service component. Among other things, if the underlying service component plays the role of a service provider, a management agent has to know possible service levels it can offer to its consumers. Analogously, for the agent of a service consumer, it has to know the consumer's requirements on service levels for particular service providers, so that they can satisfy the consumer's overall requirements jointly. Hence, the coordinator utilises history information archived by the observer to retrieve necessary service level information.

Thirdly, the collaboration model influences the behaviour of the coordinator. In particular, the collaboration model specifies how the coordinator can allocate overall service level requirements to each particular service provider, e.g., in a strict manner with tough boundaries or in a lenient manner with tender boundaries.

With these inputs, the coordinator initiates negotiation threads separately with all related service providers to reach an agreement with each of them. In each negotiation thread, the management agent of a consumer negotiates with the agent of one of its providers. That is, each negotiation thread consists of a bilateral negotiation with respect to multiple QoS parameters. Thus, the coordinator is responsible to carry out these parallel negotiation threads and consolidate the resulted negotiation outcomes. In case that one or more negotiation threads fail to reach an agreement, the coordinator has to roll back eventual side effects of those negotiation threads. Among other things, the coordinator has to withdraw agreements that have been successfully negotiated.

It is worth noting that based on the central role of the coordinator in a management agent, it can also apply some other possible negotiation scheme. In particular, the coordinator can conduct a multilateral negotiation with all its services providers. In this case, it merges all parallel negotiation threads into a single negotiation thread. This negotiation scheme gives leeway to the coordinator to find optimal trade-offs considering all QoS parameters. However, in comparison to this negotiation scheme, the scheme applied in the present thesis with separated negotiation threads ensures maximal flexibility to maintain negotiated agreements. In particular, negotiated agreements can be enforced independently from one another. In case an existing agreement has to be renegotiated due to agreement violation, the affected agreement can be refreshed without having to renegotiating others.

Furthermore, the negotiation scheme with a single negotiation thread will be only beneficial, if all service providers involved in a negotiation thread are cooperative. That is, they are ready to donate part of their own utilities in favour of other service providers in the thread. For example, this assumption is only valid, if all service providers belong to the same organisation and follow a common operational goal. However, in a heterogeneous SOE, service components cannot be assumed as being cooperative in their collaborative behaviour.

Thirdly, a multilateral negotiation results in a single SLA for all service providers. In a heterogeneous SOE, it is common that service providers involved by a service component belong to different organisational units with different interests. In this case, a single SLA does not solve interest conflicts among service providers involved, in particular from the viewpoint of business-related QoS parameters. Among other things, it is not explicitly specified by a single SLA how revenues generated by all service providers are shared among them. Therefore, a single SLA is not specific enough to regulate all provider/consumer relationships of a single service component.

Therefore, in comparison to other negotiation schemes, the bilateral negotiation scheme with separated negotiation threads is mostly suitable for the coordinator.

Negotiator

Bilateral negotiation is carried out between negotiators of two corresponding management agents. To this end, the negotiator in a management agent applies a particular negotiation protocol that specifies a range of rules to regulate how it should behave in the course of negotiation. That is, a negotiation protocol determines how a negotiator sends an offer to its counterpart, what it should do with an incoming offer, and how it can commit to an agreed contract with its negotiation partner. The iterated negotiation protocol applied in the present thesis is described in detail in Section 6.5. By following the negotiation protocol, two management agents carry out a bilateral negotiation on service levels. The negotiation process leads to either an agreement specifying particular service levels for service delivery, or a cancelation of the entire negotiation thread if they cannot find a compromise within the given time limit.

In addition, all communication between two negotiators is carried out via a Web service-based interface, the *collaboration interface*. Hence, another responsibility of the negotiator is to implement and provide the necessary Web service interface based on existing interoperable Web service specifications. As such, two negotiators can unambiguously interact with each other in a flexible and loosely coupled manner.

Decision Maker

The *decision maker* is the brain of the *negotiator*. That is, for each incoming SLA offer, the decision maker determines how the negotiator should handle the offer. To this end, the decision maker is equipped with utility functions to estimate benefits of SLA offers for the respective management agent. In addition, it is aware of preferences of its corresponding negotiator on negotiation issues (i.e., QoS parameters with service level objectives). Hence, for each incoming offer, the decision maker can determine how far the offer is away from its expectations. By using such information, it can determine whether to accept an incoming offer or to propose a new counter offer to its counterpart.

The collaboration model controls how the decision maker perceives incoming offers. The collaboration model specifies a set of QoS parameters that are of importance to guarantee global business objectives. Hence, the decision maker correspondingly weights these QoS parameters in calculation of utilities. That is, the decision maker intends to preserve values of more weighted QoS parameters in the course of negotiation. By doing this, high-level business objectives are incorporated seamlessly into a negotiation process and into the resulting SLAs, too.

The other focus of the decision maker is to determine counter offers in the course of negotiation. In a bilateral negotiation between two management agents, it is not expected that these agents exchange their preferences on negotiation issues a priori. In a heterogeneous SOE, this requires an additional trust infrastructure that ensures that management agents are trustworthy and can trust each other. However, such a trust infrastructure is often missing in a real-world SOA-based system. In this case, the decision maker has to generate counter offers in absence of preference information of its negotiation partner. In order to reach an agreement, the decision maker has to perceive negotiation preferences of its counterpart and proposes offers that are as attractive as possible to its counterpart.

SLA Life Cycle Manager

If a service consumer can reach agreements successfully with each of its service providers, these resulting SLAs are going to be applied to the underlying service components. From this point in time, the service consumer and its provider(s) establish loosely coupled provider/consumer relationships governed the negotiated SLAs. Hence, the main task of the respective management agent changes from negotiating SLAs with related agents to maintaining the negotiated SLAs locally. During this process, the *SLA life cycle manager* establishes a transition between the global collaboration part and the local management part within the management agent. It forwards collaboration results in terms of SLAs to the underlying observer/controller instance for enforcement, and receives control actions from the observer/controller instance (e.g., to renegotiate a particular SLA), which in turn leads to further collaborative activities in the collaboration manager.

As the name says, the functionality of the SLA life cycle manager follows the life cycle of SLAs, as introduced in Section 3.2.4. Hence, the life cycle manager is responsible to negotiate, establish, enforce, and terminate SLAs along their complete life cycle.

The life cycle manager triggers negotiation processes that are carried out by the co-ordinator. SLAs resulting from negotiation processes are returned back to the life cy-cle manager. From this point in time, the life cycle manager continues maintaining life cycles of these negotiated SLAs. To this end, the life cycle manager hands over nego-tiated SLAs to the observer/controller instance to enforce them. This enforcement process is described in detail in Section 5.2.4 and Section 5.2.5.

The observer/controller instance has also a channel to back couple to the life cycle manager. Under certain circumstances, the controller can select and execute control actions via the SLA life cycle manager. For example, if a service provider is no longer able to satisfy a given SLA with its consumer, the respective controller can trigger the SLA life cycle manager to solve the problem by collaborating with other related com-ponents. A possible strategy in this case is to renegotiate the violated SLA with the affected consumer. Alternatively, the SLA life cycle manager can begin to renegotiate SLAs with the component's own providers and thus delegate the solution of its per-formance problems to them. Hence, in addition to local configuration possibilities provided by the service component, the channel back coupling to the SLA life cycle manger gives the observer/controller instance the possibility to enforce negotiated SLAs through collaboration on the global level.

Furthermore, the SLA life cycle manager exposes a set of collaboration interfaces based on Web services to related management agents. Via these interoperable collabo-ration interfaces, the SLA life cycle manager can interact with other related agents to maintain SLAs during their life cycles. For example, management agents can use the interfaces to annul existing SLAs or arrange their activities to terminate expired SLAs.

5.2.4 Observer

The observer is the part in the management agent that senses runtime behaviour of the underlying service component. To this end, the observer consists of several functional components:

- to collect management information from the underlying SuOC,
- to quantify it to composite metrics,

- and to use such metrics to analyse and predict runtime behaviour of the corresponding component.

Figure 5-7 illustrates the internal structure of the observer and its interactions with other components within a management agent.

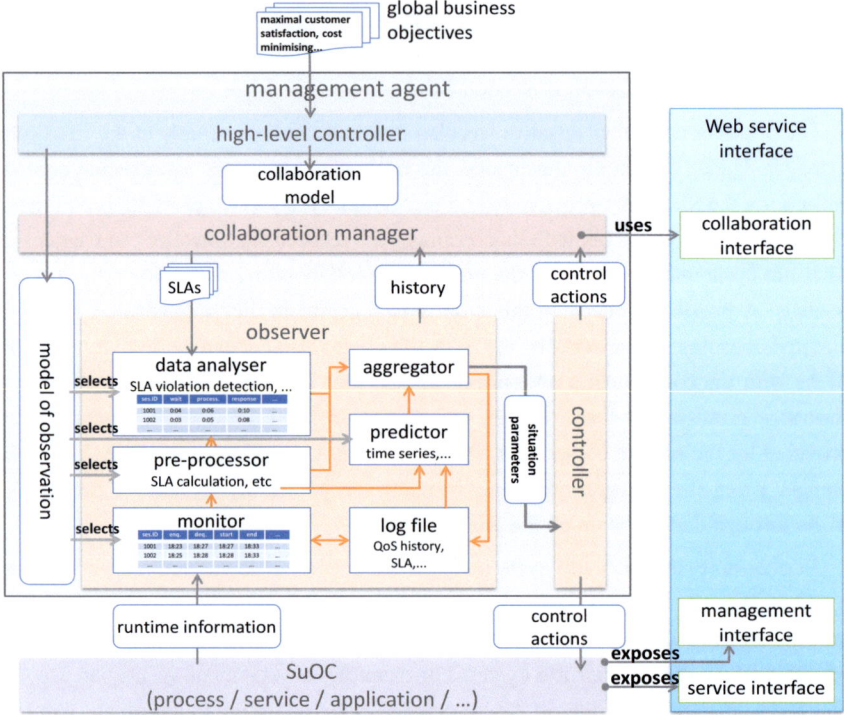

Figure 5-7: Structure of the observer in the management agent

The observer collects low-level metrics from the SuOC and consolidates them to high-level situation parameters step-by-step. The remainder of this section is concerned with the capabilities of internal components of the observer and outlines their interactions.

Model of Observation

The *model of observation* derived from global business objectives provides the observer with various ways how to monitor the underlying service component. Among other things, the model specifies a set of QoS parameters that are of particular interest for the observer/controller instance for enforcing negotiated SLAs. That is, the model restricts with its instructions the set of raw data that the observer collects from the underlying component. Considering that a service component exposes both relevant and irrelevant management information to management applications, this measure is of particular importance to increase efficiency of the observer/controller instance. Specifically, an observer/controller instance is expected to make real time decisions to control the underlying service component. Therefore, situation parameters delivered by the observer must be precise, compact, and clear. To this end, the observer uses the model of observation to limit the state space, which the controller has to exploit for decision-making, to a minimal size.

The model of observation interacts with several components in the observer to guide their operations. These components work with metrics on different abstraction levels, varying from raw management information like session information (e.g., start, end, session id, etc.) to high level composite metrics like service level attributes (e.g., mean response time of a service component). Therefore, the model of observation has to deal with models on different abstraction levels. In particular, the model of observation must be aware of relationships between these models, so that it can switch correctly and unambiguously between them. For example, to calculate response times of service invocations, the observer needs to know their start and end times. Hence, the model of observation must link low-level metrics, such as the start and the end of particular service invocations, to high-level metrics, such as response time.

In addition, the model of observation has to interpret QoS parameters derived from global business objectives correctly, in particular in the context of the underlying service component. For example, the term *response time* may be interpreted as time-to-complete for service invocations in Web services, or as network latency in network components for transferring data. Hence, the model of observation has to be aware of the context of the underlying SuOC, in order to know the correct meaning of the corresponding terms in the local context.

Therefore, the model of observation is equipped with an ontology globally standardised across the entire SOE. Alternatively, this requirement can be met by a global ontology service that delivers necessary models on request. By using a global ontology, the model of observation identifies all related QoS terms and their meanings in dependence of the context of the underlying service component. Moreover, the model of observation is aware of transitions between related QoS terms from different layers, as shown in Figure 5-8. The observer is responsible to build high-level situation parameters out of a range of basic metrics collected from the underlying SuOC. To this end, the model of observation delivers a set of transition directives to guide how low-level technical metrics can be consolidated systematically to service level metrics. Hence, a transition directive specifies a set of low-level metrics that are required to calculate a high-level metric and the necessary formulas to convert them.

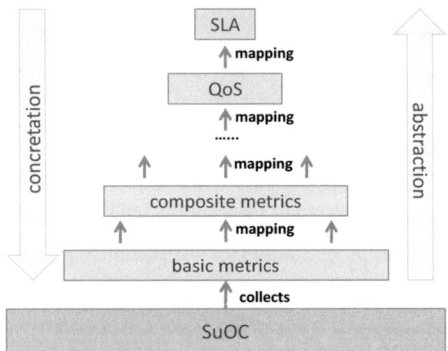

Figure 5-8: Hierarchy of metrics in the model of observation

For example, a transition directive can state that a service response time is calculated by estimating the difference between start and end of a corresponding service request. In this case, a transition directive determines relationships between the terms *response time*, *request start*, and *request end*. It states how the response time of a service request can be computed in relationship to the start and the end of the request.

On top of a global QoS ontology and the input from the high-level controller, the model of observation derives a set of sub-models for the functional components in the observer:

- *Monitor*: The model of observation specifies the scope of observation in terms of basic metrics and sampling frequencies of these metrics. It is noteworthy that these basic metrics are domain specific. They are selected from the ontology in dependence of the underlying SuOC. Furthermore, these metrics are still conceptual terms and have no reference to the concrete service component in the underlying SuOC. For example, the metric request start is used as an abstract term and is not correlated with a specific Web service or a business process.

- *Pre-processor*: The model of observation determines a set of mechanisms to pre-process collected basic metrics at runtime. In general, selection of these mechanisms is based on the specific characters of corresponding basic metrics. For example, the model of observation can guide the pre-processor to use a smoothing function (e.g., moving average) to remove noises from a given data set of response time. Furthermore, the model of observation delivers the pre-processor necessary models (i.e., transition directives) to calculate QoS parameters out of collected basic metrics. For each QoS parameter, the model of observation states the set of related basic metrics, and the functions to estimate QoS values based on these basic metrics.

- *Data analyser*: The model of observation provides the data analyser with necessary models to map QoS parameters to service levels and to evaluate them (e.g., for detecting SLA violations). It links composite QoS parameters to terms specified in an SLA on the service level. As such, the data analyser can use the provided guidance to evaluate calculated QoS values against service level objectives in the SLA for possible violations.

- *Predictor*: The model of observation also specifies the necessary mechanisms to predict runtime behaviour of the underlying service component in the next sampling period. These mechanisms are determined depending on the characteristics of the corresponding QoS parameters. For example, a time series analysis can be used to predict the development of response time due to its strongly time-dependent pattern (e.g., peak time during business hours and off-peak time in the evening).

Monitor

The monitor is one of the two interfaces in the observer/controller instance facing the underlying service component. From the model of observation, the monitor receives a range of abstract basic metrics that it has to fill with values collected from the service component at runtime. Moreover, the monitor has to interact with concrete service components (e.g., Web services, business applications, network routers, etc.) that provide heterogeneous manageability interfaces. The monitor is responsible to retrieve heterogeneous management information from underlying managed objects of the service component and map them to homogeneous basic metrics defined by the model of observation. To this end, the monitor utilises a range of additional adapters to collect management information and to convert them to the desired metrics as defined in the models.

Each of these adapters is designed depending on the manageability interfaces of the underlying service component. Therefore, it is aware of the set of managed objects that the instrumented service component exposes via its manageability interface, and the ways to retrieve information of these managed objects at runtime.

Typical examples of managed objects are CIM managed objects of technical components [DMTF99], e.g., *Win32_LogicalDisk* for a logical disk as a managed object in the operating system Windows. Another example can be the Web Service Resource Framework (WSRF) [OAS06] in combination with WSDM. In this case, managed objects are modelled as distributed resource objects that are accessible via Web services. It is noteworthy that modern technical components, both software-centric and hardware-centric, are delivered with standard-based and/or proprietary instrumentation interfaces. Such interfaces enable authorised external applications to get an insight into internal operational states of those components. For example, Windows Performance Counters provide a platform to create and retrieve performance-related information for a range of software products on the Windows platform [Mir10].

Hence, it is assumed in the present thesis that all service components in an SOE are instrumented with corresponding management standards. Via appropriate manageability interfaces, management agents can collect relevant management information from those service components at runtime. Then, the monitor converts collected raw data to desired basic metrics as specified by the model of observation. These unified metrics are then forwarded to the pre-processor for further processing and to the log file for archiving.

In addition to the scope of basic metrics, the model of observation also specifies sampling frequencies of those metrics. A sampling frequency defines how often the monitor should retrieve management information from the underlying service component. Sampling frequencies are determined with respect to the characteristics of the SuOC and the management agent. In general, the monitor can adopt the following interaction patterns:

- *Pull*: In this interaction pattern, a management agent plays an active role in the communication. It determines time schedules to get management information from the SuOC at runtime, mostly at regular intervals. The pull pattern is easy to implement, provides however a less efficient way for the management agent to monitor the SuOC. In particular, pulling regularly runtime information from the SuOC causes unnecessary processing efforts for a management agent, even if there are no changes in the operational state of the SuOC.

- *Push*: The push pattern is also known as the "publish/subscribe" pattern. In this pattern, the SuOC publishes a range of management information that is normally organised according to some given criteria, such as contents, topics, or categories. A management agent can select a set of management information that is of interest to it. In contrast to the pull pattern, the management agent only get related information pushed by the SuOC, if there are any updates in the corresponding managed objects. Hence, this pattern allows management agents monitoring relevant information that is of real interest to them efficiently, and thus reducing the overhead to process unnecessary requests. In addition, the push pattern establishes a loosely coupled relationship between the SuOC and its management agent that makes operation of a management agent independent from the underlying SuOC. The management agent can continue operating in the management overlay, even if the underlying SuOC is temporarily offline, and vice versa.

- *Polling*: The polling pattern is an improved version of the pull pattern. In contrast to the pull pattern, a management agent does not regularly query the SuOC for management information. Instead, it polls regularly on the remote SuOC for changes. A management agent only starts reading management information from the SuOC, if there have been any changes in the operational state of the SuOC in the past sampling interval. Hence, the polling pattern increases the efficiency of a management agent to process monitored information.

To summarise, the monitor collects heterogeneous management information from the underlying service component and converts them to homogeneous basic metrics as specified by the model of observation. From this viewpoint, the monitor acts as a kind of adapter that connects homogeneous management agents with heterogeneous service components.

Log File

The log file is responsible to archive all basic and composite metrics (e.g., session information, QoS history, and so on) measured and processed by the observer for later use. In particular, archived measurements are used to support activities of the management agent, whose functionalities rely on such history information of the past.

In the generic observer/controller architecture, the log file serves as the database for the predictor. For a given metric, it can deliver the history of different time windows. Such historical information is of particular interest for the predictor, which applies e.g. time-series analysis to forecast the development of a given metric in the future.

Moreover, as mentioned previously, the log file also delivers historical information to the collaboration manager to support its activities. The coordinator in the collaboration manager utilises historical service level information to estimate capabilities of the underlying service component. Furthermore, history information about particular service types gives the coordinator the necessary decision support to allocate appropriate non-functional requirements to corresponding service providers.

Pre-Processor

The pre-processor is responsible to convert and consolidate basic resource-centric metrics collected by the monitor into appropriate more abstracted data types that the data analyser can use. To this end, the pre-processor leverages two types of tools to compute composite metrics: *data smoothing* and *data consolidation*.

Measurement data collected by the monitor from the SuOC is subject to continuous influences of the environment on the corresponding service component. Hence, such measurement data may contain noise that prevents the observer from getting an accurate overview of the operational state of the SuOC. To this end, the pre-processor utilises different algorithms to smooth incoming data sets that the monitor collects from the underlying SuOC during a pre-defined sampling period. Algorithms used to smooth data sets depend on the type of management data they contain.

For example, to calculate completion time of service invocations, a management agent generally estimates time differences between the start and the end of service invocations. However, in case of service timeout, the end of an affected service invocation can be the point in time, at which the service component recognises the service timeout. Hence, time differences calculated in this case can be multiples of regular service completion time. This leads to a noisy peak in the data set that falsifies calculation of mean service completion time. Hence, the pre-processor can use a moving average to smooth a given data set of service completion time. It calculates the unweighted mean of all completion times within a fixed time window.

The other task of the pre-processor is to consolidate smoothed measurement data to composite metrics towards service level QoS parameters. To this end, the pre-processor utilises guidance provided by the model of observation to compute composite QoS metrics based on basic metrics. As stated before, such guidance specifies the set of basic metrics involved, and the functions used to calculate composite metrics.

For a given set of measurement data concerning service invocation details (e.g., start time t_{start}, end time t_{end}, session id, etc.), the guidance specifies that mean response time of a service provider is the average of all smoothed response times that are calculated by computing time differences between t_{start} and t_{end}. Another example can be that the rate of successful service invocations is the quotient of the number of successful service invocations among the total number of service invocations.

To conclude, the pre-processor is the part of a management agent that is responsible for data consolidation. The major focus of the pre-processor is to calculate composite metrics in terms of QoS parameters based on basic metrics collected from the underlying SuOC. Necessary directives to build composite metrics are provided by the model of observation on top of a global QoS ontology. In addition, the pre-processor uses data smoothing algorithms to improve the quality of the consolidated data.

Data Analyser

The data analyser is concerned with validating the runtime operational state of the underlying SuOC against service level targets defined in an SLA to detect SLA violation. To this end, the data analyser gets composite metrics in terms of QoS parameters from the pre-processor and the negotiated SLAs from the collaboration manager as input. In addition, the model of observation delivers models for the data analyser to associate composite metrics and service level targets in an SLA. Furthermore, the model of observation specifies priorities of particular service level targets to detect SLA violation. Based on these inputs, the data analyser has to determine whether some negotiated service level target(s) were violated in the previous sampling period.

To detect potential SLA violations, the data analyser compares calculated QoS values with service level targets defined in an SLA. Given a set of QoS parameters $\{1, 2, ..., n\}$, let q_i be the value of the parameter i calculated by the pre-processor. Furthermore, let q_i^t be its arranged service level target for the corresponding QoS parameter, then the *degree of fulfilment* f_i of a single service level target i is defined as:

$$f_i = \begin{cases} q_i/q_i^t & \text{if the QoS parameter i is increasing} \\ q_i^t/q_i & \text{if the QoS parameter i is decreasing} \end{cases}$$

Herein, a QoS parameter is increasing, if a higher value of the parameter is desired, such as availability or throughput for a consumer. Vice versa, a QoS parameter is decreasing, if a lower value is desired, such as response time for a consumer. It is obvious that a service level target i is met by a given operational state, if its degree of fulfilment is greater than or equal to 1 (i.e., $f_i \geq 1$). Analogously, a given service level target is not met, if the degree of fulfilment is less than 1. Based on f_i, the *overall degree of fulfilment* f of an SLA is defined as follows:

$$f = \sum_{i=1}^{n} \omega_i \cdot (f_i)^r$$

$$(3.3.7)$$

ω_i determines the relative *weight* of the parameter i in the calculation of the overall degree of fulfilment, with $\sum_{i=1}^{n} \omega_i = 1$. The parameter r is the *strictness factor* of the calculation of the overall degree of fulfilment that is defined as follows:

$$r = \begin{cases} 0 & \text{if the calculation is strict and } f_i \geq 1 \\ 1 & \text{if the calculation is strict and } f_i < 1 \\ 1 & \text{if the calculation is lenient} \end{cases}$$

Therefore, a strict calculation can detect an SLA violation, as soon as one or more service levels falls short of their targets. This can be easily proven with the help of the formula (3.3.7). Without loss of generality, it is assumed that a single service level target $k \in \{1, 2, ...n\}$ is not met (i.e., all other service level targets are met), then the overall degree of fulfilment is less than 1:

$$f = \sum_{i=1}^{n} \omega_i \cdot (f_i)^r = \sum_{i=1}^{k-1} \omega_i \cdot (f_i)^r + \omega_k \cdot (f_k)^r + \sum_{j=k+1}^{n} \omega_j \cdot (f_j)^r$$

$$= \sum_{i=1}^{k-1} \omega_i \cdot (f_i)^0 + \omega_k \cdot (f_k)^1 + \sum_{j=k+1}^{n} \omega_j \cdot (f_j)^0$$

$$= \sum_{i=1}^{k-1} \omega_i + \omega_k \cdot (f_k) + \sum_{j=k+1}^{n} \omega_j$$

$$< \sum_{i=1}^{k-1} \omega_i + \omega_k \cdot 1 + \sum_{j=k+1}^{n} \omega_j$$

$$= \sum_{i=1}^{n} \omega_i$$

$$= 1$$

With a strict strategy, a negotiated SLA is considered as not met, as soon as a single service level target is violated by a given operational state. In contrast, in case of a lenient strategy, the calculated overall degree of fulfilment may not immediately be less than 1, if one of the arranged service level targets is not met. In particular if that violated target is weakly weighted in the calculation, it has less impact on the overall calculation. In addition, non-fulfilment of a service level target can be compensated by other service level targets, which are (over-)fulfilled by a given operational state.

Thus, with different calculation strategies, the data analyser can flexibly determine whether an arranged SLA is considered as not met by a given operational state of the SuOC. In particular, the weights assigned to the QoS parameters allow the analyser to incorporate priorities of particular QoS parameters derived from global business objectives into estimation of the overall degree of fulfilment. This ensures that results of analysis done by the data analyser comply permanently with the global objectives.

Predictor

The predictor provides a management agent with insight into the future development of the underlying service component, in particular from the viewpoint of non-functional QoS parameters. Together with the metrics processed by the pre-processor and the data analyser, predicted future system states serve as the base for the controller to make decisions. Hence, an accurately and precisely predicted future system state is crucial for the controller to choose foresighted control actions for the underlying service component. This helps to increase the probability of the controller to prevent occurrence of non-desired system states and reduces SLA violations proactively.

The predictor can utilise a set of mathematical and statistical models to give both qualitative and quantitative estimation of future system state. As initial input, the predictor gets instructions from the model of observation specifying a set of QoS parameters and appropriate prediction algorithm(s) to predict them. It is obvious that a prediction algorithm used for a given QoS parameter depends strongly on the characteristics of the parameter. While development of system loads of a CRM system has a strongly time-related pattern (e.g., peak time during business hours, and off-peak time in the evening), development of availability of a system is not directly related with the time. Hence, to predict future development of system loads, the predictor has to use a multi-dimensional quantitative prediction algorithm that takes the parameter time into its prediction model. In contrast, to predict availability of a system, the predictor may need a simulated system model. By using the simulation model, the predictor can estimate dependences between various systems components and their impact on the overall system availability.

Additionally, the predictor builds its prediction process on top of historical data. As mentioned before, the log file acts as the data archive in a management agent and stores historical basic/composite data. Such history information is provided to the predictor as time series. Depending on the time horizon of the corresponding prediction algorithm (e.g., short, middle, or long term), time series consisting of historical data reflect behaviour of the corresponding data (or QoS parameters) during the specified time horizon in the past.

In brief, the predictor is responsible to estimate future development of the system state based on known history data. By analysing given time series using mathematical or statistical models, the predictor is expected to address development trends of the system state in the forthcoming sampling period(s), either in a qualitative or quantitative manner.

Aggregator

As the name says, the aggregator has the task to aggregate all analysis results from the observer to unified situation parameters. Situation parameters contain the current system fingerprint of the SuOC consisting of information that the controller needs to make decisions. To this end, the aggregator consumes analysis results from the pre-processor, the data analyser, and the predictor. Hence, for each QoS parameter specified in an SLA, the aggregator creates a separate data vector. A data vector consists of the current values calculated by the pre-processor, the degree of fulfilment computed by the data analyser, and the predicted values estimated by the predictor. Hence, the resulting situation parameters are composed of a set of data vectors, where each data vector contains information of a corresponding QoS parameter. In addition, the situation parameters contain the overall degree of fulfilment of the SLA.

By using the situation parameters, the controller is aware of the current state of the SuOC. In particular, it can determine whether the arranged SLA was violated by the underlying service component in the previous sampling period. This information helps the controller to concentrate on a very limited set of facts for making decisions.

5.2.5 Controller

Upon receiving situation parameters, the controller exploits a set of control actions it can execute. It triggers some appropriate control actions matching the observed operational state of the underlying service component. Control actions executed are expected to influence runtime behaviour of the underlying service component in compliance with arranged service levels of the collaboration manager. By selecting and performing appropriate control actions on the service component, the controller ensures enforcement of the agreed service level targets in the SLAs proactively.

To this end, the controller must be able to correlate states in the state space accurately with appropriate actions in the action space. The state space is spanned by states exposed by the service component via its manageability interface. Similarly, the action space is spanned by control actions that the service component makes available for external management applications. It is noteworthy that dimensions of the state space and the action space depend on the set of QoS parameters that the model of observation derived from the global business objectives. To this end, the model of observation considers the global business objectives and SLAs negotiated by the collaboration manager. This helps the observer to limit the state space to a minimal set, which the controller has to explore for making decisions.

Correlations between states and actions imply an understanding of the underlying service component by its corresponding management agent. For each situation parameter reported by the observer, the controller can consult its local rule base consisting of such correlations to choose an appropriate action. Hence, in order to control the underlying service component in compliance with given SLAs, the controller has to find a way to correlate system states and actions.

As depicted in Figure 5-9, the controller leverages a two-level structure to build up its rule base consisting of correlations between states and actions. Level 1 attempts to provide a response to reported situation parameters in real-time. Hence, it contains a mapping component that maps situation parameters to available control actions and a *rule performance evaluation* to assess the performance of executed control actions. However, for mission-critical service components, it is not desired that the controller performs any control action on those components that may decrease their service levels or even lead to damages in the system due to limited or inaccurate knowledge. Hence, the mapping rules must meet a certain level of quality, before they are applied to the real system. It is the task of level 2 to generate such accurate mapping rules. It employs a rule adaptation module in combination with an offline simulation model of the SuOC to explore unknown areas in the state space.

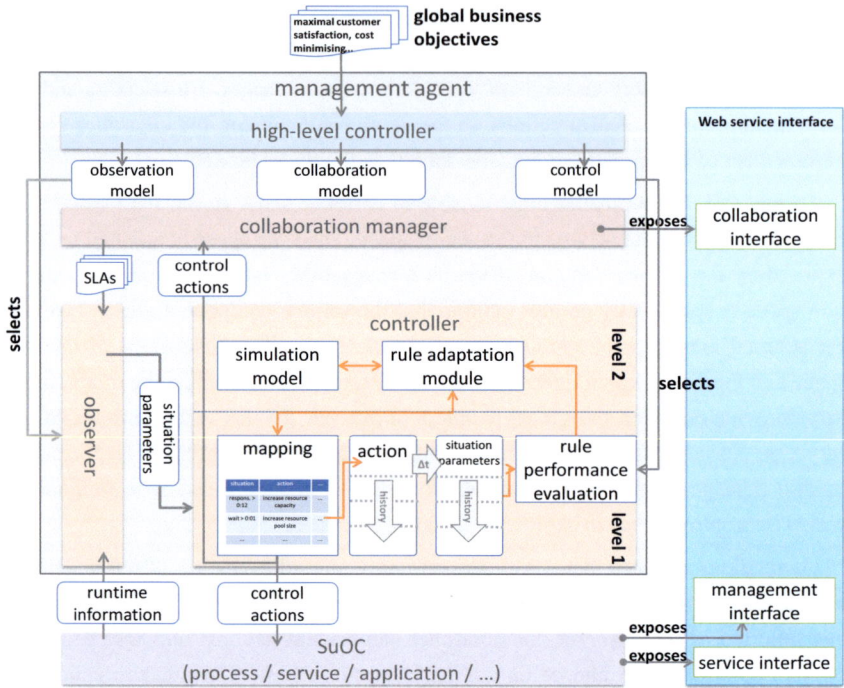

Figure 5-9: Structure of the controller in the management agent

The remainder of this section focuses on the two-level structure of the controller. Among other things, it outlines generally the set of control actions that the controller can execute to enforce SLAs with respect to global business objectives. In addition, level 1 and level 2 are introduced in detail to show how a management agent can build up its rule base to control the underlying service component.

Control Actions

Via control actions, the controller of a management agent can influence the runtime behaviour of the underlying service component and/or other related service components to enforce arranged SLAs. Generally, a management agent can employ two categories of control actions for this purpose, namely *local* actions and *collaboration-based* actions.

Obviously, a management agent can leverage the manageability interface of the underlying service component to modify its behaviour towards desired service level targets. By doing this, a management agent changes configurations of the service component directly to manipulate its behaviour. Specific types of control actions that the manageability interface provides depend on implementation details of the corresponding service instance. For example, in order to modify responsiveness of a service instance, a Web server can change processing priorities or queuing strategies of incoming requests for the corresponding service instance. Hence, local control actions enable a management agent to change operational states of the underlying service component by modifying its local resources and technical capabilities.

Local control actions have often limited capabilities to change runtime behaviour of a service component. In particular, if a service component has to share limited technical resources among a set of service instances, its management agent may run out of possibilities to influence runtime behaviour of particular service instance locally. As discussed in Section 4.1, runtime behaviour of a service component depends not only on itself, but also on behaviour of its service providers. Therefore, it is possible that a management agent manipulates the runtime behaviour of its service component by influencing runtime behaviour of its service providers. By doing this, a management agent can reach its local goal by collaborating with other related management agents.

A critical aspect that must be kept in mind is autonomy of service components, as discussed in Section 2.1.1. Service autonomy determines that a management agent cannot send directives to other related service components and expects that they are willing to follow those directives. Instead, a management agent has to build desired collaborative activities based on negotiation that respects the autonomy of other related components. In order to change runtime behaviour of the underlying service components, the corresponding management agent has to renegotiates with its service providers with updated negotiation conditions. These updated negotiation conditions reflect the most recent demands of the service component. If a management agent can reach new SLAs with the updated conditions, it succeeds in influencing behaviour of its own service component by changing that behaviour of its service providers. From this viewpoint, several service components work collaboratively to realise desired runtime behaviour of a single service component. Otherwise, a management agent is forced to violate the contract with its service consumer and to renegotiate a new SLA containing less restricted service level targets.

It is worth noting that although both local actions and collaboration-based actions can influence runtime behaviour of the underlying service component, they are however not equivalent regarding their efficiency. Due to the direct management relationship between a management agent and its service component, local control actions achieve quick and precise changes in the runtime behaviour of the component. Such changes take place normally almost in real-time and, therefore, are mostly desired for mission-critical service components. In contrast, collaboration-based control actions involve a range of additional service components in the renegotiation process, where a successful outcome with renegotiated SLAs is not guaranteed. Furthermore, the time needed for renegotiating SLAs and applying renegotiated SLAs causes undesirable delays and overheads that are crucial for mission-critical service components. Hence, collaboration-based control actions are less efficient in comparison to local actions.

Hence, the controller has to incorporate this difference into its decision-making process. In order to achieve quick and precise changes in the service component, the controller prefers to exhaust at first local possibilities that the underlying service component directly provides, before it begins to collaborate with other related components via negotiation. This ensures that a management agent can enforce SLAs with its service consumer as quick as possible.

Level 1

Level 1 is the part in a management agent that responds quickly to situations in the service component. The controller makes decisions based on its existing rule base consisting of accurate correlations between system states and possible control actions. To build up as well as evolve correlations in the knowledge base, the construction of level 1 follows the concept of reinforcement learning.

As depicted in Figure 5-9, correlations between system states and control actions are stored in a *mapping table*. Each rule in the table maps a possible system state of the service component to one or more executable actions. For example, a service instance violates the predefined service level target for response time and there are free processing capacities that can be assigned to the service instance. In this case, an appropriate control action may be to increase the processing capacity of the respective service instance.

Furthermore, to reflect accuracies of correlation rules, each rule is assigned with a fitness value that is estimated based on a management agent's experience so far with the service component.

For an incoming situation parameter, level 1 consults the mapping table to select the best-assessed rule matching the situation parameter, and forwards the selected action to either the SuOC or the collaboration manager. The simple construction of the mapping table ensures that a management agent can respond quickly to situations in the SuOC.

For each executed control action selected by level 1, the controller has to estimate the quality of the rule. Hence, it evaluates the resulting effects in the underlying SuOC and updates fitness value of the corresponding correlation rule with the help of evaluation results. To this end, level 1 keeps track of control actions executed at time t and situation parameters reported by the observer at time $t + \Delta t$ in its history data. These pairs of control actions and resulting situation parameters are evaluated to update accuracies of corresponding correlation rules. The rule performance evaluation module carries out all these activities to estimate correctness of correlation rules against capabilities of corresponding control actions to enforce negotiated SLAs.

In addition, other optimisation aspects can be incorporated into the evaluation process of the rule performance evaluation module. For example, in order to avoid over- or under-utilisation of local resources, the evaluation process can estimate the utilisation rate of local technical resources against the overall degree of fulfilment of the SLA. Evaluation results can be used to update fitness values of corresponding correlation rules. In this way, a management agent can fine tune the correlation rules to ensure that the underlying service component leverages its local resources efficiently and sparingly.

Level 2

As discussed in the previous section, level 1 builds its decision-making process on top of a set of existing correlation rules. Hence, the control loop in level 1 is concerned with exploiting performance of these existing correlation rules. Exploring new correlation rules for the mapping table is however not done by level 1. This design consideration is made because newly generated correlation rules (e.g., by using genetic operators) do not satisfy the necessary level of quality to control the underlying service component directly. Such generated rules may even contain wrong directives that may lead to serious damages on the SuOC.

Therefore, in order to ensure certain quality level for the correlation rules in level 1 while keeping these rules up-to-date with the ever-changing environment (i.e., with respect to unknown situations in the environment), the controller employs an additional level, level 2, to generate new rules for these unknown situations with certain quality level.

Level 2 has the responsibility to explore the state space for previously unknown correlations between situations and actions. To this end, level 2 applies methods from machine learning and performs offline learning against an abstracted model of the real SuOC. As depicted in Figure 5-9, based on existing correlation rules, the *rule adaption* module uses genetic operators (such as crossover and mutation [Mit97]) to generate new correlation rules.

Applying newly generated correlation rules directly to real-time systems is critical for runtime operation of the underlying service component. Hence, level 2 employs an addition module, the *simulation* model, to evaluate these rules in an offline manner. The simulation model, as the one introduced later in Section 7.2, allows simulating possible outcomes of new correlation rules, before they are applied directly to real systems. By doing this, wrong correlation rules that may lead to damages in the underlying service component are proactively removed from the rule set. This ensures that correlation rules already reach some desired quality level, before they are added to the mapping table of level 1 for application.

In this way, level 2 ensures the quality of the correlation rules in the rule base. Together with level 1, they provide a learning-based control mechanism to enforce the runtime behaviour of the underlying SuOC.

5.2.6 Design Rationale

This section introduces the architecture of a management agent. The main objectives of designing a management agent are:

- first collaborative activities on the global level to arrange service levels for service consumption,
- and secondly controlled self-organisation of the underlying service component in compliance with arranged contracts on service levels.

Hence, the design of a management agent utilises a clear separation of concerns to address those design objectives. The high-level controller and the observer/controller instance establish controlled self-organisation in the local context of a service component. The high-level controller along with the collaboration manager facilitates coordination and collaboration of the respective management agent with related agents in the environment. This separation of concerns enables a clear design of a management agent and increases modality of its subcomponents.

With respect to the requirement analysis in Section 4.3, the design of a management agent addresses the requirements as follows:

- By using manageability interfaces exposed by a service component, a management agent (i.e., the observer of the agent) can actively monitor the operational state of the underlying service component (i.e., the SuOC). With appropriate models to link monitored information to service level objectives, a management agent can draw conclusions on runtime behaviour of its service component on the service level.

- With continuous observation and control of a service component by the observer/controller instance, a management agent can affect runtime behaviour of the service component proactively to enforce negotiated service level targets. Hence, managing the underlying service component is driven by SLAs that a management agent closes with its providers/consumers.

- The interface to an external high-level control instance (i.e., human participants) allows influencing the behaviour of a management agent with external business objectives. The high-level controller derives corresponding control models out from these external objectives and applies them to the functional components of a management agent. By doing this, a management agent can align its behaviour to global business objectives in the environment.

- The collaboration manager allows a management agent to explore its environment and to establish as well as maintain relationships with related service components in the environment. Via the collaboration manager, management agents of related service components are aware of existence of one another and can interact with one another in a coordinated manner.

- Collaboration between management agents is carried out by using automated negotiation. Outcomes of such negotiation activities are SLAs that regulate obligations and expectations of these agents in the course of service consumption. In particular, these contracts specify the desired behaviour of the related service components on service level. Hence, these contracts are used by a management agent, i.e., the observer/controller instance, as operational objectives to control the underlying service component.

- The collaboration manager exposes their local capabilities, i.e., for automated negotiation and management of SLA life cycle, via a set of interfaces based on Web service. Interoperable standards used in the Web service-based interfaces ensure that management agents can interact with one another, in spite of heterogeneity of their underlying service components.

In a word, the architecture of a management agent, based on the generic observer/controller architecture, establishes controlled self-organisation in alignment with given business objectives. In addition to the observer/controller architecture, a management agent focuses particularly on the collaboration aspect of a service component with its providers/consumers. The interdependent nature of service components determines that all related components have to collaborate with one another in a coordinated manner, so that they can jointly contribute to desired global behaviour of the entire environment. The collaboration manager in a management agent addresses this aspect by providing the necessary capabilities to cover the complete life cycle of service levels, in particular for automated negotiation of SLAs.

5.3 Summary

Managing service levels of service components within an SOE is challenging. Heterogeneity of service components and inherent complexity of such management tasks prevent an establishment of comprehensive approaches for service level management. In particular, human participants are heavily involved in this process. Hence, in order to cope with the complexity and to increase agility of such an SOE in spite of continuous changes, the present thesis proposes the approach to solve the problem using controlled self-organisation. The core of the approach is the concept of collaborative and self-organising management agents. This chapter has introduced the architecture of a management agent and has explained how management agents can work together to enable automated service level management in service-centric environments.

The agent-oriented design of the management overlay allows service components to maintain their autonomy while still having the possibility to collaborate with other related components to coordinate their activities. Furthermore, the service-oriented structure of the management overlay complies with scalability and dynamism of the underlying service-oriented layer. Within the management overlay, each management agent collaborates with other related management agents to arrange service level objectives via automated negotiation. As soon as SLAs are established, a management agent utilises the observer/controller instance to enforce these SLAs. This self-organising enforcement process is guided by external business objectives, thus the behaviour of the entire overlay remains controllable for human participants.

Chapter 6   Collaboration between Agents

"知己知彼，百战不殆。"

—【孙子兵法，孙子】

"Precise knowledge of oneself and of the counterpart leads to victory."

(The Art of War, Sun Tzu, ca. 544-496 B.C.)

Collaboration between related service components builds the foundation of the self-organising end-to-end SLM approach of the present thesis. The distributed and recursive nature of an SOE requires tight cooperation between all related service components, in order to conjointly realise the overall operational goals of the entire environment. In Chapter 5, the structure of an organic SOE with an agent-oriented design has been introduced, and SLA-centric collaboration between management agents in such an organic environment was outlined. In the following, the present chapter is concerned with details of collaborative interactions between management agents and explains how end-to-end SLM can be supported by collaboration in an organic SOE.

In particular, this chapter focuses on automated negotiation of SLAs between a service consumer and its providers, which is crucial for establishing service relationships dynamically and adaptively in an organic SOE. As introduced in Section 3.2, SLAs are formal contracts governing provider/consumer relationships in an SOE. From this viewpoint, SLAs protect interests of all contract parties by means of ensuring mutually agreed service-level objectives. Hence, efficient negotiation of SLAs is essential for organising a dynamic and loosely coupled SOE.

Therefore, this chapter is structured as follows: after a brief overview in Section 6.1, Section 6.2 addresses the target negotiation scenarios of the present thesis in detail. Section 6.3 analyses those negotiation scenarios and determines the type of automated negotiation that can be applied to enable end-to-end SLM in an SOE. Section 6.4 outlines the underlying mathematical model based on the bilateral negotiation model introduced in Section 3.3.1, while Section 6.5 is concerned with the negotiation protocol to facilitate bilateral negotiation between management agents. In particular, the characteristic recursive constructs of an SOE, where a service component can simultaneously act as a service consumer and a service provider, demand an appropriate negotiation protocol other than those that are common. Section 6.6 describes negotiation strategies of management agents to find optimised SLA offers in the course of negotiation. In particular, this section addresses how to fine-tune negotiation strategies so that resulting agreements between a consumer and its providers can contribute to overall business objectives. At last, Section 6.8 summarises the chapter.

6.1 Collaboration Overview

The distributed nature of SOEs requires that autonomous service components have to collaborate with one another to reach common goals. Collaboration between service components may be carried out in a varying way. Since the focus of the present thesis is to automate end-to-end SLM in an SOE, this chapter is concerned with collaborative activities between service components to facilitate the life cycle of SLAs as introduced in Section 3.2.4, such as arranging new service level targets, establishing negotiated agreements, or terminating expired agreements. Hence, this section is organised following the life cycle of SLAs, and outlines the underlying collaborative activities involved throughout its different phases.

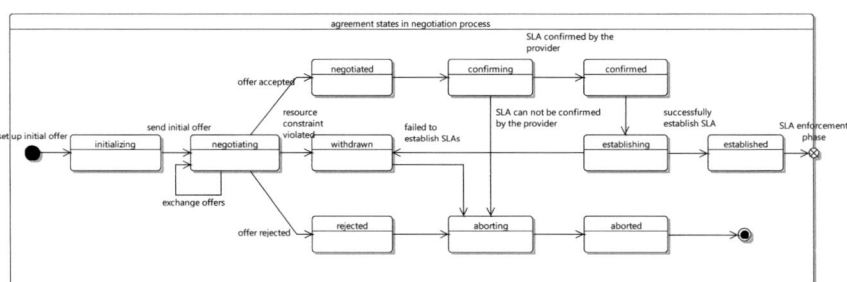

Figure 6-1: Collaboration to negotiate and establish new SLAs

Before a service component, i.e., the management agent of the component, can actively enforce an SLA, this SLA has to be arranged with its related service components. During this procedure, related service components negotiate with one another to regulate their expectations and obligations with respect to service level objectives. Figure 6-1 depicts such a negotiation process as a state diagram from the viewpoint of the life cycle of a single agreement and specifies all possible states of an agreement in the course of negotiation.

A negotiation process is triggered by an initial offer sent by a service consumer to a respective service provider. From this point in time, the two management agents are related and enter into a collaboration phase, until one management agent decides to exit it. In the following alternating negotiation process, the *negotiating* state remains unchanged while alternating offers are exchanged. If one negotiation participant aborts the negotiation thread due to some resource constraints, such as limited negotiation time, the state of the agreement is changed from *negotiating* to *withdrawn*. Similarly, if a management agent rejects an incoming offer depending on its negotiation constraint (e.g. the predefined negotiation deadline), the state of the agreement is changed from *negotiating* to *rejected*, too. In both cases, the management agents are about to abort the corresponding negotiation thread by updating the state of the agreement to *aborting*. This allows affected negotiation participants to perform clean-up tasks to close the corresponding thread, such as freeing local computational resources used in the negotiation. Afterwards, the agreement's state is changed to *aborted* and the complete negotiation process is terminated.

Alternatively, if a negotiation participant accepts an incoming agreement from its counterpart, it changes the agreement's state from *negotiating* to *negotiated*. In the following steps, the service provider in the negotiation starts to confirm the negotiated agreement on its part with its providers (cf. Section 6.5 for more information on this procedure). If the service provider can successfully arrange in turn agreements with its providers to support the negotiated agreement, it changes the agreement's state to *confirmed* and the negotiation process is closed. Otherwise, it aborts the negotiation thread by changing the agreement's state to *aborting*, which leads to a termination of the complete negotiation process.

As soon as an SLA is negotiated between two management agents, they begin to establish it in their local environments. This process is composed of activities to configure local resources in alignment with service level targets specified in the SLA. Hence, this process is only carried out in the local context of the respective service components. No interactions are expected between the related management agents in the course of this phase. If one of both agents runs into trouble when it tries to allocate necessary resources to enforce the SLA, it can communicate with its counterpart to withdraw the negotiated SLA. Otherwise, the corresponding SLA is marked as *Established* and both management agents pass into the SLA enforcement phase.

Figure 6-2 illustrates the activities involved in the *enforcement* and *termination* phases. In fact, the observer/controller instance of a management agent plays a major role during both phases. As discussed in Section 5.2.4 and 5.2.5, by continuous monitoring and control of the underlying service component, the observer/controller instance ensures that runtime behaviour of a service component complies with its negotiated SLA.

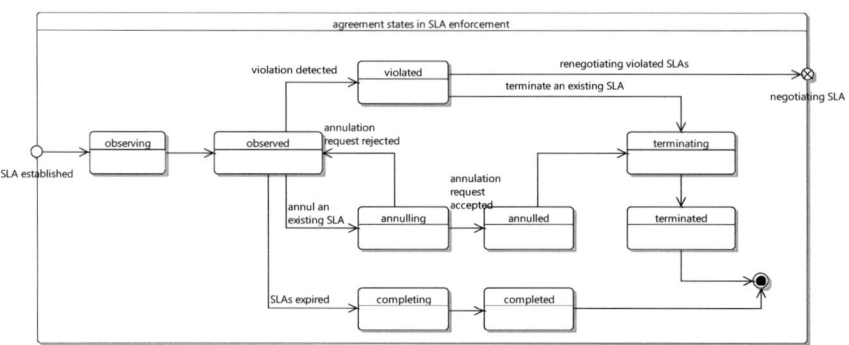

Figure 6-2: Collaboration to enforce and terminate existing SLAs

The *enforcement* phase follows the previous negotiation phase. At the beginning of the enforcement phase, the negotiated SLA has been established in the underlying service component. Hence, the observer/controller instance has to be configured to observe the service component. During this phase, the state of the established SLA is changed to *observing*. As soon as the observer/controller instance is ready to actively monitor and control the service component, the SLA's state is updated to *observed*. This indicates that the respective SLA is actively enforced by the management agent from this point in time.

If, in the course of SLA enforcement, a management agent observes an inevitable violation in spite of its local control activities, it marks the state of the respective SLA as *violated*. In this case, the management agent has to collaborate with the agent of the service provider/consumer at the other end of the affected SLA to solve this problem. To this end, it can either renegotiate the affected SLA with its counterpart, or arrange with its counterpart to terminate the SLA. An early termination of a violated SLA requires affirmations of both management agents. As soon as the counterpart confirms early termination of the affected SLA, both management agents mark its state as *terminated* and break off the provider/consumer relationship between them.

However, a management agent can also terminate an SLA ahead of the arranged expiration deadline, even if the corresponding SLA is not violated by either the provider or the consumer. For example, if a service provider anticipates an inevitable SLA violation (e.g., limited availability of technical resources during planed power outage of the infrastructure), it can collaborate with its service consumers to proactively prevent damages in the environment. To this end, a management agent can arrange with its counterpart to annul an established SLA. If both parties agree to the suggested annulation, the affected SLA is marked as *annulled* and both parties begin to terminate the corresponding partnership. Otherwise, if the annulation request is not accepted by the other party, the affected SLA remains untouched. In this case, the SLA is further monitored and enforced actively by both parties.

As soon as the expiration deadline specified in an established SLA has been exceeded, both negotiation parties begin to compete the SLA. To this end, a management agent frees resources reserved for the corresponding service instance. After that, the corresponding SLA is marked as *completed* and both service components end their provider/consumer relationship.

So far, this section has introduced a set of collaborative activities between a service provider and its service consumer to set up, establish, enforce, and terminate SLAs. Apart from the local activities performed by a management agent to establish and enforce SLAs, most of the collaborative activities between management agents are concerned with set-up of SLAs. That is, how a service provider can align its service capabilities to service expectations of a service consumer, in particular in terms of service level objectives.

In such a process, both service provider and service consumer have their predefined preferences on a set of service level objectives. Hence, the focus of the process is to find a mutually acceptable compromise while taking preferences of both parties into consideration. Therefore, the remainder of this chapter focuses on automated negotiation of SLAs between service providers and service consumers (as indicated by the negotiating state in Figure 6-1) and outlines how such a negotiation process can be carried out reliably and efficiently. Section 6.2 outlines the essential negotiation scenarios considered in the present thesis and addresses their characteristic differences that distinguish them from other similar scenarios in the field.

6.2 Negotiation Scenarios

This section addresses the major negotiation scenarios between a service consumer and its service providers in a self-organising SOE. For simplicity, it is assumed that all service components can communicate with one another via Web service interfaces, as discussed in Section 5.1. Further aspects within Web service communication, such as security, transactional behaviour, and reliability, are not considered in the scope of this section. These aspects are easily covered by utilising corresponding Web service standards in the communication channel. For example, WS-Security [NKMH06] can be adopted to secure communication channels between service components, and WS-Coordination [FJ09] can be applied to coordinate the behaviour of several related components.

Furthermore, it is assumed that each service component knows its potential providers (i.e., negotiation partners). This assumption can be fulfilled by using appropriate service discovery approaches with given syntactical, semantic, or QoS-based criteria. For example, Ding, Liu, and Schmeck introduce a service discovery approach combing both semantic and syntactic search to increase accuracy of discovery results [DLS10]. In their model, each service consumer maintains a local discovery table consisting of references to potential service providers matching a given set of search criteria. By doing this, a service consumer is aware of service providers that can provide exact services that the consumer needs. Similar approaches are the WebPeer introduced by Li et al. [LZW+05] with a peer-to-peer service discovery platform or a user-centric Web service community proposed by Liu et al. that searches for potential service providers by using similarity measurement mechanisms [LGH09].

Without loss of generality, it is assumed that each service component in an SOE has provider/consumer relationships with service components in its direct neighbourhood, i.e., service components located in the direct upper or lower layer. Each service provider may serve several service consumers simultaneously; vice versa, each service consumer may involve several service providers at the same time.

As already discussed in Section 3.1, runtime behaviour of a particular service component, in particular in terms of service level objectives, depends strongly on those of its providers. Depending on a consumer's usage pattern of services, i.e., how services are involved into the consumer's runtime process, services exert influence of a different intensity on a consumer's runtime behaviour. For example, if a Web service is hosted by a single server, then its runtime performance depends only on its sole host-ing server. However, if a Web service is hosted by two load-balanced servers, where incoming requests are distributed uniformly to one of the servers, then performance of the Web service depends on the composite performance of its both hosting servers. Therefore, in order to estimate composite QoS of service providers and their influence on their consumer, composition patterns outlining relationships between a service consumer and its services providers must be investigated. Section 6.6.1 addresses common composition patterns within an SOE in detail.

As discussed in Chapter 5, managing service levels of an SOE is modelled as a multi-agent approach in compliance with the decentralised and autonomous nature of service components in the environment [LTS08]. Each component in the environment is managed by an agent adopting an observer/controller instance. A management agent monitors its respective service component and controls the component in com-pliance with given business objectives. In addition to the layered structure of the envi-ronment, all management agents are organised in a management overlay, where rela-tionships between service components in the SOA environment are fully mapped to their respective management agents in the overlay layer (see also Figure 5-1). Man-agement tasks within the global context, such as negotiation between a consumer and its service providers, are accomplished within the overlay layer through interactions between respective management agents.

Applying a multi-agent approach in the management overlay results in a homoge-neous agent landscape with respect to roles and capabilities of management agents in the environment. That is, management agents are homogeneous with respect to their management tasks and their capabilities. Secondly, service-oriented design of the management overlay endows management agents with the features of service-orientation. Among other things, these are autonomy, loose coupling, and dynamism. In addition, further characteristics distinguishing the negotiation scenario of the pre-sent thesis from other similar scenarios are:

- The focus of SLA negotiation is to iteratively establish SLAs between related service components across the complete SOE, so that given service level objec-tives of a particular business process can be fulfilled. In this context, underly-ing service components are expected to conjointly support the given end-to-end service level constraints of a business process. This aspect allows an adaptive and dynamic management of related service components using automatically negotiated SLAs. In case of changes in the environment or within a particular service component, supporting components can adapt to those changes by re-negotiating affected SLAs in an automated manner.

- An agent's negotiation behaviour is influenced by its social context within the management overlay. There are two general agent types, namely cooperative agents and self-interested agents. Cooperative agents usually belong to the same organisation and therefore are willing to contribute to global business objectives. Self-interested agents are less cooperative and hence more utility-oriented. In general, such agents are located in an external organisation and may have their own business objectives.

- All management agents are autonomous, i.e., each agent has its own negotiation preferences and negotiation behaviours (e.g., negotiation strategies, decision-making models, etc.). Such information is private and not shared with other agents in the management overlay. Hence, an agent has only incomplete information about its counterparts as a guideline for its negotiation strategies.

- Each service component is aware of its operational state through the observer/controller instance of its management agent in the reference architecture (cf. Section 5.1 and [LTS08]). This provides the prerequisite for monitoring runtime behaviour of a service component, which is crucial for estimating values of service level objectives at runtime.

- A service component can be both a service provider and a service consumer in different negotiation contexts at the same time. Recursive constructs of service components as both a service provider and a service consumer in an SOE complicates the negotiation scenarios. In particular, a service component has to confirm that its own providers can support the SLA it negotiates with its consumer, before it commits to the SLA.

- As discussed in Section 3.2.3, QoS parameters of an SLA can be either quantitative (cost, throughput, availability, etc.) or qualitative (security, service compliance, etc.). For simplicity, only quantitative QoS parameters are considered in the negotiation scenarios. However, qualitative QoS parameters can be easily transformed to quantitative parameters by using a mapping function that maps a finite set of qualitative values to a continuous value range. For example, such a function can map various security levels of a service provider, from synchronous encryption on network level to PKI-based encryption on message level, to a continuous range of quantitative values, e.g., [0,1]. In this way, qualitative QoS parameters can be included in a negotiation process, too. The only prerequisite to enable such a mapping function is that both negotiation parties must have a common understanding of the mapping function and its input and output. This prerequisite can be met by a global ontology service, as discussed in Section 3.1.

• Furthermore, it is assumed that a consumer and its providers have conflicting interests on QoS parameters; otherwise, both parties can simply reach an agreement by choosing their common optimum in their negotiation space.

In short, automated negotiation within a decentralised SOE involves a set of inter-organisational and hence heterogeneous service components to conjointly guarantee given end-to-end QoS requirements of a business process. In comparison to other point-to-point negotiation scenarios from the research field, the negotiation scenarios, on which the present thesis focuses, span all logical layers of an SOE in an end-to-end manner. Among other things, negotiation scenarios of the present thesis are character-ised by their iterated negotiation processes involving all related service components with both the roles of a service provider and a service consumer.

6.3 Design Considerations

As discussed in the previous section, the basic negotiation scenario of the present the-sis is concerned with a service consumer that negotiates with each of its service pro-viders in a separate negotiation thread. However, how such a negotiation thread is car-ried out between a service consumer and its providers is subject to a range of design considerations with respect to the characteristics of end-to-end SLM within an SOE. Hence, this section focuses on those design considerations and outlines the constraints of automated negotiation of SLAs in such a self-organising environment.

Mediation: mediated negotiation requires a dedicated mediator in the environment and a corresponding trust infrastructure established within the environment. Since a mediator receives negotiation preferences from two management agents and tries to find a mutually acceptable compromise based on the given preferences, an underlying trust infrastructure is indispensable to build trust relationships between management agents as well as between those agents and their mediator. Only a working trust infra-structure can guarantee that each party involved in a negotiation thread (i.e., a man-agement agent or a mediator) is trustworthy for other parties.

However, in a self-organising SOE, a mediated negotiation is not applicable. First, a trust infrastructure requires additional infrastructural components that would have to be available in each SOE, but this prerequisite is not always given in practice. Furthermore, in case that an SOE spans several trust infrastructures, it requires considerable effort to establish trust relationships across different trust infrastructures. Secondly, a centralised negotiation approach with third-party mediators does not comply with the distributed nature of an SOE. Typical problems of centralised approaches, like performance bottleneck or single-point-of-failure prevent an active adoption of mediated negotiation in a large-scale SOE. Hence, the present thesis adopts direct negotiation between service providers and service consumers without mediators.

Bilateral vs. multilateral negotiation: the next essential design consideration is that of how many management agents are involved in a single negotiation thread. Theoretically, either a service consumer can negotiate with a single service provider, which forms a bilateral negotiation; or a service consumer can negotiate simultaneously with a set of service providers in a single negotiation thread, which forms a one-sided multilateral negotiation. Both negotiation styles have their advantages and disadvantages. Bilateral negotiation is easy to implement and to assess. When a management agent makes a statement, it can expect a timely response from the counterpart. In contrast, multilateral negotiation allows a consumer to reach a possibly better negotiation result by taking advantage of competitive situations between various service providers.

Obviously, a multilateral negotiation is much more complex than a bilateral one. It has to consider a variety of interests of all parties involved in the process. The large number of potential trade-offs that a management agent has to consider increases exponentially with the number of negotiating parties involved in the process. This leads to the fact that a management agent needs to explore a larger negotiation space to take interests of all parties into account. In addition, a management agent must maintain a much more complicated communication protocol to enable a multilateral negotiation. In contrast, a bilateral negotiation employs a straightforward conversation to exchange views and arguments of agents. Moss pointed out that a multilateral negotiation needs much more negotiation rounds to reach an agreement, if any, than a bilateral negotiation with the same negotiation constraints [Mos02].

With respect to the desirable properties of negotiation mechanisms (cf. Section 2.3.3), in particular communicational efficiency and computational efficiency, bilateral negotiation is used to design automated negotiation of SLAs between a service consumer and its service providers. It leads to a more probable convergence of a negotiation process within a reasonable time slot. Moreover, a set of SLAs resulting from several negotiation threads gives a service consumer more flexibility to maintain them at runtime. Since each service provider is associated with a dedicated SLA, a service consumer can flexibly renew or modify it, if necessary. For example, a service consumer can update a dedicated SLA in case of SLA violation, without having to adjust its SLAs with other service providers that are not affected by the SLA.

Single-issue vs. multi-issue negotiation: in a bilateral negotiation, two management agents can bargain either over a single QoS parameter in one of a sequence of negotiation threads or over multiple QoS parameters simultaneously in a single thread. In contrast to single-issue negotiation, multi-issue negotiation allows management agents to facilitate a negotiation process by exploiting optimal trade-offs among several QoS parameters. That is, management agents can fine-tune values between several QoS parameters within an SLA proposal to generate offers that are more attractive to their counterparts. Hence, for the purpose of the present thesis, bilateral multi-issue negotiation is considered.

Criticality of time: in a business-critical service-oriented system, timely response of the system is crucial for experiences of end users with the system. This implies that negotiation processes in the underlying infrastructure must be brought to an end within a predictable time slot. Hence, a negotiation process is limited in time. Each management agent has a predefined deadline for negotiation. In the course of negotiation, as soon as the deadline is exceeded and no mutually accepted agreement has been reached, the respective negotiation process will be terminated. It is noteworthy that two negotiating agents may have defined different negotiation deadlines, depending on their local negotiation preferences. In this way, it can be ensured that a negotiation process terminates definitively after some time units.

Information situation: as aforementioned in Section 2.1.1, service components in an SOE are autonomous. That is, they are responsible for designing, implementing, and provisioning their own services. Therefore, each management agent is not expected to expose its internal implementation, in particular its negotiation preferences, to other related management agents in the management overlay. Furthermore, in a large-scale SOE, a management agent is unlikely to have perfect knowledge about its environment, in particular those service components in the environment, with which it has provider/consumer relationships. The large scale of such an environment prevents a management agent from acquiring perfect information about its surroundings.

Therefore, without loss of generality, this thesis focuses on bilateral negotiation in an incomplete information situation, where related management agents do not share their negotiation preferences with one another.

Negotiation access: as assumed in Section 6.2, each service component negotiates only with a selected set of potential service providers, which match some predefined (non-)functional requirements of the consumer. Hence, from this viewpoint, this thesis focuses on an open negotiation process. A service component can join a negotiation process as a potential service provider, if it fulfils the given (non-) functional require-ments of a consumer.

Theoretical foundations: a theoretical foundation determines the way, in which two management agents can negotiate with each other. As introduced in Section 2.3.3, there are in general three different negotiation mechanisms: game theoretical, heuris-tic, and argumentation-based. The choice of a negotiation mechanism depends on the characteristics of the negotiation scenarios, among other things:

- It is a bilateral negotiation between a service consumer and its provider.

- Negotiating management agents know exactly what they have and what they want. In other words, through continuous observation of a service component by the observer/controller instance of the respective management agent, the component knows its (non-)functional capabilities to provide its services. Such preference information is fixed in the course of a negotiation process.

- Management agents have an exact way to estimate the quality of a given SLA. By doing this, they can assess the benefits they would gain from a given SLA, and compare them with their own expectations in order to make decisions.

- As aforementioned, management agents have only incomplete information about their counterparts.

Approaches based on game theory expect a perfect information situation for both negotiation parties and assume that both management agents have complete knowledge of the outcome space. Hence, with respect to the incomplete information situation of a management agent about its counterpart, game theoretical approaches cannot be applied in the assumed scenarios. Without perfect information about oneself and its counterpart in terms of negotiation preferences, two management agents can-not apply a game theoretical approach to bargain over a range of QoS parameters and reach a global equilibrium.

Argumentation-based approaches provide means to incorporate additional information (i.e., arguments) in outgoing proposals to changes the counterpart's negotiation space by altering its preferences. Hence, argumentation-based approaches require
additional communication efforts to exchange such advertising information. Furthermore, these approaches demand additional mechanisms to allow management agents
to argue their beliefs and other attitudes during a negotiation process. This leads to
additional communicational and computational overhead.

Secondly, as in human argumentation, rational agents may trick their counterparts
in order to gain an unfair advantages. Hence, this demands an additional trust infrastructure in an SOE to build up trust-worthy relationships between management
agents. However, as aforementioned, such a trust infrastructure is not always available
in an SOE. In particular, for a large environment spanning a set of trust infrastructures, it is also challenging to create a trust federation across all related domains.

Thirdly, argumentation-based approaches assume that a rational management agent
can modify its preferences upon reception of advertising arguments from its counterpart. For a service consumer, its negotiation preferences are derived from given busi-
ness/operational objectives, which cannot simply be changed without consultation
with its high-level control instance, e.g., human participants. Similarly, a service provider derives its preferences from its local technical capabilities. Changing negotiation
preferences means that a service provider has to change its local technical capabilities
in compliance with its new preferences. Such actions are, however, associated with
additional effort and are therefore not always applicable on the fly, in particular if a
service provider has locally only limited technical resources.

By comparing the characteristics of the negotiation scenarios of the present thesis
and the ones of various theoretical foundations to enable negotiation, it is obvious that
heuristic approaches are most applicable for the purpose of this thesis. Game theoretical approaches fail because of their requirement of a perfect information situation of
both negotiating agents about their negotiation preferences. Similarly, argumentation-
based approaches are unsuitable in the present case, because those approaches assume
that both negotiating agents can change their preferences upon receiving appropriate
argumentations.

Summarising all design considerations above, a service consumer and its providers
employ *bilateral*, *multi-issue*, and *non-mediated* negotiation to regulate their differences of opinions in terms of service level objectives. Each management agent has its

private negotiation preferences derived from either external directives or runtime history observed by the observer/controller instance. A negotiation thread is *limited in time*, which ensures termination of a negotiation process. The actual negotiation process is carried out by using a *heuristic* negotiation model that is introduced in detail in Section 6.4.

6.4 Mathematical Model

The previous sections have introduced the negotiation scenarios and outlined the fundamental design considerations to facilitate automated negotiation between related service consumer and service provider. In a basic negotiation scenario, a service consumer negotiates simultaneously in several separated negotiation threads with all its service providers on several pre-determined QoS issues. Hence, this section focuses on the basic negotiation model based on the model introduced by Sierra, Faratin, and Jennings [SFJ97] (cf. Section 3.3.1) to enable bilateral multi-issue negotiation.

The present thesis considers a bilateral negotiation between the management agent c of a service consumer and the management agent p of its provider (i.e., management agent $i \in \{c, p\}$) on multiple QoS parameters $\{1, 2, ..., n\}$ of an SLA, such as availability, response time, or throughput. Each QoS parameter $j \in \{1, 2, ..., n\}$ has a continuous value range $[min_j, max_j]$, where $min_j \in \mathbb{R}$, $max_j \in \mathbb{R}$, and $min_j < max_j$. In addition, it is assumed that for the same QoS parameter j, the value ranges of both negotiation parties have overlaps, i.e., $[min_j^c, max_j^c] \cap [min_j^p, max_j^p] \neq \emptyset$. This constraint is ensured by incorporating QoS evaluation into the service discovery process, as discussed by Ding, Liu, and Schmeck [DLS10].

Each management agent i has a predefined negotiation deadline $t_{max}^i \in \mathbb{R}^+$, until which the respective management agent can exchange SLA proposals with its counterpart. In other words, a given deadline defines a maximal amount of time that a management agent can spend to reach an agreement with its counterpart. In the course of negotiation, an SLA proposal sent from a management agent a to a management agent b in a negotiation thread at time t is denoted as $x_{a \to b}^t$, where $a, b \in \{c, p\}$, $a \neq b$, and $t \in [0, \min(t_{max}^a, t_{max}^b)]$. Each SLA proposal is composed of a set of QoS values, i.e., $x_{a \to b}^t = (x_{a \to b}^t[1], x_{a \to b}^t[2], ..., x_{a \to b}^t[n])$, where $x_{a \to b}^t[j]$ specifies the value of the QoS parameter j in the agreement sent at time t and $x_{a \to b}^t[j] \in [min_j^a, max_j^a]$.

In order to estimate the level of satisfaction of a particular management agent for a given SLA, it leverages various utility functions. In this case, the utility of a given SLA is the weighted sum of utilities of all QoS parameters in the agreement. To this end, for each QoS parameter $j \in \{1, 2, ..., n\}$, a management agent $i \in \{c, p\}$ has a corresponding utility function $V_j^i(x) : [min_j^i, max_j^i] \rightarrow [0, 1]$ that maps the value of a QoS parameter into a real-valued utility from the range $[0, 1]$. For a particular management agent i, an agreement x is preferable than another agreement x', if the utility of x is higher than that of x'.

Depending on a management agent's preferences, utility functions can have very different shapes in their value range. For simplicity, the present thesis considers only monotone utility functions. That is, for a management agent i, a utility function $V_j^i(x)$ implies that, for two values $x[j]$ and $x'[j]$ with $x[j] \leq x'[j]$,

$$\begin{cases} V_j^i(x[j]) \leq V_j^i(x'[j]) & \text{if QoS parameter } j \text{ is increasing} \\ V_j^i(x[j]) \geq V_j^i(x'[j]) & \text{if QoS parameter } j \text{ is decreasing} \end{cases}.$$

In this case, a QoS parameter j is *increasing* if the resulting utility increases if the value of the parameter increases, such as availability for a consumer; and vice versa *decreasing* if the estimated utility decreases if the parameter's value increases, such as cost for a consumer. Obviously, increasing and decreasing are two relative properties that must be viewed from the viewpoint of a particular management agent. For example, while cost is a decreasing QoS parameter for a service consumer, it is an increasing one for a service provider. This fact denotes clearly conflicting interests of a consumer and its providers on the same QoS parameter. Because a service provider perceives for the same QoS parameter exactly the opposite as its consumer does, they have competitive relationships on values of the same QoS parameter.

To estimate precisely utility of a given QoS parameter j for a management agent i, the negotiation model uses a family of polynomial functions as follows, with $\alpha \in \mathbb{R}^+$:

$$V_j^i(x[j]) = \begin{cases} \left(\frac{max_j^i - x[j]}{max_j^i - min_j^i} \right)^\alpha & \text{if QoS parameter } j \text{ is decreasing} \\ \left(\frac{x[j] - min_j^i}{max_j^i - min_j^i} \right)^\alpha & \text{if QoS parameter } j \text{ is increasing} \end{cases}. \tag{15.4.1}$$

Since the function family $V_j^i(x[j])$ in (15.4.1) is monotone, a management agent i gets the maximal utility and the minimal utility at the boundaries of its value range for the QoS parameter j. That is, for an increasing QoS parameter, its utility increases monotonically from 0 to 1 as the corresponding parameter value increases from min_j^i

to max_j^i, with $V_j^i(min_j^i) = 0$ and $V_j^i(max_j^i) = 1$; vice versa, for an decreasing QoS parameter, its utility decreases monotonically from 1 to 0 as the parameter value increases from min_j^i to max_j^i, where $V_j^i(min_j^i) = 1$ and $V_j^i(max_j^i) = 0$.

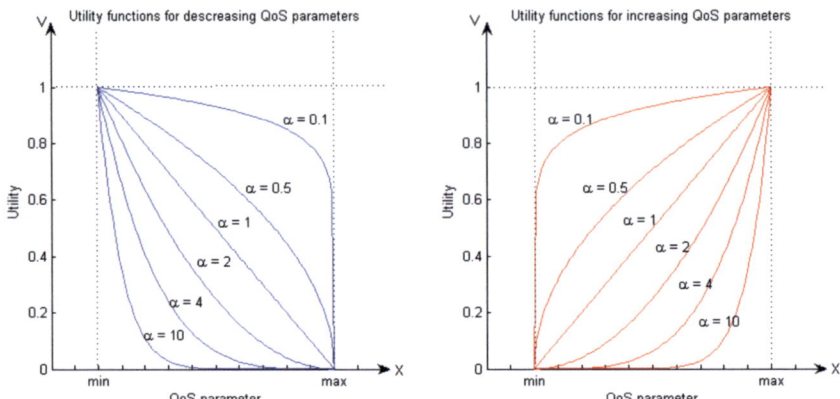

Figure 6-3: Utility functions for increasing and decreasing QoS parameters

Of course, it is possible to use utility functions other than (15.4.1) for negotiation scenarios in this section, such as by using exponential functions. The major consideration to choose a utility function is whether the selected utility function can reflect appropriately preferences that an agent has on a particular QoS parameter. (15.4.1) represents an infinite number of possible utility functions with different behaviour patterns, as illustrated in Figure 6-3. The parameter $\alpha \in \mathbb{R}^+$ determines different behaviour patterns of utilities as the corresponding QoS parameter's value changes.

In the case that $\alpha = 1$, $V_j^i(x[j])$ is linear and monotone. Hence, changes of a QoS parameter's value are proportional to changes of its utility. By assigning α with values other than 1, a management agent can model various behaviour patterns to reflect its preferences on the particular QoS parameter. For example, for a *decreasing* QoS parameter with $0 < \alpha < 1$, the utility function returns high utilities at the lower bound of the value range. As the QoS parameter's value approaches the maximal value max, the estimated utility falls quickly against 0 (as shown in Figure 6-3, in particular by the curve with $\alpha = 0.1$). Similarly, for $\alpha > 1$, as QoS values increase from min to max, utilities fall at once against 0, even at the lower bound of the value range. In Figure 6-3, the curve with $\alpha = 10$ depicts this behaviour clearly.

Hence, the function family in (15.4.1) specifies three general types of change behaviours of utilities: a *proportional* type with $\alpha = 1$, a *conservative* type with $0 < \alpha < 1$ that lets a management agent to preserve high utilities until the value range is almost exhausted, and the *conceding* type with $\alpha > 1$ where a management agent gives up its utilities very quickly in the course of negotiation.

As aforementioned, utility of a given agreement x is the weighted sum of utilities of all QoS parameters in the agreement, i.e.,

$$V^i(x) = \sum_{1 \leq j \leq n} \omega_j^i V_j^i(x[j])$$

(15.4.2)

In (15.4.2), $j \in \{1, 2, ..., n\}$ and $\sum_{1 \leq j \leq n} \omega_j^i = 1$. Obviously, different utility functions span negotiation spaces with different curvature. To better illustrate impact of utilities functions on the perception of management agents of a given SLA, Table 6-1 specifies a sample negotiation scenario between a service consumer c and its provider p to reach an agreement on two QoS parameters: response time and availability. The negotiation space of a management agent is characterised by its boundary values of the value ranges for the corresponding QoS parameters.

Table 6-1: Sample QoS parameters to illustrate utility functions

	response time				availability			
	weight	type	minimal	maximal	weight	type	minimal	maximal
agent c	0.5	decreasing	$min_1^c = 3$	$max_1^c = 8$	0.5	increasing	$min_2^c = 0.96$	$max_2^c = 0.99$
agent p	0.5	increasing	$min_1^p = 5$	$max_1^p = 10$	0.5	decreasing	$min_2^p = 0.95$	$max_2^p = 0.999$

For simplicity, the sample negotiation scenario assumes that both QoS parameters are equally weighted in the utility calculation. Therefore, with respect to (15.4.2), both a service consumer and its service provider can estimate utilities of a given agreement x using the following formulas:

$$\begin{cases} V^c(x) = 0.5 \cdot \left(\frac{max_1^c - x[1]}{max_1^c - min_1^c}\right)^\alpha + 0.5 \cdot \left(\frac{x[2] - min_2^c}{max_2^c - min_2^c}\right)^\alpha = 0.5 \cdot \left(\frac{8 - x[1]}{8 - 3}\right)^\alpha + 0.5 \cdot \left(\frac{x[2] - 0.96}{0.99 - 0.96}\right)^\alpha \\ V^p(x) = 0.5 \cdot \left(\frac{x[1] - min_1^p}{max_1^p - min_1^p}\right)^\alpha + 0.5 \cdot \left(\frac{max_2^p - x[2]}{max_2^p - min_2^p}\right)^\alpha = 0.5 \cdot \left(\frac{x[1] - 5}{10 - 5}\right)^\alpha + 0.5 \cdot \left(\frac{0.999 - x[2]}{0.999 - 0.95}\right)^\alpha \end{cases}$$

(15.4.3)

Based on (15.4.3), Figure 6-4 illustrates the perception of a service provider (i.e., by means of utilities) of a given SLA within its negotiation space in dependence of different values of α.

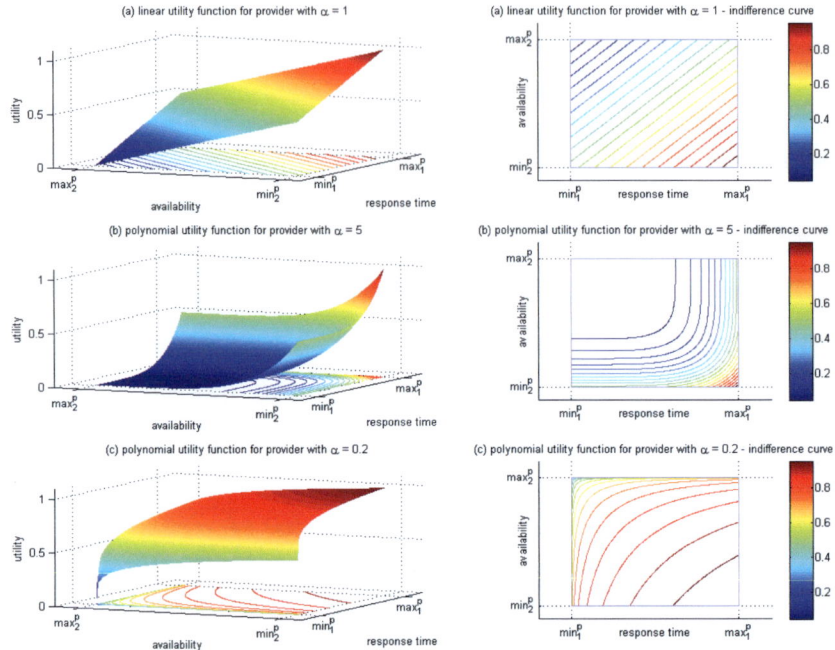

Figure 6-4: Illustration of utility functions with different α

To make the impact of α on utilities clearer, Figure 6-4 shows three different utility functions from each utility function type with $\alpha = 0$, $\alpha = 5$, and $\alpha = 0.2$. The charts on the left illustrate the distribution of utilities in relationship to varying value combinations of response time and availability within the negotiation space specified in Table 6-1. In order to make the distribution of utilities more clear, the charts on the right depict the projection of corresponding surfaces on the plane of response time and availability, where the lines/curves in the charts are indifference curves. That is, all value combinations of response time and availability on a same indifference line/curve have the same utility. The colour depth of a indifference line/curve specifies its utility in compliance with the colour bar.

As seen in Figure 6-4, while a linear utility function with $\alpha = 1$ spans a plane in the negotiation space, utility functions with $\alpha \neq 1$ span curved surfaces instead. The form and intensity of curvature of these surfaces depends on the value of α. A utility functions with $\alpha > 1$ spans a convex surface in the space. The larger the value of α, the more intensive is the convexity of the surface. In contrast, a utility function with

$0 < \alpha < 1$ spans a concave surface in the space. The smaller the value of α, the more intensive is the concavity of the surface.

The meaning of different α is not limited to different shapes of corresponding utility functions in the negotiation space. Moreover, different utility functions enable a management agent to model its preferences individually within its negotiation space. Areas with high utilities are mostly desired by a management agent, while areas with low utilities are less desirable.

Another aspect of utility functions is dynamic transition of utilities from desired areas to less desirable areas within a negotiation space. As aforementioned, a management agent has to concede from its best case (i.e., $V(x) = 1$) to its worst case (i.e., $V(x) = 0$) in the course of negotiation. With different utilities functions, a management agent can realise different transition behaviour during this process. With a convex shape in the negotiation space (i.e., $\alpha > 1$, as illustrated by the charts (b) in Figure 6-4), a management agent is willing to give up a large amount of utility already at the very beginning of a negotiation process. In contrast, with a concave shape in the negotiation space (i.e., $0 < \alpha < 1$, as shown by the charts (c) in Figure 6-4), a management agent tries to preserve most of its utilities towards the end of a negotiation process, whereupon it concedes more quickly in favour of its counterpart.

To sum up, utility functions determine how a management agent moves from its best case to its worst case within a given negotiation space. For a given utility function, a negotiation space is composed of indifference curves/surfaces within it. An indifference curve/surface consists of an infinite number of value combinations that have the same utility for a particular management agent. As depicted in Figure 6-4, different utility functions induce a variety of shapes of indifference curves in a negotiation space, in dependence of the value of α.

Indifference curve/surfaces play an important role to facilitate automated negotiation of SLAs. It is obvious that in order to accelerate a negotiation process, both negotiating management agents are engaged to propose SLA offers as attractive as possible to their counterpart. The fact that for a given utility there are an infinite number of SLAs (i.e., various value combinations of all QoS parameters) that can be proposed by a management agent increase greatly the flexibility and degree of freedom of an agent to determine the best proposal for its counterpart. In this process, a management agent has to find a single point on the indifference curve/surface of a given utility, which can provide utility as high as possible to its counterpart. Based on the concept of indifference curve/surface, Section 6.7.2 discusses various trade-off strategies to facilitate a negotiation process.

6.5 Negotiation Protocol

A negotiation protocol specifies how two management agents interact with each other to find mutually acceptable agreements at runtime. In particular, such a protocol defines how an agent can initialise a negotiation process and how agents can exchange their proposals interactively. There are several established negotiation protocols in the field, such as the FIPA Iterated Contract Net Interaction Protocol mentioned before [FIP02b]. These protocols are designed majorly for multilateral negotiation scenarios, where a single agent interacts simultaneously with a set of agents to find mutually acceptable solutions. In addition, these protocols are not sufficient for the negotiation scenarios introduced in Section 6.2.

In particular, existing negotiation protocols do not address the following two important aspects with respect to characters of an SOE:

- A service component in an SOE can be both a service consumer and a service provider at the same time. For example, an application server provides hosting services to Web services and consumes hardware services from the underlying infrastructure layer at the same time. In this case, the application server negotiates with Web services as a service provider and in turn with the underlying infrastructure layer as a service consumer. Since non-functional behaviour of an application server in terms of service level objectives (e.g., performance, security, etc.) is supported by its providers, there is a correlation between the SLA closed between an application server and its hosted Web services and the SLAs arranged between the application server and its supporting servers. Due to this correlation, a service component has to ensure that a contract with its consumer can be fully supported by its own service providers.

- As mentioned in Section 6.2, in order to get maximal flexibility, a service component closes an SLA with each of its providers separately. As aforementioned, service levels of a service component's providers influence the ones that this component provisions to its consumer. From this viewpoint, if a service component runs several negotiation threads simultaneously with its providers, it has to coordinate these parallel negotiation threads. The purpose of such coordination is to ensure that the resulting agreements from all parallel negotiation threads comply with the QoS requirements that a service component's consumer has.

Based on the previous considerations, a *coordinated* and *iterated* negotiation protocol is designed to facilitate negotiation activities between management agents across a given SOE, as illustrated in Figure 6-5. In contrast to others, the negotiation protocol introduced in this section is adapted in accordance with the hierarchical structure of a service-oriented system, where business processes are supported by a set of underlying service components in the system.

Initially, a business process gets external operational objectives in terms of QoS requirements as initial input. External operational objectives define the desired behaviour of a particular business process, in terms of a set of service level objectives, such as minimal availability, maximal response time, or maximal service cost for executing a business process. Such non-functional requirements specify boundary conditions for the runtime behaviour of a business process. Hence, such requirements specify negotiation spaces of a business process for the set of QoS parameters.

In addition to these external operational objectives, a business process is given a set of business objectives as initial input. High-level business objectives allow external high-level control instances (e.g., human participants) to influence the negotiation behaviour of a business process and other related service components. For example, business objectives can determine priorities of particular QoS parameters in the course of negotiation. By doing this, management agents handle the preferred QoS parameters more sparingly than the less preferred QoS parameters. That is, management agents concede more liberally in less preferred parameters in favour of preferred ones, so that they can reach values for the favoured QoS parameters as good as possible.

With these initial inputs, a business process triggers the overall negotiation process. Figure 6-5 shows the sequence diagram of such an iterated and coordinated negotiation process of a service consumer with its provider. Negotiation activities are carried out between a service consumer (*Component A* in Figure 6-5) and a service provider (*Component B* in Figure 6-5). In the course of negotiation, *Component B* has both the role of a *provider* and the role of a *consumer*, as discussed in Section 3.1.2. Therefore, Component B has two parallel time lines in the sequence diagram in Figure 6-5, in order to distinguish its activities with different roles. The same applies to Figure 6-6, showing the confirmation phase of the negotiation protocol.

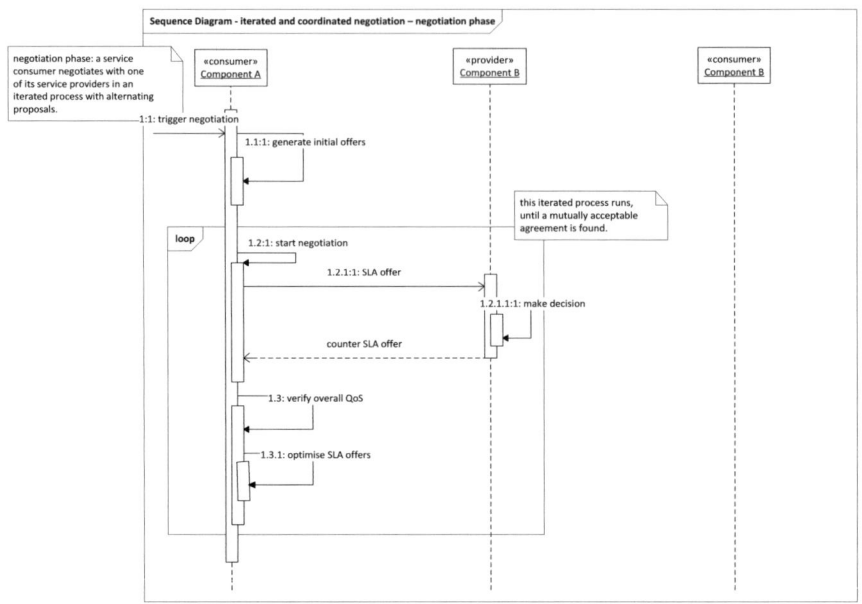

Figure 6-5: Iterated and coordinated negotiation protocol – the negotiation phase

The first phase of the negotiation protocol is the negotiation phase. The main objective in this phase is to set up a mutually acceptable agreement between a service consumer and its provider. To trigger a negotiation process, a service consumer (*Component A* in Figure 6-5) generates an initial offer for each of its providers (*Component B* in Figure 6-5). Initial offers are generated based on given operational objectives with respect to composition patterns specified in the environment model (see Section 6.6.1). Afterwards, it starts several parallel negotiation threads, where in each thread the service consumer negotiates only with a single service provider.

The actual negotiation process in a thread is an iterative process with alternating offers between the consumer and its provider. Initially, the consumer behaves as a proposer and makes an initial offer. After having received this SLA offer, the provider consults its local negotiation strategies to decide whether to accept it. In case that the provider rejects an incoming offer, it proposes a counter offer and sends this as a new proposal back to the consumer. Upon receipt of a counter offer, the consumer leverages its local decision maker to find its optimal action – namely either to accept the offer or to generate a counter offer.

Before a consumer sends a counter offer to its respective negotiation partner, it optimises the offer with respect to the global business objectives and the consumer's local experiences so far with the particular counterpart. The objective of such optimisation is to find optimal trade-offs between various QoS parameters by keeping utilities of respective agreements unchanged. For example, if a global business objective focuses on providing customers with services for maximal customer satisfaction (e.g., high availability and low response time), then a possible trade-off for a consumer is to reduce the assigned value for response time by simultaneously increasing service cost in the agreement. Section 6.7.2 discusses such trade-off strategies in details.

After having optimised the outgoing counter offers, a consumer sends the offers to its respective counterparts and the negotiation process thereupon goes into the next round. This is an iterative process, until either both the consumer and the provider reach a consensus on the given QoS parameters or the negotiation process is aborted due to the violation of some predefined constraints (e.g., negotiation time-out).

If a set of mutually acceptable agreements is found between a consumer and its provider(s), the confirmation phase begins. Figure 6-6 illustrates the interactions between a service consumer and its provider as well as between the provider and the provider's providers.

The focus of the confirmation phase is to verify that the agreements resulting from the previous phase can be supported by a provider's underlying service components. In other words, a service provider can only commit to an SLA negotiated with its consumer, if this SLA is also supported by its own provider(s) in turn.

Hence, this phase is concerned with the service providers rather than the service consumer. A service provider (*Component B* in Figure 6-6) must ensure that it has the ability to support service level objectives specified in the agreement with its consumer, in particular with respect to its own service providers. Therefore, it changes its role from *provider* of the previous phase to *consumer* in this phase and negotiates in turn with its service providers by using the service level targets specified in the agreement resulting from the previous phase as its operational objectives.

It is noteworthy that a service provider may have its own business objectives in this phase other than the one used in the previous negotiation phase. It depends on the organisational affiliation of the service provider. This determines if a service provider has to follow the same business objectives as its consumer.

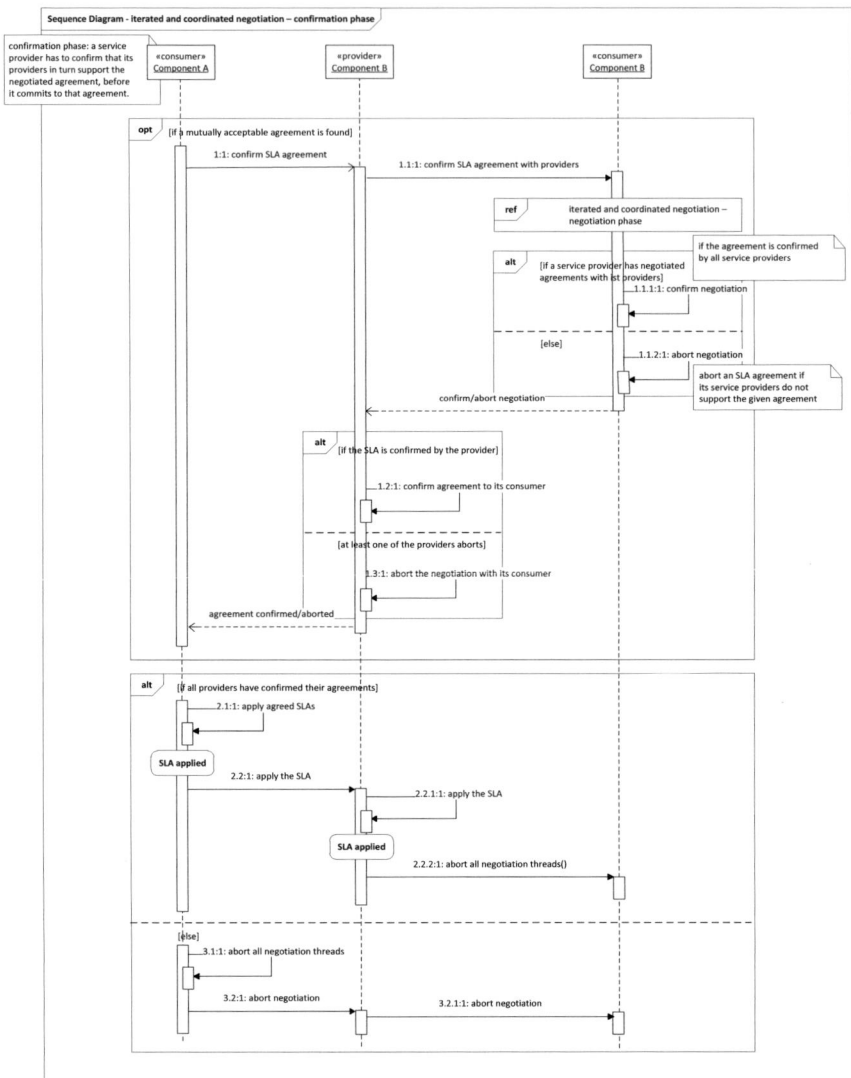

Figure 6-6: Iterated and coordinated negotiation protocol – the confirmation phase

With operational objectives and business objectives as inputs, a service provider starts a negotiation process in its local context as a service consumer. In this way, the negotiation initialised by the consumer of the service provider is propagated to the providers of the service provider. Putting this recursive scheme into the global context of an SOE, this mechanism allows a negotiation process initialised by a particular business process being recursively propagated across the complete environment, from the highest business process layer down to the lowest infrastructure layer.

If a service provider can reach agreements with its providers and the resulting agreements meet the QoS constraints specified in the agreement from the previous negotiation phase, it is going to commit to this agreement with its consumer. Of course, this process is omitted, if a service provider (e.g., an infrastructural service component) does not utilise any further services from other service components in the same environment. Correspondingly, if a service consumer is invoked by other components in the system, it has therefore on its part outstanding agreements to confirm. In this case, a service consumer is going to responds to its consumers in turn, in dependence of confirmations it receives from its service providers. In this way, outcomes of negotiation processes in the lowest infrastructure layer can be propagated bottom-up to the initialising process in the highest process layer in the environment.

Upon receiving the confirmation from all service provider(s), a business process closes the corresponding negotiation thread and begins to set up the SLA in its local runtime environment, as discussed in the SLA lifecycle in Section 3.2.4. Upon receiving the message, that a service consumer has applied a negotiated SLA, a provider begins to set up the SLA in its local environment, too. If it utilises any other services from the underlying service components, the corresponding service component informs its service providers to close the negotiation threads between them. By doing this, negotiated SLAs are set up recursively top-down from the initialising business process to the lowest infrastructural providers.

However, in case that at least one of its service providers fails to confirm its SLA, a service consumer aborts all negotiation threads with its providers, even if some providers in other threads have confirmed their SLAs. In case that a service provider has some confirmed SLAs on its part with its providers, it forces its service providers to close the negotiation threads between them by withdrawing the confirmation. Simultaneously, if a service consumer provides services to other service components in the upper layer, it aborts the negotiation threads with its service consumers, too. By doing this, a single negotiation failure between a single provider/consumer pair is propagated across the complete environment.

In addition, the negotiation process illustrated in Figure 6-5 and Figure 6-6 is a co-ordinated process. In this case, a consumer plays the role of a coordinator throughout the negotiation phase. It triggers the negotiation phase by initialising a set of parallel negotiation threads with its providers. In this way, a consumer can actively involve all related service providers into its negotiation process. In addition, a consumer is responsible to control the negotiation process in dependence of the outcomes of all negotiation threads. In case that one or more negotiation threads are aborted due to some unexpected events, a consumer has to inform all other service providers, e.g., by aborting the respective negotiation threads with them. Otherwise, as soon as a consumer has successfully reached a consensus on service level objectives with all its service providers, it has to close all negotiation threads by informing the related service providers to apply the negotiated SLAs.

By following this negotiation protocol at runtime, the initial negotiation process started by a business process is recursively propagated top-down to all related service components in the underlying layers. Vice versa, outcomes of negotiation processes are recursively fed back bottom-up to the initialising process again. At the end of such a chained negotiation process across all related service components in the environment, either each consumer/provider pair in the system has a mutually accepted and confirmed SLA; or there are no established SLAs between related service components along the vertical dependence chains. In this way, a business process can ensure that all supporting service components in the underlying layers can contribute to the service level constraints it receives from its consumers.

Rationale. The negotiation protocol described in this section takes the characteristics of negotiation scenarios introduced in Section 6.2 into consideration. Given a predefined SOE and a set of service requirements (i.e., operational objectives) for particular business processes on top of the environment, the negotiation protocol guides service components to negotiate service levels with their respective service providers, so that all resulting SLAs across the environment are able to support conjointly the overall non-functional requirements on the complete environment.

Coordinating activities of a service consumer enables a partly centralised optimisation of SLAs with respect to global business objectives, while keeping actual negotiation processes simple and flexible by using bilateral multi-issue negotiation between a service consumer and its provider. In addition, the confirmation process of a negotiated SLA forces a service provider to extend a negotiation process to its service providers. From the viewpoint of the recursive construction of an SOE, where a service component can simultaneously be a provider and a consumer, this mechanism allows a business process to propagate a negotiation process iteratively across the complete SOE down to service components in the infrastructure layer.

In order to meet given operational objectives on a particular service component, the negotiation protocol allows a service component to decompose its operational objectives in terms of QoS requirements progressively into several sub-requirements for each of its supporting service components in the environment. By doing this, a business process delegates part of its responsibility to enforce its operational objectives to its supporting service components.

The key requirement to apply the iterated and coordinated negotiation protocol introduced in this section is that a service component can decompose given overall operational objectives in terms of QoS requirements with respect to its service providers by some means. Obviously, such a decomposition process must take the nature of a target SOE into considerations, in particular, (expected) runtime behaviour of related service components in the environment. Secondly, a service consumer must be able to aggregate QoS dimensions of its service providers to ensure that they can satisfy the overall QoS requirements at runtime. Therefore, in the following, the underlying composition and decomposition schemas are discussed. These schemas are crucial for a service component to determine its negotiation spaces with its service providers.

6.6 Negotiation Space

As mentioned in the previous section, the key challenge for a consumer to apply the iterated negotiation protocol is to determine negotiation spaces for each particular service provider at runtime. A service consumer has to ensure that its negotiation spaces align with the non-functional requirements it has. That is, resulting SLAs based on these negotiation spaces can support sufficiently the non-functional requirements. Therefore, it has to split its non-functional requirements for each of its service providers. However, this task is not trivial. Theoretically, a service consumer has an infinite number of possibilities to decompose given non-functional requirements. Therefore, it has to take the nature of each service provider into consideration, so that the resulting requirement for each service provider complies with its real behaviour pattern.

To this end, this section investigates composition and decomposition schemas for a selected set of QoS parameters, namely *availability*, *cost*, *response time*, and *throughput*. While *availability* addresses reliability of a service by estimating its online probability, *response time* and *throughput* cover the performance aspect of a service. In contrast, *cost* investigates the business aspect of service consumption in an SOE. These QoS parameters are selected based on their types and their relevance to service invocations in an SOA. From this aspect, schemas discussed in this section are representative for other QoS parameters. Based on them, schemas for further QoS parameters can be derived easily.

Hence, this section is organised as follows: Section 6.6.1 outlines the basic composition patterns used in the present thesis. These patterns are important to determine relationships between involved service providers. Section 6.6.2 is concerned with decomposition schemas for the aforementioned QoS parameters, while Section 6.6.3 focuses on composition schemas for them. Finally, Section 6.6.4 outlines how these composition and decomposition schemas can be utilised by a service consumer to determine negotiation spaces for its service providers.

6.6.1 Composition Patterns

In the context of business process management, workflow patterns addressing relationships of process activities are exhaustively analysed, such as in the work of van der Aalst, Barros, Hofstede, and Kiepuszewski [ABHK00, AHK+03]. Work with similar focuses is conducted in the context of service composition [JRM05]. Figure 6-7 illustrates an example of such a workflow with several workflow patterns.

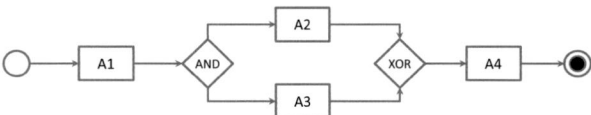

Figure 6-7: Sample workflow with workflow patterns

The activity A1 is the first activity in the workflow. An AND-pattern specifies that the main process flow is split into two parallel activities A2 and A3 that are executed simultaneously after the activity A1. A XOR-pattern indicates that there is an exclusive choice between the sub-process flows A2 and A3. Only one of both sub-process flows can be continued by the main process flow, while the other one is aborted. After the XOR join, the main flow continues with the activity A4, before the complete workflow terminates.

Similarly, the business logic of a service consumer can be expressed using a workflow consisting of a range of *composition patterns*. Each workflow addresses chronological concerns of service invocations of a service component. That is, a workflow states how business logics of the underlying service components (i.e., service providers) are involved into the business logic of a service consumer in a chronological order. In this context, it is of particular interest to control how a logic flow can be passed to the next activity at runtime. Therefore, in order to model different relationships between predecessor and successor activities in a business logic, the present thesis aligns its definitions of composition patterns to the BPMN's definitions of gateways [OMG09].

In BPMN, gateways are used to define types of logic flow behaviour within a business process, such as branching, merging, and joining. They specify a range of gating mechanisms that supervises the logic flow at a gateway, i.e., whether logic flows can be merged or split on a range of outgoing paths. In general, BPMN distinguishes between three basic gateway types: *exclusive*, *inclusive*, and *parallel*. In the following, these gateway types are introduced in combination with their corresponding composition patterns in the present thesis.

In an *exclusive* gateway, only one of the alternative (incoming or outgoing) paths will be taken by the gateway. To determine which path to use, an exclusive gateway evaluates a predefined condition using its current operational context. The evaluation result leads either to one of the paths or to a default path.

Correspondingly, a composition pattern *XOR* is defined to reflect the same branching/merging behaviour, as illustrated in Figure 6-8. In an XOR composition pattern, only a single service provider among all service providers will be invoked by a consumer. Depending on the particular business logics of a service component, an XOR pattern can be used to realise different scenarios with exclusive choice. The most common scenario is a conditional evaluation of execution context within a business process in the process layer. In addition, this composition pattern can be used to realise redundancy behaviour in other layers to increase reliability of particular service component. For example, a single Web service is hosted on two or more identical Web servers. Hence, an incoming request for the Web service is passed to one of those servers. The decision, which Web server to use for an incoming service request, depends on the current workload of the servers. In any case, only one of the service providers is selected exclusively to handle an incoming service request.

Given an XOR pattern with m outgoing/incoming paths, in order to reflect precisely the branching/merging behaviour of the pattern, each outgoing/incoming path is associated with a probability value p_i with $\sum_{i=1}^{m} p_i = 1$ (as shown in Figure 6-8). A probability value indicates the transition probability of the respective path that it is selected by an XOR pattern at runtime. These probability values are calculated at runtime by a management agent, based on a set of usage data of the pattern. In order to keep such probability values up-to-date, they are re-calculated regularly after a pre-defined time period, using statistics collected during this period. Alternatively, re-calculating transition probabilities can be done using statistics collected during a sliding window of a predefined size, which helps to reduce the influence of noise in the calculation.

To distinguish exclusive gateways from scenarios, where more than one path is selected, BPMN introduces the *inclusive* gateway. In comparison to an exclusive gateway, all outgoing/incoming paths in an inclusive gateway are evaluated for selection. Paths matching a predefined condition expression are activated by an inclusive gateway to continue its process flow.

Based on an inclusive gateway, a second composition pattern *OR* is defined. In contrast to an XOR pattern, this composition pattern allows a service consumer to model the kind of branching/merging behaviour, where one or more service providers are consumed at the same time. For example, a business process may utilise simultaneously several Web services out of a predefined set of services. Determining the set of Web services to invoke depends on evaluation results of predefined conditional expressions in the context of a particular process instance. All paths with positive evaluation results are activated by an OR pattern. Hence, an OR pattern can be considered as a generalised form of an XOR pattern.

Given an OR pattern with m outgoing/incoming paths, each path within the pattern is introduced with a weight w_i with $\sum_{i=1}^{m} w_i = 1$, as shown in Figure 6-8. In contrast to transition probabilities of paths in an XOR pattern, weights indicate the ratio of invocations of a respective service provider among all invocations of service providers within a given time period. Hence, the weight of a service provider is estimated by calculating the quotient of the number of invocations of the respective service provider and the total number of invocations of all service providers involved in an OR pattern during a predefined time slot. Such statistical information is collected and calculated by a management agent at runtime.

To model the branching/merging behaviour that all service providers are required to pass a gateway, BPMN introduces the *parallel* gateway. A *parallel* gateway creates several parallel flows out of a single process flow or merges several parallel flows into a single process flow. In a merging gateway, termination of all incoming parallel flows is required by the gateway in order to continue with the next activity in the process flow.

Correspondingly, a third composition pattern *AND* is introduced, where all parallel service providers are invoked by a consumer at the same time. In an AND pattern, a consumer waits for responses from all its service providers, before it moves forward to the next activity in its business logic. Correspondingly, each path in an AND pattern has the same probability of 100% to be activated at runtime.

The last composition pattern introduced is a SEQ pattern, where a service consumer invokes a range of service providers one after another in a sequential and predefined order. Obviously, the transition probability between two successive service invocations is always 100%.

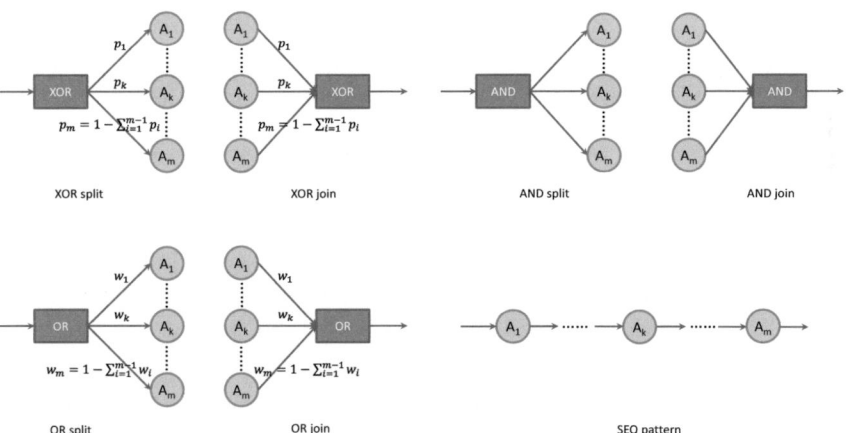

Figure 6-8: Composition patterns in business logics

Figure 6-8 illustrates all composition patterns defined in the present thesis to model invocation behaviour of a service consumer at runtime. It is noteworthy that all composition patterns except the SEQ pattern can be used either as a split gateway or as a join gateway to model invocation behaviour. For example, in order to improve responsiveness of a service consumer, it can invoke several redundant service providers using the same service request. A service consumer can take the first incoming service response to continue its logic flow. Other responses arriving after this point in time will be discarded by the consumer. In this case, the service consumer combines an AND split to start a set of parallel service invocations and an XOR join to exclusive select an incoming responses.

Based on the composition patterns introduced in this section, a service component can model its business logic (i.e., invocation behaviour) in terms of chronological invocations of service providers in the underlying layers. In particular, it is possible to address the order and the relationships of service invocations, which play a crucial role to delegate an appropriate portion of non-functional requirements to a particular service provider at runtime. In addition, there are nine possible combinations of the splitting/joining gateways illustrated in Figure 6-8, i.e., XOR-XOR, XOR-AND, XOR-OR, AND-XOR, AND-AND, AND-OR, OR-XOR, OR-AND, OR-OR. However, some of them do not make sense from the viewpoint of business logic. For example, an XOR split pattern cannot be followed by an AND pattern.

Hence, in the remainder of this chapter, only the following composition patterns are considered:

- XOR-XOR, i.e., an XOR split in combination with an XOR join: the exclusive choice of a service provider takes place at the XOR split pattern.

- AND-XOR, i.e., an AND split in combination with an XOR join: all service providers are invoked by a consumer. It performs an exclusive choice among all responses at the XOR join.

- AND-OR, i.e., an AND split in combination with an OR join: all service providers are invoked by a consumer. It selects a set of responses in dependence of its current operational context.

- AND-AND, i.e., an AND split in combination with an AND join: responses of all service providers are required by a consumer to continue its logic flow.

- OR-OR, i.e., an OR split in combination with an OR join: only some of a given set of service providers are selected by a consumer at the OR split.

- OR-XOR, i.e., an OR split in combination with an XOR join: a consumer invokes a selected set of service providers and makes an exclusive choice among all responses of these selected providers.

Figure 6-9 illustrates an example of the business logic of a service component with various composition patterns. In addition to local activities that the service component performs in the layer n, it consumes services from the underlying layer $n + 1$ to realise its business logic.

The business logic starts with two sequential invocations of the service component S_1 and the local activity L_1. After this, it splits its logic flow into two parallel sub-flows with an AND split pattern. That is, the main logic flow has to wait for further execution, until both sub-flows have completed their activities. The upper sub-flow in the figure splits its flow into two further sub-flows with an XOR split. In other words, only one of the activities L_2 and S_3 will be executed in the upper sub-flow. In the lower sub-flow, the service S_2 is consumed. After both sub-flows have completed their execution, they return to the main logic flow, where the service S_4 is consumed in a sequential order in the flow. The complete business logic terminates after the service consumption of S_4.

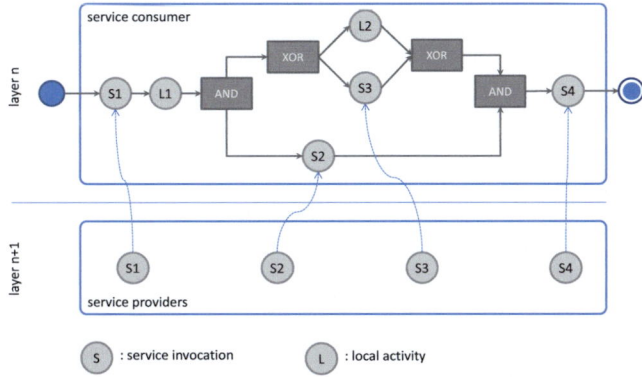

Figure 6-9: Sample business logic with composition patterns

Modelling the business logics of a service component by means of composition patterns is crucial for determining negotiation spaces for its service providers. Structural analysis of business logics allows a service component to precisely determine the impacts of particular service providers on its local behaviour, in particular with respect to its non-functional behaviour. For example, behaviour (e.g., response time) of the XOR-XOR composition in Figure 6-9 depends on the probabilities that both activities L_2 and S_3 are executed at runtime. However, this relationship changes, if both activities are composed with an AND-AND pattern instead of an XOR-XOR pattern.

In this case, response time of the composition is determined by the activity that takes longer for execution.

Therefore, the following sections focus on the impacts of different composition patterns on non-functional behaviour of a service consumer. In particular, the following sections investigate relationships between the overall QoS values of a composition pattern and the QoS values of each particular service provider within the pattern by means of composition and decomposition schemas.

6.6.2 Decomposing QoS Requirements

As aforementioned, the prerequisite to utilise the negotiation protocol introduced in Section 6.5 is the ability of a service component to decompose QoS requirements for each of its service provider. This task is however not trivial. It has to take the nature of each service provider into consideration, so that the resulting sub-requirements comply with the behaviour pattern of the respective provider. For example, a service consumer needs two service providers to accomplish its task and it can pay maximally 100 cost units for consuming these services. Theoretically, there are an infinite number of possibilities to distribute 100 cost units between its two providers, but not all of them are reasonable from the viewpoint of negotiation. That is, assuming that both service providers have similar service charges, then a distribution with 50 cost units for each provider is more likely to be acceptable for the involved parties than a distribution with 10 cost units for one provider and 90 cost units for the other one. Analogously, if the average service charges of both service providers have a relation of about 1:2, then distributing cost units equally between them is not applicable. Hence, decomposing QoS requirements of a service consumer to construct negotiation spaces has to take behaviour patterns of respective service providers into consideration.

The key challenge to decompose QoS requirements is to determine appropriate portions of QoS requirements for each service provider. Ideally, each functional dependence between a service consumer and one of its service providers can be associated with a kind of impact factor that specifies how far the respective provider affects the overall QoS behaviour of the consumer. However, such impact factors are hard to estimate. In particular, due to the large number of various types of QoS parameters that a service consumer has to deal with, a generic way to establish such impact factors is hard to define. Depending on the particular type of a QoS parameter, it may require a different decomposition schema. From this viewpoint, generic impact factors for all QoS parameters are not applicable.

Therefore, instead of using a generic mechanism to decompose given QoS requirements, a consumer has to consider each QoS parameter separately with respect to the following aspects:

- Characteristics of a QoS parameter: for example, service response time T_r is calculated by determining the time difference between sending a service request at t_{input} and receiving a corresponding service response from a provider at t_{output}, namely $|t_{output} - t_{input}|$. Therefore, the total service response time of two sequential service invocations could be determined by adding the response time of these two service invocations. However, this schema cannot be applied to statistically computed QoS parameters, such as availability. As discussed in Section 3.2.3, availability of a service provider is the probability that the provider is accessible in a given period, namely $\frac{t_{up}}{t_{up}+t_{down}}$. In contrast to response time, availability of a composition consisting of sequential service invocations cannot be estimated by simply summing up the availabilities of both service providers. Instead, it is the product of availability of all service providers, which addresses the probability that all service providers are simultaneously accessible within the given time slot.

- Composition patterns, which specify functional dependences between a service consumer and its providers, as introduced in Section 6.6.1. Obviously, even with the same set of service providers, different composition patterns result in a different composite QoS behaviour on the consumer level.

- Behaviour patterns of a particular service type as well as a particular service provider. Such behaviour patterns state how a particular service provider or a service type behaved in previous sessions. For example, historical QoS information may contains average response time of a particular service provider or of all service providers of the same type in previous session(s). To decompose overall QoS requirements between several service providers, a service consumer incorporates such historical QoS information as reference of behaviour patterns of a given service provider to decompose overall QoS requirements for it. Obviously, the more precise such historical information is, the more accurate are the decomposition results for the provider.

Therefore, in order to decompose overall QoS requirements for particular service providers, a service consumer needs to determine behaviour patterns of the corresponding service providers (or of their service types) in terms of service level objectives, composition patterns organising these service providers, and characteristics of QoS parameters involved.

A management agent is aware of behaviour patterns of a service provider as well as a service type. As discussed in Section 5.2.4, a management agent collects management information from the underlying service component, including information about invocations of its service providers. Invocation information can be distinguished on three different levels: *instance level*, *provider level*, and *service-type level*. In other words, information on the instance level is associated with a particular instance of a provider. Historical information on the provider level is associated with a particular service provider. Hence, such information is calculated across all instances of a corresponding service provider. Similarly, information on the service-type level is associated with a particular service type and is estimated based on information collected across all service providers of the same type.

Differentiation between three levels of details allows a management agent to determine behaviour patterns of a given service provider as precisely as possible. It is obvious that information on the instance level is the most precise and reflects the exact behaviour of a particular service instance. This delivers therefore an accurate base to determine the extent of the influence that a service provider has on the overall behaviour of its consumer, in particular with respect to given QoS requirements. Behaviour patterns consolidated based on provider level information helps a management agent to estimate runtime capacities of a particular provider. In case that no instance level and provider level information is available for a given service provider, a management agent uses information on the service-type level in its decomposition process. Under the assumption that service providers have similar implementation complexity for the same service type, such service-type level information delivers at least approximate reference values for a given service provider.

It is noteworthy that service level management is a dynamic process within a running service-oriented system. That is, collected information to estimate behaviour patterns of a service component evolves in the course of system operation. Continuous monitoring of an underlying service component allows a management agent to continuously improve its knowledge about a particular service provider instance. For its service component, incorrect decomposition of service requirements based on imprecise information of a corresponding service provider at the beginning can be gradually improved based on an increasingly accurate knowledge base, e.g., by renegotiating less accurate SLAs in case of violations. Section 8.3 addresses this scenario in detail and outlines the process towards stable SLAs.

Given a service consumer c with its service providers $\{1, 2, ..., m\}$ and a set of QoS parameters $\{1, 2, ..., n\}$, let $\{h_1^c[j], h_2^c[j], ..., h_m^c[j]\}$ be the observed average values at the instance level for a particular QoS parameter $j \in \{1, 2, ...n\}$, $\{h_1^p[j], h_2^p[j], ..., h_m^p[j]\}$ be the corresponding average values at the provider level, and $\{h_1^s[j], h_2^s[j], ..., h_m^s[j]\}$ be the average values at the service-type level, then historical information that the consumer c uses for a service provider $i \in \{1, 2, ..., m\}$ in the decomposition schemas is defined as:

$$h_i[j] = \begin{cases} h_i^c[j] & \text{if } h_i^c[j] \neq null \\ h_i^p[j] & \text{if } h_i^p[j] \neq null \text{ and } h_i^c[j] = null \\ h_i^s[j] & \text{if } h_i^s[j] \neq null, h_i^p[j] = null, \text{ and } h_i^c[j] = null \end{cases} \tag{6.6.1}$$

That is, if instance-specific historical information is available, this information is used; otherwise, less-accurate provider-specific information about a corresponding service provider is used as a reference, if it is available. If both types of information are not available, then historical information on service-type level is used as reference.

Secondly, each management agent is aware of the business logic of its underlying service component. In particular, such business logic consists of composition patterns that organise chronological service invocations of underlying service providers. As discussed in Section 5.2.3, the collaboration manager of a management agent maintains relationships of its underlying service component to other related components in the environment. In addition, the collaboration manager is aware of the set of service providers, with which a management agent has to negotiate an SLA.

Hence, given appropriate behaviour patterns as well as composition patterns of all related service providers, and a set of QoS parameters, a service consumer can start a decomposition process to determine how it can delegate part of its QoS requirements to its service providers. To this end, this section defines a range of decomposition schemas for the selected QoS parameters. In the remainder of this section, let x_c be the QoS requirements for a given set of QoS parameters $\{1, 2, ..., n\}$ of a consumer, and x_i be the decomposed QoS values for the activity $i \in \{1, 2, ..., m\}$ in the composition pattern. Each activity can be either an invocation of the service of an underlying service component, or an invocation of a local service capability.

Availability

As discussed in the previous section, depending on composition patterns, availability of a service consumer is determined either by all of its providers or by a particular provider at runtime.

In the patterns AND-AND and SEQ, where availability of a consumer $x_c[j]$ (i.e., the QoS parameter $j \in \{1, 2, ...n\}$ is availability) depends on availabilities of all involved service providers $x_i[j]$ with $i \in \{1, 2, ..., m\}$, composite availability of a consumer and availabilities of all service providers satisfy the following conditions:

$$\begin{cases} x_1[j] \cdot x_2[j] \cdot ... \cdot x_m[j] = x_c[j] \\ |\ln x_1[j]| \cdot h_1[j] = |\ln x_2[j]| \cdot h_2[j] = ... = |\ln x_m[j]| \cdot h_m[j]. \end{cases} \tag{6.6.2}$$

In (6.6.2), $h_i[j]$ is the historical information of the service provider i for the QoS parameter j. From the second condition in (6.6.2) it can be derived that for any two service invocation activities $a, b \in \{1, 2, ..., m\}$ with $a \neq b$:

$$\begin{aligned} &|\ln x_a[j]| \cdot h_a[j] = |\ln x_b[j]| \cdot h_b[j] \\ \iff &-\ln x_a[j] \cdot h_a[j] = -\ln x_b[j] \cdot h_b[j] \text{ with } \ln x_i[j] \leq 0 \text{ for } x_i[j] \in [0, 1] \\ \iff &\ln x_a[j] \cdot h_a[j] = \ln x_b[j] \cdot h_b[j] \\ \iff &\ln x_a[j] = \ln x_b[j] \cdot (h_b[j]/h_a[j]) \\ \iff &e^{\ln x_a[j]} = e^{\ln x_b[j] \cdot (h_b[j]/h_a[j])} \\ \iff &e^{\ln x_a[j]} = (e^{\ln x_b[j]})^{(h_b[j]/h_a[j])} \\ \iff &x_a[j] = x_b[j]^{h_b[j]/h_a[j]} \end{aligned} \tag{6.6.3}$$

By applying (6.6.3) to the first condition of (6.6.2), one gets that for a given activity $i \in \{1, 2, ..., m\}$:

$$\begin{aligned} &x_1[j] \cdot x_2[j] \cdot ... \cdot x_i[j] \cdot ... \cdot x_m[j] = x_c[j] \\ \iff &x_i[j]^{h_i[j]/h_1[j]} \cdot x_i[j]^{h_i[j]/h_2[j]} \cdot ... \cdot x_i[j] \cdot ... \cdot x_i[j]^{h_i[j]/h_m[j]} = x_c[j] \\ \iff &x_i[j]^{\sum_{k=1}^{m} \frac{h_i[j]}{h_k[j]}} = x_c[j] \\ \iff &x_i[j] = x_c[j]^{\sum_{k=1}^{m} \frac{h_i[j]}{h_k[j]}} \end{aligned} \tag{6.6.4}$$

Using (6.6.4), a consumer can compute the corresponding requirement for availability of each activity that is bound to the current consumer via either an AND-AND or an SEQ composition pattern, where composite availability of the consumer depends on all its service providers.

In the composition patterns XOR-XOR, AND-XOR, as well as OR-XOR, availability of a consumer depends on that of a selected activity in the pattern. That is, an appropriate decomposition schema has to take into consideration the probability, with which the corresponding service provider $i \in \{1, 2, ..., m\}$ will be selected by an XOR join at runtime. Hence, the following conditions apply to a consumer and its involved activities with respect to their availabilities:

$$\begin{cases} p_1 \cdot x_1[j] + p_2 \cdot x_2[j] + ... + p_m \cdot x_m[j] = x_c[j] \\ \frac{x_1[j]}{h_1[j]} = \frac{x_2[j]}{h_2[j]} = ... = \frac{x_m[j]}{h_m[j]} \end{cases} \quad . \tag{6.6.5}$$

That is, the composite availability of a consumer depends proportionally on availabilities of all involved activities with respect to their probabilities for being invoked at runtime. By solving the second condition in (6.6.5), it can be derived that for any two activities $a, b \in \{1, 2, ..., m\}$ with $a \neq b$:

$$x_a[j] = \frac{h_a}{h_b} \cdot x_b[j]. \tag{6.6.6}$$

By combining (6.6.6) with the first condition in (6.6.5), it can be derived that for a given activity $i \in \{1, 2, ..., m\}$:

$$\begin{aligned} x_c[j] &= p_1 \cdot \frac{h_1[j]}{h_i[j]} \cdot x_i[j] + p_2 \cdot \frac{h_2[j]}{h_i[j]} \cdot x_i[j] + ... + p_i \cdot \frac{h_i[j]}{h_i[j]} \cdot x_i[j] + ... + p_m \cdot \frac{h_m[j]}{h_i[j]} \cdot x_i[j] \\ &= \frac{(p_1 \cdot h_1[j] + p_2 \cdot h_2[j] + ... + p_i \cdot h_i[j] + ... + p_m \cdot h_m[j])}{h_i[j]} \cdot x_i[j] \\ &= \frac{\sum_{k=1}^{m} p_k \cdot h_k[j]}{h_i[j]} \cdot x_i[j] \\ \Longleftrightarrow x_i[j] &= \frac{h_i[j]}{\sum_{k=1}^{m} p_k \cdot h_k[j]} \cdot x_c[j] \end{aligned} \quad .$$

For the patterns discussed so far, they allow to estimate precisely how probable it is for a particular activity to be invoked by a consumer instance at runtime. By using these estimated probabilities, it is possible to determine to which extent a respective service invocation influences the overall behaviour of a composition pattern, in particular from the viewpoint of non-functional aspects. However, in a composition pattern consisting of an OR split/join, it is not possible to estimate invocation probabilities for particular service invocations. For each single consumer instance, there can be a range of possible combinations of several parallel executed service invocations. Each of these possible combinations is an element in the power set of all activities $\{A_1, A_2, ..., A_k, ..., A_m\}$ except the empty set. Hence, for a service consumer, it is only possible to estimate probabilities of occurrence of a particular set from the power set. This, however, does not help to estimate precisely the extent of influence of a particular service invocation on the overall behaviour of the composition at runtime.

Therefore, instead of estimating decomposed values for involved activities directly in an AND-OR or OR-OR pattern, these patterns are at first transformed to an equivalent structure consisting of patterns that allow precise estimation of decomposed values, as illustrated in Figure 6-10.

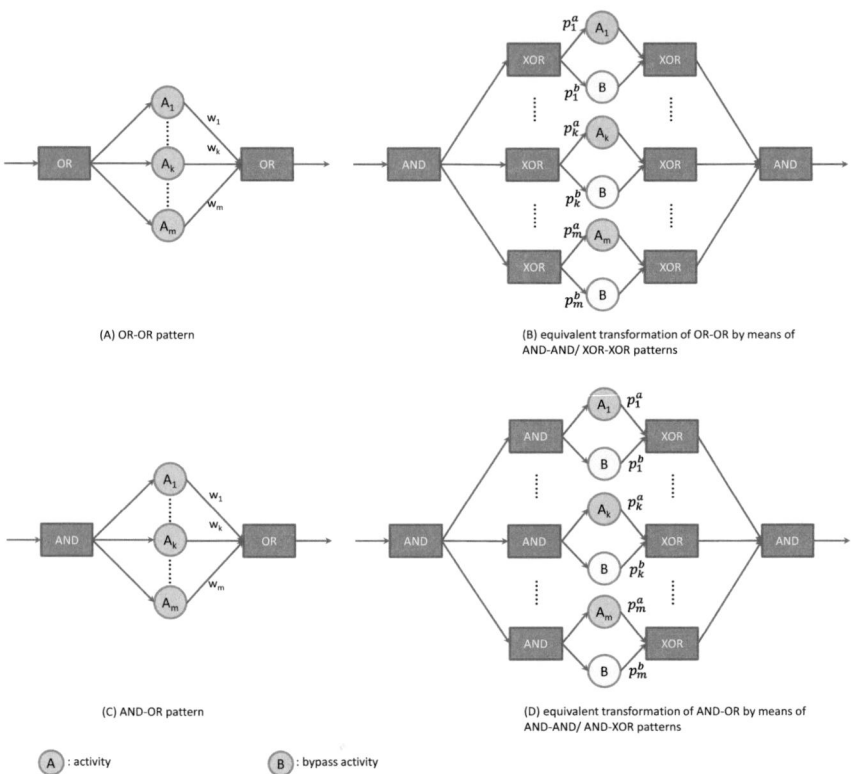

(A) OR-OR pattern

(B) equivalent transformation of OR-OR by means of AND-AND/ XOR-XOR patterns

(C) AND-OR pattern

(D) equivalent transformation of AND-OR by means of AND-AND/ AND-XOR patterns

(A) : activity   (B) : bypass activity

Figure 6-10: Transformation of AND-OR / OR-OR patterns

On the left are the OR-OR and AND-OR patterns, whose difference in behaviour is the point in time, at which evaluation of predefined conditions takes place. In an AND-OR pattern, an evaluation of operational context takes place, after all activities have been completed. In contrast, an OR-OR evaluates predefined conditions before invoking selected activities.

Hence, the AND-OR pattern and the OR-OR pattern are handled separately. Illustration (B) in Figure 6-10 depicts the equivalent transformation of an OR-OR pattern by means of a set of AND-AND and XOR-XOR patterns. In the transformation, each branch in the original OR-OR pattern is replaced by an XOR-XOR pattern, which decides based on runtime operational context either to activate the branch (i.e., invoke the corresponding activity) or to bypass the branch. Hence, the activity of an i-th XOR-XOR branch has a probability of p_i^a to be activated at runtime. Correspondingly, the same XOR-XOR pattern also has a probability of p_i^b with $p_i^a + p_i^b = 1$ to be bypassed by the pattern at runtime. All XOR-XOR patterns are combined by an AND-AND pattern. That is, all XOR-XOR patterns are activated by an AND split. Results of all XOR-XOR patterns are merged by an AND join.

In this way, relationships between availabilities of related service invocations and the overall availability of an OR-OR pattern can be determined by considering respective relationships in its replacement structure. For each XOR-XOR branch with service invocation of activity i, its composite availability $x_i^r[j]$ can be determined by using:

$$x_i^r[j] = p_i^a \cdot x_i[j] + p_i^b \cdot 1 = p_i^a \cdot x_i[j] + p_i^b. \tag{6.6.7}$$

Here, $x_i[j]$ is the availability of the activity $i \in \{1, 2, ..., m\}$. Furthermore, it is assumed that a bypass activity has the availability of 1.

By considering each XOR-XOR branch as a composite activity in an AND-AND pattern, the overall availability of the AND-AND pattern $x_c[j]$ satisfies the following conditions:

$$\begin{cases} x_1^r[j] \cdot x_2^r[j] \cdot .... \cdot x_m^r[j] = x_c[j] \\ |\ln x_1^r[j]| \cdot h_1^r[j] = |\ln x_2^r[j]| \cdot h_2^r[j] = ... = |\ln x_m^r[j]| \cdot h_m^r[j]. \end{cases} \tag{6.6.8}$$

Here, $h_k^r[j]$ is the historical average availability of a corresponding XOR-XOR branch and can be estimated analogously to (6.6.7) with: $h_i^r[j] = p_i^a \cdot h_i[j] + p_i^b$, where $h_i[j]$ is the average availability of the i-th activity from the history.

By solving (6.6.8) in a similar manner as in (6.6.2), the composite availability of a XOR-XOR branch with the activity $i \in \{1, 2, ..., m\}$ is given by:

$$x_i^r[j] = x_c[j]^{1/\sum_{k=1}^{m} \frac{h_i^r[j]}{h_k^r[j]}}. \tag{6.6.9}$$

By combining the formulas of (6.6.7) and (6.6.9), one can get that for a given activity i of an OR-OR pattern, its respectively decomposed availability can be calculated by:

$$x_i^r[j] = p_i^a \cdot x_i[j] + p_i^b = x_c[j]^{1/\sum_{k=1}^m \frac{h_i^r[j]}{h_k^r[j]}}$$

$$\Longleftrightarrow x_i[j] = \frac{x_c[j]^{1/\sum_{k=1}^m \frac{h_i^r[j]}{h_k^r[j]}} - p_i^b}{p_i^a}$$

As aforementioned, the last pattern, the AND-OR pattern, differs from an OR-OR pattern in the point in time to evaluate conditional expressions of each branch. Hence, in its replacement structure, as depicted in illustration (D) in Figure 6-10, each branch is replaced by an AND-XOR pattern. This ensures that each activity involved in an AND-OR pattern is always invoked before evaluating its corresponding conditional expression, as defined in an AND-OR pattern.

Correspondingly, both the service activity i and the bypass activity in the i-th AND-XOR pattern are assigned respectively with two probability values p_i^a and p_i^b. The value p_i^a indicates the chance that the branch with the service activity is selected by the XOR join of the corresponding AND-XOR pattern at runtime. Similarly, p_i^b shows the probability that the result of service invocation i is discarded by the XOR-join. Furthermore, all AND-XOR patterns are combined by an AND split and merged by an AND join. This ensures all AND-XOR branches are activated at runtime, analogously to the behaviour of an AND-OR pattern.

Hence, the composite availability of an AND-XOR branch can be estimated using:

$$x_i^r[j] = p_i^a \cdot x_i[j] + p_i^b \cdot 1 = p_i^a \cdot x_i[j] + p_i^b. \tag{6.6.10}$$

Since all AND-XOR branches are combined by an AND-AND pattern, the overall availability of the pattern and availabilities of all AND-XOR branches satisfy the same conditions as in (6.6.8) and (6.6.9). Therefore, availability of each service activity i can be estimated out of the overall availability $x_c[j]$ using:

$$x_i[j] = \frac{x_c[j]^{1/\sum_{k=1}^m \frac{h_i^r[j]}{h_k^r[j]}} - p_i^b}{p_i^a} .$$

Here, $h_i^r[j]$ is the composite availability of an AND-XOR branch with service invocation of the provider i and is given by:

$$h_i^r[j] = p_i^a \cdot h_i[j] + p_i^b.$$

Cost

Cost is a QoS parameter that depends on the number of services invoked by a service consumer: the resulting composite cost of a service consumer is the sum of service costs of all service invocations. As already mentioned before, in the composition patterns AND-XOR, AND-OR, AND-AND, and SEQ, all service activities specified in the patterns are invoked by a consumer. Therefore, the composite cost $x_c[j]$ of a service consumer and the cost of all service invocations satisfy the following conditions:

$$\begin{cases} x_1[j] + x_2[j] + \dots + x_m[j] = x_c[j] \\ \frac{x_1[j]}{h_1[j]} = \frac{x_2[j]}{h_2[j]} = \dots = \frac{x_m[j]}{h_m[j]} \end{cases}. \tag{6.6.11}$$

For two given service activities $a, b \in \{1, 2, \dots, m\}$ and $a \neq b$, it can be derived from the second condition in (6.6.11) that

$$x_b[j] = \frac{h_b[j]}{h_a[j]} \cdot x_a[j]. \tag{6.6.12}$$

For an activity i, the first condition in (6.6.11) can be transformed as follows:

$$x_1[j] + x_2[j] + \dots + x_i[j] + \dots + x_m[j] = x_c[j]$$

$$\Longleftrightarrow \frac{h_1[j]}{h_i[j]} \cdot x_i[j] + \frac{h_2[j]}{h_i[j]} \cdot x_i[j] + \dots + \frac{h_i[j]}{h_i[j]} \cdot x_i[j] + \dots + \frac{h_m[j]}{h_i[j]} \cdot x_i[j] = x_c[j]$$

$$\Longleftrightarrow \frac{h_1[j] + h_2[j] + \dots + h_i[j] + \dots + h_m[j]}{h_i[j]} \cdot x_i[j] = x_c[j]$$

$$\Longleftrightarrow x_i[j] = \frac{h_i[j]}{h_1[j] + h_2[j] + \dots + h_i[j] + \dots + h_m[j]} \cdot x_c[j] \tag{6.6.13}$$

$$\Longleftrightarrow x_i[j] = \frac{h_i[j]}{\sum_{k=1}^{m} h_k[j]} \cdot x_c[j].$$

For an XOR-XOR pattern, where only a single selected activity is invoked by a consumer, it applies in general that cost of any service invocation i fulfils the condition: $x_i[j] \leq x_c[j]$ with $i \in \{1, 2, \dots, m\}$. That is, cost of any service activity i involved in an XOR-XOR pattern is equal to or less than the composite cost of the pattern. Hence, additional information is required to estimate $x_i[j]$ more precisely. As aforementioned, it is possible to estimate the probability that an activity is invoked by a consumer. Hence, it satisfies the following conditions:

$$\begin{cases} p_1 \cdot x_1[j] + p_2 \cdot x_2[j] + \dots + p_m \cdot x_m[j] = x_c[j] \\ \frac{x_1[j]}{h_1[j]} = \frac{x_2[j]}{h_2[j]} = \dots = \frac{x_m[j]}{h_m[j]} \end{cases}. \tag{6.6.14}$$

The first condition states that composite cost of a service consumer is the sum of service cost of all service invocations with respect to their respective invocation probabilities at runtime. The second condition determines that invocation cost of a service activity i is proportional to its average invocation cost in the past. Hence, given two activities $a, b \in \{1, 2, ..., m\}$ and $a \neq b$, it can be derived from the second condition in (6.6.14) that

$$x_a[j] = \frac{h_a[j]}{h_b[j]} \cdot x_b[j]$$

By applying this term into the first condition in (6.6.14), for a given service activity i, it can be transformed as follows:

$$p_1 \cdot x_1[j] + ... + p_i \cdot x_i[j] + ... + p_m \cdot x_m[j] = x_c[j]$$

$$\Longleftrightarrow p_1 \cdot \frac{h_1[j]}{h_i[j]} \cdot x_i[j] + ... + p_i \cdot \frac{h_i[j]}{h_i[j]} \cdot x_i[j] + ... + p_m \cdot \frac{h_m[j]}{h_i[j]} \cdot x_i[j] = x_c[j]$$

$$\Longleftrightarrow \frac{p_1 \cdot h_1[j] + ... + p_i \cdot h_i[j] + ... + p_m \cdot h_m[j]}{h_i[j]} \cdot x_i[j] = x_c[j]$$

$$\Longleftrightarrow \frac{\sum_{k=1}^{m} p_k \cdot h_k[j]}{h_i[j]} \cdot x_i[j] = x_c[j] \tag{6.6.15}$$

$$\Longleftrightarrow x_i[j] = \frac{h_i[j]}{\sum_{k=1}^{m} p_k \cdot h_k[j]} \cdot x_c[j]$$

By comparing the results in (6.6.13) and (6.6.15), it is obvious that one can get the equation (6.6.13) by setting all invocation probabilities p_k in (6.6.15) to 1. This correlation is reasonable, since all activities in the composition patterns AND-XOR, AND-OR, AND-AND, and SEQ are executed with a probability of 100%.

For the OR-OR pattern and the OR-XOR pattern, several branches can be activated simultaneously at runtime. Hence, in order to estimate composite cost of these patterns, one has to determine the set of all possible combinations of simultaneously activated branches (i.e., the power set of all service providers $\{1, 2, ..., m\}$ except the empty set, with a total size of $2^m - 1$), and the probabilities that these combinations are activated at runtime. Hence, a management agent has to make considerable efforts to collect and aggregate relevant information from the underlying service component.

Therefore, to enable an efficient estimation of decomposed cost for service activities, the OR-OR and OR-XOR patterns are transformed firstly to equivalent structures, as done for determining decomposition schemas in the previous section.

An OR-OR pattern is replaced by a combination of XOR-XOR and AND-AND patterns, as depicted by the illustration (B) in Figure 6-10. Under the assumption that a bypass activity does not cause any service cost, each XOR-XOR branch in the replacement structure has the composite cost:

$$x_i^r[j] = p_i^a \cdot x_i[j] + p_i^b \cdot 0 = p_i^a \cdot x_i[j]. \tag{6.6.16}$$

Since all XOR-XOR branches are combined by an AND split and synchronised by an AND join, the composite cost of the entire replacement structure can be estimated as follows:

$$\begin{cases} x_1^r[j] + x_2^r[j] + \dots + x_m^r[j] = x_c[j] \\ \frac{x_1^r[j]}{h_1^r[j]} = \frac{x_2^r[j]}{h_2^r[j]} = \dots = \frac{x_m^r[j]}{h_m^r[j]} \end{cases} \quad . \tag{6.6.17}$$

Here, $h_i^r[j]$ is the composite historical information of the i-th XOR-XOR branch and is determined by $h_i^r[j] = p_i^a \cdot h_i[j]$. By solving the equations in (6.6.17), the decomposed cost for the i-th XOR-XOR branch can be determined as follows:

$$x_i^r[j] = \frac{h_i^r[j]}{\sum_{k=1}^m h_k^r[j]} \cdot x_c[j] \quad . \tag{6.6.18}$$

By combining the formulas (6.6.16) and (6.6.18), the following condition applies:

$$x_i^r[j] = p_i^a \cdot x_i[j] = \frac{h_i^r[j]}{\sum_{k=1}^m h_k^r[j]} \cdot x_c[j] \quad .$$

Therefore, the decomposed cost for invoking the service provider i can be calculated as follows:

$$\begin{aligned} x_i[j] &= \frac{h_i^r[j]}{p_i^a \cdot \sum_{k=1}^m h_k^r[j]} \cdot x_c[j] \\ &= \frac{p_i^a \cdot h_i[j]}{p_i^a \cdot \sum_{k=1}^m h_k^r[j]} \cdot x_c[j] \\ &= \frac{h_i[j]}{\sum_{k=1}^m h_k^r[j]} \cdot x_c[j] \quad . \end{aligned}$$

Similarly, an OR-XOR pattern is first transformed to an equivalent structure consisting of m XOR-XOR patterns and an AND-XOR pattern, as depicted in illustration (B) in Figure 6-11. To each XOR-XOR branch in the transformed structure, (6.6.16) can be applied to determine its composite cost, too. In addition, all XOR-XOR branches are combined by an AND-XOR pattern. That is, they are combined by an AND split and synchronised at the end by an XOR join.

For the XOR join in the AND-XOR pattern, each XOR-XOR branch has the probability of p_i to be selected by the exclusive join. Therefore, the composite cost of the entire transformed structure satisfies the following conditions:

$$\begin{cases} p_1 \cdot x_1^r[j] + p_2 \cdot x_2^r[j] + \dots + p_m \cdot x_m^r[j] = x_c[j] \\ \frac{x_1^r[j]}{h_1^r[j]} = \frac{x_2^r[j]}{h_2^r[j]} = \dots = \frac{x_m^r[j]}{h_m^r[j]} \end{cases} \quad . \tag{6.6.19}$$

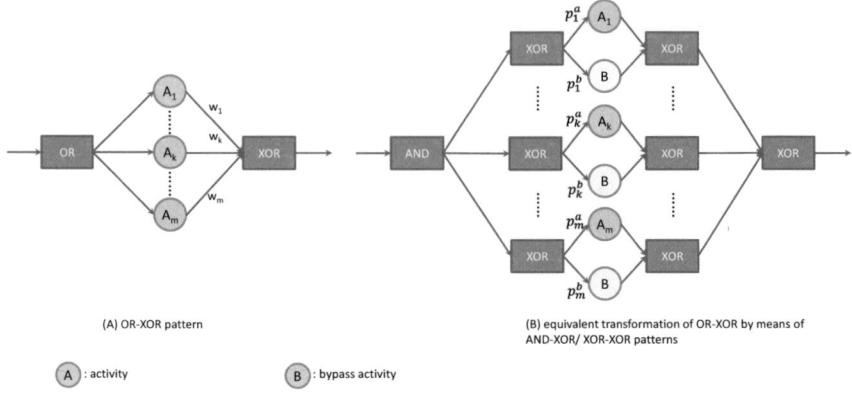

(A) OR-XOR pattern

(B) equivalent transformation of OR-XOR by means of AND-XOR/ XOR-XOR patterns

A : activity   B : bypass activity

Figure 6-11: Transformation of OR-XOR pattern

The equations in (6.6.19) can be solved in a similar way as (6.6.14). Hence, the composite cost of the i-th XOR-XOR branch can be estimated by:

$$x_i^r[j] = \frac{h_i^r[j]}{\sum_{k=1}^{m} p_k \cdot h_k^r[j]} \cdot x_c[j]$$

$$(6.6.20)$$

The composite cost of an XOR-XOR branch is also given by

$$x_i^r[j] = p_i^a \cdot x_i[j].$$

Hence, the decomposed cost for an activity $i \in \{1, 2, ..., m\}$ can be estimated as follows:

$$x_i^r[j] = \frac{h_i^r[j]}{\sum_{k=1}^{m} p_k \cdot h_k^r[j]} \cdot x_c[j] = p_i^a \cdot x_i[j]$$

$$\Longleftrightarrow x_i[j] = \frac{h_i^r[j]}{p_i^a \cdot \sum_{k=1}^{m} p_k \cdot h_k^r[j]} \cdot x_c[j]$$

$$\Longleftrightarrow x_i[j] = \frac{p_i^a \cdot h_i[j]}{p_i^a \cdot \sum_{k=1}^{m} p_k \cdot h_k^r[j]} \cdot x_c[j]$$

$$\Longleftrightarrow x_i[j] = \frac{h_i[j]}{\sum_{k=1}^{m} p_k \cdot h_k^r[j]} \cdot x_c[j]$$

Here, $h_i^r[j]$ is the historical composite average cost of the i-th XOR-XOR branch and can be determined by $h_i^r[j] = p_i^a \cdot h_i[j]$.

Response time

Response time of a service consumer depends strongly on the way, in which its service providers are invoked. If all service providers are executed in parallel, such as in the patterns with OR or AND splits, response time of the service consumer is determined by the largest response time among all service invocations, i.e., $x_i[j] \leq x_c[j]$ with $i \in \{1, 2, ..., m\}$. In an SEQ pattern, where all service providers are consumed one after another, composite response time of a consumer is determined by the sum of response times of all service invocations.

In addition, invocation probability p_i of a given activity i at runtime also influences response time of a consumer. While in composition patterns with XOR splits/joins, only a single service provider is invoked by a consumer, in all other patterns, all selected activities are invoked either simultaneously or in a sequential manner.

Therefore, it has to be distinguished between the following three different cases to get an accurate decomposition of $x_c[j]$: one case with parallel invocation of all service providers, a second case with a single invocation of a particular service provider, and a third one with sequential invocation of all service providers.

For an AND-AND pattern, response time for each service invocation can be estimated in percentage terms, with respect to their historical values:

$$\frac{x_1[j]}{h_1[j]} = ... = \frac{x_i[j]}{h_i[j]} = ... = \frac{x_m[j]}{h_m[j]} = \frac{x_c[j]}{h_c[j]}.$$

Hence, for a given service activity i, its decomposed response time is determined by:

$$x_i[j] = h_i[j] \cdot \frac{x_c[j]}{h_c[j]} = \frac{h_i[j]}{h_c[j]} \cdot x_c[j].$$

For an AND-XOR, OR-XOR, or XOR-XOR pattern, invocation probability of an activity p_i determines the extent of the influence of a respective service activity i on the overall composite response time of the pattern. Hence, this correlation satisfies the following conditions:

$$\begin{cases} p_1 \cdot x_1[j] + ... + p_i \cdot x_i[j] + ... + p_m \cdot x_m[j] = x_c[j] \\ x_1[j]/h_1[j] = ... = x_i[j]/h_i[j] = ... = x_m[j]/h_m[j]. \end{cases} \tag{6.6.21}$$

Similar to (6.6.14), the decomposed response time of a service invocation i can be estimated as follows:

$$x_i[j] = \frac{h_i[j]}{\sum_{k=1}^{m} h_k[j] \cdot p_k} \cdot x_c[j].$$

For the SEQ pattern, response time between a consumer and its providers applies the same dependence as for service cost shown in (6.6.11). That is, the composite response time of a service consumer is the sum of all response times of all service invocations involved. Hence, the decomposed response time of an i-th activity can be estimated as follows:

$$x_i[j] = \frac{h_i[j]}{\sum_{k=1}^m h_k[j]} \cdot x_c[j].$$

Decomposing the composite response time of an AND-OR or OR-OR pattern causes similar problems as decomposing the service cost for these patterns. In particular, complex procedures to determine the possible combinations of activities, and the activation probabilities of these combinations at runtime, complicate the direct estimation of decomposed values. Hence, the equivalent transformations of both patterns, as illustrated in Figure 6-10, are used to estimate decomposed response times.

In the replacement structure of an AND-OR pattern, response time of the i-th AND-XOR branch is given by:

$$x_i^r[j] = p_i^a \cdot x_i[j]. \tag{6.6.22}$$

In (6.6.22), it is assumed that a bypass activity has a response time of 0. Since all AND-XOR branches are combined by an AND split and merged by an AND join, composite response times of all AND-XOR branches satisfy the following condition:

$$\frac{x_1^r[j]}{h_1^r[j]} = \ldots = \frac{x_i^r[j]}{h_i^r[j]} = \ldots = \frac{x_m^r[j]}{h_m^r[j]} = \frac{x_c[j]}{h_c[j]}. \tag{6.6.23}$$

Here, $h_i^r[j]$ is the composite historical response time of the i-th branch and is determined by:

$$h_i^r[j] = p_i^a \cdot h_i[j].$$

By combing (6.6.22) and (6.6.23), the decomposed response time for an activity i can be calculated by:

$$x_i^r[j] = \frac{h_i^r[j]}{h_c[j]} \cdot x_c[j] = p_i^a \cdot x_i[j]$$
$$\Longleftrightarrow x_i[j] = \frac{h_i^r[j]}{p_i^a \cdot h_c[j]} \cdot x_c[j]$$
$$\Longleftrightarrow x_i[j] = \frac{p_i^a \cdot h_i[j]}{p_i^a \cdot h_c[j]} \cdot x_c[j] \tag{6.6.24}$$
$$\Longleftrightarrow x_i[j] = \frac{h_i[j]}{h_c[j]} \cdot x_c[j]$$

.

The decomposed response time for service activities involved in an OR-OR pattern can be determined in a similar way. Since response time of each XOR-XOR branch is the same as for an AND-XOR branch (i.e., (6.6.22) applies in this case), and all XOR-

XOR branches are combined by an AND-AND pattern (i.e., (6.6.23) applies here, too), decomposed response time for the i-th activity can be determined by:

$$x_i[j] = \frac{h_i[j]}{h_c[j]} \cdot x_c[j]$$

Throughput

Throughput is a QoS parameter, where the overall throughput of a consumer depends on the bottleneck of its providers. In other words, providers with the most restricted throughput rates determine the overall throughput of their consumer. Hence, except patterns containing an XOR split/join, given the composite throughput of a service consumer $x_c[j]$, throughput of all involved service activities, i.e., $x_i[j]$, is equal to or higher than the one of the consumer, namely $x_i[j] \geq x_c[j]$ for any activity $i \in \{1, 2, ..., m\}$. In composition patterns containing an XOR split/join, the composite throughput is determined not only by the throughput rates of particular service activities, but also by the probabilities that these activities are invoked at runtime. Hence, in order to get a precise decomposition of $x_c[j]$ among all service activities, one has to distinguish between two general cases: the one with invocations of all activities involved in a pattern, and the other one with invocation of a particular selected activity.

For the former case, i.e., with respect to AND-AND and SEQ patterns, throughput rates of all service invocations and the composite throughput of a consumer satisfy the following condition:

$$\frac{x_1[j]}{h_1[j]} = ... = \frac{x_i[j]}{h_i[j]} = ... = \frac{x_m[j]}{h_m[j]} = \frac{x_c[j]}{h_c[j]}$$

Hence, for an activity i, its decomposed throughput can be estimated as follows:

$$x_i[j] = \frac{h_i[j]}{h_c[j]} \cdot x_c[j]$$

For the latter case, in particular with respect to the patterns AND-XOR, OR-XOR, and XOR-XOR, throughput rates of a consumer and its providers satisfy the following conditions, with respect to the probability p_i, with which a corresponding activity i is invoked at runtime:

$$\begin{cases} p_1 \cdot x_1[j] + p_2 \cdot x_2[j] + ... + p_m \cdot x_m[j] = x_c[j] \\ \frac{x_1[j]}{h_1[j]} = \frac{x_2[j]}{h_2[j]} = ... = \frac{x_m[j]}{h_m[j]} \end{cases}$$

241

Similar to (6.6.14), for a given activity i, its decomposed throughput rate can be determined in relationship to the composite throughput rate of its consumer as follows:

$$x_i[j] = \frac{h_i[j]}{\sum_{k=1}^m p_k \cdot h_k[j]} \cdot x_c[j]$$

For the patterns AND-OR and OR-OR, both replacement structures illustrated in Figure 6-10 are used to estimate relationships between the composite throughput rate of a corresponding pattern and the throughput rate of each service activity involved in the pattern. For each XOR-XOR as well as AND-XOR branch in the replacement structures, their composite throughput rates can be estimated using:

$$x_i^r[j] = p_i^a \cdot x_i[j]. \tag{6.6.25}$$

Here, the throughput rate of the bypass activity in an XOR-XOR or an AND-XOR branch is ignored in the condition. Furthermore, all XOR-XOR/AND-XOR branches are combined with an AND split and merged with an AND join. Hence, the following conditions apply between the throughput rates of the branches and the overall throughput of the replacement structure:

$$\frac{x_1^r[j]}{h_1^r[j]} = ... = \frac{x_i^r[j]}{h_i^r[j]} = ... = \frac{x_m^r[j]}{h_m^r[j]} = \frac{x_c[j]}{h_c[j]}. \tag{6.6.26}$$

Here, h_i^r is the historical composite throughput of the i-th branch and is given by:

$$h_i^r[j] = p_i^a \cdot h_i[j].$$

Therefore, by combining (6.6.25) and (6.6.26), the decomposed throughput of the i-th branch can be determined out of the overall throughput of the pattern using:

$$x_i^r[j] = \frac{h_i^r[j]}{h_c[j]} \cdot x_c[j] = p_i^a \cdot x_i[j]$$

$$\Longleftrightarrow x_i[j] = \frac{h_i^r[j]}{p_i^a \cdot h_c[j]} \cdot x_c[j]$$

$$\Longleftrightarrow x_i[j] = \frac{p_i^a \cdot h_i[j]}{p_i^a \cdot h_c[j]} \cdot x_c[j]$$

$$\Longleftrightarrow x_i[j] = \frac{h_i[j]}{h_c[j]} \cdot x_c[j]$$

Summary

To conclude, the focus of decomposition schemas is to compute QoS values for service providers out of given composite QoS values of a consumer. The decomposition schemas discussed in this section are designed to solve decomposition problems for a single composition pattern. That is, all service providers are organised by a single composition pattern. For complex hierarchical structures containing more than one composition pattern, such as the one introduced in Figure 6-9, an additional mechanism is necessary to apply the decomposition patterns introduced in this section. Section 6.6.4 addresses this question in detail and outlines how a service consumer can determine negotiation spaces for its service providers in accordance with its non-functional requirements.

6.6.3 Composing QoS Parameters

Composing QoS parameters is the inverse process of decomposing QoS requirements. It focuses on calculating composite QoS values of several service invocations from the viewpoint of a service consumer. This is of particular interest for determining an appropriate service composition based on a set of given services. For example, composing QoS parameters allows a service consumer to determine a set of appropriate service components that can jointly satisfy its non-functional requirements.

Furthermore, aggregating QoS values plays also an important role in the course of negotiation, e.g., if a service component has to ensure that QoS terms it arranges separately with its providers can satisfy the overall QoS requirements that it receives from its service consumer. In this case, a service consumer needs composition schemas to aggregate corresponding QoS values across all negotiation threads to verify them.

Composition schemas have been frequently studied in the field of business process management, e.g., in [CSM+04, JRM04, Men04, JRM05]. In these work, QoS aggregation focuses on verifying that the resulting composite service can satisfy some given QoS requirements from a non-functional point of view. However, most of the work is concerned with qualitative predication on whether aggregated QoS values can meet some given target values. In other words, they are only concerned with the question, if the given QoS requirements can be satisfied by related service components. This requirement is however not sufficient for establishing an organic SOE, where each management agent intends to precisely control runtime behaviour of its underlying service component.

Hence, a management agent needs a precise way to estimate aggregated QoS values quantitatively, which is the only way to enable a management agent to determine precisely how well the underlying service components can satisfy their consumer in terms of QoS parameters. Advanced monitoring features of a management agent allow it to observe its service providers, capture their behaviour patterns, and predict their future behaviour. This provides the necessary foundation to quantitatively compose QoS parameters. This section focuses on these composition schemas for the selected set of QoS parameters, namely availability, cost, response time, and throughput.

Given a service composition c with a range of service activities $\{1, 2, ..., m\}$, let x_i be the QoS values of an activity i, and x_c be the QoS values of the service composition c, then the task of composing QoS parameters is to predict x_c based on given QoS values of its activities.

Availability

As described in Section 3.2.3, availability of a service provider denotes the probability that a service is online to process requests from its consumers. Depending on composition patterns, availability of a service consumer depends either on all of its providers (i.e., in patterns with AND split/join or in an SEQ pattern) or on part of its providers at runtime (i.e., in patterns with OR or XOR split/join).

In the AND-AND and SEQ patterns, a service composition works properly at runtime, only if all its service invocations are successful. Therefore, the composite availability $x_c[j]$ of an AND-AND or an SEQ pattern is the product of availabilities of all activities, namely $x_c[j] = \prod_{i=1}^{m} x_i[j]$.

In contrast, in the patterns AND-XOR, XOR-XOR, and OR-XOR, a service composition only depends on a particular selected service activity. That is, a service consumer is not available, if its selected service activity is not available at the time of service invocation. Hence, composite availability of a service composition is computed as the sum of availabilities of all activities with respect to their probabilities p_i to be invoked at runtime with $\sum_{i=1}^{m} p_i = 1$. That is, the composite availability in this case is given by $x_c[j] = \sum_{i=1}^{m} p_i \cdot x_i[j]$.

For the patterns AND-OR and OR-OR, availability of a service composition depends on availabilities of all activities that are selected for execution at runtime. That is, all activities within the selected set must be online, so that the corresponding service composition can finish its execution successfully. To this end, a management agent must be aware of all possible combinations of activities (i.e., the power set of $\{1, 2, ..., m\}$ except the empty set) and the probabilities for these combinations to be

selected by a composition pattern at runtime. This requires however complex procedures of a management agent to collect and aggregate related runtime information.
Hence, an efficient way is to use the equivalent replacement structures, as illustrated
in Figure 6-10.

Therefore, an OR-OR pattern is replaced by a range of XOR-XOR patterns and an
AND-AND pattern (as illustrated in Figure 6-10), where each activity of the original
OR-OR pattern is replaced by an XOR-XOR pattern together with a bypass activity.

In addition, all XOR-XOR branches are combined by an AND-AND pattern. Each
XOR-XOR branch has a composite availability of

$$x_i^r[j] = p_i^a \cdot x_i[j] + p_i^b \cdot 1 = p_i^a \cdot x_i[j] + p_i^b,$$

where p_i^a is the probability that an activity i is invoked by the OR-OR pattern at
runtime, and p_i^b is the corresponding invocation probability for the bypass activity.
Since all XOR-XOR branches are combined with an AND split and synchronised with
an AND join, the composite availability of the entire replacement structure can be
determined by:

$$x_c[j] = \prod_{i=1}^{m} x_i^r[j] = \prod_{i=1}^{m} (p_i^a \cdot x_i[j] + p_i^b)$$
.

Analogously, an AND-OR pattern can be transformed to a structure consisting of a
set of AND-XOR and an AND-AND patterns (as depicted in Figure 6-10), where each
activity is replaced by an AND-XOR pattern together with a bypass activity. Hence,
each AND-XOR branch has a composite availability of $x_i^r[j] = p_i^a \cdot x_i[j] + p_i^b$.

Similar to the OR-OR pattern, all AND-XOR branches are combined by an AND-
AND pattern. Hence, the composite availability of the equivalent transformation is
given by:

$$x_c[j] = \prod_{i=1}^{m} x_i^r[j] = \prod_{i=1}^{m} (p_i^a \cdot x_i[j] + p_i^b)$$
.

Cost

Cost of a service composition depends on the number of services it consumes at
runtime. Therefore, the resulting cost of a service composition is the sum of service
cost of all service invocations. In the composition patterns AND-AND, AND-XOR,
AND-OR, and SEQ, all activities are invoked at runtime. Hence, the composite cost

$x_c[j]$ of the corresponding pattern is given by $x_c[j] = \sum_{i=1}^{m} x_i[j]$, where $x_i[j]$ denotes the cost for invoking the activity i in the pattern.

For the patterns OR-OR, OR-XOR, and XOR-XOR, the composite cost of these patterns depends not only on service costs of particular activities, but also on the probabilities that these activities are invoked at runtime. Hence, for an XOR-XOR pattern, its composite service cost can be determined by:

$$x_c[j] = \sum_{i=1}^{m} p_i \cdot x_i[j].$$

Here, p_i is the probability that the i-th activity is selected and invoked by an XOR-XOR pattern at runtime.

For the patterns OR-OR and OR-XOR, their equivalent transformations illustrated in Figure 6-10 and Figure 6-11 are used. In the replacement structure for an OR-OR pattern, each XOR-XOR branch has the composite cost of

$$x_i^r[j] = p_i^a \cdot x_i[j] + p_i^b \cdot 0 = p_i^a \cdot x_i[j].$$

It is assumed that a bypass activity does not cause any service cost. Since all XOR-XOR branches are synchronised by an AND-AND pattern, the composite cost of the entire replacement structure is given by:

$$x_c[j] = \sum_{i=1}^{m} x_i^r[j]$$
$$= \sum_{i=1}^{m} p_i^a \cdot x_i[j] \quad .$$

Similarly, in the replacement structure for an OR-XOR pattern, each XOR-XOR branch has the composite cost of $x_i^r[j] = p_i^a \cdot x_i[j]$. In addition, all XOR-XOR branches are combined by an AND split and merged by an XOR join. Under the assumption that each XOR-XOR branch has the probability of p_i to be selected by the XOR join, the composite cost of the transformation can be determined by:

$$x_c[j] = \sum_{i=1}^{m} p_i \cdot x_i^r[j]$$
$$= \sum_{i=1}^{m} p_i \cdot p_i^a \cdot x_i[j] \quad .$$

Response time

Response time of a service composition refers to the time elapsed between the time starting a new instance of the composition and the time at which the respective instance terminates. In comparison to cost, response time is strongly affected by parallelism of service invocations. If several activities are invoked simultaneously, composite response time is determined by the largest response time among all service invocations. Therefore, in the composition pattern AND-AND, the composite response time of a service composition is determined by $x_c[j] = max\{x_1[j], x_2[j], ..., x_m[j]\}$. In contrast, for an SEQ pattern, where all activities are invoked in a sequence, response time of the composition is determined by the sum of response times of all service invocations, namely $x_c[j] = \sum_{i=1}^{m} x_i[j]$.

For other patterns, the probabilities, with which the respective activities are invoked at runtime, have to be considered. They directly influence the overall response time of a service composition. Hence, for the patterns AND-XOR, OR-XOR, and XOR-XOR, where each activity in the composition pattern has a probability of p_i to be selected at runtime, their composite response time can be estimated by:

$$x_c[j] = \sum_{i=1}^{m} p_i \cdot x_i[j]$$
.

Similar to service cost, in order to estimate the composite response time of an AND-OR or an OR-OR pattern, their equivalent transformations illustrated in Figure 6-10 are used. Thus, in the replacement structure of an OR-OR pattern, each XOR-XOR branch has a composite response time of $x_i^r[j] = p_i^a \cdot x_i[j]$, under the assumption that a bypass activity has a response time of 0. In addition, all XOR-XOR branches are combined with an AND-AND pattern. Hence, the overall response time of the replacement structure is given by:

$$x_c[j] = max\{x_1^r, x_2^r, ..., x_m^r\}$$
$$= max\{p_1^a \cdot x_1[j], p_2^a \cdot x_2[j], , ..., p_m^a \cdot x_m[j]\}.$$

Analogously, in the replacement structure of an AND-OR pattern, each AND-XOR branch has a response time of $x_i^r[j] = p_i^a \cdot x_i[j]$. Since all AND-XOR branches are combined by an AND split und merged by an AND join, the overall response time of the transformed structure is determined by:

$$x_c[j] = max\{p_1^a \cdot x_1[j], p_2^a \cdot x_2[j], , ..., p_m^a \cdot x_m[j]\}.$$

Throughput

Throughput of a service composition denotes the number of service requests that it can process per time unit. Obviously, the service activities with the lowest throughput determine the overall throughput of a corresponding service composition. Hence, in an SEQ pattern, where all activities are invoked in a sequential order, the service activity with the lowest throughput forms the bottleneck of a composition. Hence, the composite throughput in this case is $x_c[j] = min\{x_1[j], x_2[j], ..., x_m[j]\}$.

The same applies to an AND-AND pattern, where all branches in the pattern are synchronised by an AND join. Therefore, the service invocation with the lowest throughput rate regulates the overall throughput of the composition, namely $x_c[j] = min\{x_1[j], x_2[j], ..., x_m[j]\}$.

For the patterns AND-XOR, OR-XOR, and XOR-XOR, a composition's throughput depends on the throughput of the service activity it selects. Therefore, with respect to probabilities p_i, with which an activity i will be activated by a composition at runtime, the overall throughput of the composition is given by $x_c[j] = \sum_{i=1}^{m} p_i \cdot x_i[j]$.

For the patterns AND-OR and OR-OR, their replacement structures illustrated in Figure 6-10 are used. In the equivalent transformation of an OR-OR pattern, each XOR-XOR branch has a composite throughput of $x_i^r[j] = p_i^a \cdot x_i[j]$. Furthermore, all XOR-XOR branches are combined by an AND-AND pattern. Hence, the overall throughput of the replacement structure is given by:

$$x_c[j] = min\{x_1^r[j], x_2^r[j], ..., x_m^r[j]\}$$
$$= min\{p_1^a \cdot x_1[j], p_2^a \cdot x_2[j], ..., p_m^a \cdot x_m[j]\}.$$

Analogously, in the equivalent transformation of an AND-OR pattern, each AND-XOR branch has a composite throughput of $x_i^r[j] = p_i^a \cdot x_i[j]$. Since all AND-XOR branches are synchronised by an AND-AND pattern, the overall throughput of the transformed structure can be determined by:

$$x_c[j] = min\{x_1^r[j], x_2^r[j], ..., x_m^r[j]\}$$
$$= min\{p_1^a \cdot x_1[j], p_2^a \cdot x_2[j], , ..., p_m^a \cdot x_m[j]\}.$$

Using composition schemas

In the previous discussion, it has been assumed that all service providers are organised by a single composition pattern with respect to a single service consumer. However, in practice, a service consumer may have a hierarchical structure of composition patterns, such as illustrated by the sample scenario in Figure 6-9. In that scenario, a service consumer invokes services from four different service providers one after another. The first two invocations are done sequentially. Afterwards, the execution flow is split into two parallel threads synchronised by an AND-AND pattern. The upper thread splits in turn into two parallel sub-flows with a relationship of exclusive choice, whose result is merged with the result of the lower thread S2 by an AND join. The execution flow terminates after the invocation of the activity S4 in the graph. Obviously, the composition schemas introduced in the previous sections alone are not sufficient to calculate composite QoS of complex hierarchical structures with more than one composition patterns. Therefore, an additional mechanism is necessary to handle this issue.

A possible approach to solve the problem is a *graph reduction algorithm* that is usually used in BPM to verify correctness of business workflows, such as in the work of Sadiq and Orlowska [SO00] or Lin, Zhao, Li, and Chen [LZLC02]. The basic idea of graph reduction is to apply a set of predefined reduction rules to a given business process, until the process cannot be reduced any more.

By considering the business logic of a service consumer as a directed acyclic graph, it is possible to apply the same algorithm to business logics. The goal is to simplify the structure of a service consumer's business logic, so that a direct estimation of composite QoS values is possible. To this end, the seven composition patterns identified in this section are used as *reduction rules*. These composition schemas are utilised repeatedly on a given business logic of a service consumer, as long as there are constructs in the structure that can be reduced. At the end, a business logic can be reduced to a single atomic activity. Then, the QoS of this remaining activity represents the composite QoS of the corresponding service composition, i.e., business logic.

Figure 6-12 shows the process to reduce the business logic of a service consumer illustrated in the sample scenario of Figure 6-9. In the first step, the XOR-XOR pattern with the activities L2 and S3 is reduced. The resulting composite activity L2/S3 is then reduced together with the activity S2 according to the AND-AND pattern. At last, the composite activity L2/S3/S2 is reduced with the activities of S1, L1, as well as S4 in accordance with the SEQ composition pattern. Since in each reduction step, only a single composition pattern is involved, it is possible to calculate the intermediate composite QoS values with respect to a single composition pattern. In the end, the resulting composite QoS of the atomic activity that is left represents the composite QoS values of the corresponding service composition.

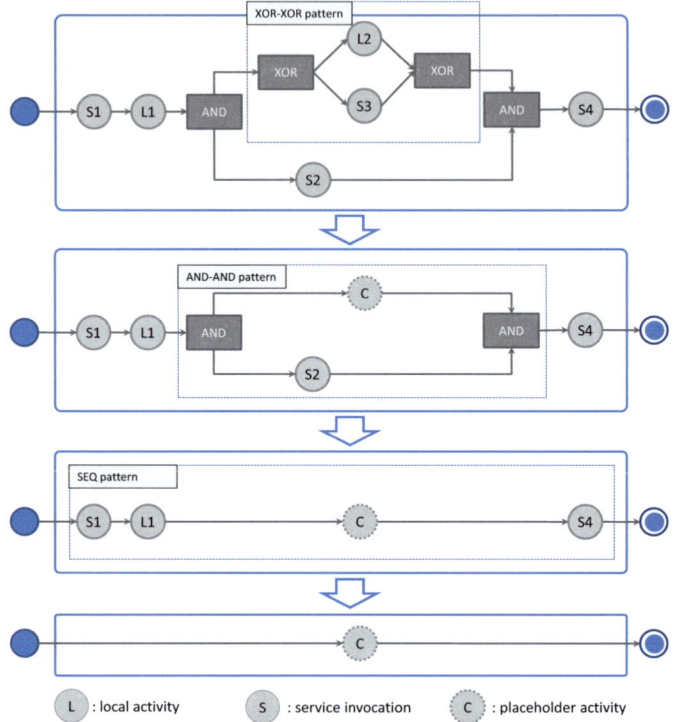

Figure 6-12: Applying composition schemas to complex service logics

6.6.4 Determining Negotiation Space

Composition and decomposition schemas defined in the previous sections cover a simple service composition with respect to the composition patterns introduced in Section 6.6.1. However, business logics of service components within an SOE usually contain more than one composition pattern. Hence, an additional mechanism is re-quired to enable a service component to decompose its end-to-end service-level re-quirements appropriately to each related service provider involved in its business log-ic. This prerequisite is crucial for a service component to determine its negotiation spaces with those service providers.

To this end, a two-phase QoS decomposition mechanism is introduced, as illustrated in Figure 6-13. The first phase is concerned with reduction of a given business logic in terms of composition patterns introduced in Section 6.6.1. The second phase is the inverse procedure of the first phase. Its focus is to decompose given service-level requirements for the atomic activity by means of the decomposition schemas introduced in Section 6.6.2.

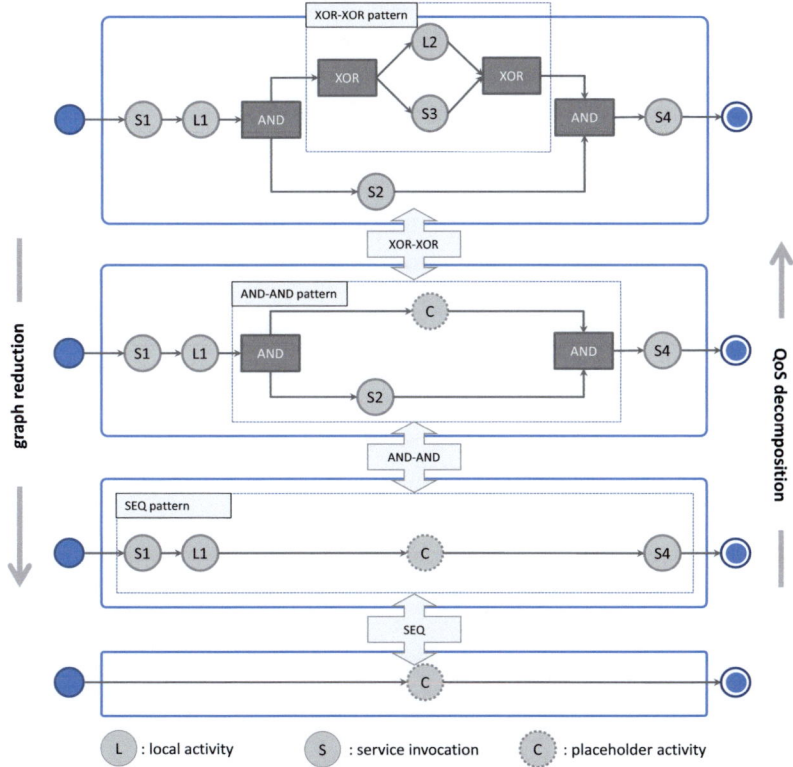

Figure 6-13: Decomposing QoS requirements for a service consumer

The first step is to reduce a given business logic by identifying the seven composition patterns in the structure and replacing them with a placeholder activity. This placeholder activity represents the composite QoS of the complete structure being replaced. This step will be repeated in the logic until a single atomic activity is left. At the end, the single atomic activity has the end-to-end QoS requirements of the service consumer.

Figure 6-13 illustrates the top-down graph reduction phase with a sample scenario. For example, the nodes L2, and S3 are organised by an XOR-XOR pattern. Correspondingly, these nodes are reduced and replaced by a placeholder activity C1. This composite node represents the two nodes in the resulting graph and has therefore the composite QoS of them. This reduction step can be applied to the sample business logic repeatedly – in accordance with the composition patterns identified in the graph. At the end of the reduction phase, a single composite node C3 is left. This node has the complete end-to-end QoS requirements that the original business logic has.

In the second phase, decomposition schemas are applied to the graph in the reverse order, in which the graph is reduced in the first phase. Initially, the atomic activity is assigned with the end-to-end QoS requirements on the corresponding service component. Depending on the composition pattern of the structure that the atomic activity represents, a suitable decomposition schema can be selected and applied to decompose the atomic activity. After that, each activity gets its QoS requirements derived from the overall requirements on the composite placeholder. Since decomposition schemas consider historical performance information of a particular activity to decompose QoS requirements, it can be ensured that QoS requirements assigned to an activity comply with its technical capabilities.

In the example illustrated in Figure 6-13, after applying the decomposition schema SEQ on the activity C3, the child nodes S1, L1, C2, and S4 are assigned with QoS requirements complying with collected historical QoS information about them. This step will be repeated as long as there are composite placeholders in the graph. At the end, the reduced atomic activity at the beginning of this phase is restored to the original business logic, where each activity in the logic is assigned with appropriate QoS requirements derived from the end-to-end service-level requirements. These requirements denote non-functional requirements on corresponding service providers invoked by the respective service component. In particular, these requirements specify the upper and lower limits of the related QoS parameters for the corresponding service provider. Therefore, a consumer can use this information to determine negotiation spaces for corresponding providers.

It is noteworthy that, to be more precise, negotiation spaces determined by the two-phase decomposition mechanism refer to particular provider instances of a consumer.

That is, in case that a service provider offers several instances to a consumer (e.g., instances with different service level options), a consumer arranges a separate agreement with each of these instances. Such a differentiating strategy allows a service provider to tailor its service offers to specific needs of its consumer.

In addition, a service consumer can invoke the same service instance several times, in particular, if these service invocations are located in different composition patterns. In this case, it is possible that negotiation spaces with different upper and lower QoS limits are determined for the same service instance, for example due to imprecise historical QoS information used for the decomposition process. In order to solve conflicts between various negotiation spaces for the same service instance, it is defined that the negotiation space with the most restricted conditions is used in the negotiation process with the corresponding service instance. That is, among all upper limits retrieved by the decomposition process, the smallest upper limit is used as the upper limit for the new negotiation space. Analogously, the largest one among all lower limits is used as the lower limit of the negotiation space. By doing this, it can be ensured that the determined negotiation space satisfies non-functional requirements for all invocations of the same service instance.

6.7 Negotiation Strategy

As described in Section 3.3, negotiation strategies are responsible to decide whether an incoming offer can be accepted. In case of counter offers, negotiation strategies help a management agent to determine how they should be constructed in conformance with given business objectives. Altogether, a negotiation strategy consists of the following three aspects: a *decision-making* strategy to decide whether to accept an incoming offer, a *conceding* strategy to determine the extent of *concessions* in utility in a negotiation step, and a *trade-off* strategy to find optimal agreements in favour of the counterpart and with respect to global business objectives.

Section 3.3.2 introduces the interpretation function (3.3.2) of Sierra et al. The interpretation function follows a simple decision strategy: for each incoming offer, a counter offer will be generated. If the incoming offer has a higher utility than the counter offer, the respective management agent will accept the offer. Otherwise, the agent proposes the generated offer as its counter offer. In the present thesis, this decision-making strategy is adopted by a management agent to decide on acceptance of an incoming offer.

The foundation of such a decision-making strategy are conceding strategies and trade-off strategies. The fact that each agent is not aware of preferences of its negotiation partner determines that each agent has to maintain and utilise its local strategies to find a mutually acceptable agreement. At best, such local strategies can take negotiation behaviour of the counterpart into consideration, and thus accelerate the overall negotiation process. Efficient conceding strategies and trade-off strategies can lead to shorter negotiation time and better negotiation results. Hence, this section focuses on both strategies and outlines them in the context of automated negotiation of SLAs.

6.7.1 Conceding Strategy

In general, a conceding strategy specifies how a rational management agent moves in a negotiation space away from its optimum in favour of its counterpart. Due to the fact that both negotiation parties have conflicting interests on negotiation issues and each of them starts with their respective optimum (i.e., $V_a(x^1_{a \to b}) = 1$ for a management agent a) into a negotiation thread, both parties have to move towards each other in order to reach an agreement. As such, each management agent has to concede in utility in favour of its counterpart. This provides the prerequisite for both management agents to find a consensus on the given objectives in the course of negotiation.

Another substantial aspect of concession is to determine the extent of concession of a management agent in each negotiation round. As illustrated in Figure 6-14, a management agent moves on a negotiation plane spanned by two sample QoS parameters x_1 and x_2. As each management agent starts from its optimum (i.e., $V_a(x^1_{a \to b}) = 1$) in a negotiation, conceding strategies guide the agent to move from its optimum towards the worst case x with $V_a(x) = 0$. In the course of negotiation, conceding strategies are used to determine how much utility an agent is willing to concede in favour of its negotiation partner, so that the probability that the generated counter offer will be accepted by the negotiation partner, is as high as possible. By doing this, an agent reduces its expectation on values of QoS parameters, in each concession step.

As discussed before, missing knowledge of an agent about its negotiation partner's preferences makes it impossible to propose an optimal offer to its counterpart. Furthermore, an adequate conceding strategy should produce suitable concession pressure on the agent's negotiation behaviour. To this end, such a conceding strategy can take factors of a negotiation process into consideration, such as time left until a given deadline or negotiation behaviour of its counterpart so far. For example, given a negotiation deadline, a management agent may have larger pressure to reach an agreement towards the end of negotiation; correspondingly, it tends to make more concessions on utility in favour of its negotiation partner.

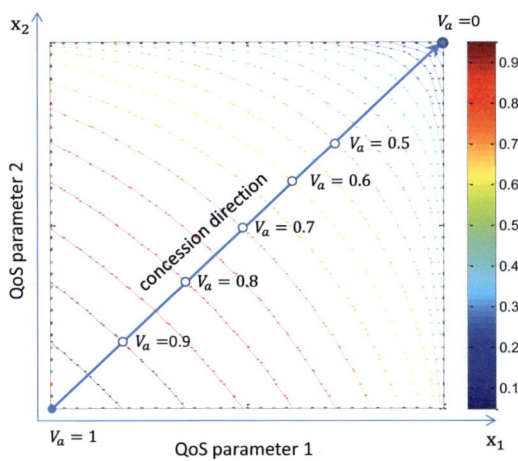

Figure 6-14: Illustration of utility concession in a sample negotiation space

Hence, the present thesis adopts the conceding strategies introduced by Sierra et al. in Section 3.3.2 as the general framework to calculate the extent of concession of an agent. In particular, the following two types of conceding tactics are focused on from the viewpoint of a management agent:

- *time-dependent* tactics that assess the extent of concession for a particular QoS parameter $i \in \{1, 2, ..., n\}$ in relationship with the current negotiation time. This allows a management agent to model its negotiation behaviour in dependence of negotiation time.

- *behaviour-dependent* tactics that assess the extent of concession according to the negotiation behaviour of an agent's negotiation partner. By considering environmental conditions, i.e., negotiation behaviour of its counterpart, an agent can adapt its negotiation behaviour dynamically.

Resource-dependent tactics are less relevant for a management agent to negotiate SLAs. It is assumed that a management agent has the necessary resources to perform negotiation-centric activities. In case that a service component has restricted resources (e.g., a network connectivity device with limited computational power), this restriction can be relaxed by delegating related activities (i.e., negotiation-centric activities) to an external trusted management agent. Therefore, scenarios where a management agent has only limited computing and memory capabilities are not considered in the present thesis.

At runtime, a management agent can combine both types of conceding tactics to use several criteria simultaneously to support its decision-making process. As discussed before, the focus of using conceding strategies is to determine the extent of concession of utility in each step. However, values of QoS parameters in a generated SLA offer are set without having taken the behaviour of an agent's counterpart or the global business objectives into consideration. Hence, the following section focuses on trade-off strategies aiming at optimising outgoing offers dynamically in dependence of environmental information that a management agent perceives in the course of negotiation, such as the observed negotiation behaviour of an agent's counterpart.

6.7.2 Trade-off Strategy

Conceding strategies enable an agent to compute its proposals based on some given conceding tactics. However, the focus of conceding strategies is to determine extent of concession on utilities in each negotiation step – with the intention that by reducing its own expectations on related QoS parameters, its opponent may accept a proposed offer in the next step. That is, a management agent has to decide how much it is willing to move away from its optimum so that it can reach an agreement as fair as possible for its opponent. In addition, further aspects involved in a negotiation process, such as how a calculated QoS values may be perceived by its counterpart, is not covered by conceding strategies.

As discussed in Section 6.4, for a given utility, there is an infinite set of combinations of QoS values in the negotiation space. Hence, as soon as a management agent has determined the utility of an outgoing offer, it has to choose a counter offer among all possible trade-offs. A *trade-off* is referred to as reducing utility of some QoS parameter(s) while increasing utility of some other QoS parameter(s) of a given agreement, so that the total utility of the agreement remains unchanged. For example, a consumer can increase the cost for shorter response time in an offer without changing the offer's utility. Since trade-offs may be perceived differently by an agent's counterpart (i.e., they have different utilities for the counterpart), a management agent has to find optimal trade-offs that are as attractive as possible for its counterpart and thus increase the overall social welfare of the negotiating agents. Furthermore, trade-offs that may induce higher utilities for the opposite party raise the probability to reach a mutually acceptable agreement more quickly. Hence, efficient trade-off strategies are essential for a management agent to facilitate a negotiation process.

Figure 6-15 illustrates the negotiation space of a service consumer and its provider spanned by two sample QoS parameters. The convex/concave curves in the negotiation space are indifference curves for the consumer/provider. It is assumed that the last incoming offer sent by the provider in the previous negotiation round is not satisfactory and the consumer is going to propose a counter offer to its opponent. Furthermore, it is assumed that the management agent of the consumer has determined the utility of the outgoing offer by using its conceding strategies.

The three points A, B, and C are located on the same indifference curve. That is, A, B, and C have the same utility for the consumer. Theoretically, the consumer can arbitrarily choose one of these three offers (as well as all other value combinations on the same indifference curve) as its counter offer to the provider, since from the viewpoint of the consumer, none of the offers brings either more or less utility for it. However, the offers A, B, and C have very different significance in the global context, if the negotiation spaces of both the consumer and the provider are considered.

It is obvious that the provider will not accept the three offers in the next negotiation round, since they are located outside its negotiation space. However, the offer B is the most appropriate one for the provider. It is the most promising offer that is closest to a possible consensus in the common negotiation space. Both offers A and C direct further negotiation into areas that are even farther away from the common negotiation space, which decreases the probability of an early consensus. Concisely, the major goal of a trade-off strategy is to identify a point on the indifference curve of a given utility, which can accelerate the respective negotiation process by leading it towards the common negotiation space. At the same time, it is expected that such a trade-off search is aligned with global business objectives.

The sample scenario illustrated in Figure 6-15 shows that the obstacle in finding optimal trade-offs consists in the incomplete information situation that an agent has about its counterpart. The only information available for an agent for making decisions is the history of SLA offers proposed by its opponent in the negotiation thread so far. Further information, such as the negotiation space of its opponent, is unknown to a management agent. Without such information, an agent cannot make a precise decision from a global viewpoint. Hence, a management agent needs a trade-off strategy that can propose a counter offer as accurately as possible despite its the incomplete negotiation information about its negotiation partners.

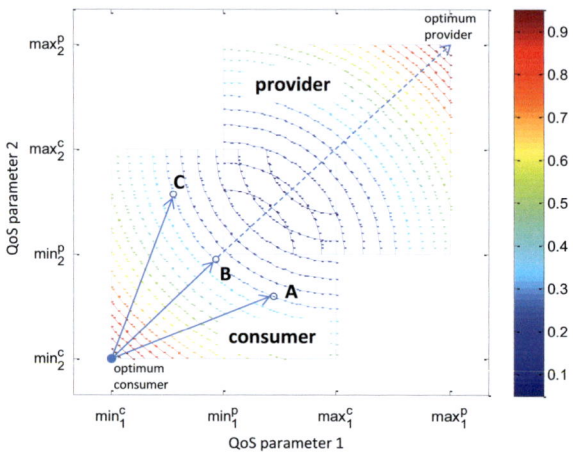

Figure 6-15: Illustration of the trade-off strategy of a management agent

In general, a trade-off strategy has to incorporate the following four aspects into the decision-making process:

- A trade-off should be located in the opponent's acceptable value ranges as probably as possible. This is the prerequisite that a counterpart will accept the proposed offer. For example, in the sample scenario in Figure 6-15, offers A and C do not fulfil this requirement, while offer B is a possible candidate for a successful trade-off.

- A trade-off should be as attractive as possible for an agent's opponent. This forces an agent to align its trade-off process with the request of its opponent.

- Even if an agent cannot find a trade-off that can be accepted by its opponent at once, it should ensure that the selected trade-off provides a good foundation for the further negotiation process. For example, by comparing the offers B and C in Figure 6-15, offer B provides a better base for further negotiation offers than offer C. By choosing offer B, it can be expected that the next offer proposed by the consumer could reach the common negotiation space in compliance with the first aspect.

- A trade-off should be selected with respect to global business objectives. This allows two negotiating agents to align their negotiation behaviour in compliance with given global business objectives.

As aforementioned, a management agent can only rely on SLA offers it received from its opponent as references to select an optimal trade-off out of an infinite set of candidates. Hence, a reasonable way is to find appropriate trade-offs by getting the search process geared to offers it received from its opponent. In other words, a management agent tries to find a trade-off similar to incoming offers from its opponent. This helps an agent to align its trade-off search to expectations of its opponent expressed in terms of SLA offers.

Faratin, Sierra and Jennings [FSJ00] introduced a similarity-based approach to find optimal trade-offs for counter offers. Their algorithm uses fuzzy-similarity to find issue assignments for a counter offer. However, their approach assumes that both agents know each other's preferences in the negotiation space. Furthermore, their approach requires suitable fuzzy rules to estimate the extent of similarity between offers, which is not always available in SLA negotiation. Since a desired trade-off strategy in the present thesis can only use the history of incoming offers as well as global business objectives to find an optimal trade-off, the approach proposed by Faratin et al. cannot be applied to negotiation scenarios handled in this thesis. Hence, a more general approach is necessary to generate counter offers based on the limited information that a management agent has about its opponent, with respect to the four aspects discussed previously for optimal trade-offs.

In the negotiation space spanned by QoS preferences of two negotiating agents, a common property of each arbitrary point in the space is its distance to any other point in the space. Analogously, among all points of the same indifference curve, the distance of each point to an incoming offer, i.e., a fixed point in the space, can be estimated, too. In addition, information needed to calculate the distance between a trade-off and an incoming offer, namely QoS values of the respective SLAs, is available to each agent. Hence, a distance-based approach for estimating similarity is much more promising than other approaches, such as the one proposed by Faratin et al. using fuzzy logic.

Given an offer $x_{b \to a}^{t-1}$ sent from an agent b to an agent a with $x_{b \to a}^{t-1} = (x_{b \to a}^{t-1}[1], x_{b \to a}^{t-1}[2], ..., x_{b \to a}^{t-1}[n])$, the distance of the counter offer $x_{a \to b}^{t} = (x_{a \to b}^{t}[1], x_{a \to b}^{t}[2], ..., x_{a \to b}^{t}[n])$ is defined as the Euclidean distance between them, namely:

$$D(x_{b \to a}^{t-1}, x_{a \to b}^{t}) = \|x_{a \to b}^{t} - x_{b \to a}^{t-1}\| = \sqrt{\sum_{j=1}^{n}(x_{a \to b}^{t}[j] - x_{b \to a}^{t-1}[j])^2} \quad . \qquad (6.7.1)$$

For example, two management agents negotiate on response time and availability. Then the distance between two SLAs offers $x_{b \to a}^{t-1} = (65, 0.998)$ and $x_{a \to b}^{t} = (89, 0.971)$ at time t can be calculated with:

$$D(x_{b \to a}^{t-1}, x_{a \to b}^{t}) = \sqrt{(89 - 65)^2 + (0.998 - 0.971)^2} = 24.000014$$

From this example, it is obvious that different QoS parameters have different impact on the distance, depending on the scale of their value ranges. For example, while availabilities vary mainly on a scale of 10^{-2}, response time varies on the level of 10^{-3} seconds. Furthermore, the scale of a particular QoS parameter depends strongly on the measurement unit it uses. For example, response time can be measured in milliseconds as well as in seconds. Hence, there is a difference of 10^3 between the same values expressed in different measurement units.

This difference in scales leads to the situation that by using (6.7.1) to determine the Euclidean distance between two SLA offers, changes of QoS parameters with large scales, such as response time, causes more considerable changes of the distance than QoS parameters with small scales, such as availability. Obviously, this behaviour of distance calculation is not desired, because it neglects changes of QoS parameters with small scales, even if these parameters are higher weighted in the estimation.

Hence, a second distance, the normalised Euclidean distance, is introduced to avoid this undesired behaviour. A normalised Euclidean distance is calculated with respect to the two initial offers of the management agents as reference points. Given the initial offer $x_{c \to p}^{0}$ sent by a consumer c at $t = 0$ and the initial offer $x_{p \to c}^{1}$ sent by a provider p at $t = 1$, the normalised Euclidean distance is defined as follows:

$$D_{norm}(x_{b \to a}^{t-1}, x_{a \to b}^{t}) = \sqrt{\sum_{j=1}^{n}(\frac{x_{a \to b}^{t}[j] - x_{b \to a}^{t-1}[j]}{x_{c \to p}^{0}[j] - x_{p \to c}^{1}[j]})^2} \quad . \qquad (6.10.1)$$

Here, a and b are two management agents with $a, b \in \{c, p\}$ and $a \neq b$. A normalised Euclidean distance reduces the impacts of various scales of QoS parameters by estimating the relative distance of two given QoS values compared to the absolute distance between the two initial offers. By doing this, QoS parameters with small scales are treated just as fair in the distance estimation as those with large scales.

As discussed before, a management agent is aware of the offers exchanged so far with its counterpart in the negotiation thread. In addition, it is assumed that a management agent has utilised some conceding strategy in advance to obtain an initial offer as input for the trade-off search. To this end, the following formula (as discussed in Section 3.3.2) is used to calculate an initial offer, where the time-dependent concession factor $\alpha_j^a(t)$ is determined by a conceding strategy in dependence of both the time left until a given negotiation deadline as well as the negotiation behaviour of an agent's counterpart:

$$x_{a \to b}^t[j] = \begin{cases} min_j^a + \alpha_j^a(t) \cdot (max_j^a - min_j^a) & \text{if } V_j^a \text{ is decreasing} \\ min_j^a + (1 - \alpha_j^a(t)) \cdot (max_j^a - min_j^a) & \text{if } V_j^a \text{ is increasing} \end{cases}$$

Given these preconditions, a trade-off strategy can be reduced to a search problem in the negotiation space that aims at finding some optimal points matching given conditions. To this end, a range of possible search algorithms can be applied by a management agent, such as greedy algorithms, evolutionary algorithms, and so on. However, an appropriate search algorithm has to address the following aspects:

- It should be simple in design and resource saving in implementation. An SLA negotiation between a consumer and a provider is normally carried out under real-time conditions. Hence, by considering a given negotiation deadline, a trade-off search must not be too expensive (i.e., too time consuming) for an agent.

- Secondly, in a multidimensional negotiation space with several QoS parameters, there may be not only a global optimum, but also several local optima. Hence, an appropriate search algorithm must be capable of escaping from local optima in the course of trade-off search.

By considering both aspects, Simulated Annealing is chosen to implement trade-off search in a multidimensional negotiation space. First, it is a generally applicable and easy to implement algorithm based on probabilistic approximation. Secondly, Simulated Annealing can escape a local optimum by using probability-based movement from one point to another in the negotiation space. This is the most essential point that makes Simulated Annealing applicable for trade-off search in a multidimensional negotiation space.

Table 6-2: Search algorithm based on simulated annealing to find trade-offs

```
procedure find trade-off offer
begin
  GET initial offer x by using conceding strategies

  // set parameters for simulated annealing
  // t: iteration time, Tmax: max temperature, Tmin: min temperature
  // T: current temperature
  SET t = 0, Tmax = Γ, Tmin = Γ', T = Tmax

  // start simulated annealing search loop
  while (T ≥ Tmin) do

    // find an alternative SLA offer in the neighbourhood
    SET x' = neighbour(x, t, S)

    // evaluate the SLA offer
    if ( eval(x') ≤ eval(x) ) then
      x = x' // do a movement in the neighbourhood
    else if ( random[0,1) < e^(eval(x)-eval(x'))/T ) then
      x = x' // do a movement in spite of worse evaluation result
    end if

    // annealing temperature
    // γ: decay rate for the temperature from Tmax to Tmin
    T = Tmax · e^(-t·γ), t = t + 1
  end while
end
```

In order to apply the search algorithm described in Table 6-2 to a management agent, the following issues must be addressed:

- *Neighbourhood of an SLA offer*: a management agent has to be able to determine feasible neighbours of a given SLA offer in the negotiation space.

- *Evaluation function for SLA offers*: a management agent has to be able to evaluate two given SLA offers and determine the better one in compliance with some given criteria.

As discussed in Section 6.6, the negotiation space of a management agent is always continuous. Hence, this provides additional flexibility to determine the neighbourhood of a given SLA offer.

Table 6-3 lists the procedure to obtain a neighbourhood of a given SLA offer. In general, a neighbour is generated by randomly selecting a QoS parameter, changing its value, and adjusting another randomly selected QoS parameter to compensate the utility change, so that the overall utility remains unchanged at the end. By doing this, a management agent can ensure that the neighbour SLA found in this way is located on the same indifference curve/plane as the given SLA offer.

Table 6-3: Algorithm to determine a neighbour of a given SLA offer

```
procedure neighbour(x, t, S)
// x: given SLA offer, t: current iteration, S: negotiation space
begin
  // neighbour: neighbour of the given offer x
  SET neighbour = x

  // size(x): the number of QoS parameters in the offer x
  // determine a random index between 0 and size(x)-1
  SET idx₁ = random[0, size(x)-1]

  // determine a random index of the compensation QoS parameter
  SET idx₂ = idx₁
  while (idx₂ = idx₁) do
     SET idx₂ = random[0, size(x)-1]
  end while

  do
     SET value₁ = neighbour(idx₁), value₂ = neighbour(idx₂)

  // determine change for the first QoS parameter in dependence of iteration time
  // determine change range between the upper and lower limits of the parameter

  // S(idx₁)ᵤₚₚₑᵣ: the upper limit of the parameter idx₁ in the negotiation space
  // S(idx₁)ₗₒwₑᵣ: the lower limit of the parameter idx₁ in the negotiation space
  // γ: constant decay rate for the size of change range
     SET range = |S(idx₁)ᵤₚₚₑᵣ - S(idx₁)ₗₒwₑᵣ| · e⁻ᵗ·γ/2
     SET change = random(-range, range) // determine a random change in the value
range
     SET neighbour(idx₁) = value₁ + change // change the value

  // compensate for change of the first QoS parameter idx₁
     SET compensation = compensate(x, neighbour(idx₁)) //calculate the value of idx₂
     SET neighbour(idx₂) = value₂ + compensation // change the value of idx₂
  // repeat the previous steps, if the neighbour is not located in S
  while (neighbour ∉ S )

  RETURN neighbour
end
```

The algorithm in Table 6-3 returns a neighbour of a given SLA offer in the negotiation space. In the following step, a management agent has to find out if the neighbour found is better than the current offer with respect to some given criteria. To this end, it utilises the evaluation function $eval(x)$ to estimate the offer's quality. A management agent can leverage various trade-off strategies to evaluate a given SLA offer.

Trade-off strategy 1 - alignment to initial offers: in this strategy, an agent uses the two initial offers $x_{c \to p}^0$ and $x_{p \to c}^1$ as fixed reference points in the space and tries to find a trade-off with minimal distance to them. Therefore, the evaluation function for this strategy is defined as follows:

$$eval(x_{a \to b}^t) = D_{norm}(x_{c \to p}^0, x_{a \to b}^t) + D_{norm}(x_{p \to c}^1, x_{a \to b}^t) \qquad (6.10.2)$$

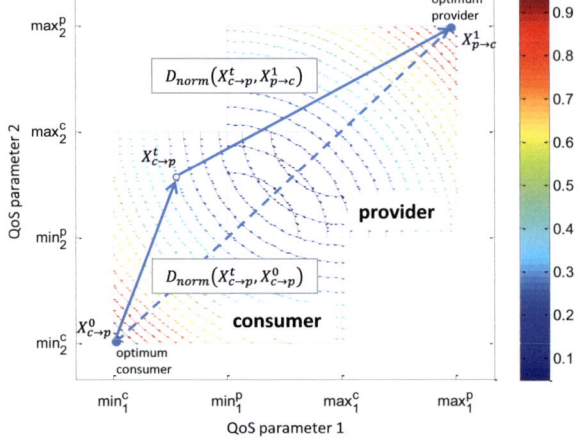

Figure 6-16: Trade-off strategy – alignment to both initial offers

Figure 6-16 illustrates this trade-off strategy with alignment to both initial offers. Since initial offers represent the optimal SLAs that both negotiation partners prefer, this strategy allows a management agent to construct an offer with respect to its counterpart. In particular, by heading counter offers towards the initial offer of the opponent agent, a management agent can ensure that its offers can reach the unknown negotiation space of the counterpart in the course of negotiation. This provides the essential prerequisite for an agent to reach a consensus with its counterpart.

A limitation of this strategy is its static alignment to two fixed reference points in the negotiation space. Fixed reference points reduce the dynamic aspect of SLA negotiation between management agents. In particular, counter offers proposed by following this strategy do not take the up-to-date intention of its counterpart into consideration, which is normally expressed in terms of incoming offers. Since incoming offers other than the initial offer are not involved in the evaluation function, their impacts are unconsidered in the decision-making process of an agent.

Trade-off strategy 2 - alignment to the last incoming offer: in this strategy, a management agent aligns its search for trade-offs to the last incoming offer $x_{b \to a}^{t-1}$ from its negotiation partner. In the search process, an agent tries to find an optimal trade-off in its negotiation space that has minimal distance to the last incoming offer. Hence, the evaluation function for this strategy is given by:

$$eval(x_{a \to b}^t) = D_{norm}(x_{b \to a}^{t-1}, x_{a \to b}^t).$$

Figure 6-17 illustrates the strategy with alignment to the last incoming offer. In comparison to the previous trade-off strategy, this strategy uses in each negotiation round a new reference point in the negotiation space. Since a rational management agent is expected to propose an offer matching its own negotiation preferences, each incoming offer represents the most recent intention of an agent's counterpart to reach a consensus. Hence, aligning trade-off search to the last incoming offer allows a management agent to update its negotiation behaviour dynamically in accordance with the behaviour of its counterpart.

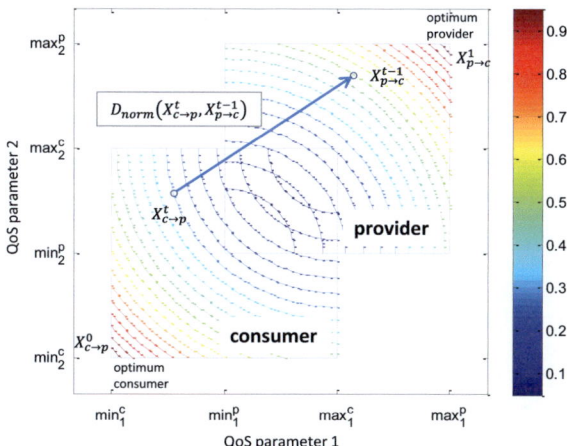

Figure 6-17: Trade-off strategy – alignment to the last incoming offer

A limitation of the both previous strategies is their apparent lack of consideration of given business objectives in trade-off search. Both strategies consider only offers exchanged between both management agents so far in a negotiation thread. Additional criteria derived from business objectives do not influence the negotiation behaviour of a management agent.

Trade-off Strategy 3 – alignment to both the last incoming offer and an agent's own initial offer: this strategy combines the previous trade-off strategies and uses the last incoming offer as a dynamic reference point and the agent's own initial offer, either $x^0_{c \to p}$ or $x^1_{p \to c}$, as a fixed one. Therefore, a management agent tries to find an optimal trade-off in the indifference curve that has minimal distance to both reference points.

That is, the evaluation function for this strategy is given by:

$$eval(x^t_{c \to p}) = D_{norm}(x^{t-1}_{p \to c}, x^t_{c \to p}) + D_{norm}(x^0_{c \to p}, x^t_{c \to p})$$

for the consumer agent c or

$$eval(x^t_{p \to c}) = D_{norm}(x^{t-1}_{c \to p}, x^t_{p \to c}) + D_{norm}(x^1_{p \to c}, x^t_{p \to c})$$

for the provider agent p.

Figure 6-18 illustrates the trade-off strategy 3. In contrast to both previous strategies, this strategy incorporates the advantages of both strategies. First, aligning with the last incoming offers enables a management agent to update its negotiation behaviour depending on that of its counterpart. Secondly, using the own initial offer as a reference offer ensures that an agent's counter offer also keeps the own optimum offer in mind. However, similar to both previous strategies, a management agent does not take given business objectives into consideration.

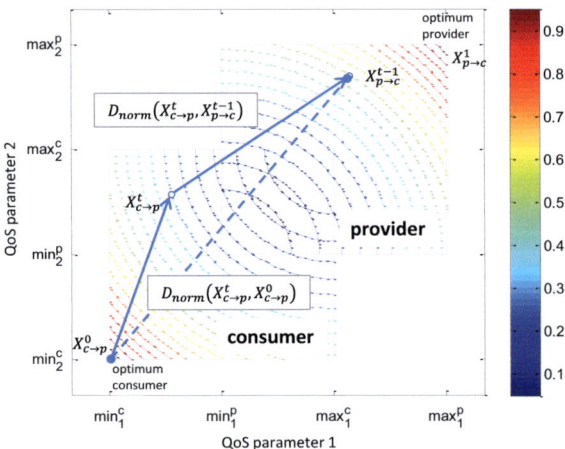

Figure 6-18: Trade-off strategy – alignment to the last incoming offer and the own initial offer

Trade-off strategy 4 - combined strategy with respect to given business objectives: by using this strategy, a management agent tries to combine the second trade-off strategy with given business objectives. To this end, a management agent divides the set of QoS parameters into two groups: one group with QoS parameters that are of relevance to satisfy given business objectives and the other group with QoS parameters that are not covered by business objectives. Hence, the trade-off search is correspondingly split into two search phases.

In the first phase, an agent first tries to find trade-offs in compliance with its business objectives. That is, a management agent seeks to optimise trade-offs with respect to the group of QoS parameters related to business objectives. For example, a given business objective of "increasing customer satisfaction" covers QoS parameters concerned with user experiences, such as response time or availability of a service component. Hence, a management agent optimises at first these QoS parameters and finds trade-offs with response time as low as possible and availability as high as possible. At the end of the first phase, QoS parameters related to business objectives have fixed values that are used to construct the outgoing counter offer.

In the second phase, an agent continues to optimise the remainder of the QoS parameters that are not considered in the first phase. That is, it keeps the QoS values determined in the first phase unchanged and tries to find offers in the negotiation space that have minimal distance to the last incoming offer. In this process, the neighbourhood of a given offer is determined by varying the QoS values that have not been fixed in the first phase.

After both phases, a management agent has an outgoing offer which satisfies the given business objectives and is simultaneously as close as possible to the last incoming offer. In this way, a management agent takes both global business objectives and local negotiation behaviour of its counterpart into consideration.

6.7.3 Concluding Remarks

Negotiation strategies determine the negotiation behaviour of a management agent. To generate an attractive offer for the negotiation partner, a management agent has to cover two different aspects:

- estimate the utility of the next offer, and

- find appropriate value assignments so that the resulting offer is attractive for the negotiation partner.

Since both management agents are not aware of the negotiation preferences of their counterparts, they can only use heuristic approaches to presume the negotiation behaviours of their negotiation partners. Conceding strategies target the first aspect and estimate the extent of concession on utility in each negotiation step. Depending on negotiation time and other criteria, a management agent determines how far it is willing to move away from its optimum in the negotiation space. However, conceding strategies are more utility-centric and do not take the most recent negotiation behaviour of an agent's negotiation partner into consideration.

Hence, the concrete value assignment for each QoS parameter is determined by trade-off strategies. With a given utility, trade-off strategies search in the negotiation space for appropriate value assignments by considering previous incoming offers, even in the absence of knowledge about its counterpart. Since trade-off strategies incorporate the most recent negotiation situation into the search process of a management agent, they can find trade-offs with a higher potential to accelerate the overall negotiation process.

6.8 Summary

The core of the self-organising end-to-end SLM approach introduced in the present thesis is collaboration between related management agents. For given service level requirements in an SOE, the recursive nature of the environment requires seamless cooperation of related service components within the environment. Each service component is expected to contribute to the overall service level requirements. However, the heterogeneous and autonomous nature of service components prevents direct arrangement of service level objectives between a service provider and a service consumer. Therefore, the present thesis proposes a generic approach that uses SLAs as homogeneous messages between related service components to facilitate the overall SLM process in the environment.

This chapter is dedicated to SLA-centric collaboration between related service components, namely automated negotiation of SLAs between them. Firstly, negotiated SLAs allow a service component to maintain its autonomy in collaboration by incorporating its preferences into a respective negotiation process. Secondly, abstracted

SLAs do not refer to any individual implementation and configuration of related service components. Hence, they enable related service components to collaborate on a higher level of abstraction, in spite of the heterogeneous nature of those components.

Hence, this chapter addresses a set of relevant aspects to enable automated negotiation of SLAs. Section 6.2 outlines the negotiation scenarios considered in the present thesis and distinguishes them from other related research in the field. Based on such negotiation scenarios, Section 6.3 outlines considerations with regard to the design of the automated negotiation process between a service consumer and its provider. Among other things, this section identifies the negotiation process as a bilateral multi-issue negotiation between two rational agents.

In order to facilitate such an automated negotiation, Section 6.4 introduces the underlying mathematical model. Among other things, this section specifies possible utility functions that a management agent can use to estimate the quality of a given SLA. In addition, this section outlines the concept of indifference curves/planes in negotiation space, which forms the foundation for determining optimal trade-offs for a given SLA.

Section 6.5 addresses the macroscopic aspect of SLA-centric collaboration and introduces an iterated and coordinated negotiation protocol to guide interactions between two related service components in the course of negotiation. In particular, the iterated mechanism of the negotiation protocol allows a business process as the top-most component in an SOE to propagate a SLA negotiation process across the complete environment down to the lowest service components. This feature is crucial to make the negotiation protocol applicable to an SOE with recursive constructs.

In contrast, Section 6.6 and Section 6.7 are concerned with the microscopic aspects of collaboration and outline how a management agent can negotiate with another agent. To this end, Section 6.6 discusses how a service consumer can determine its negotiation spaces for its service providers. In particular, this section describes how a service consumer can derive reasonably those negotiation spaces from its service level requirements in dependence of behaviour patterns of its providers. The last section in the chapter, Section 6.7 focuses on the dynamic aspects of automated SLA negotiation and introduces several negotiation strategies that a management agent can apply to generate SLA offers to its counterpart. In particular, this section introduces several trade-off strategies that help a management agent to dynamically align its SLA offers to the negotiation behaviour of its counterpart as well as to global business objectives.

Part III

Evaluation

Chapter 7   Evaluation Environment

"工欲善其事，必先利其器。"

―【论语·卫灵公，孔子】

"Good preparation is prerequisite to the successful execution of a job."

(Analects of Confucius, Confucius, ca. 551 - 479 B.C.)

This chapter focuses on the evaluation environment used to assess the feasibility of the approach introduced in the present thesis. This thesis proposes to solve automated end-to-end SLM on two different levels: SLA-driven self-organisation of a service component on the local level and negotiation-based collaboration between service components on the global level. Hence, an appropriate evaluation environment has to provide corresponding capabilities in its test bed with respect to both realisation levels of the approach.

Therefore, a fundamental requirement on an appropriate evaluation environment is that it should deliver an operating SOE, which can be flexibly configured in accordance with particular evaluation objectives. Obviously, physical environments with real world technical components satisfy this prerequisite only to a limited extent. In particular, despite high cost to set up such a physical environment, physical service components cannot be configured flexibly to cope with varying demands of evaluation experiments. In contrast, a simulation-based evaluation environment can set up certain evaluation scenarios quickly with reasonable efforts. Particularly, such a simulated environment can be configured flexibly to meet given objectives of evaluation experiments. Therefore, the remainder of the chapter is concerned with the simulated evaluation environment designed and implemented for the present thesis.

Correspondingly, the remainder of the chapter is organised as follows: Section 7.1 gives an overview of the simulation environment and its architecture. Section 7.2 is concerned with the detailed modelling of the simulation environment and outlines how the simulation environment is designed to construct a simulated SOE. Section 7.3 focuses on simulation of a single service component and outlines how a service component can model its runtime behaviour by means of workflows. In particular, this section addresses how a service component can invoke other service components involved in its business logic. Section 7.4 is concerned with the microscopic simulation of a service component. It describes how a service component can simulate its local resources to generate runtime workloads, which are crucial for estimating service level behaviour of a service component. The last section summarises the chapter.

7.1 Overview

The evaluation environment aims at providing an appropriate test bed for assessing the feasibility of the approach introduced in the present thesis. Particularly, it is desired that the evaluation environment can provide a simulated SOE in an efficient manner. Hence, this section introduces the overall architecture of the evaluation environment and outlines interactions between the integral parts of the evaluation environment.

With respect to the main purpose of the evaluation environment to evaluate the approach proposed in this thesis, the following objectives must be covered:

- An appropriate evaluation environment should provide a flexible simulation environment for creating a virtual SOE with respect to the design principles of service-orientation, as described in Section 2.1.1. A real-world SOE is driven by requests of business processes. Hence, a simulated SOE has to reproduce this typical behaviour of a real SOE. That is, interactions between supporting service components of a business process are triggered by service requests sent to the process.

- Secondly, non-functional service level objectives are associated with the microscopic runtime behaviour of a service component. Hence, a simulated service component has to produce runtime workloads, from which QoS values can be derived. To this end, a simulated service component has to be given corresponding processing capacities to handle incoming requests.

- Thirdly, a simulated SOE has to provide necessary interfaces for integrating management agents. In particular, a simulated service component has to expose its runtime information to its management agent. In addition, it should comply with control actions suggested by its management agent.

Based on these considerations, an evaluation environment with flexible expandability is designed and implemented, as illustrated in Figure 7-1.

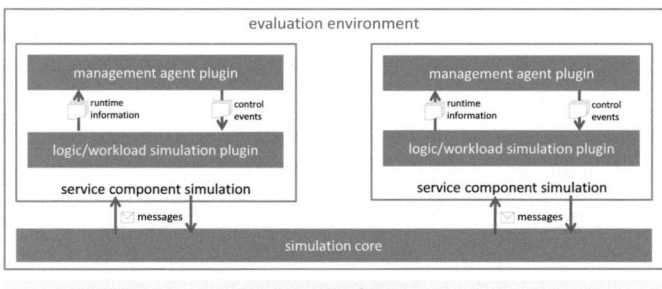

Figure 7-1: Overview of the evaluation environment

The entire evaluation environment is built on top of a simulation framework – Repast Simphony [NCV06]. Repast Simphony is a Java-based modelling system. It supports flexible development of simulation scenarios consisting of a set of interacting agents. With respect to the agent-oriented design of the management overlay (see also Section 5.1), it is reasonable to adopt Repast Simphony as the base to build the evaluation environment consisting of a set of distributed and interacting self-organising service components. The evaluation environment was built on top of Repast Simphony 2.0 Beta released on December 3, 2010.

On this simulation base, the evaluation environment is composed of four interconnected simulation modules: *simulation core*, *service component simulation*, *logic/workload simulation* plugin, and *management agent* plugin. The simulation core is the foundation of the evaluation environment. It provides an extendable infrastructure for hosting other simulation modules by means of a message-based communication channel. In this way, any simulation module can interact with other related modules by exchanging messages.

On top of the simulation core, the *service component simulation* module is responsible to define an abstract service component within a simulated SOE. It specifies the properties of the corresponding service component, such as component ID, its runtime state, and its connection to the global SOE. Several instances of the *service component simulation* module can interact with one another by exchanging messages via the simulation core. It is noteworthy that this simulation module defines a service component on an abstracted level. It does not implement any specific capability of a particular service component with respect to business logics.

In order to realise an extendable service component, the service component simulation module utilises a plugin-based architecture. A plugin is a self-contained module that can be used to extend capabilities of a simulated service component. For example, a service discovery plugin can enable service components to perform distributed service discovery. In this way, a service component can be extended with specific capabilities depending on objectives of particular evaluation scenarios.

For the purpose of the present thesis, several plugins have been designed and implemented. The remainder of this chapter focuses on two plugins that are related to the evaluation scenario of this thesis: a *logic/workload simulation plugin* that induces the microscopic behaviour of a service component and a *management agent plugin* that applies the agent architecture introduced in Section 5.2.1. The *logic/workload simulation plugin* provides an abstracted service component with capabilities to simulate specific business logic and technical resources. Section 7.3 and Section 7.4 introduce the detailed implementation of the *logic/workload simulation plugin* in detail.

7.2 Simulation Model

Figure 7-2 illustrates the constructs of the simulation modules and their interactions with one another. In a simulated SOE, there are altogether four types of service components: *process* component, *service* component, *application* component, and *infrastructure* component – according to the definition of a service-oriented environment in Section 3.1. Each of those abstracted service components employs a single instance of the *logic/workload simulation* module and a single instance of the *management agent* module.

An instance of the *logic/workload simulation* module is composed of two integral parts: a *business logic component* and a *resource simulation component*. A *business logic component* implements the logic of a given service component. Similar to the definition of a business process, it defines a set of tasks of the respective service component. Those tasks are organised by means of composition patterns introduced in Section 6.6.1. Such composition patterns define chronological and logical execution orders between related tasks of a given component.

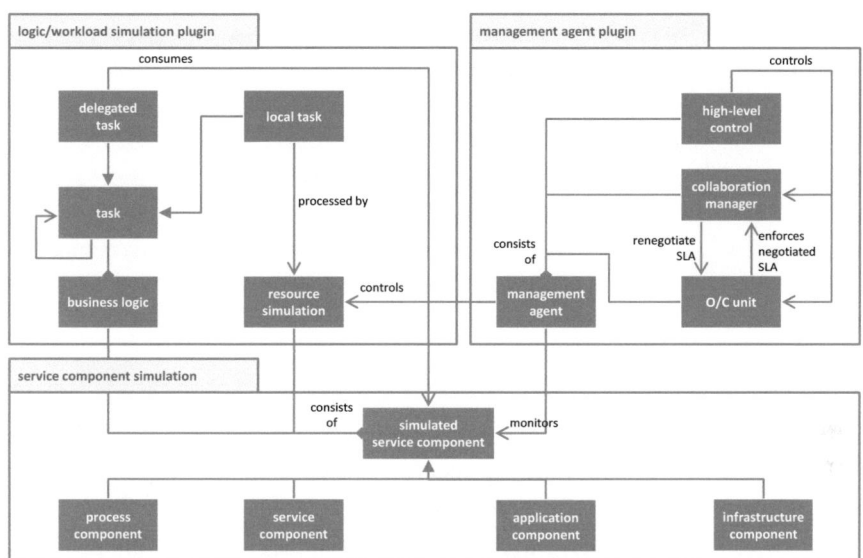

Figure 7-2: Model of the evaluation environment

A business logic distinguishes between two general task types: *delegated* tasks and *local* tasks. A delegated task is an activity that should be processed by another service component (i.e., a service provider). It indicates a provider/consumer relationship between the current service component as a service consumer and another component as a service provider. In contrast, a local task is an activity that will be processed by the respective service component itself. In this process, processing a local task causes consumption of local technical resources and induces various aspects associated with resource consumption, such as consumption cost, processing time, and resource usage.

Hence, the *logic/workload simulation module* employs a second component – a *resource simulation component* – to simulate local resources of a service component. The *resource simulation component* maintains a range of configurable local resources to process tasks of the respective service component. As such, it simulates the role of a task processor and handles assigned tasks according to its local processing capacities. Such processing capacities can be flexibly adjusted in depending on given external directives.

As aforementioned, a self-organising SOE utilises management agents to manage processing capacities of service components. Hence, each *simulated service component* is equipped with a management agent applying the agent architecture introduced in Section 5.2.1. To this end, a *management agent plugin* is designed and implement-ed in the evaluation environment. It is composed of an *O/C unit* and a *collaboration manager*. Behaviour of both components is controlled by a *high-level control compo-nent*. The control component is given an abstract business objective, from which it derives operative directives for the *O/C unit* and the *collaboration manager*. Among other things, the *high-level control component* specifies the priorities of service level objectives involved in the SLM. The *O/C unit* uses those priorities to determine the overall degree of fulfilment of a given SLA, as described in Section 5.2.4. Similarly, the *collaboration manager* applies those priorities to determine its preferences of ser-vice level objectives in the course of negotiation.

The *collaboration manager* implements automated negotiation of SLAs in the management agent, as described in Chapter 6. Via the *collaboration manager*, the management agent can negotiate with another related management agent in an auto-mated manner. The resulting SLA is then forwarded to the *O/C unit* for enforcement.

An instance of the *management agent plugin* monitors runtime behaviour of a *simulated service component*. That is, it observes how a *simulated service component* behaves in the course of interactions with other related service components. Based on runtime information that the *management agent* collects from the *simulated service component*, the *O/C unit* consolidates the collected information to situation parame-ters that address service level behaviour of the respective service component. These situation parameters together with the SLA delivered by the *collaboration manager* serve as the basis for decision-making processes of the *management agent*, i.e., the *O/C unit* of the agent.

Control actions proposed by the *O/C unit* are executed by the management agent upon the *resource simulation component*. Those control actions aim mainly at adjust-ing processing capacities of the service component, which leads in turn to changes in the component's behaviour on the service level. Alternatively, the *O/C unit* can also utilise the *collaboration manager* to renegotiate a violated SLA, if it determines that the resource simulation component runs out of its local resources. In this case, the *col-laboration manager* interacts with the respective service component to rearrange a new agreement.

7.3 Logic Simulation

As discussed in Section 6.6.1, business logic of a service component can be modelled in terms of composition patterns. Those composition patterns define the chronological order, in which a service component invokes either a local activity or a delegated activity offered by another service component. In this way, a service component implements its capability either by itself or by one of its service providers. As such, a service component delegates part of the realisation of its capability to the particular service provider. Hence, by modelling runtime behaviour as a workflow, a simulated service component can involve a set of related service components in its realisation – just as a real-world service component does.

In order to execute a workflow, a simulated service component needs an appropriate workflow engine. During simulation, such a workflow engine should be able to load a workflow from a given document (e.g., a BPMN document), instantiate it, and control the workflow instance throughout its life cycle. With regard to the evaluation environment of the present thesis, an appropriate workflow engine has to meet the following requirements:

- It should have a light footprint. This ensures that such an engine can be integrated as a programming module into a simulated service component.

- It should utilise an extensible XML document to describe its workflow instead of hard coding them directly in the source code. This requirement makes sure that evaluation scenarios can be flexibly modified in dependence of respective objectives, without having to recompile the complete environment after each change.

- Workflow documents used should be easily extensible with customised workflow elements, especially with respect to the composition patterns defined in Section 6.6.1. This ensures that the composition and decomposition schemas defined in Section 6.6.2 and Section 6.6.3 can be applied directly without any modification.

With respect to these considerations, most of the mainstream business process management (BPM) systems [SH10] can be omitted because of their heavy footprint and poor support for being integrated directly into the evaluation environment. Advanced features of such BPM systems, such as persistence of workflow instances or rich interaction interfaces, are not required in the implementation of the evaluation environment. For the purpose of the present thesis, a simple open source workflow engine, Sarasvati workflow engine [Sar11], is adopted. In comparison to mainstream BPM systems, it is rather a programming module capable of being integrated into an existing environment as a lightweight workflow engine.

The core of Sarasvati is based on graph execution. Therefore, a workflow is expressed as a directed graph consisting of *nodes* and a set of *arcs* connecting those nodes. Similar to the concept of petri net, Sarasvati utilises tokens to mark the current operational state of a workflow. The activity associated with a node will be executed, if the node receives a token passed from its predecessor. After its execution, it passes its token to the next node in the logic flow.

To control the logic flow between nodes, Sarasvati introduces the concept of *guard*. A guard has a similar role as gateways in BPMN. It is used to control branching/merging behaviour of a node in a workflow. With an appropriately configured guard, a workflow can discard, bypass, or activate one or more selected nodes to continue its logic flow.

In contrast to other workflow engines, the actual strength of Sarasvati workflow engine is its extensibility with customised workflow elements. A Sarasvati workflow can be extended with additional information according to particular target scenarios. In the context of the present thesis, the Sarasvati workflow engine is used to model the business logic of a service component. Hence, with respect to the specific characters of a business logic, this thesis extends a Sarasvati workflow as follows:

- A node is extended with a custom section describing artefacts associated with the corresponding task of a node. As mentioned in Section 7.2, a task can be either a local one or a delegated one. For a local task, the custom section defines the average payload of the task and its repeat times. For a delegated task, the custom section defines the remote logic of an external service component that the task should invoke.

- The guard of a node is extended with the composition patterns AND, XOR, and OR introduced in Section 6.6.1. In addition, each guard is associated with a conditional expression that determines, in case of conditional composition patterns (i.e., XOR and OR), which branches among all existing branches should be activated in the logic flow.

Table 7-1 describes the business logic in Figure 6-9 as a Sarasvati workflow.

Table 7-1: Sample logic definition as a Sarasvati workflow

```
1)   <process-definition name="process1"
           xmlns="http://sarasvati.googlecode.com/ProcessDefinition">
2)     <node name="start" isStart="true">
3)       <arc to="ref_S1" />
4)     </node>
5)     <node name="ref_S1" type="task">
6)       <arc to="ref_L1" />
7)       <custom>
8)         <callAgent>S1</callAgent>
9)         <callLogic>S1_1</callLogic>
10)        <callingAgent>process1</callingAgent>
11)        <taskName>ref_S1</taskName>
12)        <taskDesc>calls the logic S1_1 of the service component S1</taskDesc>
13)      </custom>
14)    </node>
15)    <node name="ref_L1" type="task">
16)      <arc to="branch_AND" />
17)      <custom>
18)        <taskName>task_L1</taskName>
19)        <taskPayLoad>2500.0</taskPayLoad>
20)        <taskRepeatTimes>2</taskRepeatTimes>
21)        <taskDesc>executes with average payload of 2500</taskDesc>
22)      </custom>
23)    </node>
24)    <node name="branch_AND">
25)      <guard>isAND</guard>
26)      <arc to="branch_XOR" />
27)      <arc to="ref_S2" />
28)    </node>
29)    <node name="ref_S2" type="task">
30)      <arc to="Join_AND" />
31)    </node>
32)    <node name="branch_XOR">
33)      <guard condition="random">isXOR</guard>
34)      <arc to="ref_S3" />
35)      <arc to="ref_L2" />
36)    </node>
37)    <node name="ref_L2" type="task">
38)      <arc to="Join_XOR" />
39)    </node>
40)    <node name="ref_S3" type="task">
41)      <arc to="Join_XOR" />
42)    </node>
43)    <node name="Join_XOR" isJoin="true">
44)      <arc to="Join_AND" />
45)    </node>
46)    <node name="Join_AND" isJoin="true">
47)      <arc to="end" />
48)    </node>
49)    <node name="end" />
50)  </process-definition>
```

It is noteworthy that for simplicity some irrelevant XML elements are eliminated in the workflow. The business logic is defined for the service component *process1* (cf.

line 1). As aforementioned, the whole business logic is organised as a graph with a start node (i.e., the node with the attribute *isStart="true"*, cf. line 2) and an end node (i.e., the last node in the graph, cf. line 50). Between two related nodes, there is a directed arc, where the node at the beginning is the predecessor of the node at the end. A node may have a guard defined in it (cf. line 25), which controls either the branching or the joining behaviour of the logic flow at the node.

The node of the task *ref_S1* (cf. lines 5~14) defines a delegated task of the service component. In this node, *process1* invokes the logic *S1_1* (cf. line 9) of the service component *S1* (cf. line 8). It is worth noting that in the current implementation of the logic simulation, all logics defined for a service component are invoked without any input parameters. This implementation decision is made to simplify the simulated provider/consumer relationship, because a service invocation with input/output parameters follows the same processing scheme as an invocation without those parameters. Furthermore, it is defined that all logic invocations are synchronous. That is, after having sent a request to a service component, the respective service consumer has to wait for the response, before it can continue with its logic flow.

The node for the task *ref_L1* (cf. lines 15~23) defines a local task of the service component. As aforementioned, in order to estimate QoS behaviour of a simulated service component, it has to produce some workload, as a real-world service component does. To this end, a local task has two corresponding properties. The first one is to define the average payload of executing the corresponding task (cf. line 19). It determines in general the amount of effort that the underlying simulated resource needs to process the task. The second one is to define the number of executions of the current task (cf. line 20).

Another customised element is the *guard* element in the logic definition. For example, line 25 of Table 7-1 defines an AND-guard at the node *branch_AND*. In this case, both arcs defined in the node (cf. lines 26 and 27) are activated by the workflow engine to continue the logic flow.

Similarly, line 34 defines an XOR-guard of the node *branch_XOR*. In contrast to an AND-guard, this node exclusively selects one of its two arcs to continue the logic flow. The decision, which arc should be activated, depends on the evaluation result of the attribute *condition* of the guard. In the example logic, the guard uses a random function (cf. line 33) to determine the outgoing arc. In other words, both arcs have equal probability to be activated during simulation.

At a glance, a business logic is the part in the evaluation environment that realises the request-driven behaviour of a real-world SOE. By executing a business logic, the evaluation environment involves not only the owner component of the logic into the simulation process, but also all of its service providers. In this way, all related service components can be successively incorporated into the simulation at runtime. The next requirement is that such service invocations have to induce workloads of respective service components, which is covered in the following section.

7.4 Workload Simulation

Workload simulation is concerned with microscopic simulation of runtime behaviour of a service component. In particular, workload simulation addresses how a service component processes incoming service requests with realistic workloads. Since invoking the logic of a given service component is associated with consumption of underlying technical resources, this section describes how a service component can simulate technical resources locally and how it processes an incoming service request by using these resources.

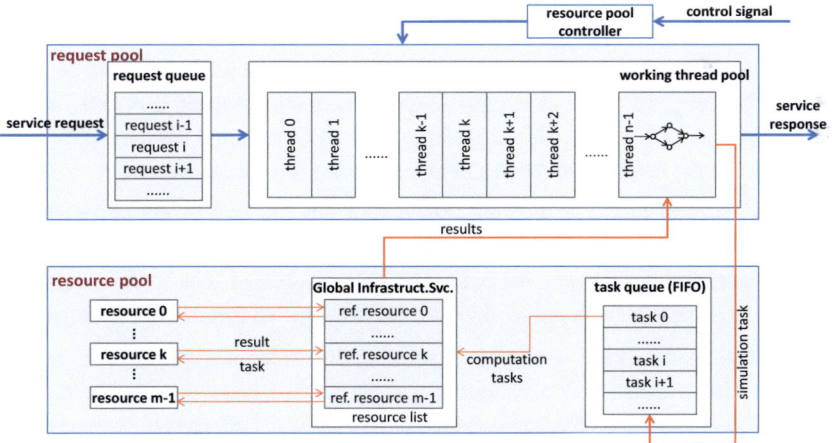

Figure 7-3: Resource simulation in the evaluation environment

Figure 7-3 illustrates the internal structure of resource simulation in the evaluation environment. The structure is composed of two parts. The first part, the *request pool*, is responsible for organising a range of working threads and determines how incoming service requests are distributed to these working threads. The second part in the resource simulation addresses the internal implementation of the *resource pool*. Among other things, this part manages a range of simulated resources and determines how a local activity is distributed to these resources.

Each incoming service request is added to a first-in-first-out (FIFO) request queue, where all requests wait to be processed by the service component. For simplicity, all requests in the request queue have the same priority for processing. A service request has to wait, until it is distributed based on the FIFO principle to a working thread that becomes available.

The working thread pool maintains a range of n working threads. It is responsible for organising the life cycle of these working threads, including initialising them, assigning service requests to them, collecting processing results, and terminating them after use. A working thread is exclusively allocated to a single service request each time. After having finished processing a request, a respective working thread is returned to the thread pool, where the pool can assign another service request to it.

A working thread executes the business logic of a service component. Hence, each working thread maintains locally a running instance of the Sarasvati workflow engine. In order to process an incoming service request, a respective working thread loads the logic specified by the request into the workflow engine and initiates it:

- For a delegated task defined in the business logic, the working thread generates a corresponding service request as specified in the delegated task to the respective service provider. Upon receiving the service response from the provider, it passes the response to the business logic to continue its execution.

- For a local task, the working thread forwards the task to the underlying resource pool, where the task is processed by a simulated resource in the pool. Processing results from the resource pool are returned back to the corresponding business logic in the working thread to trigger its further execution.

- At the end of logic execution, a working thread terminates the corresponding service instance and generates a dummy service response. This response is forwarded to the thread pool, which in turn forwards the service response to the corresponding service consumer in the environment.

The resource pool simulates a set of m technical resources of a service component. To this end, the resource pool utilises the GridSim toolkit to model and simulate distributed resources [BM02]. GridSim is originally designed to enable simulation of a distributed grid environment. As such, it provides a comprehensive platform to simulate artefacts within a distributed grid environment, such as distributed resources, resource brokers, applications, and users. Among other things, GridSim allows modelling heterogeneous types of technical resources either in a time-shared or space-shared mode. Each simulated resource can have different processing capacities defined in terms of Million Instructions per Second (MIPS). The implementation of the evaluation environment was built on GridSim Toolkit 5.0 beta, released on September 24, 2009, and has been tested on GridSim Toolkit 5.2, released on November 25, 2011.

For the purpose of the present thesis, only the part of the GridSim toolkit for modelling and simulating resources is used. It is utilised by the resource pool to define and simulate the set of technical resources of a service component. To this end, each service component uses a configuration file to define its set of technical resources, as illustrated by the sample XML file in Table 7-2.

Table 7-2: Resource definition of a service component in the evaluation environment

```
1)  <?xml version="1.0"?>
2)
3)  <resource-definition name="infrastructure1">
4)    <resource>
5)      <architecture>Sun Ultra</architecture>
6)      <OS>Solaris</OS>
7)      <machineList>
8)        <machine id="0">
9)          <pe id="0" MIPS="377"/>
10)         <pe id="1" MIPS="377"/>
11)         <pe id="2" MIPS="377"/>
12)         <pe id="3" MIPS="377"/>
13)       </machine>
14)     </machineList>
15)     <allocationPolicy>SPACE_SHARED</allocationPolicy>
16)     <timeZone>9.0</timeZone>
17)     <costPerSec>3.0</costPerSec>
18)   </resource>
19) </resource-definition>
```

The definition file specifies resources for the service component *infrastructure1* (cf. line 3). The resource runs on the hardware architecture of Sun Ultra and the operating system Solaris (cf. line 5 and 6). The resource is composed of one single machine with four processing elements. Each processing element represents a CPU unit and has a predefined processing capacity. For example, the processing elements in Table 7-2 all have a capacity of 377 MIPS (cf. lines 9~12). Computational tasks are assigned to processing elements in a space-shared manner (cf. line 15). In this case, the resource follows a simple allocation policy of FIFO to assign a task to a single processing element.

Another interesting aspect of the resource definition is service cost. The definition file specifies cost per second (cf. line 17 in the sample file) for consuming the resource. As such, the total cost of processing a single task is calculated with respect to the total number of time units used to process a task and the basic cost per time unit.

Based on the simulated resources, the resource pool processes computational tasks submitted by working threads. As specified by the sample logic in Table 7-2, each computational task is submitted with two properties: average payload of the task and the number of repeats. The actual payload of the task is determined by the resource pool on the fly. To this end, the resource pool defines two variation parameters v_{up} and v_{down}, with $0 \leq v_{up}, v_{down} \leq 1$. The actual payload ρ of a given task with an average payload of $\overline{\rho}$ is then determined by:

$$\rho = (1 - v_{down} + (v_{down} + v_{up}) \cdot r) \cdot \overline{\rho} \qquad (10.4.1)$$

In (10.4.1), r is a random double that is uniformly distributed between 0 and 1. By applying (10.4.1), the actual payload of a task is located between $(1 - v_{down}) \cdot \overline{\rho}$ and $(1 + v_{up}) \cdot \overline{\rho}$. With the calculated payload, the respective task is submitted to a simulated resource in the resource pool for processing. The resource pool maintains a global infrastructure service, which contains references to all simulated machines. The global infrastructure service distributes computational tasks to those machines and returns processing results to the invoking working thread. Among other things, a processing result contains detailed information describing how the corresponding task is processed, such as the execution start/end times, the CPU time used, the average cost per second, and the total processing cost of the task.

To summarise, the logic/workload simulation module can actively model and execute the business logic of a service component with an individual workload. Therefore, a service component in the evaluation environment can produce individual runtime behaviour based on its business logic and its local resources. By observing runtime information of such a simulated service component, a management agent can estimate the service level behaviour of a respective service component, including its response time, throughput, availability, and service cost during a sampling period. This runtime information enables a management agent to reactively manage its underlying service component, in particular with respect to SLAs it closes.

7.5 Summary

This chapter introduces the evaluation environment designed and implemented for the present thesis. Evaluating the approach proposed by this thesis requires an appropriate evaluation environment that can flexibly reproduce the runtime behaviour of an SOE. Since physical evaluation environments are expensive and difficult to maintain, and do not provide the desired flexibility, the present thesis adopts a simulation-based environment for evaluating the approach.

The evaluation environment utilises an architecture that is extendible by means of plugins. On top of an abstract simulation core, the evaluation environment can be extended by additional plugins that provide the evaluation environment with new capabilities. For the purpose of the present thesis, two plugins are developed to facilitate negotiation-based SLM in an SOE: the logic/workload simulation plugin and the management agent plugin.

The logic/workload simulation plugin focuses on simulating runtime behaviour of a single service component, both on the macroscopic as well as microscopic level. To this end, this plugin models the business logic of a service component as a workflow and employs a workflow engine to execute it at runtime. In this way, invoking a simulated business process involves all supporting service components in the underlying layers of the SOE. From this viewpoint, the simulated evaluation environment can reproduce the request-driven macroscopic aspects of an SOE on the global level.

In addition, the logic/workload simulation plugin models and simulates local technical resources of a service component. On top of such resources, a service component processes its local activities and individually produces workloads as a real-world service component does. Such workload information can be used by the management agent plugin to assess runtime behaviour of the corresponding service component on the service level.

In a word, the evaluation environment provides a flexible and extendible simulation-based test bed for assessing self-organising SLM in an SOE. Model-based configuration files allow constructing a range of varying SOE scenarios depending on the respective evaluation objectives.

Chapter 8   Evaluation Results

> *"持之有故，言之成理。"*
>
> ——【荀子・非十二子】
>
> *"It is reasonable to say things with solid judgement."*
>
> (Xun Zi, ca. 312-230 B.C.)

This chapter provides the evaluation results to support the approach proposed in the present thesis. As described in Chapter 7, the evaluation environment implements the architecture of a management agent described in Section 5.2. On top of the generic observer/controller architecture, an additional collaboration layer is built in the management agent to facilitate collaboration between related service components.

Therefore, the focus of the evaluation experiments conducted is twofold. First, the ability of the proposed model to enable automated bilateral multi-issue negotiation is evaluated. Secondly, the negotiation model is incorporated into the global context of an SOE and it is evaluated, how negotiation-based collaboration between service components can facilitate the management of the entire SOE.

Hence, the remainder of the chapter is organised as follows: Section 8.1 outlines the design considerations of the evaluation experiments. In particular, this section addresses the objectives of the experiments and explains how they relate to one another. Section 8.2 is concerned with the experimental results showing the performance of the automated negotiation model. Section 8.3 provides the evaluation results to demonstrate the applicability of the overall approach in an SOE.

8.1 Experimental Design

As aforementioned, the focus of the evaluation experiments is to assess the feasibility of the approach proposed in the present thesis. As such, a range of experiments with varying configurations has been conducted. Thus, for a clear experimental design, the present thesis follows the guidelines summarised by Montgomery [Mon09]:

- recognition of and statement of the problem,
- selection of the response variable,
- choice of factors, levels, and ranges,
- choice of experimental design,
- performing the experiments,
- statistical analysis of the data,
- and conclusion and recommendation.

The first four guidelines aim at performing a structured pre-experimental planning, while the last three guidelines address conduction of experiments and processing of experimental results. This section is concerned with the first four guidelines for a clear experimental design.

Statement of the problem: as stated in the motivation of this chapter, the key issue of the evaluation is to assess the feasibility of the multi-level SLM approach. That is, the target problem of the experiments is concerned with whether the collaboration-based concept can accelerate management of service components of an SOE in an automated manner. Thus, the goals of the experiments are as follows:

- to investigate the influence of various negotiation strategies on the negotiation outcomes,
- to investigate the influence of negotiation behaviour of a management agent on its counterpart,
- to investigate the influence of global business objectives on the negotiation outcomes,
- to investigate the feasibility of the composition/decomposition schemas introduced in Section 6.6,
- to investigate the feasibility of the negotiation protocol introduced in Section 6.5,
- and to investigate the influence of the collaboration-based SLM approach on the overall performance of an SOE.

Response variables: according to the guidelines of Montgomery [Mon09], response variables are necessary to measure the performance of the experimental outcomes. In the present thesis, they are needed to estimate the performance of the negotiation model and the overall effectiveness of the collaboration-based SLM approach. The present thesis uses the following measures:

- the number of negotiation rounds needed to reach an agreement, if any,
- the utilities of the resulting SLAs, if any, for both management agents,
- and the efficiency of the resulting SLAs.

To assess the feasibility of the approach, the present thesis estimates the runtime behaviour of related service components. By observing the changes of runtime behaviour of service components in relationship to their workloads, it is possible to draw a conclusion on the effectiveness of the collaboration-based SLM approach.

Choice of evaluation objectives: in the evaluation environment, a range of varying configurations influences the values of the response variables listed above. Therefore, it is reasonable to define the set of varying configurations depending on the respective evaluation objectives. Figure 8-1 illustrates the main objectives that the conducted evaluation experiments aim to cover.

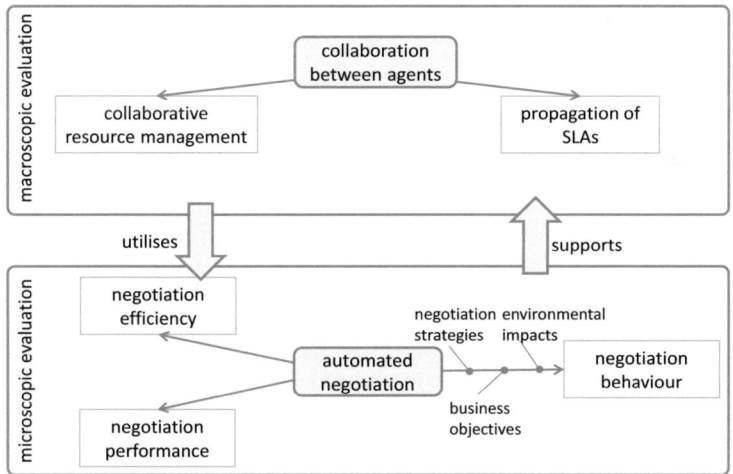

Figure 8-1: Objectives of the evaluation experiments

In general, these objectives are classified into two categories: *microscopic* evaluation and *macroscopic* evaluation. Microscopic evaluation aims at verifying the proposed approach of *automated negotiation* on the level of a single management agent. In particular, experiments of this category address how varying configurations of the proposed negotiation model influence the negotiation outcomes. Among other things, the following objectives are considered in this category:

- *Negotiation behaviour* of a management agent is subject to a range of internal and external influence factors. Internally, a management agent's behaviour is determined by its *negotiation strategy*. Externally, an agent's negotiation behaviour is influenced by given *business objectives* and by its *environment*. Business objectives guide a management agent to determine its preferences on service level objectives. Similarly, environmental impacts, in particular those of an agent's counterpart, influence its behaviour. Among other things, willingness of an agent's counterpart for cooperation determines largely if an agent can assert its preferences in the negotiation.

- The second objective is *efficiency* of automated negotiation between two agents. This objective covers mainly *efficiency* of the introduced negotiation strategies to generate socially fair SLAs. By comparing those results with Pareto optimal offers, it is possible to determine the quality of the resulting SLAs, in particular with respect to the social welfare of the results for both negotiation agents. In this way, it is also possible to investigate how far the introduced negotiation strategies can derive socially fair SLAs for both agents, even under the condition of an incomplete information situation.

- The last objective is the *performance* of the introduced automated negotiation model. In this case, it is of interest to investigate how far the introduced negotiation strategies can guide the two service components towards reaching an agreement, despite their incomplete information situation.

In contrast to the microscopic evaluation, the macroscopic evaluation focuses on the overall applicability of the negotiation-based multi-level SLM approach to facilitate *collaboration between agents*. That is, on top of automated negotiation, the macroscopic evaluation investigates how the iterated and coordinated negotiation protocol can be applied to an SOE to support multi-level SLM. Therefore, evaluation experiments in this category are organised with respect to the following two negotiation scenarios:

- The first negotiation scenario, *propagation of SLAs*, is the most basic one to prove the feasibility of the approach. This scenario investigates how end-to-end service level requirements on a business process can be propagated systematically to the supporting service components in the underlying layers.

- The second negotiation scenario, *collaborative resource management*, aims at demonstrating the strength of the proposed approach to facilitate flexible and efficient management of technical resources across several related service components. Combining with controlled self-organisation, automated negotiation allows a management agent, if necessary, to dynamically distribute its workloads to its supporting service providers depending on their most recent runtime behaviour.

By summarising the evaluation objectives, essential factors that influence the response variables of the evaluation experiments can be determined. Montgomery distinguishes between *nuisance factors* and *potential design factors*, which in turn can be either *design factors*, *held-constant factors*, or *allowed-to-vary factors* [Mon09].

In the present thesis, random seeds used for simulating resources in GridSim as well as for simulating entities in Repast Symphony are the nuisance factors. In addition, the evaluation environment employs a range of held-constant factors, such as the number of negotiating management agents, their business logics, and relationships between them, are kept constant across all evaluation experiments. Hence, these factors are of less interest to the response variables.

Similarly, there is a range of allowed-to-vary factors in the evaluation environment, such as the way to estimate distance between two given offers in a negotiation space (i.e., either pure Euclidean distance or normalised Euclidean distance). These factors have fewer impacts on the response variables. Therefore, these factors are not investigated in the present thesis in detail.

The more interesting factors are design factors that are selected for study in the evaluation experiments. That is, the set of configurations in the evaluation environment that influences the response variables identified above. The following configurations are of particular interest for evaluation:

- negotiation strategy (i.e., conceding strategy and trade-off strategy) employed by a management agent,
- utility functions used by a management agent,
- willingness of a management agent to cooperate with its counterpart,
- and business objectives given by a high-level control instance.

Choice of experimental designs: depending on the desired objectives of the respective evaluation experiments, the choice of the experiment designs determines how these experiments are conducted. With respect to both microscopic and macroscopic evaluation, it is obvious that they do not share the same goal. While macroscopic evaluation focuses on the feasibility of the multi-level SLM approach, microscopic evaluation is concerned with performance of the automated negotiation model.

Hence, microscopic evaluation is conducted as a parameter study by varying a design factor while holding all other design factors constant. In order to reduce the impacts of variances and standard errors caused by the simulation environment, each experiment will be repeated 10 times using the same configurations and the average outcomes out of 10 runs are used as the final results.

In contrast, macroscopic evaluation aims at demonstrating the applicability of the introduced multi-level SLM approach. Hence, it is of interest to investigate runtime behaviour of the selected service components within an SOE with respect to the response variables mentioned before.

Based on those considerations regarding experimental design, a range of experiments are carried out in the simulated evaluation environment. The following sections provide the experimental results. Section 8.2 focuses on experiments for the microscopic evaluation, while Section 8.3 provides an insight into experimental results of the macroscopic evaluation.

8.2 Automated Bilateral Negotiation

This section provides the experimental results to investigate the performance of the automated negotiation model. The results are presented with respect to the evaluation objectives discussed in the previous section. Section 8.2.1 investigates the basic negotiation behaviour of a management agent by employing varying negotiation strategies, while Section 8.2.2 is concerned with evaluating social welfare of a negotiation process. The last section outlines the performance of the negotiation model in a quantitative manner.

As stated in the experimental design, each experiment evaluates only a single design factor, while all other design factors are held constant. In each experiment, one service consumer and one service provider are involved. The negotiation space of the respective service component is listed in Table 8-1. In order to keep the evaluation results clear, this section considers only two QoS parameters, *response time* and *cost*.

It is assumed that both negotiating service components have the same units for the QoS parameters.

Table 8-1: Negotiation space used to evaluate automated negotiation

	response time		cost	
	minimal	maximal	minimal	maximal
consumer	60	100	130	170
provider	95	135	105	145

In all evaluation experiments, if not stated otherwise, the negotiation strategy of the consumer is fixed. It follows a simple time-dependent conceding strategy to determine its offers. That is, the consumer reduces linearly its expectation on utility in each step by a certain amount until the end of the negotiation. In addition, both management agents employ a linear utility function as introduced in Section 6.4. In the utility functions, both QoS parameters have equal weights. The negotiation deadline is set to 60 negotiation rounds. In the course of negotiation, both management agents propose alternating SLA offers to their counterpart, until a mutually acceptable offer is found. Hence, each agent has the possibility to make 30 proposals, before the negotiation thread is aborted due to timeout.

8.2.1 Negotiation Behaviour

The focus of this section is to evaluate the negotiation behaviour of the service provider with different negotiation configurations, while in each experiment only a single negotiation configuration is changed.

Influence of Negotiation Strategy

This section evaluates the impact of negotiation strategies on the negotiation behaviour of a management agent. Therefore, the service provider is configured with varying negotiation strategies, i.e., conceding strategies and trade-off strategies. As aforementioned, the service consumer employs a simple time-dependent conceding strategy.

Figure 8-2, Figure 8-3, Figure 8-4, and Figure 8-5 illustrate the negotiation behaviour of the service components with varying configurations. In each figure, the chart on the left, *the negotiation behaviour chart*, shows the negotiation behaviour of both management agents in the negotiation space spanned by the two QoS parameters, response time and service cost. The chart in the middle, *the utility chart for the consum-*

er, illustrates the consumer's perceptions of the offers in terms of utilities. Similarly, the chart on the right, *the utility chart for the provider*, illustrates the utilities of those offers from the viewpoint of the provider. To distinguish between offers proposed by the consumer and those proposed by the provider, a consumer offer is marked as a blue circle, while a provider offer is marked as a red star. This convention applies to all figures in the remainder of this thesis, if not stated otherwise.

In all figures, it is clear to see that in order to reach a compromise, both the provider and the consumer have to concede by giving up a certain extent of utility in favour of their counterpart in each step. Secondly, it can be observed how the management agents move away from their optimum offers towards the optimum offers of their negotiation partners. Both of them provide the prerequisite to find a mutually acceptable agreement through negotiation.

Figure 8-2 illustrates the negotiation behaviour of management agents that apply conceding strategies only. The provider utilises the time-dependent conceding strategy to calculate its offers. Herein, a management agent only cares about the remaining time to the given negotiation deadline. Based on this time estimation, a management agent calculates the extent of utility it is going to give up in its next offer. Other aspects, such as the assignments of both QoS parameters in the incoming offers are not considered during this process.

Figure 8-2: Evaluation of conceding strategies with time-dependent tactics

Therefore, in the behaviour chart of Figure 8-2, it can be observed that both management agents move directly from their respective optimum offers to their worst offers. During this process, both management agents pass the common negotiation space without touching it. Therefore, the negotiation process is aborted after the given negotiation deadline without reaching an agreement.

The utility chart of the *consumer* shows how the service consumer reduces its expectation on utility in each round and how the service provider increases the utilities of its offers in favour of the service consumer. The change of utility occurs linearly to the change of time. The same change behaviour can be observed in the utility chart of the provider, too. Both management agents reduce their utilities from 1 to 0 in the course of negotiation. After that, the negotiation process is aborted due to timeout.

The conceding strategies determine only utilities of outgoing offers depending on the remaining time. The largest shortage of the conceding strategies is that they take barely the intention of the negotiation partner in terms of incoming SLA offers into consideration. Hence, as already motivated in Section 6.7, in order to get more promising offers, trade-off strategies are applied to incorporate external information into the search process, such as negotiation history, or business objectives.

Figure 8-3 illustrates the negotiation behaviour of a service provider that applies the trade-off strategy with alignment to both initial offers. That is, the service provider aligns its trade-off search to the initial offers of both management agents, i.e., $X^0_{c \to p}$ and $X^1_{p \to c}$. As mentioned before, the initial offer represent the optimum QoS values of the respective management agent. Therefore, alignment to initial offers ensures that a management agent can provide offers with respect to the optimum SLA of its negotiation partner.

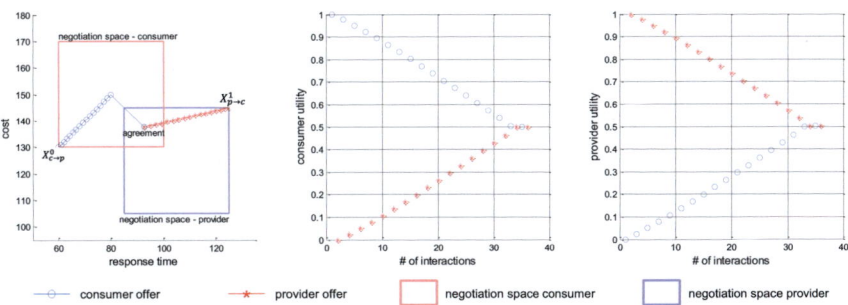

Figure 8-3: Evaluation of trade-off strategy with alignment to both initial offers

As shown in the behaviour chart in Figure 8-3, the service provider tends to place its offers along the line connecting the initial agreements. As long as the given deadline is not exceeded, the service provider can reach the joint negotiation space sometime in the course of negotiation. From this point of view, this strategy increases the possibility of convergence of a negotiation process. The utility charts illustrate how both negotiating service components move toward each other by giving up a certain amount of utility in each negotiation round. In contrast to the experiment with pure conceding strategies, the trade-off strategy applied guides the provider towards the common negotiation space. This establishes an essential prerequisite for reaching an agreement between the consumer and the provider.

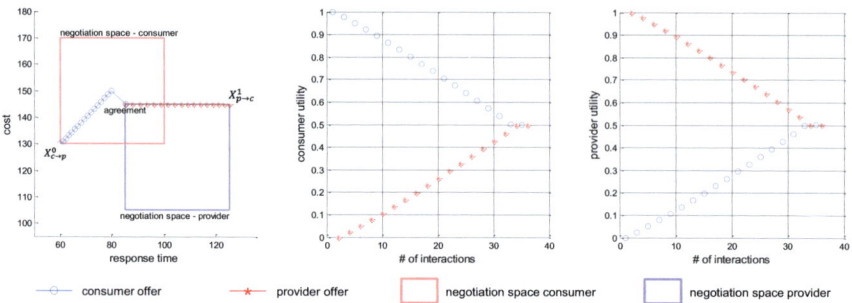

Figure 8-4: Evaluation of trade-off strategy with alignment to the last incoming offer

A shortage of the trade-off strategy applied in the previous experiment of Figure 8-3 is its lack of dynamic. The service provider uses both initial offers as fixed reference points and calculates its offers only based on these points. Incoming offers that often represent the most recent intentions of the counterpart are not considered in this process. Hence, Figure 8-4 depicts the evaluation result of the trade-off strategy with alignment to the last incoming offer.

In this strategy, the service provider aligns itself to the most recent needs of its negotiation partner, i.e., the service consumer, instead of to the optimum SLA of the consumer. This change in the negotiation strategy introduces more dynamics to the trade-off search, so that the provider can propose a more attractive offer to its partner in dependence of the most current request of the partner.

Reflected in the negotiation behaviour of the provider (see the behaviour chart in Figure 8-4), the service provider tends to place its offers on the upper boundary of the negotiation space. This strategy enables the service provider to find the shortest way to reach the common negotiation space. In this case, each proposed offer of the service provider is aligned with the most recent proposal of the counterpart.

By reviewing the two trade-off strategies evaluated previously, it is worth noting that both trade-off strategies have their strength and shortage. Aligning with the initial offers allows a management agent to find quickly the common negotiation space. This behaviour provides an important prerequisite to reach an agreement. Aligning with the most recent offer enables a management agent to adapt itself to the intent of the counterpart dynamically. Hence, the last trade-off strategy evaluated in this section combines both previous trade-off strategies. It uses the last incoming offer of the counterpart as a dynamic reference point and its own initial offer as a fixed reference point. Figure 8-5 illustrates the results of the experiments for this trade-off strategy.

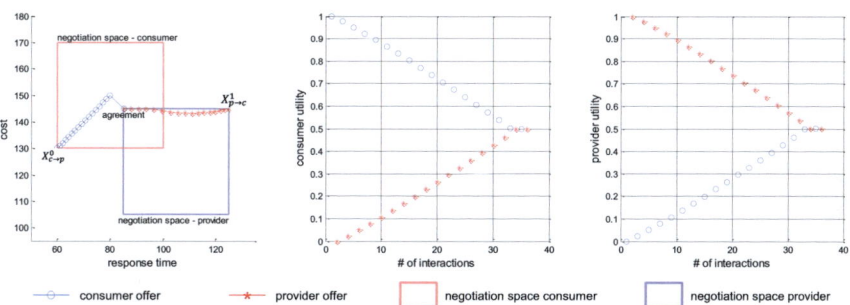

Figure 8-5: Evaluation of trade-off strategy with alignment to the last incoming offer and the own initial offer

By applying this strategy, the service provider tends to place its offers along the line connecting its own initial offer $X^1_{p \to c}$ and the last incoming offer. In this way, the service provider ensures that it takes the most recent intent of the counterpart into consideration, while keeping its own optimum SLA (i.e., the initial offer) in mind. In comparison with the behaviour charts of both previous trade-off strategies, in particular that in Figure 8-5, it is observable that at the beginning of negotiation, the service provider heads out to the offers of the consumer and moves slightly away from the upper bound of the negotiation space. As the consumer nears the joint negotiation space, the provider moves back to the upper bound of its negotiation space, until it reaches an agreement there with the consumer.

By considering the negotiation behaviour of all negotiation strategies, it is clear that appropriate negotiation behaviour of a management agent is crucial for reaching an agreement. In particular, the negotiation behaviour of pure conceding strategies (as illustrated in Figure 8-2) shows that reducing an agent's expectation on utility is not sufficient for reaching an agreement. The more important aspect is that a negotiation strategy can guide a management agent towards the joint negotiation space with its counterpart. This should takes place in spite of the incomplete information situation of the agent.

All the three trade-off strategies evaluated in this section can fulfil this requirement. As shown in the evaluation experiments, they enable a management agent to stepwise reach the joint negotiation space only by consulting offers proposed by its counterpart. In the experiments, all service providers applying a trade-off strategy have successfully negotiated agreements with their consumers within the predefined deadline.

Moreover, all resulting SLAs from the experiments with a trade-off strategy have the same utility. Similarly, the service provider needs the same number of negotiation rounds to reach an agreement. It is noteworthy that this is only a special case. It is determined by the specific combination of the negotiation spaces, the utility functions, as well as the business objectives applied in the experiments. In fact, as shown later in Section 8.2.3, different trade-off strategies may achieve varying performance depending on the respective negotiation scenarios.

Influence of Utility Functions

Utility functions determine how a management agent perceives an SLA. Hence, this section evaluates the influence of various utility functions on the agent's perception of SLAs. The evaluation experiments utilise the same negotiation space as in the previous section. The service consumer is configured with a linear utility function. All QoS parameters have equal weights in the utility calculation. In addition, both service components utilise the same time-dependent conceding strategy, where each service component concedes in an QoS parameter j with respect to the negotiation time t and the given negotiation deadline $t_{max} = 30$:

$$x_{a \to b}^t[j] = \begin{cases} min_j^a + \frac{t}{t_{max}} \cdot (max_j^a - min_j^a) & \text{if } V_j^a \text{ is decreasing} \\ min_j^a + (1 - \frac{t}{t_{max}}) \cdot (max_j^a - min_j^a) & \text{if } V_j^a \text{ is increasing} \end{cases}.$$

By applying this conceding strategy, a management agent moves uniformly from its optimum SLA with a utility of 1 to its worst case with a utility of 0, as shown in the negotiation behaviour charts in Figure 8-6 and Figure 8-7. In this way, it is possible to evaluate the change of utilities in the complete negotiation space of a management agent.

In both evaluation experiments, the service consumer employs a linear utility function to estimate the utility of an offer. Therefore, in the utility charts of the consumer in both figures, it is observable that the utilities of the offers proposed by the consumer itself change linearly from 1 to 0. Similarly, the utilities of the offers proposed by the provider change linearly from 0 to 1.

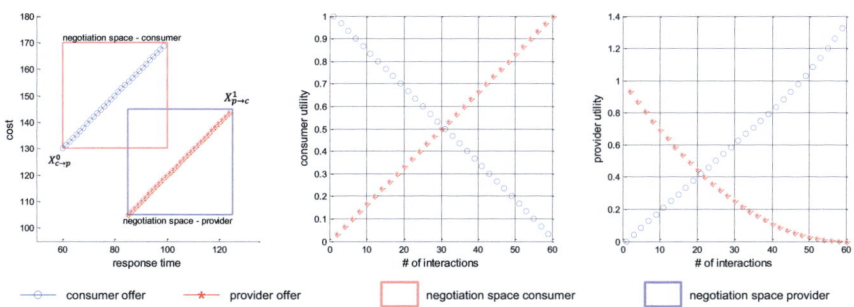

Figure 8-6: Evaluation of polynomial utility function with $\alpha = 2$

The service provider in the evaluation experiment depicted in Figure 8-6 employs a polynomial utility function with $\alpha = 2$:

$$V_j^i(x[j]) = \begin{cases} \left(\frac{max_j^i - x[j]}{max_j^i - min_j^i} \right)^2 & \text{if QoS parameter } j \text{ is decreasing and } max_j^i \geq x[j] \\ -\left(\frac{x[j] - max_j^i}{max_j^i - min_j^i} \right)^2 & \text{if QoS parameter } j \text{ is decreasing and } max_j^i \leq x[j] \\ \left(\frac{x[j] - min_j^i}{max_j^i - min_j^i} \right)^2 & \text{if QoS parameter } j \text{ is increasing and } x[j] \geq min_j^i \\ -\left(\frac{min_j^i - x[j]}{max_j^i - min_j^i} \right)^2 & \text{if QoS parameter } j \text{ is increasing and } x[j] \leq min_j^i \end{cases}$$

The utility chart of the provider in Figure 8-6 shows that in contrast to the consumer, the provider tends to give up more utility already at the beginning of a negotiation process. As time approaches the given negotiation deadline, the provider begins to slow down its concession in utility.

It is noteworthy that different utility functions allow management agents to individually determine their perception of SLA offers. For example, with its linear utility function, a service consumer perceives the incoming offers proposed by the service provider as linearly changing, although from the viewpoint of the service provider, it has strongly conceded utility to its counterpart already at the beginning of the negotiation process.

Similar behaviour can also be observed in the second evaluation experiment depicted in Figure 8-7. In this experiment, the service provider is equipped with a polynomial utility function with $\alpha = 0.5$:

301

$$
V_j^i(x[j]) = \begin{cases}
\left(\dfrac{max_j^i - x[j]}{max_j^i - min_j^i} \right)^{0.5} & \text{if QoS parameter } j \text{ is decreasing and } max_j^i \geq x[j] \\[2ex]
-\left(\dfrac{x[j] - max_j^i}{max_j^i - min_j^i} \right)^{0.5} & \text{if QoS parameter } j \text{ is decreasing and } max_j^i \leq x[j] \\[2ex]
\left(\dfrac{x[j] - min_j^i}{max_j^i - min_j^i} \right)^{0.5} & \text{if QoS parameter } j \text{ is increasing and } x[j] \geq min_j^i \\[2ex]
-\left(\dfrac{min_j^i - x[j]}{max_j^i - min_j^i} \right)^{0.5} & \text{if QoS parameter } j \text{ is increasing and } x[j] \leq min_j^i
\end{cases}
$$

The utility chart of the provider in Figure 8-7 shows that by applying this utility function, the service provider intends to preserve its utility at the beginning of the negotiation. As time approaches the given time limit, the service provider begins to make larger concessions. This conceding behaviour is completely different from the one of the provider in the previous experiment. Nevertheless, the consumer perceives the same linear change of utilities for the offers proposed by the service provider.

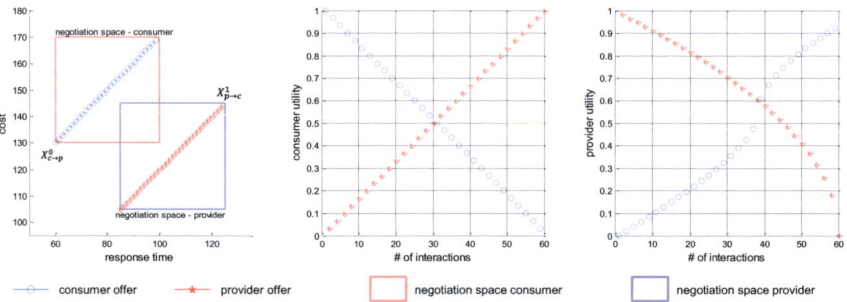

Figure 8-7: Evaluation of polynomial utility function with $\alpha = 0.5$

In short, utility functions allow management agents to determine their negotiation behaviour individually. However, it is worth noting that a concession made by a service component may not be perceived or honoured in the same way by its counterpart. It depends strongly on how the counterpart configures its own utility function.

Influence of Business Objectives

As stated in Section 5.2.2, business objectives guide the runtime behaviour of a management agent. In particular, they specify the priorities of service level objectives in the negotiation and enforcement phases of SLAs. In this section, influences of business objectives on the negotiation behaviour of a management agent are evaluated.

In order to better illustrate the experimental results, the negotiation scenario used in the previous sections is modified as given in Table 8-2:

Table 8-2: Negotiation space used to evaluate business objectives

	response time		cost	
	minimal	maximal	minimal	maximal
consumer	60	100	130	170
provider	95	135	155	195

Both service components use a linear utility function in the negotiation. In addition, the service consumer employs the trade-off strategy with alignment to both initial offers. Similarly, the service provider utilises the trade-off strategy with alignment to the most recent incoming offer. The negotiation deadline remains 60 negotiation rounds, as in the previous experiments.

The experiments evaluate the followings three business objectives:

- a business objective with equal emphasis on service cost and response time,
- a business objective with emphasis on service cost,
- and a business objective with emphasis on response time.

It is noteworthy that the service consumer and the service provider both follow the same business objective. For example, for the business objective with emphasis on service cost, the QoS parameter service cost is higher weighted than response time for both negotiation parties. From this viewpoint, a kind of competition relationship exists between both parties.

Figure 8-8 illustrates the negotiation behaviour of the service provider with the three business objectives mentioned before. The utility charts for the service consumer and the service provider are skipped in the figure.

Figure 8-8 (A) shows the behaviour of the provider that weights both QoS parameters equally. Therefore, the management agent of the provider places its offers uniformly along the diagonal of the negotiation space. Figure 8-8 (B) depicts the behaviour of the provider with emphasis on service cost. In contrast to the previous provider, this time the service provider tries to preserve the optimum value of service cost by staying at the upper boundary of the negotiation space for the first few offers. Herein, the service provider makes larger concessions in terms of response time, so that it can avoid concessions in the prioritised service cost. After that, the respective management agent reaches the turning point, where it has to begin to concede also in service cost. Otherwise, the respective management agent may not reach the joint negotiation space with the service consumer.

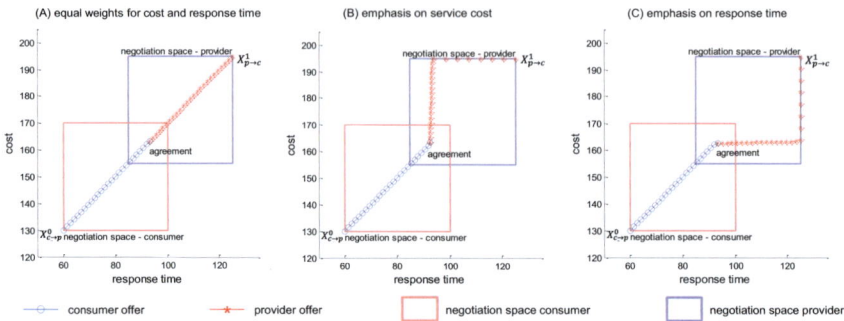

Figure 8-8: Evaluation of business objectives

Similarly, Figure 8-8 (C) illustrates the behaviour of the service provider with emphasis on response time. In this experiment, since response time is weighted stronger than service cost in utility calculation, the service provider tends to preserve the optimum value of response time by moving on the right boundary of the negotiation space until the turning point. After that, it has to leave the right boundary and move towards the joint negotiation space in order to reach an agreement there.

In brief, business objectives guide how a management agent behaves in the negotiation space. If appropriately configured, business objectives allow a management agent to preserve values of stronger weighted QoS parameters in the course of negotiation, which influences particularly the assignments of those QoS parameters in the resulting SLAs.

Influence of Cooperation between Agents

Willingness of a counterpart to cooperate in a negotiation process is crucial for a management agent to achieve its negotiation goals. Ideally, if a management agent places an emphasis on some QoS parameters, a cooperative counterpart should place its emphasis on some other QoS parameters and try to compensate its loss of utilities on these parameters. This section evaluates the influence of cooperation between management agents on the resulting SLAs.

The evaluation experiment uses the same negotiation scenario as in the previous section. The service consumer and the provider employ the same trade-off strategy with alignment to the last incoming offer of the counterpart. Moreover, both management agents use linear utility functions in their negotiation process. The global business objective is cost-first. That is, service cost is emphasised by the management agents in the negotiation.

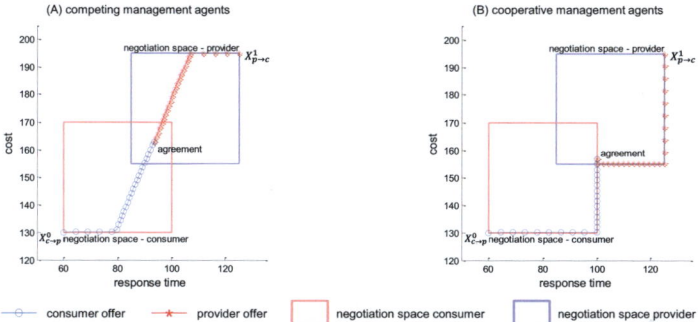

Figure 8-9: Evaluation of agent cooperation with competing and cooperative service providers

In addition, the service consumer remains unchanged in all evaluation experiments. The service provider changes its willingness to cooperate during the experiments. Figure 8-9 depicts the behaviour of both management agents in the evaluation experiments. In Figure 8-9 (A), the service provider applies the strategy to compete against the service consumer. That is, the service provider also places its emphasis on service cost and tries to achieve a service cost as high as possible. In contrast, the service consumer tends to hold the value of service cost as low as possible. Hence, there is a competition between the consumer and the provider for service cost. Reflected in negotiation behaviour, both management agents tend to hold their optimum values for service cost as long as possible (as illustrated in Figure 8-9 (A)), until they have to leave their respective optimum for service cost in order to get a compromise in the joint negotiation space.

In contrast to the negotiation behaviour in Figure 8-9 (A), Figure 8-9 (B) shows the behaviour of a cooperative service provider. That is, in favour of the service consumer, the service provider does not place its emphasis on service cost. Instead, it prefers to achieve a higher response time than a higher service cost. Correspondingly, as depicted in Figure 8-9 (B), the service consumer can exhaust at first its reserve of response time, before it has to concede in service cost. Similarly, the service provider concedes at first largely in service cost, before it has to concede in response time. By comparing the resulting SLAs of both experiments, the service consumer achieves lower service cost in the resulting SLA with a cooperative service provider. Analogously, the service provider also achieves a higher response time.

In brief, a cooperative management agent respects the negotiation preferences of its counterpart. This measure helps to increase the social welfare of both management agents. Both negotiating parties can accomplish satisfying assignments of QoS parameters they prefer. Correspondingly, the resulting SLAs have higher utilities for both parties than those with a competing negotiation partner.

8.2.2 Efficiency of Resulting SLAs

The previous section is concerned with evaluating the negotiation behaviour of management agents with varying negotiation configurations. Particularly, it focuses on the capabilities of the negotiation strategies to guide a management agent to move towards the common negotiation space and to reach an agreement there. Hence, the evaluation experiments in the previous section address only the process to reach an agreement. It lacks an evaluation of the efficiency of the process as well as the resulting SLAs, which is covered in this section.

Figure 8-10 visualises the results of an evaluation experiment, where the service consumer is configured with the trade-off strategy to align its trade-off search to the last incoming offer of the provider. The provider follows the simple time-dependent conceding strategy to generate its offers.

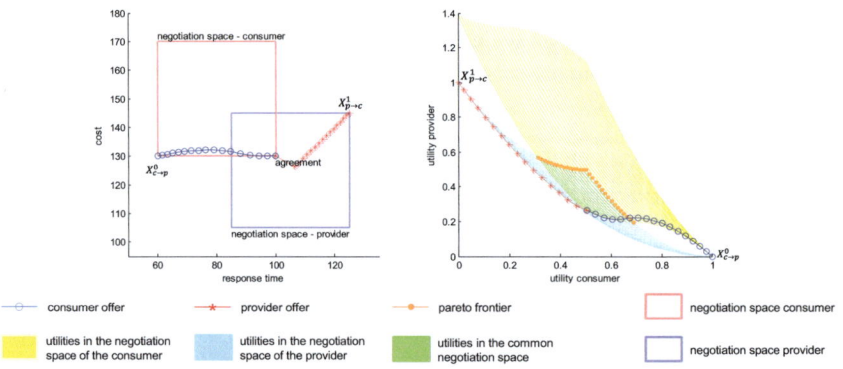

Figure 8-10: Changes in utilities of service components in the course of negotiation

The utility chart on the right of Figure 8-10 illustrates the change of the utility of the consumer in relationship to the utility of the provider. The yellow area is composed of utilities of both management agents in the negotiation space of the consumer, while the blue area consists of utilities of the agents in the negotiation space of the provider. Utilities of the agents in the common negotiation space are marked by the green area. In the utility chart, it is clear to see how both management agents move away from their optimum offers in the negotiation space towards each other.

The more interesting aspect in the utility chart is the Pareto optimal offers in the negotiation spaces, in particular in the common negotiation space of both management agents. It is noteworthy that the Pareto optimal offers are referred in the context of the common negotiation space. It is obvious that a Pareto optimal offer in the common negotiation space must not be Pareto optimal in the negotiation space of one of the management agents. Since both management agents are seeking a compromise in the common negotiation space, it is reasonable to compare an offer with Pareto optimal offers in the common negotiation space.

In the utility chart in Figure 8-10, the orange points in the common negotiation space indicate the Pareto frontier. Logically, points on the Pareto frontier dominate all other offers below as well as on the left of the frontier. Therefore, an ideal negotiation strategy should not only guide a management agent to move into the common negotiation space. It should also try to reach an agreement on the Pareto frontier, or at least near the Pareto frontier. This additional capability of a negotiation strategy is crucial to increase the total social welfare of both management agents.

In order to evaluate the efficiency of the negotiation strategies introduced in the present thesis, this section conducts a series of evaluation experiments with varying negotiation strategies. The experiments use the negotiation scenario given in Table 8-1. Both management agents utilise linear utility functions in their negotiation processes. All QoS parameters are weighted equally in the experiments. In addition, both management agents compete against each other in the negotiation space.

For simplicity, the evaluation results in the figures only illustrate the changes in utility of the consumer and the provider in the experiments. In each experiment group with three different experiments, the service consumer is configured with a fixed negotiation strategy. The service provider changes its negotiation strategy in each experiment. In addition, since time-dependent conceding strategies propose each time an offer with fixed assignments of QoS parameters, they do not incorporate any dynamic aspects into the negotiation process.

Therefore, conceding strategies are not considered in the evaluation experiments of this section. All other trade-off strategies are evaluated in the experiments.

Figure 8-11 illustrates the experimental results using a service consumer with alignment to the last incoming offer. In order to reach a Pareto optimal offer, both management agents have to keep their offers near the Pareto frontier. Although this measure cannot lead to a direct agreement with the counterpart, it retains the probability to reach an agreement on the Pareto frontier. As soon as a management agent crosses the Pareto frontier in the course of negotiation, it begins to propose offers that are dominated by some Pareto optimal offers in the frontier.

Figure 8-11 (A) illustrates the negotiation process with a provider that aligns its trade-off search to the most recent counter offer of the consumer. With the help of this trade-off strategy, the service provider is able to place its offers on the Pareto frontier. Similarly, the service consumer that applies the same trade-off strategy can also hold its offers above the Pareto frontier. Correspondingly, both management agents reach a Pareto optimal agreement.

Figure 8-11 (B) shows the negotiation process with a provider that applies the trade-off strategy with alignment to the last incoming offer of the consumer as well as to the provider's own initial offer. As shown in the figure, the service provider moves along the boundary of the negotiation space below the Pareto frontier. Therefore, in order to reach an agreement with the provider, the consumer has to pass the Pareto frontier. Though this step helps the service consumer to reach an agreement with the provider, the resulting SLA is far away from the Pareto frontier. Therefore, it is less efficient with respect to the total social welfare of both agents.

Figure 8-11 (C) shows the negotiation process with a provider that aligns its trade-off search to both initial offers. Similar to the process shown in Figure 8-11 (B), this trade-off strategy does not help the service provider to hold its offers on the Pareto frontier. Correspondingly, both management agents only reach an agreement below the Pareto frontier.

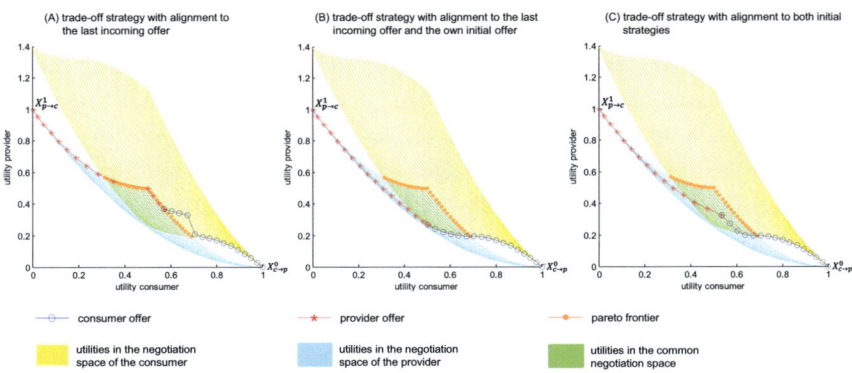

Figure 8-11: Changes in utilities - service consumer with alignment to the last incoming offer

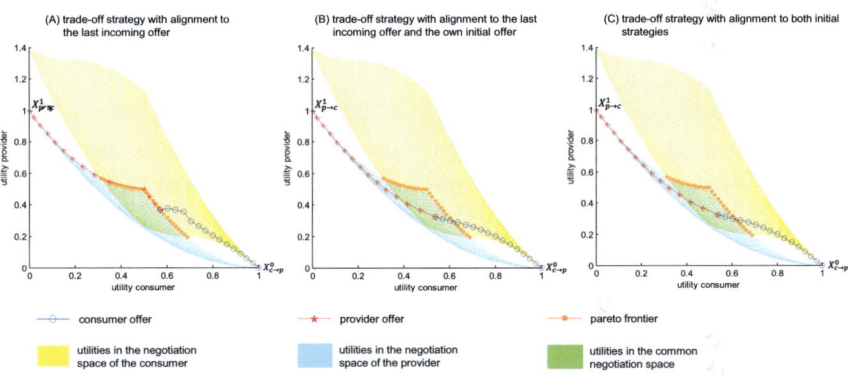

Figure 8-12: Changes in utilities - service consumer with alignment to the last incoming offer and its own initial offer

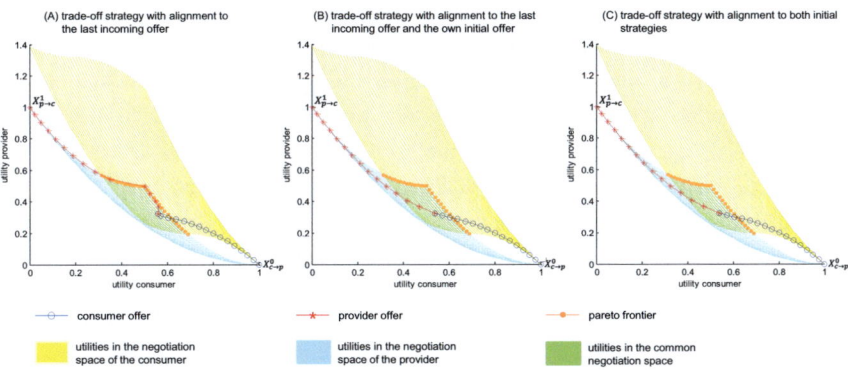

Figure 8-13: Changes in utilities - service consumer with alignment to both initial offers

Figure 8-12 shows the experimental results with a service consumer that aligns its trade-off search to the last incoming offer and its own initial offer. Figure 8-13 depicts the results of a consumer applying the trade-off strategy with alignment to both initial offers. Similar to the experimental results shown in Figure 8-11, the service provider employing the trade-off strategy with alignment to the last incoming offer can reach an agreement on as well as near to the Pareto frontier. The other trade-off strategies result in agreements that are less optimal with respect to the Pareto optimal offers.

By comparing the results from all experiment groups, it is clear that the trade-off strategy with alignment to the last incoming offer is the most efficient one among all negotiation strategies with respect to Pareto optimal agreements. Not only can it help a management agent to reach a compromise in the common negotiation space, it also ensures high social welfare of the resulting agreement for both management agents.

8.2.3 Performance Analysis

The previous sections provide qualitative evaluation of the negotiation model in the simulation environment. The experimental results are concerned with negotiation behaviour of a management agent applying varying negotiation configurations. So far, the resulting SLAs from the negotiation processes have not been evaluated quantitatively. Therefore, the present section focuses on the quantitative evaluation of the negotiation model and provides experimental results to highlight the influences of various negotiation configurations on the performance of the simulation model.

To better illustrate this influence, this section adopts a new negotiation scenario as shown in Figure 8-14.

The new scenario considers three QoS parameters in negotiation: service cost, response time, and availability. The value boundaries of the QoS parameters are set analogously to real world scenarios: the service provider offers its service with a larger spectrum of QoS values than what the service consumer desires. Other than the previous negotiation scenarios, the negotiation spaces of the consumer and the provider in the new scenario have a relatively large overlap. This desired large overlap shows the influence of varying negotiation configurations on the resulting SLAs more clearly.

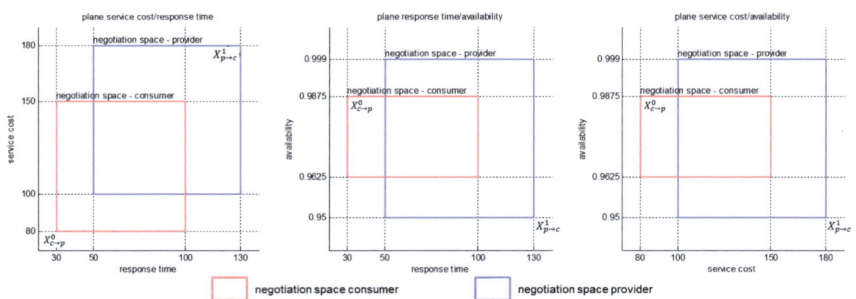

Figure 8-14: Negotiation scenario used to evaluate performance

The points $X^0_{c\rightarrow p}$ and $X^1_{p\rightarrow c}$ in the negotiation spaces are the optimum offers of the respective management agents. As aforementioned, they have to move away from their optimum offers in favour of their counterpart. Hence, the key objectives concerning evaluation of performance of the negotiation model are:

- If a particular negotiation strategy can accelerate a negotiation process.
- If a utility function can facilitate a negotiation process.
- If various business objectives have an influence on the assignments of particular QoS parameters in the resulting SLAs.
- If a cooperative management agent can influence the outcomes of the resulting SLAs.

Based on these considerations, a range of evaluation experiments with varying negotiation configurations is conducted. Table 8-3 lists the set of experimental set-ups used in these evaluation experiments. If not stated otherwise, each experiment is conducted with the same experimental set-up for 10 times. The average values of the outcomes of 10 experiments are used as the results of the experiment group. In addition, the experimental set-up is given for the provider and the consumer. For each service component, its negotiation configuration for *negotiation strategy*, *utility function*, *business objective*, and its willingness for *cooperation* is listed.

The experiment groups F1-F4 focus on the influence of negotiation strategies. Hence, the service consumer is configured with a fixed trade-off strategy that aligns its trade-off search to the last incoming offer. The service provider changes its negotiation strategy in each experiment group. All other negotiation configurations remain unchanged throughout all experiment groups. In addition, the results of the experiment groups F1-F4 serve as reference values for all other experiment groups, too.

Table 8-3: Experimental set-ups for evaluating performance

ID	consumer configuration				provider configuration			
	negotiation strategy	utility function	business objective	cooperation	negotiation strategy	utility function	business objective	cooperation
F1	counter offer	linear	average	competing	time-dependent conceding	linear	average	competing
F2	counter offer	linear	average	competing	counter offer	linear	average	competing
F3	counter offer	linear	average	competing	counter offer + initial offer	linear	average	competing
F4	counter offer	linear	average	competing	initial offers	linear	average	competing
F5	counter offer	polynom. $\alpha = 2$	average	competing	time-dependent conceding	polynom. $\alpha = 2$	average	competing
F6	counter offer	polynom. $\alpha = 2$	average	competing	counter offer	polynom. $\alpha = 2$	average	competing
F7	counter offer	polynom. $\alpha = 2$	average	competing	counter offer + initial offer	polynom. $\alpha = 2$	average	competing
F8	counter offer	polynom. $\alpha = 2$	average	competing	initial offers	polynom. $\alpha = 2$	average	competing
F9	counter offer	linear	resp. time first	competing	time-dependent conceding	linear	resp. time first	competing
F10	counter offer	linear	resp. time first	competing	counter offer	linear	resp. time first	competing
F11	counter offer	linear	resp. time first	competing	counter offer + initial offer	linear	resp. time first	competing
F12	counter offer	linear	resp. time first	competing	initial offers	linear	resp. time first	competing
F13	counter offer	linear	resp. time first	cooperative	time-dependent conceding	linear	resp. time first	cooperative
F14	counter offer	linear	resp. time first	cooperative	counter offer	linear	resp. time first	cooperative
F15	counter offer	linear	resp. time first	cooperative	counter offer + initial offer	linear	resp. time first	cooperative
F16	counter offer	linear	resp. time first	cooperative	initial offers	linear	resp. time first	cooperative
F17	counter offer	linear	resp. time first	cooperative	combined strategy	linear	resp. time first	cooperative

The experiment groups F5-F8 are concerned with the influences of utility functions. Hence, these experiment groups inherit the negotiation configurations of F1-F4 and change correspondingly their utility functions from a linear function with $\alpha = 1$ to a polynomial function with $\alpha = 2$, as stated in Section 8.2.1. Other negotiation configurations remain unchanged.

The experiment groups F9-F12 address the impacts of business objectives on re-sulting SLAs. Therefore, these experiment groups derive their configurations from the groups F1-F4 and change their business objectives from *averaged* to *response time first*. That is, response time is weighted stronger in the negotiation process than other QoS parameters.

Table 8-4: Performance evaluation in the simulation environment

ID	resulting SLA						negotiation process					
	response time		service cost		availability		# of inter-actions		provider utility		consumer utili-ty	
	∅	s.d.	∅	s.d.	∅	s.d.	∅	s.d.	∅	s.d.	∅	s.d.
F1	81.84	0.000	131.84	0.000	0.9795	0.0000	43.0	0.00	0.398	0.000	0.400	0.000
F2	91.20	3.162	142.84	3.209	0.9868	0.0001	41.0	0.00	0.433	0.000	0.400	0.000
F3	74.76	0.436	124.90	0.803	0.9717	0.0003	43.0	0.00	0.392	0.001	0.363	0.000
F4	74.02	0.768	123.92	0.479	0.9711	0.0002	43.0	0.00	0.389	0.001	0.363	0.000
F5	84.56	0.058	134.58	0.059	0.9779	0.0000	41.0	0.00	0.186	0.000	0.158	0.000
F6	99.85	0.415	148.77	0.620	0.9843	0.0000	35.0	0.00	0.283	0.002	0.253	0.000
F7	99.48	0.819	148.23	1.420	0.9842	0.0000	35.0	0.00	0.279	0.004	0.253	0.000
F8	72.64	0.875	122.65	0.532	0.9715	0.0002	43.0	0.00	0.158	0.000	0.145	0.000
F9	80.06	0.040	131.16	0.112	0.9797	0.0000	43.0	0.00	0.382	0.000	0.363	0.000
F10	80.51	0.218	149.86	0.332	0.9871	0.0001	43.0	0.00	0.402	0.002	0.364	0.003
F11	61.84	0.007	149.98	0.020	0.9625	0.0000	45.0	0.00	0.363	0.000	0.327	0.000
F12	74.79	0.283	124.70	0.373	0.9708	0.0004	45.0	0.00	0.363	0.000	0.355	0.001
F13	80.01	0.056	131.25	0.091	0.9797	0.0001	43.0	0.00	0.389	0.000	0.363	0.000
F14	50.01	0.019	141.50	0.173	0.9671	0.0001	39.0	0.00	0.468	0.000	0.490	0.000
F15	50.22	0.161	137.14	0.483	0.9645	0.0003	39.0	0.00	0.468	0.000	0.479	0.002
F16	71.10	1.529	123.94	0.764	0.9711	0.0004	41.8	1.03	0.400	0.002	0.391	0.009
F17	60.00	18.07	133.89	14.96	0.9709	0.0087	40.2	2.53	0.462	0.014	0.456	0.068

The last experiment groups F13-F16 covers the impacts of cooperation between management agents. Since with a business objective, that weights all QoS parameters equally, a cooperative service provider cannot identify the preferences of its service consumer, these experiment groups derive their configurations from the groups F9-F12, instead of F1-F4. Moreover, both management agents are configured correspond-ingly as *cooperative* in these experiments groups.

Table 8-4 summarises the experimental results of the experiment groups discussed above. For each experiment group, the resulting SLA and information about the negotiation process (i.e., *the number of negotiation rounds* to reach an agreement, the utility of the resulting SLA for the *consumer*, and the utility for the *provider*) are given in the table. Moreover, the result table contains not only the average values from the 10 experimental runs of the corresponding experiment group, but also the corresponding standard deviation of the average values.

Influences of negotiation strategies: as stated in Section 8.2.1, different negotiation strategies induce varying negotiation behaviour of a management agent. The experiment results of the groups F1-F4 show that different negotiation strategies also result in different SLAs. In general, the following influences can be observed in the experiment results:

- The trade-off strategies incorporate more dynamic into the negotiation process. The experimental result with a time-dependent conceding strategy has a standard derivation of 0. In contrast, the other experimental results with a trade-off strategy have a standard derivation larger than 0. In particular, the experiment group of the trade-off strategy with alignment to the last incoming offer has the largest standard deviation among all experiment groups.

- The trade-off strategy with alignment to the last incoming offer results in an SLA with the most utility among all experiment groups. Furthermore, the service provider applying this trade-off strategy needs the fewest negotiation rounds to reach an agreement. This shows the benefit of introducing more dynamic into the negotiation process. It grants a management agent a larger degree of freedom to respect the desires of its counterpart, while keeping its own demand on utilities unaffected.

Influence of utility functions: Section 8.2.1 studies the negotiation behaviour of management agents employing various utility functions. In particular, an agent with a polynomial utility function with $\alpha = 2$ tends to give up a large extent of utility already at the beginning of a negotiation process, while an agent with a polynomial function with $\alpha = 0.5$ rather tends to preserve its utility at the beginning of a process.

This behaviour can be observed in the experiment results, too. By horizontally comparing the experiment results of F1-F4 and F5-F8 (i.e., F1 vs. F5, F2 vs. F6, and so on), it is clear that using a polynomial utility function with $\alpha = 2$ can accelerate a negotiation process. In general, an experiment with the polynomial utility function needs fewer negotiation rounds to reach an agreement than the respective experiment with a linear utility function.

In addition, since both management agents tend to concede quickly in utility from the beginning of a negotiation process, it is clear that both management agents have less utility at the end of the negotiation process than their reference experiments with linear utility functions. Therefore, the gain of a shorter negotiation process is done at the expense of less utility at the end.

Influence of business objectives: the experiment groups F9- F12 are carried out with a global business objective that emphasises response time. Furthermore, it is noteworthy that both management agents are competing. That is, the service consumer seeks to have an assignment for the response time as low as possible, while the service provider desires to get a response time as high as possible.

Due to the competing relationship between the service consumer and its provider, the experimental results of the groups F9-F12 do not show a significant change in the assignments of response time in comparison to the corresponding results of the groups F1-F4. Indeed, the competing relationship leads to longer negotiation time and fewer utilities for both negotiating agents at the end.

Influence of agent cooperation: the experiment groups F13-F17 are concerned with the influences of cooperation between negotiating agents on the resulting SLAs. As aforementioned, cooperation between management agents is realised by configuring the negotiation preferences of the service provider on some QoS parameters other than the ones that the service consumer prefers. Therefore, these experiment groups are configured with a global business objective of response time first. That is, in contrast to competing management agents, the service consumer prefers to have an assignment for the response time as low as possible, while the service provider places its preference on some QoS parameter other than response time, for example, service availability. In this case, the service provider can offer a lower service availability to compensate for its loss in response time.

By comparing the experimental results of F13 with F1 as well as F16 with F4, it can be concluded that cooperation between management agents does not cause large changes in the value assignments of the resulting SLAs. This result is however logical. The negotiation strategies applied in both experiment groups do not grant the management agents a too large degree of freedom to act according to the business objective. Therefore, they expose some kind of static behaviour in the course of negotiation in spite of changing business objectives and willingness of a management agent to cooperate.

Instead, the experimental results of F14 and F15 show the full effects of the combination of dynamic trade-off strategies and willingness of the agents to cooperate. By comparing the results of F14 with F2 as well as F15 with F3, it is clear that this combination of negotiation configurations results in lower response time for the consumer and simultaneously lower service availability for the service provider. Moreover, the willingness of the management agents to cooperate increases the overall social welfare. The resulting SLAs have higher utilities for both management agents at the end of negotiation.

The experiment group F17 applies the trade-off strategy that combines trade-off search with business objectives, as introduced in Section 6.7.2. That is, a management agent at first determines the best assignments to the preferred QoS parameters, before it carries out trade-off search with alignment to the last incoming offer. By applying this strategy, a management agent has only a limited degree of freedom in the course of negotiation, namely on the QoS parameters that are not covered by the business objective. Correspondingly, a management agent cannot realise the full capability of dynamic trade-off search.

By comparing the experimental results of F17 and F13 with time-dependent conceding strategy, it can be seen that applying the combined trade-off strategy helps to improve the quality of the resulting SLAs for the management agents. However, the improvements are limited in comparison to the results of the experiment group F14 as well as F15.

8.2.4 Concluding Remarks

Section 8.2 aims at evaluating the performance of the automated bilateral negotiation model introduced in the present thesis. Hence, a range of experiments is conducted in the simulation environment to evaluate the model qualitatively and quantitatively.

Based on the evaluation results, it can be concluded that negotiation strategies are crucial for two negotiating management agents to reach an agreement. A conceding strategy determines the utility of an outgoing offer, in which a management agent moves away from its optimum offer in favour of its counterpart. This provides the prerequisite for reaching an agreement between two competing agents at all. However, a conceding strategy does not provide any flexibility to choose an outgoing offer. From this viewpoint, the negotiation process allows no degree of freedom for both management agents.

This drawback is covered by a trade-off strategy. Based on a counter offer calculated by a conceding strategy, a trade-off strategy allows a management agent to exhaust the potential of indifference curves. By adapting dynamically its negotiation behaviour according to the behaviour of the counterpart, a trade-off strategy can improve the quality of the resulting SLAs largely. The improvements are achieved as follows:

- Increasing probability to reach an agreement: by aligning the counter offers to the offers proposed by the counterpart, a management agent can reach the unknown common negotiation space in the course of negotiation. This is one of the prerequisites to reach an agreement.

- Reducing the number of necessary negotiation rounds: as a management agent always aligns its counter offers to the offers of its counterpart, it can propose an offer in favour of its counterpart. This helps to reduce the time needed to reach an agreement.

- Increasing utilities of the resulting SLAs: optimising the outgoing offers in favour of an agent's counterpart also increases the utilities of the resulting SLAs.

However, it is noteworthy that the convergence of a negotiation process is not always guaranteed. It depends strongly on the particular negotiation spaces and the negotiation behaviour of the two management agents. As demonstrated by the negotiation scenario in Section 8.2.1, a pure conceding strategy does not help the two management agents to reach an agreement. However, adopting a trade-off strategy enables a management agent to reach an agreement in the same scenario.

By reviewing the evaluation results in the previous sections, it is obvious that the trade-off strategy with alignment to the last incoming offer provides the best foundation to converge a negotiation process. It ensures to guide a management agent to move on as well as near the Pareto optimal frontier in the course of negotiation. This feature ensures that both management agents can reach a social welfare at the end as high as possible.

Next to negotiation strategies, other factors also influence the outcomes of a negotiation process. An appropriate utility function allows a management agent to determine individually how it is going to concede in the course of negotiation. As shown in the evaluation experiment, using a polynomial utility function with $\alpha = 2$, a management agent tends to concede greatly already at the beginning of the negotiation process. This helps to reduce the time necessary to reach an agreement.

Similarly, business objectives also influence the outcomes of a negotiation process. However, as the experimental results in Section 8.2.3 show, this applies only, if both management agents are cooperative in the negotiation process. In this case, both negotiating agents do not compete with each other for the same QoS parameter. Therefore, with a cooperative counterpart, a management agent can reach an agreement in accordance with the given business objective. In addition, this also helps to increase the utilities of the resulting SLAs for both management agents, which in turn has a positive effect on the total social welfare of the complete SOE.

8.3 Multi-Level Service Level Management

This section evaluates the overall negotiation-based SLM approach introduced in the present thesis. In contrast to the previous section, this section does not perform parameter studies on the possible configuration parameters in the simulation environment. Rather, this section focuses on the overall end-to-end SLM process within an SOE and illustrates how such an automated process can improve the responsiveness of the whole SOE.

Correspondingly, Section 8.3.1 introduces the experiment scenario modelled in the simulation environment. Section 8.3.2 provides the experimental results to show how the introduced approach can be applied in the experiment scenario to enable automated end-to-end SLM. Section 8.3.3 extends the results in Section 8.3.2 and demonstrates how the introduced approach can help service components configure their local resources depending on the change of workloads in the SOE.

8.3.1 Scenario and Experiment Set-up

Figure 8-15 illustrates the experiment scenario modelled in the evaluation environment by means of BPMN diagrams. The same scenario in the university context has been described briefly in Section 4.1. This section describes the scenario in more detail. Herein, it focuses on the interactions between the *process* layer, the *service* layer, and the *application* layer. For simplicity, the BPMN diagram in Figure 8-15 does not include the *infrastructure* layer. Furthermore, as already stated in Section 4.1, the evaluation scenario is by no means complete with respect to the real scenario developed in the KIM project [KIM10].

The consumer-facing service component in the scenario is the *competence field process*. It provides university employees with the functionality to display their respective assignments to particular competence fields. To this end, the business process utilises the *person service* to retrieve employee information for a particular person and the *competence field* service to get the corresponding assignment information for a particular employee.

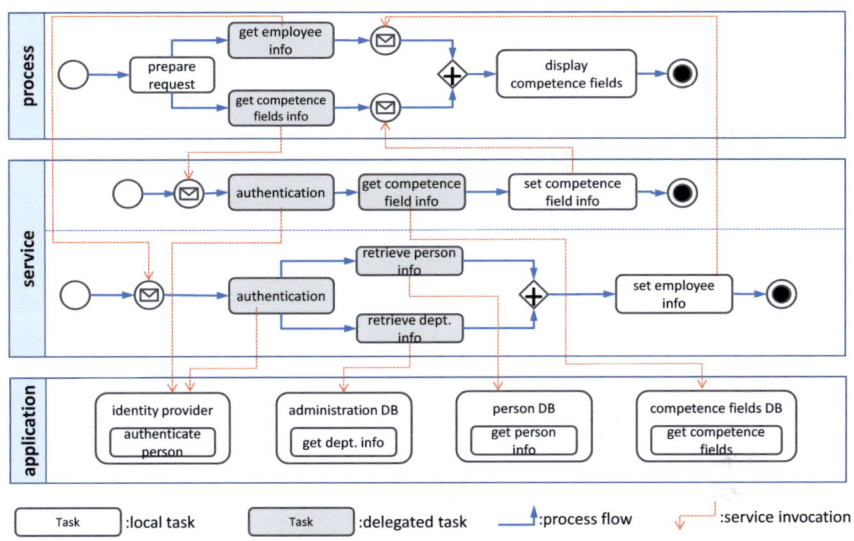

Figure 8-15: Experiment scenario in the evaluation environment

Both Web services are supported by a range of backend systems. The *person service* utilises the *identity provider* to authenticate the employee, whose information has to be retrieved from the backend database. Afterwards, the person service calls the *administration database* to get the department information and the *person database* to get the personal information of the employee. Both activities are carried out simultaneously. That is, they are composed by an AND-AND composition pattern. At the end, the results of both service invocations are combined in the last activity, before they are returned back to the calling process instance.

The *competence field* service allows retrieving the competence field information of a particular employee from the backend database. Hence, after an invocation of the *identity provider* to authenticate the service call, the service consumes the *competence field database* to retrieve the corresponding assignment information. The results are processed in the last activity, before they are passed to the respective process instance.

This experiment scenario is built in the evaluation environment. Each service component is modelled by a Sarasvati workflow. In addition, each service component is associated with a resource definition file that configures the set of technical resources available locally. By consuming the technical resources at runtime, each service component can produce appropriate service level behaviour, such as processing time, consumption cost, service availability, etc.

Moreover, each service component in the environment is configured with the same negotiation parameters:

- Each service component uses a simple linear utility function to estimate an SLA.

- Each service component uses the time-dependent conceding strategy to determine the utilities of the outgoing offers. In addition, each component utilises the trade-off strategy with alignment to the last incoming offer to enable trade-off search.

- Each service component is configured as cooperative.

- Each service component has equal preferences on the QoS parameters in the environment. For simplicity, the evaluation experiment considers only two QoS parameters: service cost and response time.

- The negotiation deadline for each service component is set to 30 time ticks.

To keep experimental results more clear, it is assumed that each service component takes exactly one simulation tick to make a negotiation decision, independently from the complexity of the decision. Furthermore, it is assumed that service invocations in the evaluation experiments are synchronous. That is, a service consumer has to wait, until the response is returned from the service provider. This assumption simplifies the calculation of QoS values during the simulation.

A further problem of the simulation runs is the historical information that a management agent needs to decompose QoS requirements for its service providers. As stated in Section 6.6.2, a management agent relies heavily on QoS information it collects in the past to determine non-functional capabilities of a particular service provider. Since each simulated service component in the evaluation environment is configured with an individual business logic and resource configuration, it is less reasonable to use the same set of historical information for all these components.

A plausible way is to adopt a training phase in each evaluation experiment. In fact, in practice, in order to better estimate the capabilities of the underlying IT infrastructure, business often utilises such a training phase of a predefined length (normally a month), in which the IT infrastructure is evaluated under various conditions. Such evaluation helps a business to determine the appropriate SLAs for its infrastructure.

Hence, before the competence field process begins to initiate a negotiation process in the simulation environment, a training phase with a length of 10,000 simulation ticks is completed. During the first 4,000 simulation ticks, each service component is configured with its minimal technical resources. During the next 3,000 simulation ticks, each component is in turn configured with its maximal technical resources. During the remaining simulation ticks until the end of the phase, each component configures its technical resources randomly. During the complete training phase, a service component, i.e., the management agent of the component, can comprehensively estimate the capabilities of each related service provider. This historical information is stored in the log file of the management agent. It is utilised by the management agent for decision-making in the actual evaluation phase, as described in Section 6.6.

8.3.2 Propagating the End-to-End SLM Process

This section provides evaluation results to demonstrate how an end-to-end SLM process can be propagated via automated negotiation across the complete SOE. As determined by the negotiation protocol introduced in Section 6.5, if a service provider receives QoS requirements from its consumer, it performs the following steps:

- Decomposing the given QoS requirements for each of its service providers. During this step, the management agent utilises the historical information about the respective service provider.

- Constructing negotiation space for each service provider. Depending on the particular type of the related QoS parameter, a management agent uses the decomposed QoS requirements as either the upper or lower boundary of the negotiation space. That is, if a QoS parameter is increasing (e.g., availability for a consumer), then the decomposed value determines the lower boundary of the negotiation space. The upper boundary of the space is set with the best availability from the historical information. Vice versa, the negotiation space for a decreasing QoS parameter can be determined in a similar way.

- Performing negotiation with the respective service provider using the previously determined negotiation space.

- If an agreement is negotiated, the respective service provider has to verify the agreement by negotiating in turn with its service providers. In this case, the negotiation process is propagated to the next layer in the simulated SOE.

- If the respective service provider can verify the agreement on its part, it confirms the agreement with the service consumer.

Therefore, the remainder of this section provides the evaluation results in two separate sections. The first part is concerned with the first three steps described above and illustrates the behaviour of a consumer with its providers. Then, the second part focuses on the last two steps and shows how a negotiation process can be propagated across the complete SOE.

8.3.2.1 Decomposing QoS Requirements

In general, each service provider in an SOE has to confirm an agreement it negotiates with its service consumer. Therefore, for simplicity, this section outlines only the decomposition and negotiation process of a service provider, the *competence field process* in the evaluation scenario, to demonstrate the applicability of the introduced approach. Decomposition processes of other service providers are done similarly.

Table 8-5 summarises the results of the decomposition and negotiation process of the *competence field process*. As illustrated by the BPMN diagram in Section 8.3.1, the *competence field process* involves a total of four activities in its business logic: *preparing request, invoking person service, invoking competence field service,* and *displaying competence fields*.

During the training phase, the management agent has collected statistics to estimate the behaviour of its activities. Among other things, it is aware of the maximal, the minimal, and the average response time and service cost for each activity. As shown in Table 8-5, each instance of the competence field process takes 198.3 simulation ticks on average. Each instance causes an average service cost of 563.4 cost units.

It is noteworthy that the management agent collects not only statistics about remote service invocations, but also those about its own local activities. These statistics allows the management agent to distribute QoS requirements correctly among all related local and delegated activities.

Table 8-5: Decomposition process of the business process in the sample scenario

activities	total		prepare request		invoke person service		invoke competence field service		display comp. fields	
	resp. time	cost	resp. time	cost	resp. time	cost	resp. time	cost	resp. time	cost
Ø history values	198.3	563.4	76.44	243.1	46.90	18.56	79.42	167.37	42.53	134.4
decomposed requirement	250	650	96.33	280.4	59.10	21.41	100.08	193.08	53.59	155.1
					min / max	min / max	min / max	min / max		
nego. space - process	-	-	-	-	20.77 / 59.10	7.32 / 21.41	35.17 / 100.08	66.02 / 193.1	-	-
					min / max	min / max	min / max	min / max		
nego. space - service	-	-	-	-	34.25 / 56.40	10.84 / 27.24	44.75 / 120.95	78.17 / 292.4	-	-
negotiated values	-	-	-	-	37.18	16.48	67.66	149.12	-	-

The target QoS requirements that the competence field process receives from its consumer are:

- Executing the competence field process should not take longer than 250 simulation ticks.

- Executing the process should not cause a cost higher than 650 cost units.

Based on the historical information and the decomposition schemas given in Section 6.2, the management agent can decompose the target QoS requirements for each activity in its business logic. For example, in order to achieve the target QoS requirements, invoking the person service should not take longer than 59.10 simulation ticks. And its consumption cost, i.e., service cost, should not be higher than 21.41 cost units.

The management agent of the competence field process uses the decomposed requirements to construct its negotiation spaces. Since both QoS parameters, response time and service cost, are decreasing for the competence field process, the decomposed QoS requirements determine the upper boundaries of the negotiation process with the respective service provider. The lower boundaries of the negotiation space are set to the best QoS values that the process achieved during the training phase. Correspondingly, a service provider (i.e., the person service or the competence field service) uses their respective best and worst QoS values during the training phase as their negotiation spaces.

After both the process and the services have determined their negotiation spaces, they begin to negotiate the two QoS parameters. As aforementioned, the process adopts two parallel negotiation threads with its both service providers. In each negotiation thread, there is a bilateral multi-issue negation over the two QoS parameters using the negotiation configurations described in Section 8.3.1.

Table 8-5 shows the resulting QoS values from the negotiation processes. After negotiation, the person service commits itself to supply its service with a maximal response time of 37.18 simulation ticks and a limit of 16.48 cost units. Similarly, the competence field service commits to an agreement with 67.66 simulation ticks and a limit of 149.12 cost units.

By comparing the resulting QoS values with the decomposed requirements, it is clear that if both service providers can deliver their services in compliance with the agreed values, the competence field process can ensure its own QoS requirements from its consumers.

8.3.2.2 Propagating the Negotiation Process

In order to cope with the recursive provider/consumer relationships in an SOE, the negotiation protocol introduced in Section 6.5 is iterative. That is, before a service provider commits to an agreement with its service consumer, it has to verify at first on its part, whether its service providers in turn support the negotiated agreement. In this way, a negotiation process initialised by a business process can be stepwise propagated throughout the complete SOE.

Figure 8-16 illustrates the negotiation process initialised by the competence field process in the SOE. The results show the negotiation processes of the involved service components within a single evaluation experiment. For simplicity, all negotiation processes are displayed side-by-side to depict their chronological order. A blue line in the figure indicates the negotiation phase of the respective service component. An orange one indicates the confirmation phase of the corresponding service component. And a dashed line states that the respective service component waits for response from its negotiation partner. Furthermore, the time axis begins at 10,000 simulation ticks. A corresponding training phase as introduced in the previous section has been carried out during the first 10,000 simulation ticks.

As shown in Figure 8-16, the negotiation process is initialised by the competence field process at simulation tick 10,000. At this point in time, the competence field process triggers two separate negotiation processes with its service providers, the person service and then competence field service. Hence, at simulation tick 10,001, both service components begin to carry out their respective negotiation processes with the competence field process.

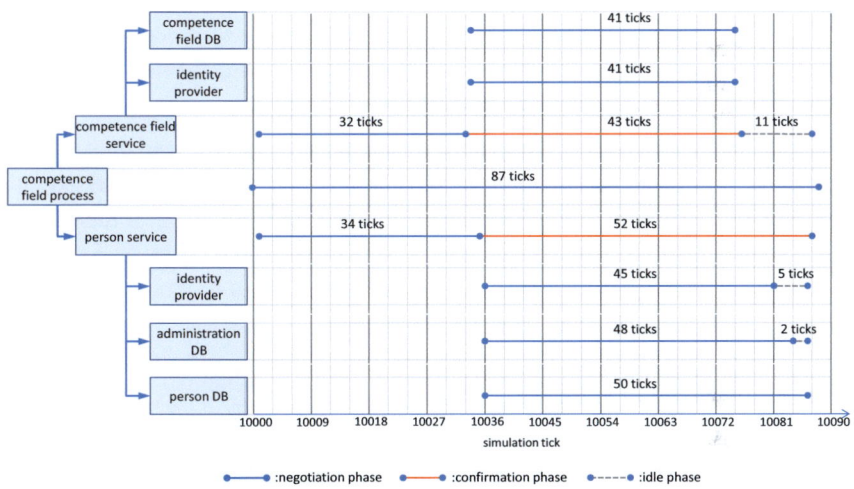

Figure 8-16: Propagation of negotiation process across the complete SOE

The competence field service uses 32 simulation ticks to find a mutually acceptable agreement with the process. After that, it begins to confirm the resulting agreement with its providers, the identity provider and the competence field database. To trigger the confirmation phase, the competence field service begins to negotiate with both of its service providers in two separate negotiation processes. Both service provides need 41 ticks to find a mutually acceptable agreement with the competence field service. Since in the evaluation scenario (see also 8.3.1) both the identity provider and the competence field database do not involve any other service providers, they commit directly to their agreements with the competence field service.

Upon receiving the confirmation messages from both service providers, the competence field service sends its confirmation message about the negotiated agreement with the competence field process. However, as introduced in Section 6.5, the competence field process coordinates the negotiation processes with its two service provider. Since the other service provider, the person service, needs more time to confirm its negotiated agreement, the competence field service has to wait for the acknowledgement from the competence field process for 11 ticks. As the competence field process also receives the confirmation message from the person service at simulation tick 10,087, the competence field process confirms the negotiated agreements on its part and terminates the overall negotiation process.

It is worth noting that although the competence field process needs a total of 87 ticks for its negotiation process, the actual negotiation times with the two service providers were 32 ticks and 34 ticks, respectively.

In short, Figure 8-16 clearly illustrates how a business process can propagate its negotiation process across the complete SOE. In this way, the business process ensures that all supporting service components in the underlying IT infrastructure are involved in the overall negotiation process. From the viewpoint of SLM, each of those service components commits with an appropriately negotiated SLA to contribute to the end-to-end service level requirements that a business process has.

8.3.3 Renegotiating SLAs

A characteristic feature of an agile IT infrastructure is that it can dynamically adjust its capabilities depending on the changing requirements from the business and the operational states of the underlying service components. From the viewpoint of non-functional requirements, an agile IT infrastructure is expected to configure its service components flexibly according to the current workload of the entire infrastructure.

In comparison to the existing approaches to enable self-organisation on a single service component, the present thesis follows a more generic and comprehensive approach. Based on local self-organisation of a service component, a service consumer can utilise automated negotiation to dynamically distribute workloads among its service providers, depending on their observed service-level behaviour in the last sampling period. This section is concerned with the evaluation results to demonstrate the capability of the introduced multi-level SLM approach of this thesis.

The evaluation scenario and the experimental set-up listed in Section 8.3.1 are applied in the evaluation environment. In addition, each management agent uses a simple strategy to organise its local technical resources:

- Initially, each management agent determines the amount of technical resources depending on the agreed response time in relation to the best response time that the service component can achieve.

- A management agent collects runtime information from the underlying service component. Among other things, it observes the processing information of each service request (the processing time, the waiting time, and the total response time) and the information about resource usage in the request pool and the resource pool (see also Section 7.4). As soon as it has collected 100 records, it initiates a new control loop to regulate the operational state of the service component.

- A management agent applies a strict policy to detect violation of response time. As stated in Section 5.2.4, an SLA is considered violated, as soon as the target value of the response time is exceeded by the measured value.

- If a measured response time exceeds 90% of the agreed response time, the management agent increases the assigned resources for the respective service instance by 10%, until all resources are assigned.

- If an agreed response time is over-fulfilled, i.e., the real response time is lower than 60% of the agreed value, then the management agent decreases the amount of technical resources assigned to the respective service instance by 10%.

- If a measured response time exceeds 90% of the agreed response time and the respective service component runs out of its local resources, it renegotiates with its service providers to rearrange the provider agreements with them.

- If a management agent fails to renegotiate SLAs with its service providers, it turns to its service consumer and renegotiates the consumer agreement.

In short, a management agent can respond to response time violations either directly by changing its local resources or by renegotiating SLAs with its service providers/consumer. In this way, a service component can solve its performance problem not only locally but also collaboratively on a global level.

The experimental results are taken after 6×10^4 simulation ticks. To produce a regular workload on the simulated SOE, the evaluation environment employs an additional consumer agent. This agent produces on a regular basis a service request on the competence field process, which in turn activates the supporting service components in the SOE. The time intervals, in which the consumer agent creates service requests, are controlled by ϕ_t. They are uniformly distributed around the average value ϕ_t. In the experiment shown in Figure 8-17, the first 1×10^4 simulation ticks are for training purpose of the management agents. In the next 3×10^4 ticks, the consumer agent generates service requests at a rate of $\phi_t = 16$. At simulation tick 4×10^4, the generation rate is reduced to $\phi_t = 8$. From this point in time, the workload of the SOE doubles.

For simplicity, the remainder of this section only focuses on the experimental results regarding the *competence field service* and its two service providers, the *competence field database* and the *identity provider*. It is noteworthy that the identity provider is invoked by two services, i.e., the competence field service and the person service. Hence, as the total workload increases in the entire SOE, the identity provider has to cope with more workload than other service components that have only a single service consumer.

Figure 8-17 depicts the average response times and the (re-)negotiated response times of the related service components in the course of the evaluation. The average response times are collected and consolidated by the respective management agents of the components. For better comparison of the results of the three related service components, the evaluation results of all components are depicted in the single figure.

Moreover, the dashed lines in the figures are the (re-)negotiated response times. Each point in the dashed lines indicates that there was a renegotiation between the service consumer, i.e., the competence field service, and its two service providers. The solid lines in the figures illustrate the changes of measured response times. Each star on the solid lines is a record of the response times measured by the respective management agent.

In general, the complete evaluation run can be divided into four phases: a *stabilisation* phase, a *stable* phase, a *workload balancing* phase after the workload is doubled, and after that a *stable* phase again, as illustrated in Figure 8-17.

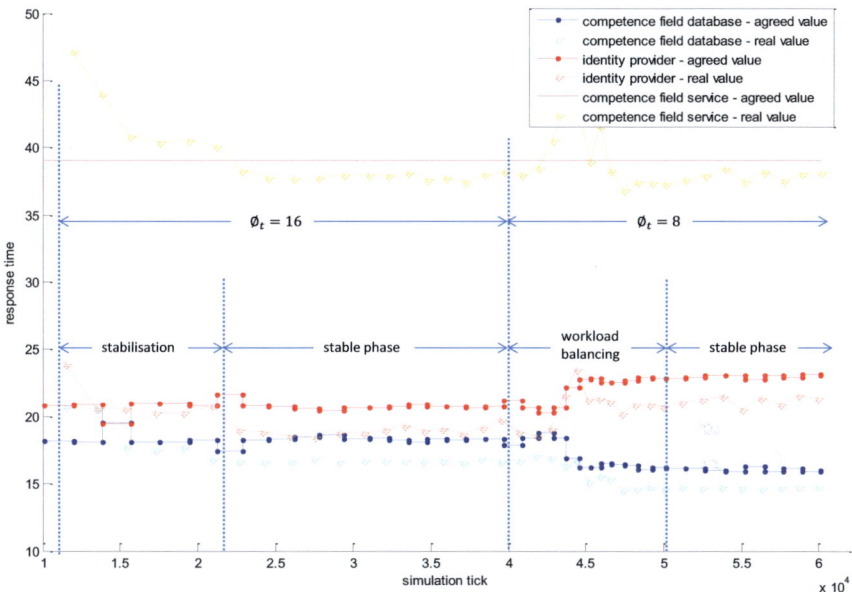

Figure 8-17: Using renegotiation of SLAs to balance workloads

In the stabilisation phase, all service components are trying to find an appropriate assignment of technical resources to their respective service instances. As shown in the figure, the first measured response times of all service components are higher than their agreed response times, respectively. Hence, both the identity provider and the competence field database try to increase their local resource assignments to avoid response time violation. In contrast, the competence field service decides to delegate the solution of this problem to its two service providers. As such, it initialises a range of renegotiation processes during the stabilisation phase with its service providers, until its response time is conform with the agreed value with the competence field process, i.e., its own consumer.

The stabilisation phase is inevitable because of the specific configuration of a service component to determine its initial amount of technical resources for the respective service instance. In the current implementation, a service component calculates the ratio between the best response time (i.e., the service instance is assigned with all resources) and the agreed response time. Then, the amount of resource assigned to the respective service instance is calculated by the product of the ratio and the total amount of resources available. This calculation estimates only approximately the amount of resources necessary to guarantee the agreed response time. Hence, the stabilisation phase is characterised by frequent renegotiation processes and large changes of response times. Of course, in practice, this phase can be substantially reduced by incorporating extensive historical information, and thus better correlation between response times and resource usages, into the calculation of the initial set of technical resources. Such information is missing in the simulated evaluation environment.

After the stabilisation phase, all service components have found their appropriate amount of resources to support the agreed response time. Hence, they enter the stable phase. As seen in Figure 8-17, the response times of all service components hardly change during this phase. Although the competence field service initialises a range of renegotiation processes, they do not significantly change the balance between the identity provider and the competence field database.

As aforementioned, from simulation tick 4×10^4 on, the total amount of service requests on the entire SOE doubles. This change leads to an increasing workloads at the service components. In particular, since the identity provider serves two service consumers in the SOE, it constitutes the bottleneck in the SOE. As seen in Figure 8-17, its measured response time increases largely around the simulation tick 4.3×10^4. The time delay of the increase in response time is caused by the buffers available in the competence field service and the competence field process. According to the control strategy of their management agents, both the service and the process try to cope with the increasing workloads by mobilising their reserves of local technical resources. Hence, as service components in the lowest layer of the SOE, both the identity provider and the competence field service experience the change in workload with a large time delay.

As the identity provider is not able to hold its response time under the agreed value and the competence field service also exceeds its agreed response time, the competence field service begins to renegotiate the SLAs with its both service providers. To this end, it takes the most recent response times of both providers as the reference values to decompose its requirement on response time. As seen in Figure 8-17, around simulation tick 4.4×10^4, the identity provider experiences a severe problem with its response time, while the competence field service can still provide its service at the same level as during the stable phase.

Therefore, the resulting agreements on response times reflect this relationship. As the identity provider has reached a higher target value for response time in the renegotiation, the competence field database has decided to deliver its service with a lower response time. From the viewpoint of the competence field service, it has managed to solve its local performance problem with support of its service providers. The distribution of the workload is based on the most recent runtime behaviour of both service providers. In this process, a service provider that shows symptoms of stress will be relieved. In contrast, a service provider that shows normal behaviour despite increasing workload will be more occupied, of course for a higher service cost.

As seen in Figure 8-17, the workload balancing phase consists of several renegotiation processes between the competence field service and its two providers. In each renegotiation process, the workload balance between both service providers is adjusted depending on the observed response times in the last sampling period. However, after the two renegotiation processes around simulation tick 4.4×10^4 with relatively large adaptations, all other renegotiation processes adjust the workload balance between both service providers only to a very limited extent. Around simulation tick 5×10^4, the stable phase follows the workload balancing phase.

Considering the agreed response times of the identity provider and the competence field database shown in Figure 8-17, it is obvious that both service providers maintain a kind of cooperative relationship with each other. As one service provider experiences a performance problem, the other provider commits to compensate the performance loss with more restricted service level targets.

In short, with automated negotiation, a service consumer can dynamically relocate its service level requirements to its service providers, depending on their most recent runtime behaviour. In this way, an SOE can efficiently respond to changes in the amount of workloads in its environment in a fully automated way.

8.4 Summary

This chapter aims at demonstrating the applicability of the approach introduced in the present thesis to enable collaboration-based multi-level SLM in an SOE. The core of the approach is automated negotiation of SLAs between two service components. Hence, after having outlined the main evaluation objectives of the experiments in Section 8.1, the following two sections evaluated the approach from both microscopic and macroscopic viewpoints.

Section 8.2 evaluated the performance of the introduced model to enable automated bilateral multi-issue negotiation between two service components. In particular, it investigated the influences of various negotiation configurations on the negotiation behaviour of the components both qualitatively (see Section 8.2.1) and quantitatively (see Section 8.2.3). Moreover, this section also investigated the efficiency of the negotiation strategies by means of Pareto-optimal offers in the common negotiation space.

The evaluation experiments showed promising results for the automated negotiation model to arrange SLAs. With appropriately configured negotiation strategies, two management agents have a large probability to reach an agreement in their common negotiation space, although both of them are not aware of the negotiation preferences of their counterpart. If both agents utilise the trade-off strategy with alignment to the last incoming offer, they can even reach a Pareto-optimal agreement at the end.

In spite of the fully automated negotiation process, a high-level control instance, e.g., a human participant, can influence the negotiation behaviour of a management agent by setting global business objectives. In this way, it can guide two management agents to reach an agreement that complies with the given business objectives.

Section 8.3 evaluated how the basic automated negotiation model can be applied to enable multi-level SLM within an SOE in a fully automated manner. This section showed that by applying the iterated negotiation protocol, a business process can gradually propagate an initial negotiation process across the complete SOE. In this way, all underlying service components that are involved to support the business process are bound to the process with an appropriately negotiated SLA. The closed SLAs are constructed depending on the processing capabilities of the particular components.

Section 8.3 also showed how collaboration-based automated multi-level SLM can be utilised to facilitate efficient resources management of the underlying service components. In particular, by dynamically renegotiating SLAs with the service providers, a service component can solve its local performance problem not only locally but also collaboratively on a global level.

In brief, the evaluation experiments in the simulated environment verify the applicability of the proposed approach to enable automated multi-level SLM. A range of evaluation results confirm the feasibility of the automated negotiation model to arrange SLAs. In addition, a first evaluation result in the simulation environment has showed the ability of the proposed approach to facilitate comprehensive resource management within an SOE in a collaborative way.

Part IV

Conclusion and Outlook

Chapter 9   Conclusion and Outlook

> "不闻不若闻之，闻之不若见之，见之不若知之，
> 知之不若行之；学至于行之而止矣。"
> ー【荀子·劝学】

> *"What I hear, I forget; what I see, I remember; what I do, I understand."*
> ー【Xun Zi, ca. 312-230 B.C.】

Businesses applying the design paradigm of service-orientation to build their IT infrastructures struggle with increasing social complexity. High heterogeneity of the involved service components prevents a comprehensive management throughout the complete SOE. Hence, this thesis has the goal to design and implement a framework to facilitate automated management of an SOE based on controlled self-organisation.

This chapter reviews the introduced approach of the present thesis and summarises its main contributions. Section 9.1 reviews the approach with respect to the objectives listed in Section 1.2.1. Among other things, it addresses how the given objectives are covered by the approach of this thesis. Section 9.2 provides an overview on possible extensions of this work.

9.1 Summary

The fundamental scenario of the present thesis is to enable seamless alignment between the business and its IT infrastructure applying the design paradigm of service-orientation. With respect to the role of IT service management as a link between business and IT, the scenario is converted to a problem of end-to-end service level management of the IT infrastructure. That is, how the underlying IT infrastructure can be appropriately configured to consistently guarantee given business/operational objectives from the business, in spite of high heterogeneity and social complexity in the infrastructure.

To this end, this thesis proposes a two-level realisation of automated end-to-end SLM based on controlled self-organisation. On the global level, a collaboration-based

335

approach is designed to enable service components to collaborate with their providers for arranging agreements on their service levels. Collaboration between service components is carried out by means of negotiation. It provides the basic means to break down high-level operational requirements of the business into low-level requirements for each involved service component, in terms of SLAs.

On the local level, each service component organises itself in compliance with the SLAs it closes with its consumers. The management agent of a service component continuously monitors the operational state of the component, analyses it, and performs, if necessary, corrective actions to control the runtime behaviour of the component. Negotiation-based collaboration between related service components provides a management agent with additional possibilities to influence the runtime behaviour of its respective service component on a global level.

In this way, global non-functional requirements on a particular business process can be ensured conjointly and continuously by a set of collaborative self-organising service components in support of the process. IT infrastructure can consistently align its runtime behaviour with given requirements from the business. Section 1.2.1 has discussed a set of objectives that a sophisticated approach to enable automated end-to-end SLM has to address. The present thesis addresses the objectives as follows:

- Autonomy of service components: In order to ensure that each service component can maintain its autonomy in the SLM process, this thesis utilises an agent-oriented design. That is, each service component is equipped with an autonomous management agent that represents the component's interests in the respective SOE. Through rational negotiation, a service component can maintain its autonomy in the course of collaboration with other related components. In addition, with respect to the distributed nature of service-oriented environments, agent-oriented design enhances the flexibility and scalability of the automated SLM approach of this thesis.

- Awareness of runtime state: Manageability interfaces offered by a service component allow the respective management agent to collect runtime information of the component. By appropriately processing and consolidating such information, the generic O/C architecture implemented in the management agent is aware of the runtime behaviour of its respective service component.

- Automated negotiation support: Collaboration between service components is carried out by means of automated negotiation. The automated negotiation model introduced in this thesis allows a service consumer to negotiate with its provider in order to find a mutually acceptable compromise between what is expected by the consumer and what can be delivered by the provider. During this bilateral negotiation process, neither of the two service components has to make concessions on its autonomy. Instead, each service component can control its negotiation behaviour individually depending on its local negotiation preferences. The negotiation strategies adopted can efficiently guide a management agent to move towards the common negotiation space in order to reach an agreement there. Herein, the convergence of a negotiation process can be guaranteed, if the respective service component employs a trade-off strategy to optimise its offers in favour of its counterpart.

- Self-adaptive SLM: This work enables self-adaptive SLM by providing the necessary technical infrastructures to support the full life cycle of SLAs. The collaboration manager in the management agent provides a service component with the capability to carry out automated negotiation processes with other related components. The O/C architecture applied allows a service component to autonomously enforce a negotiated SLA by performing appropriate action(s) to control the component's runtime behaviour. In case of changes in the environment (e.g., requirement changes, changing workload, and so on), a management agent can reactively improve the existing SLAs with respect to those changes. Herein, a management agent can either locally perform the necessary corrective actions or globally collaborate with other related components to enforce an existing SLA.

- Mapping business requirements to IT-centric metrics: The iterated negotiation protocol adopted in this thesis allows a negotiation process initialised by a business process to be gradually propagated across the complete IT infrastructure. In this way, end-to-end requirements that the business has on the entire IT infrastructure can be iteratively broken down into IT-centric requirements for each service component by means of automated SLA negotiation.

- Involving related underpinning components: By propagating a negotiation process top-down across the hierarchical structure of an SOE, all related service components in the underlying IT infrastructure are gradually included into the end-to-end SLM process.

- Heterogeneity of technical components: In order to cope with high heterogeneity within an SOE, the present thesis utilises SLAs as homogeneous messages between heterogeneous service components. On the global level, each service component interacts via interoperable Web services standards with other related components to carry out the negotiation processes. Locally, each service component individually interprets and enforces the negotiated SLAs depending on its local management standards. By doing this, the approach of the present thesis ensures maximal interoperability with minimal interference in local components. Furthermore, each service component can participate in the global SOE without having to give up its autonomy.

- Adaptive management of service components in compliance with agreed service levels: This objective is addressed by the capability of the O/C architecture to enable controlled self-organisation locally. With continuous monitoring, the observer enables a management agent to be aware of the operational state of its respective service component. For any deviation of the operational state from the agreed behaviour, the controller can perform corrective actions on the underlying service component in a timely manner. In this way, the management agent can maintain the underlying service component in compliance with agreed service levels.

Concisely, the key characteristic of the approach is to enable end-to-end SLM across all related service components by facilitating collaboration between these components. Collaborative activities between technical components are carried out by means of automated negotiation of SLAs between service providers and service consumers. In this way, end-to-end service level requirements from the business can be continuously guaranteed by the IT infrastructure without any manual efforts.

In comparison to existing approaches to enable self-organisation in SOE, in particular with respect to those introduced in Section 2.2.2, the present thesis makes the following major contributions:

- The present thesis provides a sophisticated approach to enable automated end-to-end SLM within an SOE. By applying this approach, all supporting components in the underlying IT infrastructure are involved in the overall process to ensure the end-to-end service level requirements on the entire infrastructure. Herein, runtime behaviour of each service component is specified precisely by a mutually accepted SLA.

- The present thesis focuses on facilitating collaboration between service components by using automated negotiation. Each service component is modelled as a fully rational agent that can autonomously collaborate with other related service components, in particular with respect to negotiating SLAs. In this way, a service component can actively contribute to the complete SOE without having to give up control over its own technical resources.

- In comparison to a centralised management, the present thesis provides a flexible way to enable decentralised management of an SOE. Via automated negotiation, end-to-end service level requirements can be gradually propagated across the entire SOE, where at the end the runtime behaviour of each service component is regulated by a dedicated SLA. In combination with locally controlled self-organisation, a service component can enforce its runtime behaviour in alignment to its SLA.

- The present thesis realises a way to facilitate collaboration between related service components. As soon as each service component has established a stable balance between its runtime behaviour and the desired behaviour specified by the SLA, the entire SOE becomes resilient against to changes in the environment. Via automated negotiation, a service component can resolve a service level issue that it cannot deal with locally with its service providers as well as its service consumer on a global level, and in a fully automated manner.

In brief, the present thesis designs and implements an multi-level approach to enable automated end-to-end service level management. By applying controlled self-organisation, service components can flexibly adapt their runtime behaviour according to the service level objectives specified in respective SLAs. Via negotiation-based collaboration, a service component can enforce its runtime behaviour either by using its local resources or with help of its service providers.

9.2 Outlook

In addition to the contributions of this thesis, there are a range of aspects that have to be regarded in order to apply the approach introduced by the present thesis in practice. Most of the aspects raise new questions for future research in this field.

SLA-driven self-organisation of service components: an SLA specifies the service level targets that the runtime behaviour of a service component has to achieve. However, those service level targets are highly abstracted terms that do not have any reference to the specific configurations of the respective service component. Hence, in order to establish SLA-drive self-organisation, a service component has to correctly correlate the service level targets with its underpinning configurations, which is covered by the controller, i.e., the online/offline learning modules, of a respective management agent.

Autonomous learning of management agents: In practice, a service component has to face a more complicated operating environment than what a simulated environment can provide. Hence, it is desired that a management agent should employ autonomous learning to correlate the operational state with the appropriate actions. The generic observer/controller architecture provides the necessary design guidelines to incorporate the capabilities of online/offline learning in a management agent. From the viewpoint of a management agent, it is of interest to investigate how far an existing service component can be modelled as a simulated system to perform offline learning. In case that the simulated system behaviour cannot fully reflect the behaviour of the real service component, it has to be considered how a management agent can get rid of the deficits of the learned knowledge online in the real system.

Extending the negotiation scenario: The present thesis considers only the scenario that a service consumer has determined its service providers a priori to the negotiation phase. There are no competing service providers for a given business capability. Hence, the negotiation model addresses only bilateral negotiation between one service consumer and one service provider. However, in a service market where a range of service providers offers the same business capabilities for different conditions, a service consumer can usually choose one of the service providers depending on particular conditions they offers. In this case, the negotiation model can be extended to cover multi-lateral negotiation scenarios. Herein, a service consumer can bargain for a better utility among all potential providers. In this way, a service consumer can optimise its trade-off globally among several service providers.

A comprehensive semantic support: In an SOE, where a range of heterogeneous service components are involved, it is of particular importance to have a comprehensive ontology across all service components. In this way, two collaborating service components can ensure that they understand each other unambiguously. Among other things, a comprehensive semantic support should help a management agent to understand the terms, i.e., service level objectives, specified in an SLA. If necessary, a management agent can consume the semantic support to map the terms in an incoming SLA offer to its local service level objectives.

Applying the automated negotiation model in practice: As stated in Section 3.2, electronic SLAs negotiated by intelligent agents lack the necessary trust and acceptance to be applied in practice, in particular with respect to the legal aspects of such electronic SLAs. However, electronic SLAs play a fundamental role in the whole approach introduced by the present thesis. Hence, in order to apply the approach of the present thesis in practice, interdisciplinary research is required. From a judicial viewpoint, it should be clarified, to what extent intelligent agents can be held accountable for contracts they negotiate in an fully automated way. From the viewpoint of IT service management, it is necessary to develop a concept to introduce electronic SLAs into an IT infrastructure. A possible approach to establish automated negotiation can be divided into three successive steps: adopting automated negotiation as decision-making support; adopting automated negotiation in a semi-automated manner, where human participants make the final decision; and finally adopting automated negotiation directly in a fully-automated manner.

Bibliography

[ABHK00] W. Van Der Aalst, A. Barros, A. Hofstede, and B. Kiepuszewski: *Advanced Workflow Patterns*. Cooperative Information Systems, Springer, 2000, pp. 18-29.

[ACD+07] A. Andrieux, K. Czajkowski, A. Dan, K. Keahey, H. Ludwig, T. Nakata, J. Pruyne, J. Rofrano, S. Tuecke, and M. Xu: *Web Services Agreement Specification (WS-Agreement)*. http://www.ogf.org/documents/GFD. 107.pdf. 2007. Last Access on May 2010.

[ACE+03] R. Allrutz, C. Cap, S. Eilers, D. Fey, H. Haase, C. Hochberger, W. Karl, B. Kolpatzik, J. Krebs, F. Langhammer, P. Lukowicz, E. Maehle, J. Maas, C. Müller-Schloer, R. Riedl, B. Schallenberger, V. Schanz, H. Schmeck, D. Schmid, S. Preikschat, T. Ungerer, H.-O. Veiser, and L. Wolf: *VDE/ITG/GI Positionspapier Organic Computing: Computer- und Systemarchitektur im Jahr 2010*, VDE/ITG/GI, 2003.

[ADA10] ADAC: *Pannenstatistik 2009*, ADAC Motorwelt, ADAC Verlag, 2010, p. p. 17 ff.

[ADK+05] V. Agarwal, K. Dasgupta, N. Karnik, A. Kumar, A. Kundu, S. Mittal, and B. Srivastava: *A Service Creation Environment Based on End to End Composition of Web Services*. In: *Proceeding of the 14th international conference on World Wide Web*, Chiba, Japan, ACM Press, 2005.

[AFG+09] M. Armbrust, A. Fox, R. Griffith, A. D. Joseph, R. H. Katz, A. Konwinski, G. Lee, D. A. Patterson, A. Rabkin, I. Stoica, and M. Zaharia: *Above the Clouds: A Berkeley View of Cloud Computing*, University of California at Berkeley, 2009.

[AFG+10] M. Armbrust, A. Fox, R. Griffith, A. D. Joseph, R. Katz, A. Konwinski, G. Lee, D. Patterson, A. Rabkin, I. Stoica, and M. Zaharia: *A View of Cloud Computing*. Communication of ACM, 53 (4) (2010): pp. 50-58, 2010.

[AHK+03] W. M. P. V. D. Aalst, A. H. M. T. Hofstede, B. Kiepuszewski, and A. P. Barros: *Workflow Patterns*. Distributed and Parallel Databases, 14 (3) (2003): pp. 5-51, 2003.

[AK09] A. Arsanjani and N. Kumar: *SOA Reference Architecture*, The Open Group, 2009.

[Ash62] W. R. Ashby: *Principles of the Self-Organizing System*. in: H.V. Foerster, G.W. Zopf (Eds.), Principles of Self-Organization, Pergamon Press, London, UK, 1962, pp. 255-278.

[AZE+07]   A. Arsanjani, L.-J. Zhang, M. Ellis, A. Allam, and K. Channabasavaiah: *S3: A Service-Oriented Reference Architecture*. IEEE IT Professional, 9 (3) (2007): pp. 10-17, 2007.

[BAR+10]   B. Becker, F. Allerding, U. Reiner, M. Kahl, U. Richter, D. Pathmaperuma, H. Schmeck, and T. Leibfried: *Decentralized Energy-Management to Control Smart-Home Architectures*. In: *Proceeding of the 2010 International Conference on Architecture of Computing Systems (ARCS 2010)*, pp. 150-161, Hannover, Germany, Springer, 2010.

[BBC+03]   D. F. Bantz, C. Bisdikian, D. Challener, J. P. Karidis, S. Mastrianni, A. Mohindra, D. G. Shea, and M. Vanover: *Autonomic Personal Computing*. IBM System Journal, 42 (1) (2003): pp. 165-176, 2003.

[BBK+05]   S. Bouchenak, F. Boyer, S. Krakowiak, D. Hagimont, A. Mos, S. Jean-Bernard, N. D. Palma, and V. Quema: *Architecture-Based Autonomous Repair Management: An Application to J2ee Clusters*. In: *Proceeding of the 24th IEEE Symposium on Reliable Distributed Systems*, pp. 13-24, Orlando, Florida, USA, IEEE Computer Society, 2005.

[BBWL05] N. Bieberstein, S. Bose, L. Walker, and A. Lynch: *Impact of Service-Oriented Architecture on Enterprise Systems, Organizational Structures, and Individuals*. IBM Systems Journal, 44 (4) (2005): pp. 691-708, 2005.

[BC06]   J. Barr and L. F. Cabrera: *AI Gets a Brain*. ACM Queue, 4 (4) (2006): pp. 24-29, 2006.

[BCL+04]   M. J. Buco, R. N. Chang, L. Z. Luan, C. Ward, J. L. Wolf, and P. S. Yu: *Utility Computing SLA Management Based Upon Business Objectives*. IBM Systems Journal, 43 (1) (2004): pp. 159-178, 2004.

[BDHT06] S. Bouchenak, N. De Palma, D. Hagimont, and C. Taton: *Autonomic Management of Clustered Applications*. In: *Proceeding of IEEE International Conference on Cluster Computing 2006*, pp. 1-11, Barcelona, Spain, IEEE Computer Society, 2006.

[Bee79]   S. Beer: *The Heart of Enterprise*, Managerial Cybernetics of Organization 2, John Wiley & Sons, New York, 1979.

[Bee81]   S. Beer: *Brain of the Firm*, 2nd edition. John Wiley & Sons, 1981.

[Bee85]   S. Beer: *Diagnosing the System for Organizations*, John Wiley & Sons, 1985.

[BHK+04] L. O. Burchard, M. Hovestadt, O. Kao, A. Keller, and B. Linnert: *The Virtual Resource Manager: An Architecture for SLA-Aware Resource Management*. In: *Proceeding of IEEE International Symposium on Cluster Computing and the Grid 2004*, pp. 126-133, Chicago, IL, USA, IEEE Computer Society, 2004.

[BHM+04] D. Booth, H. Haas, F. McCabe, E. Newcomer, M. Champion, C. Ferris, and D. Orchard: *Web Services Architecture*, W3C, 2004.

[BKM+04] R. Barrett, E. Kandogan, P. P. Maglio, E. M. Haber, L. A. Takayama, and M. Prabaker: *Field Studies of Computer System Administrators: Analysis of System Management Tools and Practices*. In J. Herbsleb, G. Olson: *Proceeding of the 2004 ACM conference on Computer Supported Cooperative Work*, pp. 388 - 395, Chicago, Illinois, USA, ACM, 2004.

[BKNT10] C. Baun, M. Kunze, J. Nimis, and S. Tai: *Cloud Computing: Web-Basierte Dynamische IT-Services*, Informatik im Fokus, Springer, Berlin, Germany, 2010.

[BKNT10a] C. Baun, M. Kunze, J. Nimis, and S. Tai: *Ausgewählte Cloud-Angebote*. in: C. Baun, M. Kunze, J. Nimis, S. Tai (Eds.), Cloud Computing: Web-Basierte Dynamische IT-Services, Informatik im Fokus, Springer, Berlin, Germany, 2010.

[BKNT10b] C. Baun, M. Kunze, J. Nimis, and S. Tai: *Cloud Architektur*. in: C. Baun, M. Kunze, J. Nimis, S. Tai (Eds.), Cloud Computing: Web-Basierte Dynamische IT-Services, Informatik im Fokus, Springer, Berlin, Germany, 2010.

[BKNT10c] C. Baun, M. Kunze, J. Nimis, and S. Tai: *Grundlagen*. in: C. Baun, M. Kunze, J. Nimis, S. Tai (Eds.), Cloud Computing: Web-Basierte Dynamische IT-Services, Informatik im Fokus, Springer, Berlin, Germany, 2010.

[BM02]   R. Buyya and M. Murshed: *Gridsim: A Toolkit for the Modeling and Simulation of Distributed Resource Management and Scheduling for Grid Computing*. Concurrency and Computation: Practice and Experience, 14 (13-15) (2002): pp. 1175-1220, 2002.

[BMK+05] R. P. Barrett, P. Maglio, E. Kandogan, and J. Bailey: *Usable Autonomic Computing Systems: The System Administrators' Perspective*. Advanced Engineering Informatics, 19 (3) (2005): pp. 213-220, 2005.

[BMM+06] J. Branke, M. Mnif, C. Müller-Schloer, H. Prothmann, U. Richter, F. Rochner, and H. Schmeck: *Organic Computing - Adressing Complexity by Controlled Self-Orgnization*. In: *Proceeding of 2nd International*

Symposium on Leveraging Applications of Formal Methods, Verification and Validation, pp. 200-206, Paphos, Cyprus, IEEE, 2006.

[Box04]   D. Box: *A Guide to Developing and Running Connected Systems with Indigo*. MSDN Magazine, 2004 (January) (2004): pp. 23-30, 2004.

[BS08]   J. Branke and H. Schmeck: *Evolutionary Design of Emergent Behavior*. in: R.P. Würtz (Ed.), Organic Computing, Springer, 2008, pp. 123-140.

[BS97]   C. Beam and A. Segev: *Automated Negotiations: A Survey of the State of the Art*. Wirtschaftsinformatik, 39 (3) (1997): pp. 263-268, 1997.

[BSP+02] J. P. Bigus, D. A. Schlosnagle, J. R. Pilgrim, W. N. Mills, and Y. Diao: *ABLE: A Toolkit for Building Multiagent Autonomic Systems*. IBM System Journal, 41 (3) (2002): pp. 350-371, 2002.

[BSTL06] D. Bustard, R. Sterritt, A. Taleb-Bendiab, and A. Laws: *Autonomic System Design Based on the Integrated Use of SSM and VSM*. Artificial Intelligence Review, 25 (4) (2006): pp. 313-327, 2006.

[Bue06]   R. Buettner: *A Classification Structure for Automated Negotiations*. In: *Proceeding of the 2006 IEEE/WIC/ACM international conference on Web Intelligence and Intelligent Agent Technology*, Hongkong, China, IEEE Computer Society, 2006.

[But05]   I. Butters: *IT-Entscheider Versprechen Sich Vorteile von SOA*. http:// www.cio.de/technik/810811/index1.html. 2005. Last Access on May 2011.

[BV06]   V. Bullard and W. Vambenepe: *Web Service Distributed Management: Management Using Web Services (WSDM-MUWS)*, OASIS, 2006.

[BYV08]   R. Buyya, C. S. Yeo, and S. Venugopal: *Market-Oriented Cloud Computing: Vision, Hype, and Reality for Delivering IT Services as Computing Utilities*. In: *Proceeding of 10th IEEE International Conference on High Performance Computing and Communications (2008)*, pp. 5-13, Dalian, China, IEEE Computer Society, 2008.

[BYV+09] R. Buyya, C. S. Yeo, S. Venugopal, J. Broberg, and I. Brandic: *Cloud Computing and Emerging IT Platforms: Vision, Hype, and Reality for Delivering Computing as the 5th Utility*. Future Generation Computer Systems, 25 (6) (2009): pp. 599-616, 2009.

[BZS+06] A. Bouajila, J. Zeppenfeld, W. Stechele, A. Herkersdorf, A. Bernauer, O. Bringmann, and W. Rosenstiel: *Organic Computing at the System on Chip Level*. In: *Proceeding of IFIP International Conference on Very*

Large Scale Integration of System on Chip 2006, Nice, France, Springer, 2006.

[CCMW01] E. Christensen, F. Curbera, G. Meredith, and S. Weerawarana: *Web Services Description Language (WSDL) 1.1*, World Wide Web Consortium, http://www.w3.org/TR/wsdl, 2001.

[CDD02] B. Chaib-Draa and F. Dignum: *Trends in Agent Communication Language*. Computational Intelligence, 2 (5) (2002): pp. 89-101, 2002.

[CDF+01] S. Camazine, J.-L. Deneubourg, N. R. Franks, J. Sneyd, G. Theraulaz, and E. Bonabeau: *Self-Organization in Biological Systems*, Princeton University Press, Princeton, NJ, USA, 2001.

[CDS06] Y. Charif-Djebbar and N. Sabouret: *Dynamic Web Service Selection and Composition: An Approach Based on Agent Dialogues*. International Conference on Service Oriented Computing 2006, Springer, Chicago, USA, 2006, pp. 515-521.

[CG99] K. M. Carley and L. Gasser: *Computational Organisation Theory*. in: G. Weiss (Ed.), Multiagent Systems: A Modern Approach to Distributed Artificial Intelligence, MIT Press, Cambridge, MA, USA, 1999, pp. 299-330.

[CGH+05] L. Cherbakov, G. Galambos, R. Harishankar, S. Kalyana, and G. Rackham: *Impact of Service Orientation at the Business Level*. IBM Systems Journal, 44 (4) (2005): pp. 653-668, 2005.

[CKM08] F. Curbera, R. Khalaf, and N. Mukhi: *Quality of Service in SOA Environments. An Overview and Research Agenda*. it - Information Technology, 50 (2) (2008): pp. 99-107, 2008.

[CLC+06] E. Castro-Leon, M. Chang, J. Hahn-Steichen, J. He, J. Hobbs, and G. Yohanan: *Service Orchestration of Intel-Based Platforms under a Service-Oriented Infrastructure*. Intel Technology Journal, 10 (04) (2006), 2006.

[Col04] M. Colan: *Service-Oriented Architecture Expands the Vision of Web Services*. http://www.ibm.com/developerworks/library/ws-soaintro.html. 2004. Last Access on May 2010.

[CP05] M. Comuzzi and B. Pernici: *An Architecture for Flexible Web Service QoS Negotiation*. In: *Proceeding of the Ninth IEEE International Enterprise Computing Conference 2005*, pp. 70- 79, Twente, The Netherlands, IEEE, 2005.

[CSM+04] J. Cardoso, A. Sheth, J. Miller, J. Arnold, and K. Kochut: *Quality of Service for Workflows and Web Service Processes*. Web Semantics: Science, Services and Agents on the World Wide Web, 1 (3) (2004): pp. 281-308, 2004.

[Dav98] T. H. Davenport: *Putting the Enterprise into the Enterprise System*. Harvard Business Review, 76 (4) (1998): pp. 121-131, 1998.

[DCCC06] J. Dowling, R. Cunningham, E. Curran, and V. Cahill: *Building Autonomic Systems Using Collaborative Reinforcement Learning*. The Knowledge Engineering Review, 21 (3) (2006): pp. 231-238, 2006.

[Dej08] M. Dejan: *Cloud Computing: Interview with Russ Daniels and Franco Travostino*. IEEE Internet Computing, 12 (5) (2008): pp. 7-9, 2008.

[DLS05] G. Dobson, R. Lock, and I. Sommerville: *QoSOnt: A QoS Ontology for Service-Centric Systems*. In: *Proceeding of 31st EUROMICRO Conference on Software Engineering and Advanced Applications 2005*, pp. 80-87, Porto, Portugal, IEEE Computer Society, 2005.

[DLS10] D. Ding, L. Liu, and H. Schmeck: *Service Discovery in Self-Organizing Service-Oriented Environments*. In: *Proceeding of the International Workshop on Construction and Maintenance for Service-oriented Software 2010, co-located with the 2010 IEEE Asia-Pacific Services Computing Conference* Hangzhou, China, IEEE Computer Society, 2010.

[DMTF10a] Distributed Management Task Force: *Web Service for Management (WS-Management)*. http://www.dmtf.org/standards/wsman. 2010. Last Access on April 2010.

[DMTF99] Distributed Management Task Force: *Common Informaiton Model (CIM) Specification*, Distributed Management Task Force, http://www.dmtf.org/standards/cim/, 1999.

[EL04] A. Elfatatry and P. Layzell: *Negotiating in Service-Oriented Environments*. Communications of the ACM, 47 (8) (2004): pp. 103-108, 2004.

[ELMT09] J. A. Estefan, K. Laskey, F. G. McCabe, and D. Thornton: *Reference Architecture Foundation for Service Oriented Architecture*, OASIS, 2009.

[Erd09] H. Erdogmus: *Cloud Computing: Does Nirvana Hide Behind the Nebula?* IEEE Software, 26 (2) (2009): pp. 4-6, 2009.

[Erl05]   T. Erl: *Service-Oriented Architecture: Concepts, Technology, and Design*, Prentice Hall, Upper Saddle River, NJ, USA, 2005.

[Erl08]   T. Erl: *SOA: Principles of Service Design*, Prentice Hall, Upper Saddle River, NJ, USA, 2008.

[FBMV09]   M. E. Falou, M. Bouzid, A.-I. Mouaddib, and T. Vidal: *Automated Web Service Composition: A Decentralised Multi-Agent Approach*. In: *Proceeding of the 2009 IEEE/WIC/ACM International Joint Conference on Web Intelligence and Intelligent Agent Technology*, Milan, Italy, IEEE Computer Society, 2009.

[FHS+06]   J. Floch, S. Hallsteinsen, E. Stav, F. Eliassen, K. Lund, and E. Gjorven: *Using Architecture Models for Runtime Adaptability*. IEEE Software, 23 (2) (2006): pp. 62-70, 2006.

[Fia07]   J. L. Fiadeiro: *Designing for Software's Social Complexity*. Computer, 40 (1) (2007): pp. 34-39, 2007.

[FIP02a]   FIPA: *FIPA Contract Net Interaction Protocol Specification*. http://www.fipa.org/specs/fipa00029/. 2002. Last Access on May 2010.

[FIP02b]   FIPA: *FIPA Iterated Contract Net Interaction Protocol Specification*. http://www.fipa.org/specs/fipa00030/index.html. 2002. Last Access on May 2010.

[FJ09]   M. Feingold and R. Jeyaraman: *Web Services Coordination (WS-Coordination 1.2)*. http://docs.oasis-open.org/ws-tx/wstx-wscoor-1.2-spec-os.doc. 2009. Last Access on May 2010.

[FLM+06]   P. Freudenstein, L. Liu, F. Majer, A. Maurer, C. Momm, D. Ried, and W. Juling: *Architektur Für Ein Universitätsweit Integriertes Informations- und Dienstmanagement*. In R.L. Christian Hochberger: *Proceeding of INFORMATIK 2006 - Informatik für Menschen*, Dresden, Germany, Springer, 2006.

[FSJ00]   P. Faratin, C. Sierra, and N. R. Jennings: *Using Similarity Criteria to Make Negotiation Trade-Offs*. In: *Proceeding of the Fourth International Conference on MultiAgent Systems*, pp. 119-126, Boston, Massachusetts, USA, IEEE Computer Society, 2000.

[FSJB99]   P. Faratin, C. Sierra, N. R. Jennings, and P. Buckle: *Designing Responsive and Deliberative Automated Negotiators*. In: *Proceeding of AAAI Workshop on Negotiation: Settling Conflicts and Identifying Opportunities*, pp. 12-18, Orlando, Florida, USA, 1999.

349

[GCH+04]   D. Garlan, S. W. Cheng, A. C. Huang, B. Schmerl, and P. Steenkiste: *Rainbow: Architecture-Based Self-Adaptation with Reusable Infrastructure*. IEEE Computer, 37 (10) (2004): pp. 46-54, 2004.

[Gee09]   J. Geelan: *Twenty-One Experts Define Cloud Computing*. Cloud Computing Journal, 2009 (January) (2009), 2009.

[Ger07]   C. Gershenson: *Design and Control of Self-Organizing Systems*. Ph.D. Thesis, Faculteit Wetenschappen, Center Leo Apostel for Interdisciplinary Studies, Vrije Universiteit Brussel, Brussel, Belgium, 2007.

[GHN+97]   S. Green, L. Hurst, B. Nangle, P. Cunningham, F. Somers, and R. Evans: *Software Agents: A Review*, Technical Report TCD-CS-1997-06, Trinity College Dublin, Dublin, Ireland, 1997.

[GHS+04]   A. G. Ganek, C. P. Hilkner, J. W. Sweitzer, B. Miller, and J. L. Hellerstein: *The Response to IT Complexity: Autonomic Computing*. In: *Proceeding of the 3rd IEEE International Symposium on Network Computing and Applications (NCA)*, pp. 151-157, Boston, Massachusetts, USA, IEEE Computer Society, 2004.

[GKS+08]   D. Gmach, S. Krompass, A. Scholz, M. Wimmer, and A. Kemper: *Adaptive Quality of Service Management for Enterprise Services*. ACM Transactions on the Web, 2 (1) (2008): pp. 1-46, 2008.

[GRS+02]   F. E. Gillett, C. Rutstein, G. Schreck, C. Buss, and H. Liddell: *Forrester Research Techstrategy Report April 2002 - Organic IT*, Forrester Research, 2002.

[Haa09]   A. D. Haan: *A Peek Behnid the Scenes at Hotmail*, Inside Windows Live, Redmond, WA, USA, 2009.

[HAN99]   H.-G. Hegering, S. Abeck, and B. Neumair: *Integrated Management of Networked Systems : Concepts, Architectures, and Their Operational Application*, The Morgan Kaufmann Series in Networking, Morgan Kaufmann, San Francisco, CA, USA, 1999.

[Hay08]   B. Hayes: *Cloud Computing*. Communications of the ACM, 51 (7) (2008): pp. 9-11, 2008.

[HB04]   H. Haas and A. Brown: *Web Services Glossary*. http://www.w3.org/TR/ws-gloss/. 2004. Last Access on May 2010.

[HF07]   R. Heffner and L. Fulton: *Topic Overview for Enterprise Architecture Professionals: Service-Oriented Architecture*, Forrester Research, Cambridge, MA, USA, 2007.

[HG03]   F. Heylighen and C. Gershenson: *The Meaning of Self-Organization in Computing*. IEEE Intelligent Systems, 18 (4) (2003): pp. 72-75, 2003.

[HK00]   C. Herring and S. Kaplan: *Viable Systems: The Control Paradigm for Software Architecture Revisited*. In: *Proceeding of the 2000 Australian Software Engineering Conference*, Canberra, Australia, IEEE Computer Society, 2000.

[HK01]   C. Herring and S. Kaplan: *The Viable System Architecture*. In: *Proceeding of the 34th Annual Hawaii International Conference on System Sciences (HICSS-34)-Volume 9 - Volume 9*, Hawaii, USA, IEEE Computer Society, 2001.

[HLA10]   R. Heffner, S. Leaver, and M. An: *Insights for CIOs: SOA and Beyond*, Forrester Research, Cambridge, MA, USA, 2010.

[HMC08]   M. C. Huebscher and J. A. McCann: *A Survey of Autonomic Computing: Degrees, Models, and Applications*. ACM Computing Surveys, 40 (3) (2008): pp. 1-28, 2008.

[Hof06]   B. Hoffman: *Monitoring, at Your Service*. ACM Queue, 3 (10) (2006): pp. 34-43, 2006.

[Hor01]   P. Horn: *Autonomic Computing: Ibm's Perspective on the State of Information Technology*. http://researchweb.watson.ibm.com/autonomic. 2001. Last Access on March 2010.

[HP10]   HP: *The HP Converged Infrastructure*. http://www.hp.com/go/ai. 2010. Last Access on May 2010.

[HS00]   M. N. Huhns and L. M. Stephens: *Multiagent Systems and Societies of Agents*. in: G. Weiss (Ed.), Multiagent Systems - a Modern Approach to Distributed Artificial Intelligence, The MIT Press, Cambridge, MA, USA, 2000, pp. 79-120.

[Hua04]   A.-C. Huang: *Building Self-Configuring Services Using Service-Specific Knowledge*, in: S. Peter (Ed.), 13th IEEE International Symposium on High Performance Distributed Computing (HPDC-13 '04), IEEE Computer Society, Honolulu, Hawaii, USA, 2004, pp. 45-54.

[HWH08]   M. Hiel, H. Weigand, and W.-J. Heuvel: *An Adaptive Service-Oriented Architecture*. in: K. Mertins, R. Ruggaber, K. Popplewell, X. Xu (Eds.), Enterprise Interoperability III: New Challenges and Industrial Approaches, Springer, London, UK, 2008, pp. 197-208.

[IBM05]   IBM: *An Architectural Blueprint for Autonomic Computing*. http://www-
           01.ibm.com/software/tivoli/autonomic/pdfs/AC_Blueprint_White_Paper
           _4th.pdf. 2006. Last Access on March 2010.

[IBM06]   IBM: *The IBM Autonomic Computing Toolkit*. http://www.ibm.com
           /developerworks/autonomic/overview.html. 2006. Last Access on May
           2010.

[ISO05]   International Standard Organisation: *ISO 9000: Quality Management
           Systemsn - Fundamentals and Vocabulary*, ISO, 2005.

[JFL+01]   N. Jennings, P. Faratin, A. Lomuscio, S. Parsons, M. Wooldridge, and C.
           Sierra: *Automated Negotiation: Prospects, Methods and Challenges*
           Group Decision and Negotiation, 10 (2) (2001): pp. 199-215, 2001.

[JRM04]   M. C. Jaeger, G. Rojec-Goldmann, and G. Mühl: *QoS Aggregation for
           Web Service Composition Using Workflow Patterns*. In: *Proceeding of
           the Eighth IEEE International Enterprise Distributed Object Computing
           Conference*, pp. 149-159, Monterey, California, USA, IEEE Computer
           Society, 2004.

[JRM05]   M. C. Jaeger, G. Rojec-Goldmann, and G. Mühl: *QoS Aggregation in
           Web Service Compositions*. In: *Proceeding of the 2005 IEEE
           International Conference on e-Technology, e-Commerce and e-Service*,
           Hong Kong, China, IEEE Computer Society, 2005.

[KC03]   J. O. Kephart and D. M. Chess: *The Vision of Autonomic Computing*.
           IEEE Computer, 36 (1) (2003): pp. 41-50, 2003.

[KCB03]   R. Kazman, P. Clements, and L. Bass: *Software Architecture in Practice*,
           Addison-Wesley, 2003.

[KE09]   H. Kreger and J. Estefan: *Navigating the SOA Open Standards
           Landscape around Architecture*, The Open Group/OMG/OASIS, 2009.

[KIM10]   KIM: *Karlsruher Integrated InformationManagement - KIM*. http://kim.
           cio.kit.edu/. 2010. Last Access on March 2010.

[Kin95]   J. A. King: *Intelligent Agents: Bringing Good Things to Life*. AI Expert,
           10 (2) (1995): pp. 17-19, 1995.

[KJ06]   I.-C. Kim and H. Jin: *An Agent System for Automated Web Service
           Composition and Invocation*. In R. Meersman, Z. Tari, P. Herrero:
           *Proceeding of Workshops On the Move to Meaningful Internet Systems
           2006*, pp. 90-96, Montpellier, France, Springer, 2006.

[KL03]   A. Keller and H. Ludwig: *The WSLA Framework: Specifying and Monitoring Service Level Agreements for Web Services.* Journal of Network and Systems Management, 11 (1) (2003): pp. 57-81, 2003.

[KL09]   D. Krishnan and B. Lublinksy: *Debate: Is SOA Dead?* http://www.infoq.com/news/2009/01/is-soa-dead. 2009. Last Access on March 2011.

[Koc07]   C. Koch: *Beyond Execution.* CIO, 10 (6) (2007): pp. 63-68, 2007.

[Kon00]   F. Kon: *Automatic Configuration of Component-Based Distributed Systems.* Ph.D. Thesis, Department of Computer Science, University of Illinois at Urbana-Champaign, Urbana, Illinois, USA 2000.

[Lab02]   C. Labounty: *How to Establish and Maintain Service Level Agreements*, Help Desk Institute, Colorado Springs, CO, USA, 2002.

[LBKF06]   A. Ludwig, P. Braun, R. Kowalczyk, and B. Franczyk: *A Framework for Automated Negotiation of Service Level Agreements in Services Grids.* In: *Proceeding of the Workshop on Web Service Choreography and Orchestration for Business Process Management 2005*, pp. 89-101, Nancy, France, Springer, 2005.

[Len64]   G. G. Lendaris: *On the Definition of Self-Organizing Systems.* Proceedings of the IEEE, 52 (3) (1964): pp. 324-325, 1964.

[LGH09]   X. Liu, H. Gang, and M. Hong: *Discovering Homogeneous Web Service Community in the User-Centric Web Environment.* IEEE Transactions on Services Computing, 2 (2) (2009): pp. 167-181, 2009.

[LH06]   L. Liu and H. Schmeck: *A Roadmap Towards Autonomic Service-Oriented Architectures.* International Transactions on Systems Science and Applications, 2 (3) (2006): pp. 245-255, 2006.

[Lin08]   J. Lin: *A Conceptual Model for Negotiating in Service-Oriented Environments.* Information Processing Letters, 108 (4) (2008): pp. 192-203, 2008.

[LKH06]   P. Lockemann, S. Kirn, and O. Herzog: *Management Summary.* in: S. Kirn, O. Herzog, P. Lockemann, O. Spaniol (Eds.), Multiagent Engineering: Theory and Applications in Enterprises, Springer, Berlin, Germany, 2006, pp. 1-13.

[LKN+09]   A. Lenk, M. Klems, J. Nimis, S. Tai, and T. Sandholm: *What's inside the Cloud? An Architectural Map of the Cloud Landscape.* In: *Proceeding of the 2009 ICSE Workshop on Software Engineering Challenges of Cloud Computing*, Vancouver, Canada, IEEE Computer Society, 2009.

[LML05]   P. Lin, A. MacArthur, and J. Leaney: *Defining Autonomic Computing: A Software Engineering Perspective*. In: *Proceeding of the 2005 Australian conference on Software Engineering*, Brisbane, Australia, IEEE Computer Society, 2005.

[LS10]   L. Liu and H. Schmeck: *Enabling Self-Organising Service Level Management with Automated Negotiation*. In: *Proceeding of the 2010 IEEE/WIC/ACE International Conference on Web Intelligence*, Toronto, Canada, IEEE Computer Society, 2010.

[LTS07]   L. Liu, S. Thanheiser, and H. Schmeck: *Coping with the Complexity of Service-Oriented Computing Using Controlled Self-Organization*. In: *Proceeding of the Workshop Service Oriented Computing: a look at the Inside 2007 (SOC@Inside'07)*, Vienna, Austria, EU Commission, 2007.

[LTS08]   L. Liu, S. Thanheiser, and H. Schmeck: *A Reference Architecture for Self-Organizing Service-Oriented Computing*. In W. Brinkschulte, T. Ungerer, C. Hochberger, R.G. Spallek: *Proceeding of International Conference Architecture of Computing Systems – ARCS 2008*, pp. 205-219, Dresden, Germany, Springer, 2008.

[LTS09a]   L. Liu, S. Thanheiser, and H. Schmeck: *Assessing the Impact of Inherent SOA System Properties on Complexity*. In: *Proceeding of the 2009 Fourth International Conference on Internet and Web Applications and Services*, pp. 429-434, Venice, Italy, IEEE Computer Society, 2009.

[LTS09b]   L. Liu, S. Thanheiser, and H. Schmeck: *Assessing Complexity of Service-Oriented Computing Using Learning Classifier Systems*. In: *Proceeding of the ACM Symposium on Applied Computing (SAC '09)*, Honolulu, Hawaii, USA, ACM Press, 2009.

[LWJ03]   A. R. Lomuscio, M. Wooldridge, and N. R. Jennings: *A Classification Scheme for Negotiation in Electronic Commerce*. International Journal of Group Decision and Negotiation, 12 (1) (2003): pp. 31-56, 2003.

[LYFA02]   C. Liu, L. Yang, I. Foster, and D. Angulo: *Design and Evaluation of a Resource Selection Framework for Grid Applications*. In: *Proceeding of the 11th IEEE International Symposium on High Performance Distributed Computing*, pp. 63 - 72, Edinburgh, Scotland, IEEE Computer Society, 2002.

[LZLC02]   H. Lin, Z. Zhao, H. Li, and Z. Chen: *A Novel Graph Reduction Algorithm to Identify Structural Conflicts*. In: *Proceeding of 35th Annual Hawaii International Conference on System Sciences (HICSS'02)*, p. 289, Hawaii, USA, IEEE Computer Society, 2002.

[LZW+05]   R. Li, Z. Zhang, Z. Wang, W. Song, and Z. Lu: *WebPeer: A P2P-Based System for Publishing and Discovering Web Services*. In: *Proceeding of the 2005 IEEE International Conference on Services Computing*, IEEE Computer Society, 2005.

[Man09]   A. T. Manes: *SOA Is Dead; Long Live Services.* http://apsblog. burtongroup.com/2009/01/soa-is-dead-long-live-services.html.   2009. Last Access on March 2010.

[MBH+04]   D. Martin, M. Burstein, J. Hobbs, O. Lassila, D. McDermott, S. Mcilraith, S. Narayanan, M. Paolucci, B. Parsia, T. Payne, E. Sirin, N. Srinivasan, and K. Sycara: *OWL-S: Semantic Markup for Web Services*, World Wide Web Consortium, http://www.w3.org/Submission/OWL-S/, 2004.

[McF08]   Paul McFedries: *The Cloud Is the Computer*. IEEE Spectrum, 2008 (08) (2008), 2008.

[ME05]   A. Muhammad and M. Egerstedt: *Decentralized Coordination with Local Interactions: Some New Directions*. in: M. Thoma, M. Morari (Eds.), Cooperative Control, Springer, Heldelberg, 2005, pp. 455-457.

[Men02]   D. A. Menasce: *QoS Issues in Web Services*. IEEE Internet Computing, 6 (6) (2002): pp. 72-75, 2002.

[Men04]   D. A. Menasce: *Composing Web Services: A QoS View*. IEEE Internet Computing, 8 (6) (2004): pp. 80-90, 2004.

[MGI09]   N. B. Mabrouk, N. Georgantas, and V. Issarny: *A Semantic End-to-End QoS Model for Dynamic Service Oriented Environments*. In: *Proceeding of the 2009 ICSE Workshop on Principles of Engineering Service Oriented Systems*, Vancouver, Canada, IEEE Computer Society, 2009.

[MGVH04]   D. McGuinness and F. Van Harmelen: *OWL Web Ontology Language Overview*, W3C recommendation, World Wide Web Consortium, http://www.w3.org/TR/owl-features/, 2004.

[Mic04]   Microsoft: *Microsoft Dynamic System Initiative Overview*. http:// download.microsoft.com/download/e/5/6/e5656886-ad18-4afd-945f-3680278dfd58/DSI%20overview.doc. 2004. Last Access on May 2010.

[Mir10]   Microsoft: *Windows Performance Monitoring*. http://msdn.microsoft. com/en-us/library/ee663292(v=VS.85).aspx.   2010.   Last Access on August 2010.

[Mit97]   T. M. Mitchell: *Machine Learning*, McGraw-Hill, 1997.

[MKB06]   I. Mueller, R. Kowalczyk, and P. Braun: *Towards Agent-Based Coalition Formation for Service Composition.* In: *Proceeding of the IEEE/WIC/ACM international conference on Intelligent Agent Technology 2006*, Hongkong, China, IEEE Computer Society, 2006.

[MKL+06]   C. M. MacKenzie, K. Laskey, F. McCabe, P. F. Brown, and R. Metz: *Reference Model for Service Oriented Architecture*, OASIS, 2006.

[MM04]   B. Melcher and B. Mitchell: *Towards an Autonomic Framework: Self-Configuring Network Services and Developing Autonomic Applications.* Intel Technology Journal, 8 (4) (2004): pp. 279-290, 2004.

[MMTZ06]   M. Mamei, R. Menezes, R. Tolksdorf, and F. Zambonelli: *Case Studies for Self-Organization in Computer Science.* Journal of Systems Architecture, 52 (8) (2006): pp. 443-460, 2006.

[Mon09]   D. C. Montgomery: *Design and Analysis of Experiments*, 7th Edition.John Wiley & Sons, 2009.

[Moo01]   A. V. Moorsel: *Metrics for the Internet Age: Quality of Experience and Quality of Business*, HP Laboratories, Palo Alto, CA, USA, 2001.

[Mos02]   S. Moss: *Challenges in Agent Based Social Simulation of Multilateral Negotiation.* in: K. Dautenhahn, A. Bond, L. Cañamero, B. Edmonds (Eds.), Socially Intelligent Agents, Multiagent Systems, Artificial Societies, and Simulated Organizations, Springer, New York, USA, 2002, pp. 251-258.

[MS04]   C. Müller-Schloer: *Organic Computing: On the Feasibility of Controlled Emergence.* In A. Orailoglu, P.H. Chou, P. Eles, A. Jantsch: *Proceeding of the 2nd IEEE/ACM/IFIP International Conference on Hardware/software Codesign and System Synthesis*, pp. 2-5, Stockholm, Sweden, ACM Press, 2004.

[MS04a]   J. McConnell and E. Siegel: *Practical Service Level Management: Delivering High-Quality Web-Based Services*, Cisco Press, Indianapolis, IN, USA, 2004.

[MSS08]   C. Müller-Schloer and B. Sick: *Controlled Emergence and Self-Organization.* in: R.P. Würtz (Ed.), Organic Computing, Springer, 2008, pp. 81-103.

[NCV06]   M. J. North, N. T. Collier, and J. R. Vos: *Experiences Creating Three Implementations of the Repast Agent Modeling Toolkit.* ACM Transactions on Modeling and Computer Simulation, 16 (1) (2006): pp. 1-25, 2006.

[NKMH06]   A. Nadalin, C. Kaler, R. Monzillo, and P. Hallam-Baker: *Web Service Security: Soap Message Security 1.1 (WS-Security 2004)*. http://www.oasis-open.org/committees/download.php/21255/wss-v1.1-spec-errata-os-SOAPMessageSecurity.pdf. 2006. Last Access on May 2009.

[NPTT06]   A. Negri, A. Poggi, M. Tomaiuolo, and P. Turci: *Agents for E-Business Applications*. In: *Proceeding of the Fifth International Joint Conference on Autonomous Agents and Multiagent Systems*, Hakodate, Japan, ACM, 2006.

[Nwa96]   H. S. Nwana: *Software Agents: An Overview*. Knowledge Engineering Review, 11 (3) (1996): pp. 205-244, 1996.

[OAS06]   OASIS: *The WS-Resource Framework*, OASIS, http://docs.oasis-open.org/wsrf/wsrf-primer-1.2-primer-cd-02.pdf, 2006.

[OC10]   *German Priority Programme SPP 1183 Organic Computing Website*. http://www.organic-computing.de/spp. 2010. Last Access on May 2010.

[OG08]   The Open Group: *Service Oriented Infrastructure Reference Framework*, The Open Group, 2008.

[OG09]   The Open Group: *SOA Source Book: How to Use Service-Oriented Architecture Effectively*, The Open Group Series, Van Haren Publishing, Zaltbommel, Netherlands, 2009.

[OGT+99]   P. Oreizy, M. M. Gorlick, R. N. Taylor, D. Heimhigner, G. Johnson, N. Medvidovic, A. Quilici, D. S. Rosenblum, and A. L. Wolf: *An Architecture-Based Approach to Self-Adaptive Software*. IEEE Intelligent Systems and their Applications, 14 (3) (1999): pp. 54-62, 1999.

[OMG09]   OMG: *Business Process Model and Notation (BPMN) 1.2*, OMG, 2009, p. 316.

[Pap05]   M. P. Papazoglou: *Extending the Service-Oriented Architecture*. Business Integration Journal, 2005 (FEB) (2005): pp. 18-21, 2005.

[PBB+02]   D. Patterson, A. Brown, P. Broadwell, G. Candea, M. Chen, J. Cutler, P. Enriquez, A. Fox, E. Kıcıman, M. Merzbacher, D. Oppenheimer, N. Sastry, W. Tetzlaff, J. Traupman, and N. Treuhaft: *Recovery Oriented Computing (ROC): Motivation, Definition, Techniques, and Case Studies*, University of California at Berkeley, Berkeley, CA, USA, 2002.

[PBS+09]   H. Prothmann, J. Branke, H. Schmeck, S. Tomforde, F. Rochner, J. Hahner, and C. Müller-Schloer: *Organic Traffic Light Control for Urban*

Road Networks. International Journal of Autonomous and Adaptive Communications Systems, 2 (3) (2009): pp. 203-225, 2009.

[PH07]   M. P. Papazoglou and W.-J. Heuvel: *Service Oriented Architectures: Approaches, Technologies and Research Issues*. The VLDB Journal, 16 (3) (2007): pp. 389-415, 2007.

[PNT06]   M. Petsch, V. Nissen, and T. Traub: *Anwendungspotenziale von Intelligenten Agenten in Service-Orientierten Architekturen*. in: V. Nissen, M. Petch, H. Schorcht (Eds.), Service-Orientierte Architekturen: Chancen und Herausforderungen Bei Der Flexibilisierung und Integration von Unternehmensprozessen, Die Deutsche Universitäts-Verlag, Wiesbaden, Germany, 2006, pp. 167-185.

[Pol08]   D. Polani: *Foundations and Formalizations of Self-Organization*. in: M. Prokopenko (Ed.), Advances in Applied Self-Organizing Systems, Springer, London, UK, 2008, pp. 19-37.

[Pro08]   M. Prokopenko: *Design Vs. Self-Organization*. in: M. Prokopenko (Ed.), Advances in Applied Self-Organizing Systems, Springer, London, UK, 2008, pp. 3-17.

[PRT+08]   H. Prothmann, F. Rochner, S. Tomforde, J. Branke, C. Müller-Schloer, and H. Schmeck: *Organic Control of Traffic Lights*. In: *Proceeding of the 5th international conference on Autonomic and Trusted Computing*, pp. 219 - 233, Oslo, Norway, Springer, 2008.

[PSGS04]   V. Poladian, J. P. Sousa, D. Garlan, and M. Shaw: *Dynamic Configuration of Resource-Aware Services*. In: *Proceeding of the 26th International Conference on Software Engineering*, Edinburgh, Scotland, IEEE Computer Society, 2004.

[PTDL07]   M. P. Papazoglou, P. Traverso, S. Dustdar, and F. Leymann: *Service-Oriented Computing: State of the Art and Research Challenges*. IEEE Computer, 40 (11) (2007): pp. 38-45, 2007.

[RAC+02]   M. Rutherford, K. Anderson, A. Carzaniga, D. Heimbigner, and A. Wolf: *Reconfiguration in the Enterprise JavaBean Component Model*. In: *Proceeding of the 2002 IFIP/ACM Working Conference on Component Deployment*, pp. 47-54, Berlin, Germany, Springer, 2002.

[Rah04]   I. Rahwan: *Interest-Based Negotiation in Multi-Agent Systems*. PhD Thesis, Department of Information Systems, University of Melbourne, Melbourne, Australian, 2004.

[Rai82]   H. Raiffa: *The Art and Science of Negotiation*, Harvard University Press, 1982.

[Reb01]   M. Rebstock: *Elektronische Unterstützung und Automatisierung von Verhandlungen*. Wirtschaftsinformatik, 43 (6) (2001): pp. 609-617, 2001.

[Ric10]   U. M. Richter: *Controlled Self-Organisation Using Learning Classifier Systems*. Ph.D. Thesis, Fakultät für Wirtschaftswissenschaften, Karlsruhe Institute of Technology, Karlsruhe, Germany, 2010.

[RL07]   C. Rudd and V. Lloyd: *ITIL V3: Service Design Book*, 1.The Stationery Office, London, UK, 2007.

[RMB+06]   U. Richter, M. Mnif, J. Branke, C. Müller-Schloer, and H. Schmeck: *Towards a Generic Observer/Controller Architecture for Organic Computing*. In C. Hochberger, R. Liskowsky: *Proceeding of INFORMATIK 2006 - Informatik für Menschen!*, pp. 112-119, Dresden, Germany, Bonner Köllen Verlag, 2006.

[RRJ+03]   I. Rahwan, S. D. Ramchurn, N. R. Jennings, P. McBurney, S. Parsons, and L. Sonenberg: *Argumentation-Based Negotiation*. The Knowledge Engineering Review, 18 (04) (2003): pp. 343-375, 2003.

[RS05]   J. Rao and X. Su: *A Survey of Automated Web Service Composition Methods*. In J. Cardoso, A. Sheth: *Proceeding of First International Workshop Semantic Web Services and Web Process Composition*, pp. 43-54, San Diego, CA, USA, Springer, 2005.

[RZ94]   J. S. Rosenschein and G. Zlotkin: *Rules of Encounter - Designing Conventions for Automated Negotiation among Computers*, The MIT Press, 1994.

[San00]   T. W. Sandholm: *Distributed Rational Decision Making*. in: G. Weiss (Ed.), Multiagent Systems - a Modern Approach to Distributed Artificial Intelligence, The MIT Press, Massachusetts, USA, 2000, pp. 201-258.

[Sar11]   Sarasvati Project: *Sarasvati Workflow Engine*. http://code.google .com/p/sarasvati/. 2011. Last Access on February 2011.

[SC00]   A. F. Stuhlmacher and M. V. Champagne: *The Impact of Time Pressure and Information on Negotiation Process and Decisions*. Group Decision and Negotiation, 9 (6) (2000): pp. 471-491, 2000.

[Sch05]   H. Schmeck: *Organic Computing - a New Vision for Distributed Embedded Systems*. In A. Ghafoor, Uwe Brinkschulte, K. Ramamritham, R.G. Pettit: *Proceeding of the Eighth IEEE International Symposium on*

Object-Oriented Real-Time Distributed Computing 2005, pp. 201-203, Seattle, WA, USA, IEEE Computer Society, 2005.

[SFJ97]   C. Sierra, P. Faratin, and N. R. Jennings: *A Service-Oriented Negotiation Model between Autonomous Agents*. In: *Proceeding of the 8th European Workshop on Modelling Autonomous Agents in a Multi-Agent World*, pp. 17-35, Springer, 1997.

[SH10]   J. Sinur and J. B. Hill: *Magic Quadrant for Business Process Management Suites*. http://www.gartner.com/technology/media-products /reprints/oracle/article161/article161.html. 2010. Last Access on February 2010.

[SLA10]   SLA@SOI Project: *SLA@SOI Project Website*. http://sla-at-soi.eu/. 2010. Last Access on May 2010.

[SLE04]   J. Skene, D. D. Lamanna, and W. Emmerich: *Precise Service Level Agreements*. In: *Proceeding of the 26th International Conference on Software Engineering*, Edinburgh, Scotland, IEEE Computer Society, 2004.

[Smi80]   R. G. Smith: *The Contract Net Protocol: High-Level Communication and Control in a Distributed Problem Solver*. IEEE Transactions on computers, 29 (12) (1980): pp. 1104-1113, 1980.

[SMS+02]   A. Sahai, V. Machiraju, M. Sayal, A. V. Moorsel, and F. Casati: *Automated SLA Monitoring for Web Services* Management Technologies for E-Commerce and E-Business Applications, Springer, 2002, pp. 28-41.

[SO00]   W. Sadiq and M. E. Orlowska: *Analyzing Process Models Using Graph Reduction Techniques*. Information Systems, 25 (2) (2000): pp. 117-134, 2000.

[SS07]   J. Schelp and M. Stutz: *SOA-Governance*. HMD - Praxis der Wirtschaftsinformatik, 253 (42) (2007): pp. 66-73, 2007.

[SSW10]   S. K. Sia, C. Soh, and P. Weill: *Global IT Management: Structuring for Scale, Responsiveness, and Innovation*. Communication of ACM, 53 (3) (2010): pp. 59-64, 2010.

[ST09]   M. Salehie and L. Tahvildari: *Self-Adaptive Software: Landscape and Research Challenges*. ACM Transactions on Autonomous and Adaptive Systems, 4 (2) (2009): pp. 1-42, 2009.

[SV97]   A. Shleifer and R. W. Vishny: *A Survey of Corporate Governance*. The Journal of Finance, 52 (2) (1997): pp. 737-783, 1997.

[SW04]   D. Sprott and L. Wilkes: *Understanding Service-Oriented Architecture*. Microsoft Architect Journal, 2004 (Jan) (2004), 2004.

[TGWD09]   Y. Takayama, E. Ghiglione, S. Wilson, and J. Dalziel: *Human Activities in Distributed BPM*. In W. Abramowicz, L. Maciaszek, R. Kowalczyk, A. Speck: *Proceeding of Workshop Business Process, Services Computing and Intelligent Service Management 2009*, pp. 139-151, Leipzig, Germany, Gesellschaft für Informatik, 2009.

[The08]   W. Theilmann: *SLA@SOI - an Overview: Empowering the Service Economy with SLA-Aware Infrastructures*. http://sla-at-soi.eu/wp-content/uploads/2008/12/slasoi-e28093-an-overview.pdf. 2008. Last Access on May 2010.

[TLS07]   S. Thanheiser, L. Liu, and H. Schmeck: *Towards Collaborative Coping with IT Complexity by Combining SOA and Organic Computing*. System and Information Sciences Notes, 2 (1) (2007): pp. 82-87, 2007.

[TLS08]   S. Thanheiser, L. Liu, and H. Schmeck: *Selbstorganisation Durch Dezentralität–Dezentralität Durch Selbstorganisation: Auf Dem Weg Zu Einem ,Organischen 'Management von Unternehmens-IT*. In M. Bichler, T. Hess, H. Krcmar, U. Lechner, F. Matthes, A. Picot, B. Speitkamp: *Proceeding of Multikonferenz Wirtschaftsinformatik 2008*, pp. 255-266, Munich, Germany, GITO-Verlag, 2008.

[TPB+10]   S. Tomforde, H. Prothmann, J. Branke, J. Hähner, C. Müller-Schloer, and H. Schmeck: *Possibilities and Limitations of Decentralised Traffic Control Systems*. In: *Proceeding of the 2010 IEEE World Congress on Computational Intelligence (IEEE WCCI 2010)*, Barcelona, Spain, IEEE Computer Society, 2010.

[TPR+08]   S. Tomforde, H. Prothmann, F. Rochner, J. Branke, J. Hähner, C. Müller-Schloer, and H. Schmeck: *Decentralised Progressive Signal Systems for Organic Traffic Control*. In S. Brueckner, P. Robertson, U. Bellur: *Proceeding of the 2008 Second IEEE International Conference on Self-Adaptive and Self-Organizing Systems*, Venice, Italy, IEEE Computer Society, 2008.

[TYB08]   W. Theilmann, R. Yahyapour, and J. Butler: *Multi-Level SLA Management for Service-Oriented Infrastructures*. In P. Mähönen, K. Pohl, T. Priol: *Proceeding of First European Conference ServiceWave 2008*, pp. 324-335, Madrid, Spain, Springer, 2008.

[USC+08]   B. Urgaonkar, P. Shenoy, A. Chandra, P. Goyal, and T. Wood: *Agile Dynamic Provisioning of Multi-Tier Internet Applications*. ACM

Transactions on Autonomous and Adaptive Systems, 3 (1) (2008): pp. 1-39, 2008.

[Var08]   J. Varia: *Cloud Architectures*. http://jineshvaria.s3.amazonaws.com/public/cloudarchitectures-varia.pdf. 2008. Last Access on May 2010.

[VF60]   H. V. Foerster: *On Self-Organizing Systems and Their Environments*. in: M.C. Yovits, S. Cameron (Eds.), Self-Organizing Systems, Pergamon Press, London, UK, 1960, pp. 31-50.

[Vid98]   R. Vidgen: *Cybernetics and Business Processes: Using the Viable System Model to Develop an Enterprise Process Architecture*. Knowledge and Process Management, 5 (2) (1998): pp. 118-131, 1998.

[VOH+07]   A. S. Vedamuthu, D. Orchard, F. Hirsch, M. Hondo, P. Yendluri, T. Boubez, and Ü. Yalçinalp: *Web Services Policy Framework (WS-Policy)*. http://www.w3.org/TR/ws-policy/. 2007. Last Access on May 2010.

[VRM+08]   L. M. Vaquero, L. Rodero-Merino, J. Caceres, and M. Lindner: *A Break in the Clouds: Towards a Cloud Definition*. ACM SIGCOMM Computer Communication Review, 39 (1) (2008): pp. 50-55, 2008.

[W3C04]   W3C: *Web Service Architecture WS-Arch*. http://www.w3.org/TR/ws-arch/. 2004. Last Access on May 2011.

[WC09]   M. D. Weerdt and B. Clement: *Introduction to Planning in Multiagent Systems*. Multiagent and Grid Systems, 5 (4) (2009): pp. 345-355, 2009.

[WDCL08]   X. Wang, Z. Du, Y. Chen, and S. Li: *Virtualization-Based Autonomic Resource Management for Multi-Tier Web Applications in Shared Data Center*. Journal of Systems and Software, 81 (9) (2008): pp. 1591-1608, 2008.

[WH07]   D. Weyns and T. Holvoet: *An Architectural Strategy for Self-Adapting Systems*. In: *Proceeding of the 2007 International Workshop on Software Engineering for Adaptive and Self-Managing Systems*, pp. 3-11, Minneapolis, USA, IEEE Computer Society, 2007.

[Win06]   P. J. Windley: *SOA Goverance: Rules of the Game*, InfoWorld, IDG, 2006.

[WJ95]   M. Wooldridge and N. R. Jennings: *Intelligent Agents: Theory and Practice*. The Knowledge Engineering Review, 10 (02) (1995): pp. 115-152, 1995.

[WMS+10] M. Wünsche, S. Mostaghim, H. Schmeck, T. Kautzmann, and M. Geimer: *Organic Computing in Off-Highway Machines*. In: *Proceeding of Second International Workshop on Self-Organizing Architectures 2010*, Washington, DC, USA, ACM, 2010.

[Woo02] M. Wooldridge: *An Introduction to Multiagent Systems*, Wiley & Sons, Chichester, England, 2002.

[WR04] P. Weill and J. Ross: *IT Governance: How Top Performers Manage IT Decision Rights for Superior Results*, Harvard Business School Press, Boston, MA, USA, 2004.

[WS06] K. Wilson and I. Sedukhin: *Web Service Distributed Management: Management of Web Services (WSDM-MOWS)*, OASIS, 2006.

[WSW+05] J. Wildstrom, P. Stone, E. Witchel, R. J. Mooney, and M. Dahlin: *Towards Self-Configuring Hardware for Distributed Computer Systems*, Second International Conference on Autonomic Computing (ICAC'05), IEEE Computer Society, 2005, pp. 241-249.

[XHL+03] X. Dong, S. Hariri, X. Lizhi, H. Chen, M. Zhang, S. Pavuluri, and S. Rao: *Autonomia: An Autonomic Computing Environment*. In: *Proceeding of the 2003 IEEE International Performance, Computing, and Communications Conference*, pp. 61-68, IEEE Computer Society, 2003.

[YKL+07] J. Yan, R. Kowalczyk, J. Lin, M. B. Chhetri, S. K. Goh, and J. Zhang: *Autonomous Service Level Agreement Negotiation for Service Composition Provision*. Future Generation Computer Systems, 23 (6) (2007): pp. 748-759, 2007.

[ZJ89] G. Zlotkin and J. S. Rosenschein: *Negotiation and Task Sharing among Autonomous Agents in Cooperative Domains*. In: *Proceeding of the 11th International Joint Conference on Artificial Intelligence*, San Mateo, CA, USA, Morgan Kaufmann, 1989.

[ZMCW08] F. Zulkernine, P. Martin, C. Craddock, and K. Wilson: *A Policy-Based Middleware for Web Services SLA Negotiation* In: *Proceeding of the IEEE International Conference on Web Services 2008*, Beijing, China, IEEE Computer Society, 2008.

[ZR05] F. Zambonelli and O. F. Rana: *Self-Organization in Distributed Systems Engineering: Introduction to the Special Issue*. IEEE Transaction on Systems, Man, and Cybernatics - PART A: Systems and Humans, 35 (3) (2005): pp. 313-314, 2005.